HANDBOOK OF B
Third Edition

HANDBOOK OF BUDGETING
Third Edition

1997 Cumulative Supplement

Robert Rachlin
H.W. Allen Sweeny

JOHN WILEY & SONS, INC.

New York • Chichester • Weinheim • Brisbane • Singapore • Toronto

This publication is designed to provide accurate and authoritative information in regard to the subject
matter covered. It is sold with the understanding that the publisher is not engaged in rendering legal,
accounting, or other professional services. If legal advice or other expert assistance is required, the
services of a competent professional person should be sought.

Library of Congress Cataloging in Publication Data

Handbook of budgeting / [edited by] Robert Rachlin, H.W. Allen
Sweeny,—3rd. ed.
    p. cm.
  Includes bibliographical references and index.
  ISBN 0-471-57771-5 (cloth)
  ISBN 0-471-19685-1 (supplement)
  1. Budget in business. I. Rachlin, Robert, 1937–
II. Sweeny, Allen.
HG4028.B8H36 1993
658.15′4—dc20   92-39299

Printed in the United States of America

10 9 8 7 6 5 4 3 2 1

ABOUT THE AUTHORS

Robert Rachlin, President of Robert Rachlin Associates, is an internationally known author, lecturer, and consultant in the area of financial management and serves as Assistant Dean for Business Studies, Hofstra University. He has previously served as vice president of several companies in planning and budgeting capacities. Mr. Rachlin received a BBA in accounting from Pace University and an MBA in management and economics from St. John's University. He has also served as an Adjunct Associate Professor of Management at New York University, and the New York Institute of Technology. He is currently an Adjunct Professor of Management at Hofstra University. Mr. Rachlin is a frequent lecturer to professional groups, companies, and practicing professionals, and is the recipient of the "Fellow" Award for outstanding service to the planning profession by the Planning Executives Institute, an organization for which he served as New York Chapter President. He is also the author and/or co-editor of *Successful Techniques for Higher Profits, Return on Investment-Strategies for Decision-Making, Handbook of Strategic Planning, Total Business Budgeting: A Step-by-Step Guide with Forms,* and *Managing Cash Flow and Capital During Inflation.*

H.W. Allen Sweeny retired as Senior Vice President and Chief Financial Officer of Del Monte Foods when that multibillion-dollar international food company closed its world headquarters in Miami in 1990. Prior to that he served in a variety of financial development and general management positions for R.J.R. Nabisco and Exxon while living in Argentina, Colombia, Hong Kong, Japan, and the United States. Mr. Sweeny has a BS in General Business from the University of Kansas and an MBA from the Harvard Graduate School of Business Administration. He has authored and/or edited six books on accounting, budgeting, strategic planning, and financial management and has lectured and taught these subjects at the Fordham Graduate School of Business.

PREFACE

The 1997 supplement contains nine new chapters. Chapter 11A, "Budgeting Shareholder Value," describes how shareholders provide an economic measurement of business performance. Shareholder value is used to increase future growth as measured by the sum of future cash flows in today's dollars. The chapter presents a detailed analysis of how to budget and calculate and reasons why shareholder value must be part of today's budgeting process.

Chapter 18A, "Budgeting Payroll Costs," provides an in-depth review of the payroll function. Topics range from understanding the components of payroll to the relationship within the organization; from inside development to outsourcing of payroll services; from TQM techniques to putting technology to work; and of course, the relationship of the payroll function to the budgeting process.

Chapter 18B, "Budgeting the Purchasing Department and the Purchasing Process," details the major roles of the purchasing department and how to implement a budgeting process around those roles. This chapter includes sections on the description and definition of the process approach, the role of process measures, process measures, and creating the procurement process budget.

Chapter 20A, "Leasing," explores the leasing process and how the operating budget is affected. This chapter includes such topics as lease reporting, FASB 13 case illustrations, and lease analysis techniques.

Chapter 23A, "Understanding Foreign Exchange Transactions," describes how multinational companies respond on a global basis to the issues of budget control, cash management, intracompany transfers, and capital budgeting through foreign exchange transactions.

Chapter 26A, "Budgeting for Total Quality Management," provides a foundation for understanding TQM and the model for development of a budgeting system.

Chapter 27A, "Activity-Based Budgeting," presents a complete detailed study on the activity-based budgeting process, from linking strategy and budgeting to translating strategies to activities; from determining workloads to creating planning guidelines; from finalizing the budget to performance reporting. This is a state-of-the-art look at the ABB process.

Chapter 28A, "Fuzzy Logic Applied to Budgeting: An Intuitive Approach to Coping with Uncertainty," presents an alternative approach to the development of the operating budget. This chapter focuses on how managers focus on estimates of key variables using fuzzy number modeling.

Chapter 34, "Budgeting in the Biotech Industry," discusses some of the key issues to be addressed in the development of a budget for a biotech company. With a myriad of unknowns, biotech companies are faced with the problem of developing credible forecasts that prove and justify the investment to the outside providers of capital. This chapter provides the means to resolve this problem.

In addition to the nine new chapters, minor updates were made in eight chapters and a major revision to chapters 15, 18, and 29.

Plainview, New York   ROBERT RACHLIN
May 1997   Chief Editor

CONTRIBUTORS

Page ix, add after entry for James W. Anderson:

John Antos is a management consultant specializing in activity-based management, quality costs, acquisitions, planning, and modern cost systems. He consults and lectures around the world to major companies and is a recognized professional in his field. He has been a chief financial officer, director, and controller within industry and has turned around a company on the verge of bankruptcy. He has consulted on such topics as ABM, ABC, ABB, accounting systems, strategic planning, plant expansion studies, acquisitions, and marketing. Mr. Antos has an MBA in Accounting and Marketing from the University of Chicago and his BS in Business Administration from the University of Illinois-Urbana. He is also a Certified Management Accountant and a Certified Financial Planner.

Robert D. Apgood, PhD, is a leasing and financial consultant specializing in international leasing, accounting, and finance. He is a CPA and has an MBA and a PhD in accounting. Dr. Apgood has served as chairman of the Accounting Standards Committee for the broadcast industry, as vice president of finance for a broadcasting and telecommunications conglomerate, and as a full professor of accounting. In addition to his consulting practice, he is currently vice president of a high-tech bioremediation firm.

James A. Brimson is President of Activity Based Management—Institute, an international confederation of consulting, training, and software companies who specialize in activity-based management. Prior to ABM-I, Mr. Brimson served as partner-in-charge of Coopers & Lybrand L.L.P., Deloitte's worldwide activity-based management consulting practice in London, England. He also served as director of CAM-I (an international consortium) with more than 13 years of industry experience concentrating in cost management and systems development activities, primarily in the manufacturing industry. Mr. Brimson is the author of *Activity Accounting—An Activity-Based Costing Approach,* published by John Wiley & Sons, Inc., and coeditor of *Cost Management for Today's Advanced Manufacturing, The CAM-I Conceptual Design,* published by Harvard Business School Press. He has a BS from Auburn University and an MBA in quantitative science from Arizona State University.

Page ix, add after entry for Mohammad Ali Chaudry:

Charles A. Clerecuzio is an associate with Coopers & Lybrand L.L.P.'s Consulting Division, in the Integrated Health Care Consulting group, which serves the pharmaceutical, biotechnology, diagnostic, wholesaler, and healthcare industries. He assists clients with business process reengineering, manufacturing and facility strategies, reducing time to market for products, regulatory compliance, and operations management and improvement. Before joining C&L, he held positions in operations and was an engineering and production supervisor.

Page x, replace entry for Robert M. Donnelly with:

Robert M. Donnelly is with Alpha International Management.

Page x, add after entry for Robert M. Donnelly:

Ronald A. Follet is currently a principal in the RF Group, a consulting and advisory organization catering primarily to small and medium-sized companies. Prior to his consulting activities, he held senior staff positions with several high-technology companies. He consults, lectures, and writes articles for technical and industry periodicals, and has developed specialized TQM programs for specific industry implementation. He has worked with recognized leaders in the quality field, and was a contributor/collaborator on the customer quality chapter in the *Quality Handbook*. Mr. Follet has a B.S. degree in electronics engineering from the University of Rhode Island.

Page x, add after entry for Albert A. Fried:

Leonard A. Haug is the U.S. Payroll Manager for Digital Equipment Corporation. He has held other positions within Digital, and worked for Xerox Corporation and United Airlines before joining Digital. Mr. Haug is a recognized leader in the application of TQM and EFT within the discipline of payroll. He is both an author and a frequent speaker at major conferences. Under his direction, the Digital Payroll Team has become one of the premier payroll organizations among U.S. industries, and has been recognized as best-in-class by multiple independent consulting organizations and publications. Mr. Haug is an active member of the American Payroll Association (APA), serves as the chairman of the Automated Clearing House (ACH) Committee, and is a member of both the APA Board of Advisors and its Board of Contributing Writers. In April 1994, he was recognized by the APA as "The Payroll Man of the Year" for his contributions to the profession and to the association. He has a B.A. degree from North Central College and is a Certified Payroll Professional (CPP) and a Certified Six Sigma instructor.

* **William B. Iwaskow** is a diversified business executive. He was formerly an executive vice president at Hoffman-LaRoche; a division president and general manager at Allied Chemical; a director of business development and planning for the International Division of American Cyanamid; and a principal at Korn Ferry International. Mr. Iwaskow is currently an adjunct professor of management at William Paterson College; previously, he served in the same capacity at Pace University. In addition, he has conducted many management seminars and developed a variety of multimedia projects for several trade associations. Mr. Iwaskow has a broad education with degrees in engineering, business (MBA), and law. He has also received President Reagan's citation for "Private Sector Initiatives" at the White House for his raising $7 million for New Jersey doctoral engineering scholarships.

Page xi, replace entry for Eugene H. Kramer with:

Eugene H. Kramer, CPA, deceased, was a principal in the firm of E.H. Kramer and Company.

Page xi, add after entry for Jay H. Loevy:

Robert F. McElroy is a managing associate in Coopers & Lybrand L.L.P.'s Consulting Division, in the Financial Management & Business Analysis (FMBA) group, located in the New York metropolitan area. He has more than six years of consulting experience in a variety of industries, including telecommunications and chemical manufacturing. He specializes in financial process control.

* *Page xii, add after carryover entry for Athar Murtuza:*

Thomas F. Norris is a managing associate in the consumer and industrial manufacturing practice of the New York Metro Consulting office of Coopers & Lybrand. Mr. Norris has more than twenty years of experience in operations, materials management, accounting, and information technology. His experience also includes both centralized and decentralized management in global environments. He has a B.B.A. from Siena College in accounting and has both CPIM and CIRM designations from the American Production and Inventory Control Society.

Page xii, replace entry for R. Malcolm Schwartz with:

R. Malcolm Schwartz is a partner with Coopers & Lybrand L.L.P., and is responsible for the delivery of financial management consulting services in the eastern region. He also led the firmwide development of the activity-based management practice and was a principal author of *Internal Control—Integrated Framework.* He currently focuses on the consumer products industry and has clients in the public and private sectors. He has held senior management roles in finance and control, distribution, industrial engineering, and division and general management. Prior to his association with Coopers & Lybrand, he was a senior partner and chief financial officer of a major worldwide management consulting firm.

Page xiii, replace entries for Ronald K. Tucker and Vicki L. Tucker with:

Ronald K. Tucker, BBA, CPCU, ARM, Hagedorn & Company, was formerly Vice President in the Johnson & Higgins Middle Market Division, where he was responsible for new business sales activities. Mr. Tucker has served in various sales and management roles with another national broker; was responsible for wholesale and retail sales at the Rhulen Organization; has owned his own insurance agency; and has worked for two large insurers, Reliance Insurance Company and American International Group.

Vicki L. Tucker, M.S., ARM, is a risk consultant with Good Samaritan Hospital. She has developed risk management systems within the health care industry. Her prior experience includes President, Risk Management & Quality Assurance Consulting Services, Inc., and Director of Medical Staff Services/Risk Management/Quality Assurance. Ms. Tucker is currently an administrator with the Center for Rehabilitation.

Page xiv, add after entry for R. Layne Weggeland:

Glenn A. White is a senior manager in Coopers & Lybrand L.L.P.'s Consulting Division, in the Integrated Health Care Services Consulting group, located in Philadelphia. He works with pharmaceutical and biotechnology manufacturers to provide value-adding solutions in the areas of materials management, production operations, sales, marketing, financial operations, and other corporate support functions. His background includes activity-based cost management; business process reengineering; systems requirements analysis, definition, selection, and implementation; financial analysis; and operations and cost improvement.

Serge L. Wind is Assistant Controller for Financial Studies at AT&T, with responsibility for identifying and targeting financial measures, monitoring the capital and investment program, establishing financial targeting via competitor analogs, generating financial models, overseeing transfer pricing, and performing special analytical studies (including analyzing corporate mergers and acquisitions). Dr. Wind holds Ph.D. and B.A. degrees in statistics and economics, respectively, from Columbia University.

SUPPLEMENT CONTENTS

Note to the Reader: Materials new to *this* supplement are indicated by an asterisk (*) in the left margin of the contents listed below and throughout the supplement. Materials that appear only in the supplement and not in the main volume are indicated by the word "(New)" after the title.

PART II   TOOLS AND TECHNIQUES

11A   Budgeting Shareholder Value (New)
SERGE L. WIND
AT&T Company

* **14   Techniques of Scheduling Budgets**
DONALD R. MOSCATO
Iona College

PART III   PREPARATION OF SPECIFIC BUDGETS

15   Sales and Marketing Budget (Revised)
R. MALCOLM SCHWARTZ
Coopers & Lybrand L.L.P.

17   The Research and Development Budget
MAURICE I. ZELDMAN
Emzee Associates

* **18   The Administrative Expense Budget (Revised)**
R. MALCOM SCHWARTZ
Coopers & Lybrand L.L.P.
MARIA THERESA MATEO
Coopers & Lybrand L.L.P.

18A   Budgeting Payroll Costs (New)
LEONARD A. HAUG
Digital Equipment Corporation

* **18B   Budgeting the Purchasing Department and the Purchasing Process (new)**
THOMAS F. NORRIS
Coopers & Lybrand L.L.P.

20A   **Leasing (New)**
      ROBERT DALE APGOOD
      Canterbury Group

23A   **Understanding Foreign Exchange Transactions (New)**
      FRANÇOISE B. SOARES-KEMP
      Credit Suisse

24   **Budgeting Property and Liability Insurance Requirements**
      RONALD K. TUCKER
      Hagedorn & Company
      VICKI L. TUCKER
      Good Samaritan Hospital

PART IV   BUDGETING APPLICATIONS

26   **Bracket Budgeting**
      MICHAEL W. CURRAN
      Decision Sciences Corporation

26A   **Budgeting for Total Quality Management (New)**
      RONALD A. FOLLETT
      RF Group, Inc.

* 27 **Program Budgeting: Planning, Programming, Budgeting**
      WILLIAM B. IWASKOW

27A   **Activity-Based Budgeting (New)**
      JAMES A. BRIMSON
      ABM Institute
      JOHN J. ANTOS
      Antos Enterprises, Inc.

* 28 **Computer Applications in Budgeting**
      DONALD R. MOSCATO
      THOMAS POLLINA
      Iona College

28A   **Fuzzy Logic Applied to Budgeting: An Intuitive Approach to Coping
      with Uncertainty (New)**
      DONALD R. MOSCATO
      Iona College

* 29 **The Behavioral Aspects of Budgeting (Revised)**
      GYAN CHANDRA
      Miami University (Ohio)

* **33   Budgeting in the Health Care Industry**
CHRISTOPHER S. SPENCE
Ernst & Young L.L.P.

PART V   INDUSTRY BUDGETS

34   Budgeting in the Biotech Industry (New)
R. MALCOLM SCHWARTZ
GLENN A. WHITE
ROBERT F. MCELROY
CHARLES A. CLERECUZIO
Coopers & Lybrand L.L.P.

CUMULATIVE INDEX

BUDGETING SHAREHOLDER VALUE (New)

Serge L. Wind

AT&T Company

CONTENTS

11A.1 OVERVIEW OF SHAREHOLDER VALUE 1

(a) Purposes 2
(b) What Is Shareholder Value? 2
(c) Why Focus on Cash Flow? 2
(d) Two Complementary Value-Based Measures 3

11A.2 LONG-TERM VALUATION 4

(a) Shareholder Value Recapitulation 4
(b) Time Value of Money 4
(c) Cost of Capital 5
(d) Continuing Value 6
(e) Budgeting Implications 6

11A.3 ECONOMIC VALUE ADDED (EVA) 7

(a) EVA Overview 7
(b) Example of Value-Added Concept 7
(c) EVA Formula 8
(d) Implications for Value Creation 8
(e) Components of EVA—Return on Invested Capital 8

(f) Components of EVA— Invested Capital 9
(g) Operating Drivers of Value 9
(h) EVA Attributes 10

11A.4 COMPLEMENTARY MEASURES OF VALUATION 12

(a) EVA and Valuation 12
(b) Tracking by EVA 14
(c) Guide to Appropriate Uses of EVA 14

11A.5 BUDGETING SHAREHOLDER VALUE 14

(a) Business Cases 15
(b) Capital and Investment Programs 15
(c) Business Plans 15
(d) Resource Allocation 16
(e) Operating Budget Review 16
(f) Monthly Actuals Reporting 16

11A.6 SUMMARY OF BUDGET VALUATION TECHNIQUES 17

SOURCES AND SUGGESTED REFERENCES 18

11A.1 OVERVIEW OF SHAREHOLDER VALUE. Businesses that want to grow their market shares, or at least to be competitive in their markets, must improve productivity, foster innovation, and strive toward enhanced customer satisfaction. Businesses that want to grow, as manifested by these objectives, must increase investment now for the future.

As the source of much of this required funding, shareholders assess the potential increase in "value" of their investments in a business when deciding to invest or not. This assessment is based on their anticipated return and the risk they associate with it.

It is vital, then, for firms to focus on shareholder satisfaction by understanding what is important to this stakeholder. In this manner, the drivers of intrinsic value (or *shareholder value*) of the firm can be discerned and its value managed.

(a) Purposes.   Shareholder value provides the valuation of a business. The principal purposes of implementing (period) performance measurement of shareholder value are:

- To provide an economic measurement of business performance from the perspective of the shareholder.
- To supplement traditional accounting-based measures of business performance with cash flow valuation.
- To provide proper vehicles for achieving management objectives and decisions—including the planning process, resource utilization, and employee compensation—that drive creation of value.

(b) What Is Shareholder Value?   Return to the share owner is in the form of cash dividends and share price appreciation. Aside from psychic and other nonfinancial attributes of an investment, these are the only returns available to common stockholders.

The value of the shareholder investment emanates from the cash flow generated over the life of the business, assessed with the associated business risk. Thus, shareholder value—the economic measure of the value of a business—is expressed as the sum of future cash flows in today's dollars.

The cash flows are aftertax cash generated each period from the operations of the business, available to all providers of company capital. For a proper analysis of the true worth of cash flows over time, they have to be expressed in terms of today's dollars. (See § 11A.2(b) on the time value of money.)

(c) Why Focus on Cash Flow?   The concept of shareholder value is expressed in terms of cash flows, and is based on current and future cash outflows and inflows from now out to the future. We are adopting an economic perspective, in which cash outlays are delineated as the underlying components of an economic model of valuation. This framework was laid out by Rappaport and others (see Sources and Suggested References).

The emphasis on the discounted cash flow (DCF) approach versus the standard, accounting-based approach also manifests itself in the types of financial measures that are most expressive of economic performance in which investors are interested. Traditional measures, such as earnings per share and returns on equity and operating assets, do not capture all aspects of value creation, including:

- Business risk
- Investor expectations
- Time value of money.

They also often reflect the effects of leverage or the debt ratio, which is the total debt of the firm divided by total capital. Finally, they are single-period, short-term measures. We need to start concentrating on measures, such as the two value-based indicators delineated in the next section, which (unlike accounting earnings) have been found by studies to be highly correlated with stock price, an external indicator of company value.

In their book on valuation, Copeland *et al.* sum it up accurately: "Managers who use the DCF approach to valuation, focusing on long-term cash flow, ultimately will be rewarded by higher share prices. The evidence from the market is conclusive. Naive attention to accounting earnings will lead to value-destroying decisions."[1]

(d) Two Complementary Value-Based Measures.   Two measures of shareholder value will be discussed, because they are related in important ways. Both are value-based measures.

Shareholder value, based on discounted cash flows, measures total long-term value. Long-term valuation is used for:

- Evaluation of investment decisions (both capital projects and acquisitions)
- Assessment of long-term plans and projects
- Economic decision-making.

As we have seen, this measure—the investors' perception of the total worth of a company—is based on all the cash flows to be generated, in order to include all future benefits or returns, as well as costs of all current and future investments and added assets.

For both short-term planning and tracking, *Economic Value Added* or EVA, developed by Stern and Stewart, captures the value created (or depleted) during a period of business activity.[2] (A *period* is a finite time interval, like a year.) Because of its importance to planning and budgeting, EVA is more fully explained in § 11A.3.

Both measures share another key property: they distinguish between operations and financing and measure the effects of only the former in valuation. Inclusion of financing effects (such as interest and number of shares), along with traditional accounting, introduces misleading non-cash-based information in measures like return on equity and EPS.

---

[1]See Tom Copeland, Tim Koller, and Jack Murrin at 94.

[2]Joel Stern and Bennett Stewart defined a form of residual income or Economic Value Added (EVA) in two publications (see Sources and Suggested References).

The critical assertion to be developed for budgeting purposes is that EVA is particularly useful in tracking a plan's contribution to the total shareholder value. The nature of cash flows and their inherent difficulty for budgeting, coupled with the observation that the period cash flow component does not reveal the state of incremental value, combine to favor an added role for EVA. Thus, EVA, apparently relegated to a period measure of value added, takes on an important new role: short-term budget tracker of total value.

11A.2   LONG-TERM VALUATION.   In the last section, we introduced two measures: shareholder value and EVA. Shareholder value is the (long-term) valuation of a company, whereas EVA is a measure of short-term value creation for a period of business activity. Total value, or shareholder value, is always quantified at a point in time (e.g., as of this year), and value is a function of all future time periods.

(a)   Shareholder Value Recapitulation.   Long-term valuation is the best approach to linking shareholder value creation to investment decisions. We have defined *value* as the summation of all projected free cash flows for a business or project, expressed in the equivalent of today's dollars.

Free cash flow represents the aftertax cash generated each period after reinvestment from the operations—not financing—of the business. Reinvestment, from the firm's perspective, consists of net plant adds (or capital expenditures for plant and equipment), changes in operating capital (or changes in receivables and inventory less payables), and investments (or acquisitions, mergers, etc.).

Example of a Statement of Funds Flow		
Operating Income (Before Interest & Taxes)	$895	
+ Other Income (Operating)	112	
- Cash Operating Taxes Paid	(189)	
Income After Cash Taxes (Before Interest)	818	$818
- Additions to Plant Net of Depreciation	(98)	
- Additions to Operating Capital	(34)	
- Additions to Investments	—	
Reinvestment	$(132)	$(132)
Free Cash Flow		$686
= Income After Cash Taxes (before Interest) less Reinvestment		

Exhibit 11A.1.   Definition of free cash flow.

In Exhibit 11A.1, an example is shown of free cash flow, forecasted in terms of future dollars, which must be subsequently "discounted" back to today's dollars.

(b)   Time Value of Money.   The reference to "today's dollars" in § 11A.1(c) is to the economic tenet that "most people prefer to have cash now rather than later," because the cash can now be invested to produce returns unavailable if the cash flow is delayed. The time value of money derives from the cost of foregone opportunities.[3] With the cash flows forecasted in terms of future dollars, the time-value-of-money concept dictates that they must be discounted to equate them to today's dollars, thus providing an estimate of the present value of the business from each period. We will see later that risk as reflected in the cost of capital determines the discount rate.

(c) Cost of Capital. The rate used to discount future cash flows back to the present for valuation is called the *cost of capital* or *discount rate*. (See Chapter 11 for further discussion on the subject; capital itself is defined in § 11A.3(f).)

The numerical example of discounting assumes negative cash flow of $120 in the first year for an initial project investment, and positive cash flows of $80 in each of the next four years. Although the total of the five years added up to $200 in absolute dollars, that $200 is only equivalent to $110 in today's dollars. The $110 is the *present value*.

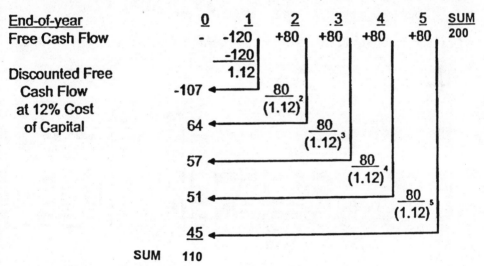

Exhibit 11A.2.   Discounted free cash flow: An example.

The cost of capital is the risk-adjusted opportunity cost for investors, or the minimum required return. The cost of capital represents the average rate of return that investors expect when they decide to invest in a company of a certain risk.

The cost of capital is the weighted average cost of debt capital supplied by bondholders and equity capital supplied by the shareholders. This weighted average cost of capital is often referred to as the *WACC*.

COST OF CAPITAL

Cost of Capital = [After-Tax Cost of Debt x % of Debt in Capital Ratio]

+

[Cost of Equity x % of Equity in Capital Ratio]

---

[3]See Tom Copeland, Tim Koller, and Jack Murrin at 75.

For debt, with interest tax deductible, the aftertax cost of debt is based on the prevailing interest rates (and the effective income tax rate). For equity, the more complicated methods described in Stewart's book[4] are needed to estimate the cost of equity of different companies. Finally, the weights are determined by the corporate objective (or sometimes the actual) debt ratio, usually determined by the treasurer of the company. The cost of equity, in essence, is an estimate of the return required by shareholders for investing in the company's common stock, based on an assessment of the level of risk in the company and other investment alternatives in the marketplace.

(d) Continuing Value.   As shown in the graphical representations of a long-term value calculation (see exhibit 11A.3), *shareholder value* is the present value of all future free cash flows. For time beyond the explicit planning period (usually 5 or 10 years), a term called *continuing value* captures the remaining future cash flows forecasted into perpetuity. Formulas for continuing value, or residual value, can be found in the valuation book by Copeland, Koller, and Murrin.[5]

• Long-term value is the present value of all future free cash flows

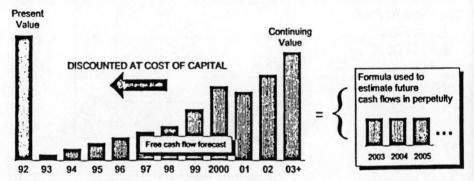

Exhibit 11A.3.   Long-term value: An illustration.

Continuing value, absolutely necessary to compute discounted cash flows, often accounts for more than 70%, and sometime more than 100%, of total value. Moreover, with even near-term forecasts often hard to estimate, the long-term-based continuing value is often difficult to estimate reliably. However, it does represent the premium investors are expecting beyond the explicit planning period.

(e) Budgeting Implications.   With the most important decisions made by company managers involving value of a pending project or business unit, accountability based on successful implementation is vital. A business plan and budget for the company must reflect the benefits and costs of those projects and business units for which value has been altered.

However, we have seen that valuation is a complex procedure, depending upon multi-years' continuing value, which is determined by imprecise parameters and

---

[4]See Bennett Stewart III, ch. 12, at 431–75 (1990).

[5]See Tom Copeland, Tim Koller, and Jack Murrin at 207–30.

accounts for the majority portion of value, and cash flow projections with start-up problems that reverberate throughout the DCF. Budget practitioners responsible for cash flow items know that actual end-of-year (or start-up) balance sheet items (known only after the budget has been approved) must be taken into account in re-estimating budget-year cash flows (like payables, receivables, additions to plant, and free cash flow).

The complexity and reliability of budgeting and tracking discounted cash flows for even the first few years leaves us amenable to other budgeting notions.

11A.3   ECONOMIC VALUE ADDED (EVA).   We have seen why shareholder value is vital in assessing a company's value over the long term. An ongoing firm needs to be able to check progress as well, and measure increases in value with a short-term measure. EVA, depicted as the most important period measure of value added (or depleted),[6] will also be seen to provide a means for effective budgeting for the DCF measure of shareholder value.

(a)   EVA Overview.   Rather than estimating total value via multi-year cash flows, Economic Value Added measures period value added to or depleted from share-holder value. It relates income statement and balance sheet activity to shareholder expectations, and uses traditional accounting information as a surrogate for cash flows. EVA is more highly correlated with stock price than are traditional measures, according to empirical studies by Stern Stewart.

The EVA formula incorporates earnings, cash income taxes, balance sheet capital, and the cost of capital so that value created is measured (positive value is created when the return on invested capital exceeds the cost of capital). EVA measures operating returns in excess of (or below) the cost of capital. (Financing impacts, such as the tax deductibility of interest expense, are excluded.)

(b)   Example of Value Added Concept.   If you borrow $100 from a bank at a 10% rate for one year, and you earn 12% return on the money through investment or the race track, you have created value for yourself. Your return exceeds the bank's cost to you by two percentage points.

If, however, with the bank cost fixed at 10%, you manage only an 8% return, you have lost money and value by two percentage points.

In an analogous fashion, if the return on invested capital (ROIC) exceeds the cost of capital, value is added. Value is depleted for the period when ROIC is less than the weighted average cost of capital (WACC).

We have already referred to the cost-of-capital component; it is more complex (e.g., two dimensions) than the cost of debt in the example, but plays a role analogous to the hurdle rate. (A *hurdle rate* is a threshold value for determining economic acceptance of a project: the return must exceed the hurdle rate.)

We now need to be a bit more precise in defining the return on capital and an explicit EVA equation.

---

[6]See Bennett Stewart III at 3–14 (1986).

(c) EVA Formula. Building into the formula the feature that EVA is positive only when the return exceeds the cost of capital, the EVA formula[7] can be written as:

EVA = [Return on Invested Capital - Cost of Capital] x Average Invested Capital

Note that EVA is an actual dollar figure, not a percentage. Its sign indeed depends on the sign of the *spread,* the difference between return and cost of capital (both percentages). Its magnitude or size depends, in large part, on average capital, which is also dollar-denominated. (*Capital* is defined in section 11A.3(f).)

(d) Implications for Value Creation. There are three basic means of securing an increase in EVA for the company, as pointed out by Stewart[8]:

An increase in EVA will result:
- If operating efficiency is enhanced
  - Rate of return on existing capital base improves

OR

- If value-added new investments are undertaken
  - Additional capital invested returns more than cost of capital

OR

- If capital is withdrawn from uneconomic activities
  - Capital withdrawn where returns are below cost of capital.

(e) Components of EVA—Return on Invested Capital. Return on invested capital (ROIC) in the EVA formula must exceed the cost of capital, the hurdle rate which we have already defined in section 11A.2(c). ROIC, also a percentage, is defined as:

$$\text{ROIC} = \frac{\text{Net operating profit after taxes (NOPAT)}}{\text{Average invested capital}}$$

NOPAT represents posttax earnings before payment of capital costs (i.e., interest and dividends). Essentially, NOPAT includes all revenues and sales net of costs and expenses, plus other operational income, less cash income taxes paid (except for the deductibility of financing-related interest). As such, NOPAT is the right measure to compare pre-capital-cost earnings with investors' costs. Cash taxes are more consistent with cash flow valuation and serve as an appropriate operating driver of EVA, because of comprehensive income taxation employed in accounting.

---

[7]Joel Stern and Bennett Stewart defined *Economic Value Added* and its concept and are responsible for its development into an important model for creating and managing value; the description of EVA in this chapter is based on the value-based framework they generated, as described in two books by Bennett Stewart.

[8]See Bennett Stewart III at 138 (1990).

(f) Components of EVA—Invested Capital. The third component of the EVA formula is average *invested capital*; it also forms the denominator of ROIC. Invested capital represents the cumulative cash invested in the company over time.

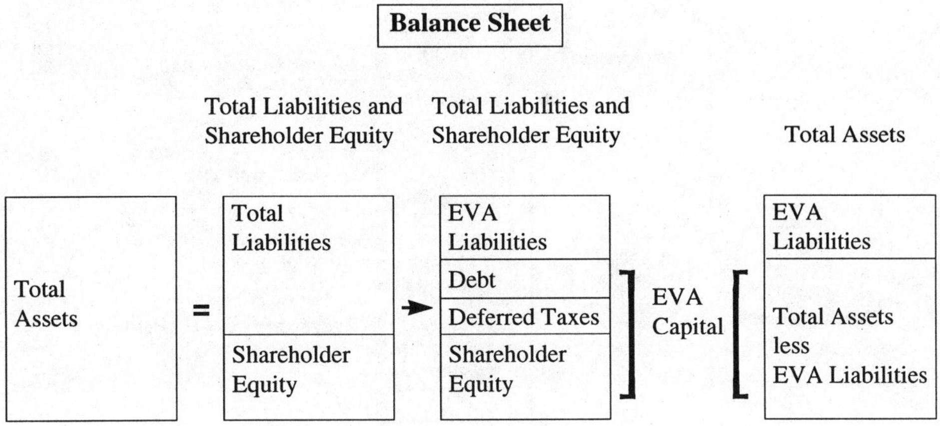

Balance Sheet

EVA Capital = Total Assets - EVA Liabilities

Exhibit 11A.4. EVA capital.

EVA capital is defined as the difference between assets and EVA liabilities (excluding debt and deferred taxes), or, equivalently, in terms of the right-hand side of the balance sheet, equity plus equity equivalents (e.g., deferred taxes), plus debt.

In both capital and NOPAT, some corresponding adjustments to each term are required to fit in the EVA formula in § 11A.3(c). Basically, as defined by Stewart,[9] most of these adjustments involve replacing book accounting value with terms that are more cash-flow or economic-based. EVA capital, including the adjustments contained in equity equivalents (e.g., deferred taxes) which convert the standard accounting book value to a form of economic book value, is a truer measure of the cash invested.

(g) Operating Drivers of Value. Key value drivers can be used effectively to include a detailed analysis of the EVA sensitivity to changes in input parameters. Operating drivers include revenue growth, NOPAT margin (i.e., NOPAT divided by revenues), capital turnover (revenues divided by average capital), and some of the other variables from the income statement and balance sheet as depicted in Exhibit 11A.5. For example, inventory turnovers and receivables turnover (or days outstanding) are operating drivers of EVA via capital.

Most of these drivers are related to return on invested capital (ROIC) via duPont decomposition or *ROIC tree*.[10] For example, NOPAT margin, times capital turnover, times the tax factor, equals ROIC.

---

[9]See Bennett Stewart III at 8–13 (1986).

[10]See Tom Copeland, Tim Koller, and Jack Murphy at 125.

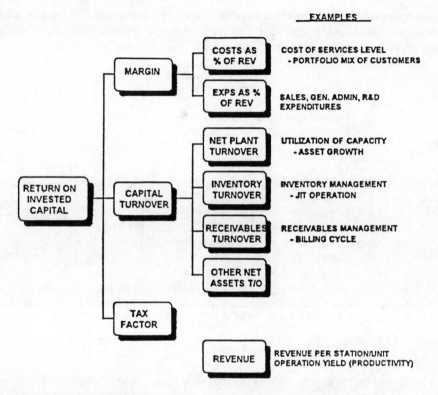

EXAMPLES

Exhibit 11A.5.   Value drivers.

Financing drivers, distinct from operating drivers, include debt ratio and amounts and costs of capital, but are not controlled by business units or profit centers.

Sensitivity analysis can be applied to valuation and associated decision-making, once the key drivers with the greatest impact on value are identified. For budgeting, the drivers can identify the source of any variance, and can be used for unit trend comparison.

(h)   EVA Attributes.   In describing Economic Value Added, its principal attribute in short-term planning is that it is "the single most important indicator of value creation. . . . EVA measures not only management's ability to manage capital efficiently, but takes into account the magnitude of capital investment as well."[11]

In addition, EVA is an indicator of the company's productivity. We usually think of a firm or industry competing in a market for products and/or services. The conceptual approach of shareholder value suggests that there is another market—the market for investor capital—in which all publicly owned companies must compete simultaneously with its other markets. (We began § 11A.1 with a discussion of the need of companies to be competitive in securing funding.)

As indicated in Exhibit 11A.6 (generated by Deo[12]), the firm strives to attain a sustainable competitive advantage in its markets for its products and services,

---

[11]See Bennett Stewart III at 3–14 (1986).

[12]Adapted from Prakash Deo's unpublished AT&T paper, "Resource Alignment" (1991).

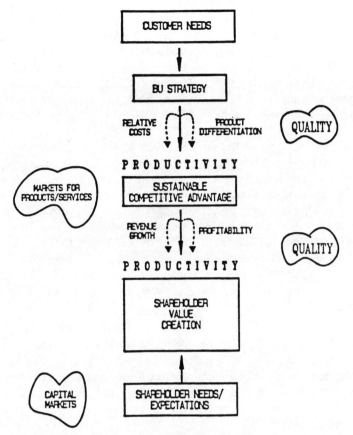

Exhibit 11A.6.   Linking customer and shareholder needs.

through product differentiation, cost minimization, and so forth, to satisfy its customers. Simultaneously, via profitability and revenue growth drivers, the firm satisfies its shareholders' expectations by value creation emanating from its products and services.

Productivity is foremost a measure of ability to create value (or output) in excess of cost (input) of generating it. Two complementary productivity measures are suggested:

1. *Operating margin*—for expense productivity and income statement efficiency
   - Pretax NOPAT divided by total revenues.
2. *Capital turnover*—for capital productivity and balance sheet efficiency
   - Revenue per average capital.

Productivity improvement is year-over-year percentage change in either measure.

Return on invested capital (ROIC) is the joint measure of operating margin and capital productivity; it reveals the company's productivity, as determined by the spread between return on capital and cost of capital, in competition for investor capital.[13]

---

[13]See Bennett Stewart III at 3–14 (1986).

EVA can also be decomposed by disaggregating financial results to delineate the impact of key operating drivers, like revenue growth, pretax profit margin per sales, cash tax rate, net operating capital (NOC) charge and plant, property, and equipment (PPE) charge. These last two drivers, proposed by Stern Stewart, represent the normalized variable (NOC/sales and PPE/sales) times the cost of capital (before taxes), and are derived from viewing EVA as residual income (of earnings in excess of capital charges); that is, EVA = NOPAT - COC x Average Invested Capital.

In the 1992 AT&T Annual Report, CFO Alex Mandl wrote that: "EVA is truly a system of measurement. It supplements traditional accounting measures of performance, giving us additional insight into our business and helping us to identify the factors that affect our performance. We have made it the centerpiece of our 'value-based planning' process. And we are linking a portion of our managers' incentive compensation to performance against EVA targets in 1993."

Moreover, EVA has the important facility of connecting forward-looking valuation to performance evaluation (via actual operating performance) over discrete periods. EVA thereby enables consistent tracking of valuation. However, first, we need to explore in more depth the relationship between the two measures, EVA and shareholder value.

11A.4   COMPLEMENTARY MEASURES OF VALUATION.

(a)   **EVA and Valuation.**   *Shareholder value* was defined in § 11A.2 as the multi-period, long-term valuation of a company (as of a point in time), whereas we have just seen that EVA measures value added to a shareholder's investment for a period (like a year or quarter).

To determine the economic value of an enterprise, operating unit, or project requires a valuation—or all-period analysis—of all future cash flows. Generally, the entity value is the future expected cash flows discounted at a rate (or cost of capital) that reflects the riskiness of the operating cash flow. In particular:

$$\text{VALUE} = \text{PV(FCF)} = \frac{\text{FCF } 1}{1+\text{COC}} + \frac{\text{FCF } 2}{(1+\text{COC})^2} + ...$$

where FCF 1, stands for the free cash flow in period 1 and PV denotes present value or discounted sum.

It is, however, true (only under some conditions) that VALUE also equals the present value of the EVAs plus initial capital CAP:

$$\text{VALUE} = \text{PV(EVA)} + \text{CAP}$$

where

$$\text{PV(EVA)} = \frac{\text{EVA } 1}{1+\text{COC}} + \frac{\text{EVA } 2}{(1+\text{COC})^2} + ...$$

Capital, defined in § 11A.3(f), is not equal to the book value of traditional accounting, but represents economic book value, where adjustments, like the deferred tax reserve, are added to book debt and equity, to allow capital to reflect a more economic and accurate base on which to earn.

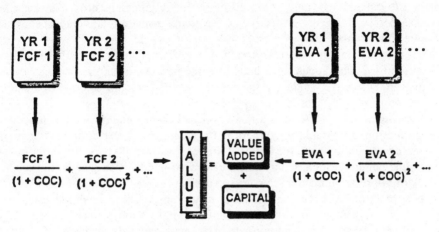

$$PV(FCF) = V = PV(EVA) + CAP$$

Exhibit 11A.7. Valuation.

Although individual-period EVA is usually different from FCF for the same period, under a specific set of assumptions, the two approaches generally yield the same value, i.e.,

$$PV\,(FCF) = PV\,(EVA) + CAP = VALUE,$$

when the amount of initial capital of the firm is added to the discounted EVA (or value added) sum.

This result is important, because it suggests that VALUE may, under certain assumptions, be calculated using EVA components (in place of cash flow) and that the definition of EVA as a period measure of value added yields the same VALUE when a discounted sum of EVA terms is taken. Shareholder value can be expressed in terms of EVA components, too.

For initial implementation, using VALUE (EVA) for valuation is not always recommended, because the set of assumptions for value equality may not be valid in all cases, and FCF-based routines are well established for project valuation in business cases in most firms. The specialized circumstances and assumptions for VALUE equality may not be applicable to the majority of projects and investments of a firm without an adjustment.

Identification and correction of any systematic difference in the VALUE determined by EVA and FCF (usually a function of project timing and start-up assumptions) may be viewed as a transition issue. As implementation takes root, the advantages of consistency—of using EVA as one common measure with a common language and framework, with operating drivers for all planning and budgeting, for both period and total value estimation—may dominate the discomfort of any needed adjustments. In addition, as shown by Worthington,[14] the contribution (as a percent of total value) from EVA continuing value will be less than the percent value attributed to the FCF continuing value; part of this effect is attributable to the role of initial capital in the EVA NPV formulation. Even with reliance on the cash flow approach to calculating value, it would be useful to complement it with the EVA approach to get a different perspective on the components of total value, specifically the value added in the early years and the continuing value.

What is interesting, however, is that the period component of PV (FCF) does not yield any information about value added for the period—but EVA does, by definition. Instead, FCF merely indicates the dependence on parent or external financing.

(b)   Tracking by EVA.   We have already touched upon some difficulties associated with budgeting and tracking valuation by cash flows: the dependence on an intractable continuing value, the impossibility of tracking all years, the shifts in cash flows in the budget year caused by actual prior year-end balance sheet variances, and the lack of information inherent in component cash flows.

A few years of EVA data, on the other hand, indicate how much value has been created by management, and thereby evaluate progress toward shareholder value. When all-period valuation is appropriate, it is recommended that EVA period measures be generated for the first three to five years of analysis, along with the multi-year valuation to supplement the FCF valuation approach and to provide a basis for meaningful budgeting and tracking. As a period performance measure, EVA connects forward-looking valuation to performance evaluation. Because EVA is not a cash flow measure, and because its period interpretation is value-oriented, it greatly facilitates period tracking of value, thereby adding "memory" to the planning process.

(c)   Guide to Appropriate Uses of EVA.   EVA is the best internal, single-period measure of value creation. However, single-period values of EVA are not to be used for critical asset or investment and project evaluation decisions, which are based on long-term value creation potential. Instead, discounted cash flow valuation utilizing net present value (NPV) is mandated for decisions involving multi-period benefits, such as business unit evaluation, lease/buy decisions, mergers and acquisitions, and strategic options assessment. (Subject to the conditions raised in § 11A.4(a), NPV based on EVA could be utilized.)

As discussed in the previous section, EVA, in addition to its primary role, can serve as a complement to discounted cash flow valuation, particularly to gauge the initial impact of the project or investment, and to track.

11A.5   BUDGETING SHAREHOLDER VALUE.   Critical investment decisions, based on long-term valuation, come in several different forms in a typical corporation (as discussed in other chapters of this book). Budgeting of these investments is often spotty, partly because it is difficult to isolate the effects of an investment project embedded in an operating unit's returns.

---

[14]Adapted from Mac Worthington's unpublished AT&T presentation, "Terminal Value Computation in Cash Flow Valuation of Business Opportunities" (1994).

(a) Business Cases.   Business cases are the fundamental support analysis for business decisions involving resource utilization. The business case process, while dealing with periodic projects and investments, must be an integral part of budgeting and planning.

Business cases for R&D and capital (additions to plant, property, and equipment) also serve as the basis for subsequent measurement and tracking actions.

As part of the financial analysis of the project, business case output should exhibit the net present value and other standard measures, as well as the EVA forecasts for the first three to five years. The latter will be compared to actuals to determine if initial additions (or depletions) from value are on schedule. Incremental cash flow effects of investment are represented, along with risks, uncertainty, and alternatives.

Review and approval procedures are usually specified by corporate governance. For example, it is an AT&T corporate requirement that a rigorous business case process drive business investment decisions. Capital investments are further discussed in chapters 19 and 20.

(b)   Capital and Investment Programs.   Potential mergers and acquisitions, divestitures, investments, and joint ventures are included in these programs, along with additions to capital (APPE) and additions to finance assets; the latter two categories are included in the program at a more aggregate level.

Consummated ventures should be tracked quarterly, comparing budget and actual values for revenues, EVA, funding, and the like.

Part of the investment analysis is an evaluation of the expected impact on the parent's reported EVA earnings after the acquisition. This assessment is usually more important than the EVA expected from the new entity itself.

Review of major investments will be based on a comparison of original enabling business case expectations with actuals. Again, comparison of the first few years' actuals versus plan EVA values is strongly recommended.

A clear understanding should exist as to the circumstances under which a potential acquisition should be included in the company and entity budgets, rather than merely covered by a separate investment program or business case. Generally, large magnitudes combined with a high degree of uncertainty result in omission of the investment from the budget, or statement of the budget with and without the investment. "Ready for approval" investments are usually reflected in the budget.

(c)   Business Plans.   As a part of the annual planning process, each business unit is expected to generate a business plan, consisting in the main of a strategic plan and a financial plan. The first year of the financial plan usually becomes next year's budget. Its monitoring and tracking are discussed in § 11A.5(e).

However, budgeting and tracking should also play a role in subsequent assessments of the business plan. To curtail undue optimism in the late years of the plan (the "hockey stick effect"), financial projections, particularly EVA and revenue, should be monitored and compared to actuals, from the second through tenth years. Such an assessment would conceivably contribute to a greater degree of comfort or discomfort for the attainability of the immediate budget year.

(d)   Resource Allocation.   Based upon resource requirements expressed in the business plans to achieve business strategies and long-term economic profits, senior management makes resource allocation decisions as a step in arriving at a budget for next year and beyond. Strategic considerations are paramount, or at least share equal billing with economic considerations in all resource allocation decisions. A business case analysis of the life-cycle cash flows indicates the economic value of a project.

Economic considerations generally can be assessed by two broad categories: benefit and efficiency measures.[15] Benefit measures reveal the cash benefit from investing in a particular proposal, expressed in dollar terms: measures include shareholder value, net present value (NPV), and discounted cash flows. Efficiency measures, expressed as a percentage, indicate how productive a project is in generating cash, relative to resource costs. A ratio of shareholder value or NPV to the present value of all cash outflows (resource expenditures) is used, as is an internal rate of return. Long-term attractiveness tends to dominate decisions, and capital projects and investments could be ranked by total value (or by value per resource input).

Translation of the consequences of resource allocation must be included in the budget. Economic impact should include impact on EVA and total value. Considerations of cash affordability for the firm must also be evaluated.

(e)   Operating Budget Review.   Once major resource allocation decisions are made, attention falls on the commitment budget. Now period measures, like EVA and FCF, are more important as indicators of value added and current cash flow than total valuation. The year-to-year change in unit EVA is as important a measure as the current level of EVA (and its sign).

The budget should pose a challenge that is achievable. If each operating unit makes its EVA level and that EVA level is viewed as a stepping stone toward maximizing shareholder value over time, the enterprise will be successful.

A budget (by year, quarter, and, usually, month) consists of parts or all of an income statement, balance sheet, funds flow, and measures (particularly, the explicit commitment measures to which compensation is tied). In this budgeting mode, EVA is the best measure.

(f)   Monthly Actuals Reporting.   Key measures compared by unit and month for budget versus actual and budget versus last year's period should include EVA, FCF, and revenue. EVA can be decomposed into its operating drivers—revenue growth, NOPAT margin, and capital turnover—and the respective variances compared to better understand shortfalls. As EVA is implemented in the company, additional critical information can be shown, such as variance in the EVA operating drivers, discussed in section 11A.3(g).

Exhibit 11A.8 displays useful information for management of budget/actual differences in EVA, underlying data, and drivers. Consolidated EVA is also shown in internal company reports as a sum of entity EVAs for actual and budget, enabling identification of entity shortfalls. A modified tree diagram, like Exhibit 11A.5, displays more value drivers, to assess the principal source of actual/budget variance.

---

[15]Adapted from Harish Chandra's unpublished AT&T memo, "Resource Allocation" (1993).

($)	Actual	Budget	Difference
Operating Income	133	139	(6)
EVA Adjustments	(11)	(9)	(2)
Adjusted Operating Income	122	130	(8)
Cash Taxes Paid	(35)	(37)	2
	----	----	----
NOPAT	87	93	(6)
Avg. Invested Capital	579	599	(20)
EVA	20	24	(4)

EVA Drivers Impact			
Change in NOPAT			(6)
Change in Adj. Operating Income		(8)	
Change in Cash Taxes Paid		2	
Change in Avg. Capital @ 11.5% Cost of Capital			2
Change in EVA			(4)

Exhibit 11A.8.   EVA year-to-date results.

11A.6   SUMMARY OF BUDGET VALUATION TECHNIQUES.   Effectively managing and measuring value calls for different, although complementary, techniques depending upon the intended use and the associated time period required. For decisions involving long-term value creation potential, the all-period FCF valuation should be utilized to estimate shareholder value. However, for budgeting purposes, the EVA annual component is particularly valuable in budgeting as a measure of value created in a period. It indicates how much value is to be created from capital by management, and thereby evaluates progress toward the all-period shareholder value.

For a single period, EVA is the best measure of value creation, and EVA should be monitored and tracked for budgeting.

Valuation must be closely linked to single-period measures of value created. When all-period valuation is required (e.g., business cases), it is recommended that EVA period measures be generated for the first three to five years of analysis to provide a basis for meaningful budgeting and tracking.

We have seen that EVA is particularly well suited to discern the drivers of EVA budget variances, especially to determine whether the income statement or balance sheet is variance-causative.

Adding measures like EVA to budget and planning processes has some practical consequences, which have been very positive. In particular, attention must be paid to balance sheets, as well as just income statements.

The use of EVA has also aided the establishment of market-facing business units and strategic business units by prescribing a meaningful sufficient set of financials and an associated measure of value-added that enables close scrutiny of the true financial performance of these discrete entities. Thus, adoption of EVA is seen as a boon to driving financials to the smallest revenue-generating units, because cash taxes and capital on the balance sheet, in addition to standard profitability, are required components at a business unit or strategic business unit level (usually characterized by separate markets, customers, products/services, competitors, and so on).

SOURCES AND SUGGESTED REFERENCES

Copeland, Tom, Koller, Tim, and Murrin, Jack, *Valuation—Measuring and Managing the Value of Companies,* John Wiley & Sons, New York, 1990.

Rappaport, Alfred, *Creating Shareholder Value,* The Free Press, New York, 1986.

Stewart, G Bennett III, *The Quest for Value,* HarperCollins, New York, 1990.

Stewart, G. Bennett III, *Stern Stewart Corporate Finance Handbook,* Stern Stewart Management Services, New York, 1986.

CHAPTER 14

TECHNIQUES OF SCHEDULING BUDGETS

Donald R. Moscato

Iona College

CONTENTS

14.2	GANTT CHARTS	1	SOURCES AND SUGGESTED REFERENCES	7
14.6A	COMPUTER SOFTWARE RESULTS (NEW)	5		

14.2 GANTT CHARTS

Page 14·2, replace bulleted list in third paragraph with:

- Consider company goals   2 days
- Evaluate existing operations   4 days
- Evaluate new business opportunities   5 days
- Derive sales forecast   3 days
- Departmental managers review sales forecast   4 days
- Prepare departmental budget proposals   7 days
- Develop implementation strategies   2 days
- Present budget to management   1 day.

Page 14·2, replace fourth paragraph with:

Exhibit 14.1 shows a plausible Gantt chart created in Microsoft Project™ for our example. Each step is represented as a bar on the chart. The left column shows the number of the tasks. The next column depicts the finish times. The next column identifies those tasks that have predecessor requirements. The final column highlights the daily schedule. Note that the analysis shows that no work is scheduled for weekends. Exhibit 14.1A presents the task sequence in the form of a more familiar calendar schedule.

Page 14•3, replace Exhibit 14.1 with:

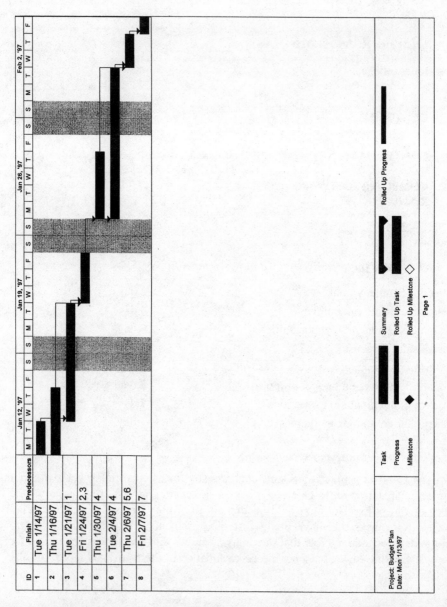

Exhibit 14.1.   Gantt Chart.

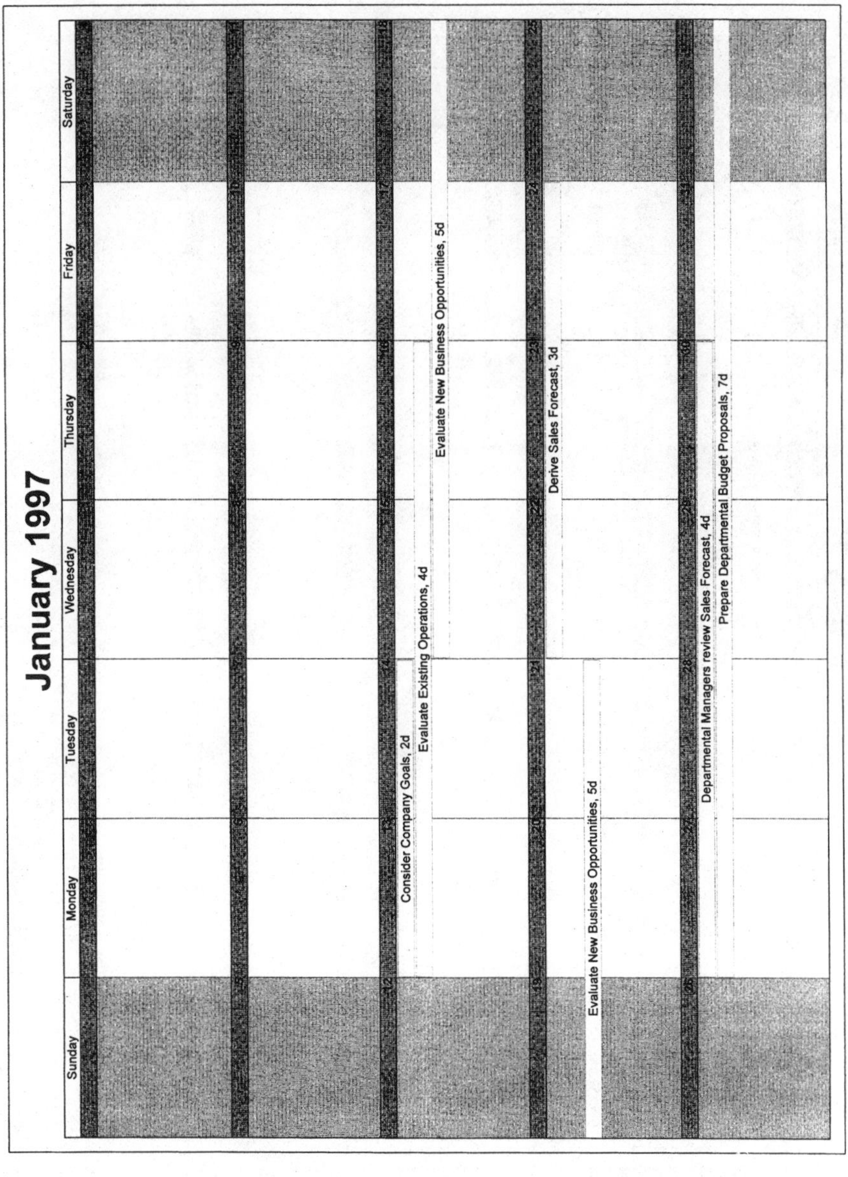

January 1997

Sunday	Monday	Tuesday	Wednesday	Thursday	Friday	Saturday

Consider Company Goals, 2d
Evaluate Existing Operations, 4d
Evaluate New Business Opportunities, 5d
Evaluate New Business Opportunities, 5d
Derive Sales Forecast, 3d
Departmental Managers review Sales Forecast, 4d
Prepare Departmental Budget Proposals, 7d

Exhibit 14.1A.   Budget calendar.

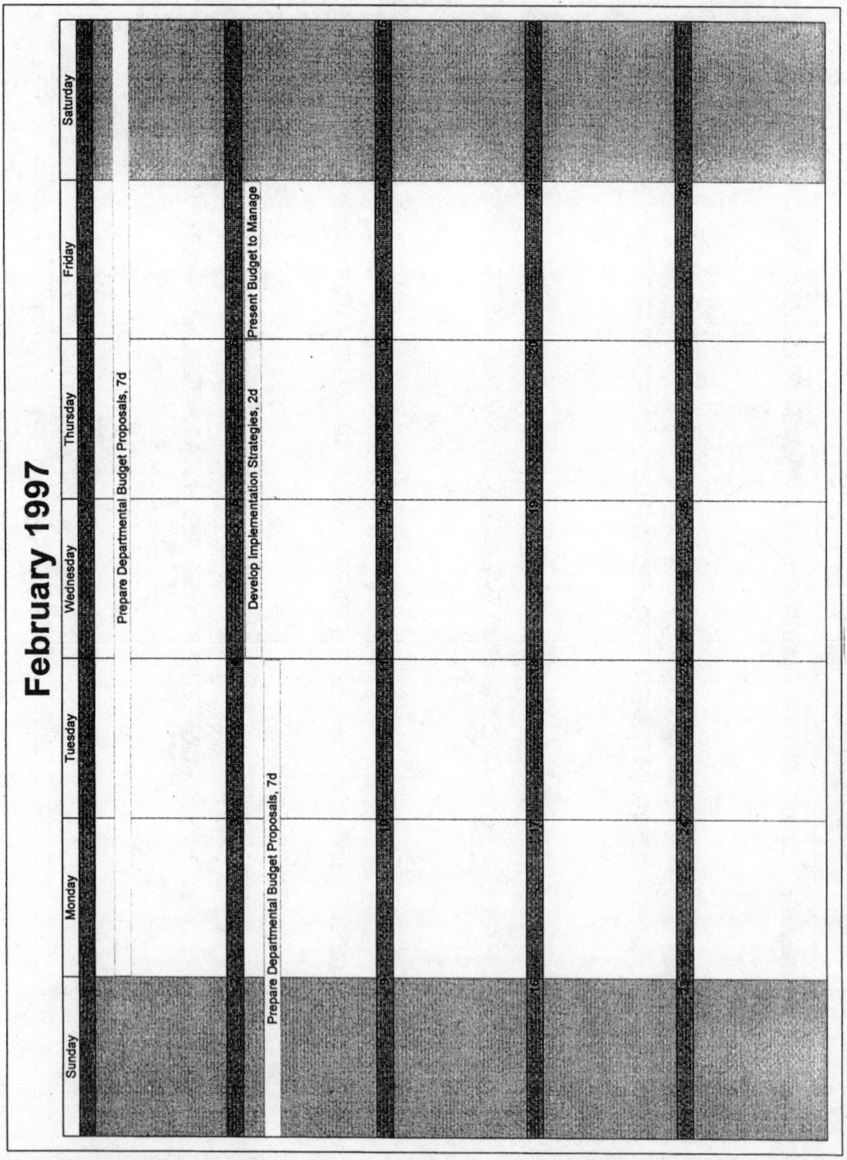

February 1997

Sunday	Monday	Tuesday	Wednesday	Thursday	Friday	Saturday

Prepare Departmental Budget Proposals, 7d

Prepare Departmental Budget Proposals, 7d

Develop Implementation Strategies, 2d

Present Budget to Manage

Exhibit 14.1A.   Budget calendar (continued).

Page 14.12, add new section before section 14.7:

14.6A   COMPUTER SOFTWARE RESULTS (New).   In this section, we present the computer results of our illustrative budget plan. Exhibit 14.9 presents the CPM chart for the example. Note the inclusion of the starting dates and the finishing dates for each task. Exhibits 14.10 through 14.12 depict a series of useful budget reports created as default reports in the Microsoft Project™ computer system. Each one is useful for project control purposes. In our example they all contain zero values because the budget plan had not been started at the time the reports were prepared. Exhibit 14.10 shows the budget plan's fixed cost, total cost, baseline values, the variance, the actuals, and any remaining costs. Exhibit 14.11 depicts the base calendar template used for the budget planning process. Exhibit 14.12 illustrates the progress of the budgeting activities in terms of the percent of each task that was completed, its cost, and the status of the work.

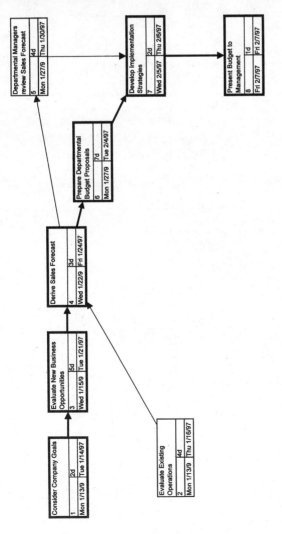

Exhibit 14.9.   CPM chart for budget schedule.

ID	Task Name	Fixed Cost	Total Cost	Baseline	Variance	Actual	Remaining
1	Consider Company Goals	$0.00	$0.00	$0.00	$0.00	$0.00	$0.00
2	Evaluate Exhisting Oper	$0.00	$0.00	$0.00	$0.00	$0.00	$0.00
3	Evaluate New Bus.Opps	$0.00	$0.00	$0.00	$0.00	$0.00	$0.00
4	Derive Sales Forecast	$0.00	$0.00	$0.00	$0.00	$0.00	$0.00
5	Depart.mental Managers review Sale	$0.00	$0.00	$0.00	$0.00	$0.00	$0.00
6	Prepare Departmental Budget Propo	$0.00	$0.00	$0.00	$0.00	$0.00	$0.00
7	Develop Implementation Strategies	$0.00	$0.00	$0.00	$0.00	$0.00	$0.00
8	Present Budget to Management	$0.00	$0.00	$0.00	$0.00	$0.00	$0.00
		$0.00	$0.00	$0.00	$0.00	$0.00	$0.00

Exhibit 14.10   Budget report.

BASE CALENDAR:	STANDARD
Day	Hours
Sunday	Nonworking
Monday	8:00AM-12:00PM, 1:00PM-5:00PM
Tuesday	8:00AM-12:00PM, 1:00PM-5:00PM
Wednesday	8:00AM-12:00PM, 1:00PM-5:00PM
Thursday	8:00AM-12:00PM, 1:00PM-5:00PM
Friday	8:00AM-12:00PM, 1:00PM-5:00PM
Saturday	Nonworking
Exceptions:	None

Exhibit 14.11   Budget plan template.

ID	Task Name	Duration	Start	Finish	% Comp.	Cost	Work
1	Consider Company Goals	2d	Mon 1/13/97	Tue 1/14/97	0%	$0.00	Oh
2	Evaluate Exhisting Oper.	4d	Mon 1/13/97	Thu 1/16/97	0%	$0.00	Oh
3	Evaluate New Business Opportunities	5d	Wed 1/15/97	Tue 1/21/97	0%	$0.00	Oh
4	Derive Sales Forecast	3d	Wed 1/22/97	Fri 1/24/97	0%	$0.00	Oh
5	Departmental Managers Review Sale	4d	Mon 1/27/97	Thu 1/30/97	0%	$0.00	Oh
6	Prepare Departmental Budget Propo	7d	Mon 1/27/97	Tue 2/4/97	0%	$0.00	Oh
7	Develop Imlement. Strat.	2d	Wed 2/5/97	Thu 2/6/97	0%	$0.00	Oh
8	Present Budget to Management	1d	Fri 2/7/97	Fri 2/7/97	0%	$0.00	Oh

Exhibit 14.12   Top level tasks.

SOURCES AND SUGGESTED REFERENCES

Page 14·12, add after Battersby entry:

Grady, Robert B., *Practical Software Metrics for Project Management and Process Improvement,* Englewood Cliffs, NJ: Prentice-Hall, 1992.

Lewis, James P., *The Project Manager's Desk Reference,* Chicago: Probus, 1993.

CHAPTER 15

SALES AND MARKETING BUDGET (Revised)

R. Malcolm Schwartz

Coopers & Lybrand L.L.P.

CONTENTS

15.1 INTRODUCTION   1

15.2 OVERVIEW OF THE BUDGET PROCESS   2

(a) A Link Between Strategic and Other Functional Plans   2
(b) Discretionary Expenses   3
(c) Operating Factors   4
(d) Culture and Management Style   5
(e) Incremental Planning and Analysis   6

15.3 SPECIAL BUDGETING PROBLEMS   7

(a) Pricing Adjustments   8
(b) Selling Expense   8
(c) Sales Promotion Expense   8
(d) Advertising Budget   9
(e) Product Development Costs   9
(f) Customer Service Expenses   10
(g) Physical Distribution   10

15.4 PERTINENT TOOLS   10

(a) Analysis of Product Life Cycles   11
(b) Marginal Analysis   11
(c) Breakeven Analyses   11
(d) Forecasting Techniques   12
(e) Sensitivity Analysis   12
(f) Bracket Budgeting   12
(g) Tactical and Strategic Pricing Techniques   12
(h) Testing Actual Performance   14

15.5 UNIQUE ASPECTS OF SOME INDUSTRIES   14

(a) Consumer Packaged Goods Firms   14
(b) Industrial Products Firms   15
(c) Retailing   15
(d) Banking   15

15.6 SUMMARY   16

SOURCES AND SUGGESTED REFERENCES   16

Pages 15 • 1 to 15 • 16, delete entire chapter and replace with:

15.1 INTRODUCTION. The sales and marketing budget is an important link with all other budgets. To make this link effective, the budget system should be based on a sound understanding of the vision, culture, and objectives of the organization; on an awareness of the relationships among business processes and with other business functions; on the ability to use external information about competitors, customers, suppliers, and public policy; and on good judgment.

The importance of these factors suggests that the sales and marketing budget process should be discussed broadly and not merely in terms of how related data should be entered, stored, and printed from a computer system. Therefore, this chapter concentrates on the following subjects:

- An overview of the budget process
- Special budgeting problems
- Pertinent tools
- Unique aspects of some industries

15.2 OVERVIEW OF THE BUDGET PROCESS. The sales and marketing budget process links to product, channels of distribution, and profit a group of largely discretionary expenses that focus on customers' acceptance—on the downstream components of the value chain. Most firms try to sell profitably what customers want, that is, what the market will bear. As a result, the sales and marketing budget is a means of integrating the functional plans as well as the process capabilities of an organization. It is important that the budget be controlled because marketing expenses, which are not only largely discretionary but also can be changed dramatically as to priorities and mix, can be misdirected quite easily.

As a result, a budget process should be in place that can be integrated with other plans and that can provide useful analyses to support the judgments of marketing planners.

(a) A Link Between Strategic and Other Functional Plans. The sales and marketing budget provides a link between the business strategy and other functional plans. The sales budget defines the level and mix of projected product and services offerings, as well as such support costs as sales organization expense and trade promotion and education programs. This information generally is developed to be consistent with the organization's overall strategic plan and to provide more detailed information for the planning period covered by the overall budget.

Much sales information traditionally is "top line" (that is, it is presented at the top of a profit and loss statement): the identification of short-term activity that it provides links the strategic plan to the budgets of other functions that support achieving the intended operating level. These other budgets include:

- **Operations (sourcing, conversion, and physical distribution).** Factors that are affected include inventory and service levels, replenishment techniques, production mix, and lengths of production runs.
- **Research and Development.** Replacing products over their life cycles, anticipating customers' wants and needs and competitors' actions, and taking advantage of technological developments should help to identify priorities for development projects as well as the funding levels.
- **Administration.** A number of these support functions—ranging from clerical activities, such as order entry and customer service, to legal specialists—can be influenced by the sales budget.
- **Capital Investment.** The needs for facilities, tooling, and equipment should be coordinated with sales activity.

- **Cash.** Inventory, accounts receivable, and accounts payable all can be affected by the sales budget.

The marketing budget in turn relates in two ways to sales plans. First, it can be driven by sales plans, as when higher volumes can cause greater expenditures for cooperative advertising. Second, it can be used to drive sales plans, as when promotional activities are planned to support sales growth or mix. The overall sales and marketing budget is therefore a means of integrating a number of plans to the strategy of the organization.

Today, many organizations think of this integration in process rather than functional terms. In such cases, plans and budgets may be process-focused rather than function-focused. A typical framework of processes and the business cycles they encompass might include:

- **Customer Management**—from offering to selling products and services
- **Product Management**—from planning through discontinuing product offerings
- **Supply Chain**—from receiving demand signals through delivering products and services, including sourcing and conversion activities
- **Development**—from considering innovations through applying them
- **Support**—all infrastructure activities.

Whether a company takes a functional or a process view, the sales and marketing—or customer and product—planning is an important link between strategy and business activities.

(b) Discretionary Expenses.   In addition to consideration of product, price, promotion, and volume, the sales and marketing budget deals with a number of expenses that are largely discretionary. Sales budgeting deals with issues such as what products are to be sold, what prices are to be charged, how customer loyalty can be encouraged, and how much volume should result.

The marketing portion of the budget considers what resources are to be used—and in what mix—to move products from the firm to its customers. Major elements of the marketing budget include:

- **Selling**—which may involve direct selling through various media, an employed sales force, sales representatives, or some combination.
- **Sales Promotion**—which often includes a combination of price and premium programs, trade shows, store fixtures, coupons, sponsorship, and the like.
- **Advertising**—which may concentrate on the image of the firm, a product line, or a brand; which may be national, regional, local, or customer-specific; and which can use various media.
- **Product Development**—which some firms consider a marketing expense, particularly for short-term efforts; and which can include new features, packaging changes, new products, and the like.
- **Customer Service**—which includes both warranty and out-of-warranty support, education, training, complaint handling, and a variety of other services.

- **Physical Distribution**—which some organizations treat as a marketing expense; and which may be handled centrally or may be spread through the regions served; other discretionary factors include how goods are shipped and whether the firm elects to use its own resources, distributors, or public warehouses.

The marketing budget considers what mix and levels of these elements will be used. Therefore the budget process should enable analyses that consider trade-offs, priorities, and contingent actions in support of the eventual agreed plan.

(c)   Operating Factors.   The budgeting process should consider a number of operating factors that shape the expenses planned for sales and marketing.

There are several different ways in which the levels of the various elements of marketing expense can be analyzed and targeted; these include historical trends, standards or benchmarks, and operating factors.

Historical trends can be applied rather simply; for example, if sales are planned to increase by 10%, then advertising can be increased by the same percentage. This approach takes little effort, but it assumes that prior levels of expenses were effective, that there are no benefits from growth, and that similar levels of expense will be needed in the future.

Standards—usually in the form of typical levels of expenses for certain industries—may be available, but because most firms have different objectives and operations they can be hard to apply. Furthermore, an industry-wide benchmark can be too broad to have useful application. At the least, if benchmarks are used, the underlying practices should be understood and applicable. Standards for marketing expenses are usually more effective for checking if the plan varies from industry practice—and for being able to understand why and the associated risks—than as a means of developing the budget.

When developing the marketing budget, it is probably more useful to analyze the underlying operating factors that drive market performance than to rely on history or on benchmarks. Examples of such drivers include:

- Market share
- New account and customer retention rates
- Customer ordering patterns (size, frequency, and mix)
- Value of the customer and value to the customer
- Competitive position
- Impact of past promotions
- Costs to acquire an account
- Sales call patterns

Exhibit 15.1 shows the impact of these and other factors on sales and marketing costs. By reviewing the factors that are important to the firm and how they relate to performance, the marketing planner likely will be able to make better recommendations regarding the amount and mix of marketing expense elements.

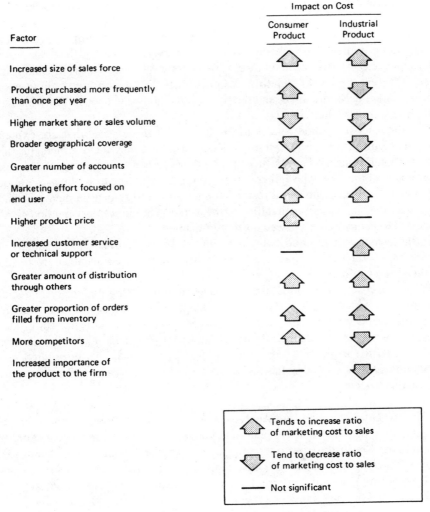

Factor	Impact on Cost	
	Consumer Product	Industrial Product
Increased size of sales force	⬆	⬆
Product purchased more frequently than once per year	⬆	⬇
Higher market share or sales volume	⬇	⬇
Broader geographical coverage	⬇	⬇
Greater number of accounts	⬆	⬆
Marketing effort focused on end user	⬆	⬆
Higher product price	⬆	—
Increased customer service or technical support	—	⬆
Greater amount of distribution through others	⬆	⬆
Greater proportion of orders filled from inventory	⬆	⬆
More competitors	⬆	⬇
Increased importance of the product to the firm	—	⬇

⬆ Tends to increase ratio of marketing cost to sales

⬇ Tend to decrease ratio of marketing cost to sales

— Not significant

Exhibit 15.1.   Impact of selected factors on sales and marketing cost.

Therefore, the budgeting system should include operating information as well as cost information.

(d)   Culture and Management Style.   The organizational architecture and the priorities that underlie the sales and marketing budget should fit with management style as well as with other processes. Because it is a means of integrating plans throughout the organization and the actions that result, it is important to consider issues of culture and management style when constructing the sales and marketing budget. These issues deal with responsibility, authority, accountability, and empowerment; the importance of sole contributors or teams; how decisions get made; and the like. Culture issues also must consider information management—efficiency, cost, integrity, and the like—so that actions can focus on what should be done and not on whose information is correct.

An important culture issue is goal-setting: some executives prefer to hold managers responsible for the actions that they directly control, whereas others want managers to be aware also of the indirect consequences. For example, promotional activity directly affects prices and volumes and may indirectly affect the costs of order entry, credit, and accounts receivable, among other activities. In dealing with these different styles of relating responsibility to the budget structure, two approaches are used, the direct and the full cost methods, the concepts of which have been discussed in earlier chapters.

The direct cost method relates to products only those costs that are expressly associated with them; in addition to product costs, these may include elements of the sales and marketing budget, such as promotional expense, cooperative advertising programs, and the like. The full cost method relates all costs to products by allocating indirect cost elements; as a result, product profitability can be measured in the same way that business profitability is measured. The direct cost method is often supported today by activity-based costing principles.

In the direct cost method, which is simpler from a performance management viewpoint, product performance is measured in terms of contribution to business overhead and profit.

Whatever costing method is used, the sales and marketing budget system should be coordinated with other systems. For example, the chart of accounts should be used effectively. With proper planning, subaccounts can be established for products, salespersons, customer classifications, promotional programs, and other categories that are useful for planning and control. Just as expenses can be related to the accounting system, operating factors can be related to other parts of the management information system.

(e) Incremental Planning and Analysis. Assuming that the sales and marketing budget is used to integrate other plans and budgets, and that the revenue and expense information is built up from operating factors, another major system feature is to allow for incremental planning. Depending on the business and industry, planning increments might include geographic regions, channels of distribution, classes of customers, and product lines.

When plans are developed incrementally, adjustments can be more focused during the review process. Key steps in budgeting incrementally include the following:

- Identify the increments
- Analyze the related operating factors
- Develop the sales and marketing plan for each increment
- Extend each increment to revenues and expense
- Sum the increments to form a base budget
- Review the base budget for consistency with the firm's strategy, for profit, for an assessment of competitive actions, and for overall affordability
- Adjust the base budget as needed and at the level of the individual increments
- Test the adjusted base budget for profit sensitivity to different levels of expense.

Finally, when the optimal incremental programs have been budgeted, and at levels that should generate desired profits, the budget can be approved and a road map will have been provided for sales and marketing efforts. This approach enables the linking of "top-down" and "bottom-up" budgeting, focused at the sales and marketing decisions. Exhibit 15.2 provides an overview of this process.

15.3 SPECIAL BUDGETING PROBLEMS. Because marketing expenditures are so discretionary and can be combined in so many different ways, it can be difficult to develop meaningful levels of expense for each element of cost. During the budgeted period, it can also be difficult to control expense levels and to adapt them to changing circumstances. This section reviews some of the more general aspects of these problems as they relate to the major cost elements.

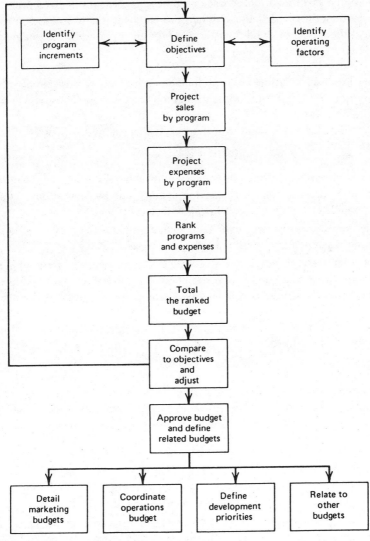

Exhibit 15.2. Approach to incremental budgeting.

(a)   Pricing Adjustments.   Planned pricing and any adjustments need to be budgeted if future revenues are to be attained and controlled.

Prices are usually developed both in relationship to costs and in response to competition. For products that have leading positions in the market, prices may be based on value to the customer.

New products can be difficult to price. At the time of initial market entry, prices are sometimes set close to cost to achieve desired volume and market share. After these goals are attained, prices might be adjusted. During the same period—as volume is growing—product costs could be declining; as a result, prices could be kept stable and profits would increase.

When prices are declining, it may be necessary to plan additional discounts. These usually can be better controlled in many companies' systems than outright price reductions because they can be recorded and tracked as expenses. Some companies overcome this limitation by tracking both standard and realized prices.

For any product for which a price change is planned, it is useful to control this by budgeting at the base price and then showing for each period in the budget the pricing adjustments that are to be made.

(b)   Selling Expense.   Selling expense includes a number of cost elements, such as salary, commissions, training, and salespersons' expenses. These costs often are associated with different sales forces for regions, classes of customers, or groups of products. Selling expense should be budgeted incrementally in ways that enable future analyses; as examples:

- Firms with large in-store sales forces may want to budget and report selling expense by department, by transaction, by day, and by time of day; data such as these enable correlating store staffing with service levels.
- Firms whose sales forces cover wide geographical areas may want to compare the times to call on customers in urban and rural areas.
- Mail order firms usually want to evaluate selling expense geographically (zip codes are often used) and by the source of the sale (which could be from a specific list of names, from particular advertising copy, or from a media placement).

The kinds of monitoring analyses that will be needed should be identified as the budget is being assembled so that techniques for reporting and control can be established.

(c)   Sales Promotion Expense.   Too often, sales promotions are undertaken to increase sales without sufficient attention to planning and controls. Lack of control can be found with sales personnel as well as with customers, as seen in the following examples:

- The internal auditor for a household products firm found that some promotional fixtures never had been placed in stores, and yet sales representatives were receiving commissions approved by the sales manager.
- When a mail order firm revised its customer list programs, it found that one customer had made a number of minor changes in his name and address to obtain more than $10,000 worth of free promotional merchandise.

Because there are few industry standards for sales promotion expense, each firm needs to use its own track record to determine what is effective. Records should be kept—and incorporated into budgets and controls—for the relationships among volume, product, media, and promotional devices. Later promotions can be correlated to benchmarks that are developed, and variances can be analyzed, as misredemption or promotional losses, as examples.

In addition to incremental planning and control of merchandise, the expenses for premiums and coupons and other elements of sales promotion also should be planned and controlled incrementally. As examples:

- Trade shows and exhibits often are planned and controlled for each instance, and analyzed in relationship to sales activity generated.
- Samples and giveaways are usually controlled by salespersons, to evaluate any unusual rates of usage.
- Fixtures often are controlled as if they were inventory, and may need accountability by both salesperson and customer.

(d) Advertising Budget.   Advertising often appears to be discretionary to management and can become one of the first elements of expense to be reduced in bad times. It therefore is important to be able to assess the effectiveness of advertising. Copy, timing, media, and placement can be important factors. The budget should be assembled so that advertising expense and sales activity can be correlated. Similarly, tests of geographical coverage, copy, and the like need to be controlled.

Control can be exercised by having the advertising organization develop standards (examples can include recall, impact, or sales percentages) for effectiveness, and then conduct tests regularly to measure that impact. Advertising expenditures by product are often published (for example, in *Advertising Age*), so that a firm's expenditures can also be compared to these external benchmarks.

Dealer cooperative advertising presents another problem in planning and control that can influence both the design of a budget system and the process of budgeting. Cooperative claims should be verified by tearsheets for print advertising and by invoices for television and radio. As a consequence, a subsystem is needed, by dealer, in regard to claimable amounts, claims pending, and claims approved and paid. The claimable amounts, which are usually based on purchases of a given product or products for a specified period, should be tracked to establish the potential expense, although actual claims paid are often much less.

Even with the use of benchmarks and analyses to explain what advertising is important and why, it still remains a discretionary expense. Occasionally, when management attempts to reduce advertising expense, it finds that commitments already have been made for future expenditures. Therefore the budget system—and the resulting controls—should incorporate plans for the timing and amount of commitments as well as expenditures.

(e) Product Development Costs.   Marketing management uses product development to procure new styles of packaging, new features, and the like. Such procurements can be internal, or items may be purchased from suppliers. In any case, development efforts and their associated costs are best controlled by project. A product development project subsystem can be used to link the research and development budget with the marketing expense budget.

(f)   Customer Service Expenses.   The influence of consumer price and value sensitivities, and the needs for differentiation in the marketplace, have caused warranty and other service programs to be expanded. Recalls and replacements have become more common. More staff is being used to answer consumers' questions, and more information is available, in return, to shape product and marketing plans.

As a result, new methods are being used to plan and control customer service expenses. Warranty expenses have usually been planned as a percentage of sales, but today more attention is being given to relating warranty expense to particular products and their sources. Recall expenses can be projected from Total Quality Management programs, and from the statistical process control activities that tend to follow. Replacement expenses can be estimated from failure rate percentages related to the product and developed in the quality control laboratory.

Comparative trends of expenses on these elements of cost should be monitored, and should be used to:

• Adjust the budget
• Provide reserves on actual performance
• Focus development activities
• Direct quality assurance actions.

(g)   Physical Distribution.   Physical distribution involves market-responsive trade-offs between service and cost. Service levels should be planned and performance monitored. Often, service can provide an important competitive advantage when price, product features, and the like are not highly differentiable among competitors.

Higher levels of inventory usually accompany better service, and with the annual costs to carry inventory often approaching 25% of inventory value, it is important to ensure that service is worth the cost. In many cases, service can be improved with the same or a reduced inventory level by planning and controlling where the inventory is located across the overall supply chain and for what product, by improving demand communications (using point-of-sale, or POS, information, for example), and by synchronizing the sourcing, conversion, and delivery activities.

As a consequence, the sales and marketing system should be linked to the inventory control system, and through it, to manufacturing and purchasing. Marketing information is needed by product and location; service as well as cost data should be planned, reported, and analyzed. A system of this sort provides the performance benchmarks related to objectives that can help to resolve the usual conflicts about inventory among marketing, finance, and operating managers.

15.4   PERTINENT TOOLS.   There are a number of techniques that are helpful in budgeting and controlling sales and marketing expense. These include:

• Product life-cycle analyses
• Marginal analysis
• Breakeven analysis

- Forecasting
- Sensitivity techniques
- Bracket budgeting
- Pricing techniques
- Performance tests.

This section discusses some of the key features of these techniques.

(a) **Analysis of Product Life Cycles.**   Each phase of a product's life cycle presents different budgeting concerns, ranging from early investment requirements and inventory to "fill the pipeline" to later issues of price and of product discontinuance. Methods need to be established in advance to determine when a product is moving from one phase to another so that:

- Strategies and budgets can be adjusted.
- Agreement can be reached on whether to extend the product's life.
- Planning guidelines can be set on removing the product from the market.

A product life cycle is usually longer than the budget period, so a product plan should be developed that relates to a series of budgets. The product plan should include information on the competitive environment because:

- Little competition may relate to the introductory phase.
- New competitors may indicate the beginning of the growth phase.
- A variety of differentiated products often shows the maturity phase.
- Identical competitive products may point to the decline phase.

The technique of monitoring products' life cycles can help to direct development efforts for differentiating and improving products and thus for extending their lives.

(b) **Marginal Analysis.**   Marginal analysis, which has been discussed previously, can be helpful for cost allocation. Different geographical or sales categories can be tested so that incremental revenue less incremental cost derived from the last unit sold in each area is equal. To illustrate marginal analysis, an advertising budget can be assigned to two categories, and then $1.00 can be transferred from the first to the second; if profit increases, then the transfer is worthwhile and should be continued until no change in profit occurs.

(c) **Breakeven Analyses.**   Breakeven analysis, which was discussed in chapter 8 and chapter 10, requires knowledge of fixed and variable costs and of contributions for individual products. With these data, the breakeven point can be calculated. The result of such an analysis may indicate that increasing the sales of selected products will help to cover fixed costs; if so, the sales and marketing budget should focus on efforts to support that objective.

(d) Forecasting Techniques.   Most firms forecast by extending historical data for themselves, for competitors, and/or for the overall industry. Some companies incorporate economic data, or have determined that there are leading indicators that help in forecasting sales, such as new home starts for heavy appliances or marriage rates for tableware. Economic data can be obtained from government publications, trade journals, industry associations, consulting firms, and banks; computer programs can be used to test historical correlations.

Many firms rely heavily on internal data for forecasting sales. Using regression analysis or other statistical techniques, a series of internal and external factors can be selected and tested to determine if they help to predict sales. Often, firms rely on simpler statistical techniques, such as moving averages.

Of course, because forecasts are never precise, it is best to rely on actual demand signals for operational and tactical actions. For planning, however, some form of forecasting usually will be needed. To deal with the uncertainty of forecasts, it is useful to consider a range of possible outcomes, with related assumptions, impacts, and probabilities of occurrence.

(e) Sensitivity Analysis.   Sensitivity analysis can be used, for example, to simulate best, likely, and worst cases before they occur. Relationships must first be understood between the conditions that are to be tested and their effects on sales, costs, and profits; these conditions could include changes in:

- The market, such as overall demand or competitive share
- The economy, such as monetary or fiscal policies or local business conditions
- The environment, including changes in life style or demographic shifts.

Sensitivity analysis is often coupled with probability techniques to answer "what if" questions. For example, a firm might want to know the impact of interest rates on cash flow—for example, at 5% interest a particular project is profitable, but at 12% interest it is not. The project can be analyzed for a series of interest rates, and a probability can be assigned to each one. An overall expected benefit thus can be determined, as illustrated in exhibit 15.3.

(f) Bracket Budgeting.   Bracket budgeting is a form of built-in contingency planning. Expenses are developed at higher and lower levels (plus or minus 10%, for example) than the base budget, and sales that are likely to result are then forecast. At a later date, if sales were to rise and management should act to maintain the higher level, the likely impact on expenses would already be understood.

If the sales budget were not achieved, the bracket budget gives management a sense of the profit impact, and a contingency plan can be installed quickly. A detailed discussion of this subject is found in chapter 26.

(g) Tactical and Strategic Pricing Techniques.   Various techniques are used for tactical pricing, which is usually practiced in times of static market conditions and growing demand. These include cost-based pricing, reaction to competitors, and penetration pricing.

Cost-based pricing rests on sound knowledge of all costs as well as effective management of costs that are allocated among products. Reaction to competitive moves has been used by smaller firms who must respond—often by charging less—to industry leaders. Penetration pricing occurs when a firm consciously reduces its usual profit objective to increase market share or to emphasize profitable aftermarket sales (selling razors to sell blades, as an example).

Strategic pricing is appropriate with slow-growing economies, changing demand levels, and stiff competition. This techniques often relates to value as perceived by the customer. For example, reformulating a product by removing an additive that did not have broad appeal could enable a price reduction with a concomitant sales gain. Strategic pricing can also relate to the pace of technological change or to the uniqueness of the product.

The Problem

Invest $33,000.

Positive cash flow is projected by year at $10,000, $10,000, $8,000, $7,000, and $5,000.

Current interest rate is 5%.

Will the investment be worthwhile if interest rates go higher?

The Sensitivity Analysis[a]

Year	Cash Flow	5%	6%	8%	10%
1	$10,000	$9,524	$9,434	$9,259	$9,091
2	10,000	9,070	8,900	8,573	8,264
3	8,000	6,910	6,717	6,350	6,010
4	7,000	5,759	5,545	5,145	4,781
5	5,000	3,918	3,737	3,403	3,105
Total cash in		$35,181	$34,333	$32,730	$31,251
Cash out		(33,000)	(33,000)	(33,000)	(33,000)
Net present value		$2,181	$1,333	$ (270)	$(1,749)

Conclusion: If interest rates approach 8%, do not do the project.

What is management's judgment on the likelihood?

The Expected Benefit Analysis

	Probability by Interest Rate				Adjusted Net Present Value
Year	5%	6%	8%	10%	
1	80%	20%	—	—	$9,506
2	80%	20%	—	—	9,036
3	—	50%	30%	20%	6,466
4	—	50%	30%	20%	5,272
5	—	50%	30%	20%	3,511
Estimated cash in					$33,791
Cash out					(33,000)
Net present value					$ 791

Conclusion: If management's judgment about interest rates is correct, do the project.

[a]Using present value technique.

Exhibit 15.3. Example of sensitivity analysis.

- For a market in which technology is expected to change in five years, product durability could be designed to that period, and price reduced accordingly.
- Unique product or service features—or the level of technical support—may enable product differentiation and value-added pricing; alternatively, store-branded products can be priced lower because they use available capacity and require less marketing expense.

In any regard, the pricing techniques that are used can influence the structure of the sales and marketing budget as well as the related systems and reports. Emphasis on cost-based pricing, for example, requires more complete cost portrayals, more emphasis of cost differentiation by product, and sensible rules for allocating fixed costs; activity-based costing is a useful supportive approach.

(h)   Testing Actual Performance.   Whatever specialized techniques are used for planning and evaluation, the system should have the ability to provide feedback. Plans to increase or decrease expense should be tested in controlled situations to measure the impact on sales.

For example, results of a market test should be compared to plan, and the budget system should be adapted accordingly. The capability of analyzing controlled changes will enable the extrapolating of results to later budget periods.

15.5   UNIQUE ASPECTS OF SOME INDUSTRIES.   Just as each firm is distinctive, so many industries have different characteristics that cause different approaches to sales and marketing budgeting. This section identifies some features of selected industries—namely, consumer packaged goods, industrial products, retailing, and banking—to illustrate some of the differences. These four industries were selected to illustrate differences resulting from products or services, from customers, and from method of distribution.

(a)   Consumer Packaged Goods Firms.   Budgets for this type of firm often begin with stated goals for market share. Strategies for product, distribution, price, copy, media, promotion, special programs, and volume are formed to reach these goals. Costs are assigned to each strategy and, along with expected volume, are compared to profit objectives. Expense levels are generally determined by a combination of experience and test marketing; external standards are rarely used to determine expense levels, but benchmarks are often used to test the reality and risk in the plan.

The budget usually links other functional plans. Marketing efforts are geared to the profit objective. The manufacturing plan provides cost information that must be assumed by marketing management. The product manager (in the marketing organization) often controls the research and development budget. Because plans are linked and the overall effort is market-driven, the marketing plan often includes a section that identifies where and how the budget should be changed if conditions warrant.

Selling efforts are often important and the sales force can be large. Pressure therefore can be created to price low, to provide substantial promotional activity, and to structure large incentive compensation programs. The trade (the direct customer) also can come to expect continuing promotions, cooperative allowances, and the like. The budget system enables management to plan and evaluate these activities and to make sure that they really are productive.

(b)   Industrial Products Firms.   The sales force is the key element in the selling of industrial products; hence the budget should be geared to provide the mix of expenses that will best support that selling effort. Underlying policies are important, such as warranty, prepaid freight, and trade-in allowance. These are often developed more to fit the company objectives than to imitate competitors' policies. Costs generally are influenced by the policies that are set. This individualized approach precludes the use of external standards to set expense levels, so an internal data base is important. Again, benchmarking and analyzing best practices are increasing in use.

Sales forecasts also are usually based on internal data. Firms with long order lead-in times can analyze their backlogs or, in some cases, the progress against completion of large jobs. Share of market information is seldom used because share tends to remain stable or is less meaningful. Most sales projections involve collecting and interpreting historical and competitive data.

The budget is usually linked with the purchasing and manufacturing plans. Occasionally, too little attention is given to linkages with service and applications engineering budgets. Sales personnel can overpromise service or product adaptability, and the support functions have difficulty in delivering what was promised; effective planning and control, coupled with procedural guidelines, can prevent problems of this sort.

(c)   Retailing.   Whereas the focus for consumer packaged goods is on the market and for industrial products is on the selling effort, for retail the budgeting focuses on the merchandise—what to sell and how it is to be sold. Key factors include fashion trends, the cycle of selling seasons, and the pressure to move inventory.

Forecasts are often quite detailed, in some cases down to item by store. Forecasts are coordinated between buyers of merchandise and store managers—the first reflects fashion trends and the second relates the merchandise to local conditions. Expenses are usually projected by store and sometimes by department. Various trade associations publish extensive data on expenses by merchandise category, by store size, and by volume. Pricing involves target and historic markups by product line, adjusted for inventory movement and promotional activity.

The budget is closely linked to buying activities. Usually, a buyer can commit only up to an inventory limit (called an "open to buy"), so merchandise must be sold to enable future merchandise to be bought. Open to buy is carefully planned and monitored. The expense budget is controlled by store management; if sales are low, steps usually are taken to reduce advertising expense or the sales force.

(d)   Banking.   Bank budgeting focuses on budgeting the differential between the costs to obtain and the costs to lend funds. Key elements of the budget include projecting availability of funds, interest rates, loan demand, deposit demand, and operating expenses.

Economics information and knowledge of the business environment are important factors in budgeting. In banking, sales information is in terms of the amount and types of loans, the interest rates that pertain, the timing of repayment, and likely loan losses.

Sophisticated forecasting and control techniques are used in regard to economic conditions, interest rates, loan demand, and consumer needs. Banks' marketing departments use research techniques (those that are traditionally used by consumer products firms) to evaluate new financial services products.

15.6   SUMMARY.   The sales and marketing budget is a key integrative device in many industries. It relates the firm's strategy to operating plans for various functions. It is a means with which to deal with a mass of external and internal data. It should link a number of subsystems for controlling elements of marketing expense and for evaluating the strategy for a product over its life cycle. Therefore, developing and maintaining a sales and marketing budget system requires a broad understanding of the overall business and its strategy and needs.

SOURCES AND SUGGESTED REFERENCES

Ahadiat, Nasrollah, "Sales Forecasting and Cash Budgeting for Automotive Dealerships," *Journal of Busines Forecasting,* Vol. 11, Issue 11, Fall 1992.

Andris, A., Mantrala, Murali, K., Prabhakant, Sinha, and Zoltners, "Impact of Resource Allocation Rules on Marketing Investment-Level Decisions and Profitability," *Journal of Marketing Research,* Vol. 29, Issue 2, May 1992.

Anonymous, "Budgeting for the Agency Sales Force," *Agency Sales Magazine,* Vol. 20, Issue 5, May 1990.

Anonymous, "The Road to Upfront: Beverages," *Mediaweek,* Vol. 3, Issue 20, May 17, 1993.

Anonymous, "Sound Budgeting Can Help Control Costs and Increase Profits; Five Basic Ways to Budget for Your Advertising Needs," *Profit-Building Strategies for Business Owners,* Vol. 22, Issue 4, April 1992.

Anonymous, "You Said It: How Do You Balance Your Sales Budget?" *Sales & Marketing Management,* Vol. 144, Issue 11, September 1992.

Anonymous, "1991 Sales Manager's Budget Planner," *Sales & Marketing Management,* Vol. 143, Issue 7, June 17, 1991.

Anonymous, "1993 Sales Manager's Budget Planner," *Sales & Marketing Management,* Vol. 145, Issue 7, June 28, 1993.

Book, Joel, "Building a Marketing Info System," *Agri Marketing,* Vol. 29, Issue 6, June 1991.

Calvin, Robert J., "Budgeting Prizes and Profits," *Small Business Reports,* Vol. 18, Issue 7, July 1993.

Chatterjee, Gopalakrishna, Rabikar, and Srinath, "A Communication Response Model for a Mature Industrial Product: Application and Implications," *Journal of Marketing Research,* Vol. 29, Issue 2, May 1992.

Donath, Bob, "Busting Budget Bean Counters," *Marketing News,* Vol. 26, Issue 18, August 31, 1992.

Doyle, Peter, and Saunders, John, "Multiproduct Advertising Budgeting," *Marketing Science,* Vol. 9, Issue 2, Spring 1990.

Falvey, Jack, "The Battle of the Budget," *Sales & Marketing Management,* Vol. 143, Issue 14, November 1991.

Fleming, Mary M.K., and Jizba, Barbara, "Promotion Budgeting and Control in the Fast Food Industry," *International Journal of Advertising,* Vol. 12, Issue 1, 1993.

Frank, Howard A., and Gianakis, Gerasimos A., "Raising the Bridge Using Time Series Forecasting Models," *Public Productiviy & Management Review,* Vol. 14, Issue 2, Winter 1990.

Howell, Keith A., "Lowe's Companies' Statistical Approach to Sales Forecasting," *Corporate Controller,* Vol. 3, Issue 5, May/June 1991.

Hudson, Phillip F., "What Would You Do?" *Bank Marketing,* Vol. 25, Issue 9, September 1993.

Hung, C.L., and West, Douglas C., "Advertising Budgeting Methods in Canada, the UK and the USA," *International Journal of Advertising,* Vol. 10, Issue 3, 1991.

Lamons, Bob, "Let's Demand Enough Money to Do the Job," *Marketing News,* Vol. 27, Issue 8, April 12, 1993.

Lynch, James, E., and Hooley, Graham J., "Increasing Sophistication in Advertising Budget Setting," *Journal of Advertising Research,* Vol. 10, Issue 1, February/March 1990.

O'Neal, Jason, "Budgeting with Trend Projection," *CFO: The Magazine for Senior Financial Executives,* Vol. 7, Issue 8, August 1991.

Pollare, Frank L., "Marketing Public Relations: Surviving the Budgeting Game," *Public Relations Journal,* Vol. 46, Issue 3, March 1990.

Rachlin, Robert, *Total Business Budgeting: A Step-by-Step Guide with Forms,* John Wiley & Sons, Inc., New York, 1991.

Shawkey, Bruce, "Building a High-Performance Budget," *Credit Union Management,* Vol. 15, Issue 8, August 1992.

Symons, Paula, "MCIFs Supply Budget Support," *Credit Union Management,* Vol. 15, Issue 8, August 1992.

Turner, James, "Budgeting Crunch Requires Creative Solutions," *Bank Marketing,* Vol. 23, Issue 9, September 1991.

Turner, James, "Budgeting Crunch Requires Creative Solutions," *Bank Marketing,* Vol. 23, Issue 9, September 1993.

CHAPTER 17

THE RESEARCH AND DEVELOPMENT BUDGET

Maurice I. Zeldman

Emzee Associates

CONTENTS

17.5 MANAGING A BUDGET   2

(b)   Budget Tracking   2

17.5 MANAGING A BUDGET

(b)   Budget Tracking

Page 17 • 37, replace Exhibit 17.24 with:

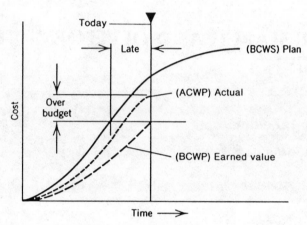

Exhibit 17.24.   Traditional reporting of plan versus actual.

CHAPTER 18

THE ADMINISTRATIVE EXPENSE BUDGET (Revised)

R. Malcolm Schwartz

Coopers & Lybrand L.L.P.

Maria Theresa Mateo

Coopers & Lybrand L.L.P.

CONTENTS

18.1 INTRODUCTION 1

18.2 THE ROLE AND SCOPE OF THE ADMINISTRATIVE EXPENSE BUDGET 2

(a) Allocating Administrative Expenses from Those Who Incur Them to Those Who Use Them 2

(b) Identifying the Value of Administrative Expenses 3

(c) What Functions Are Included in the Administrative Budget 4

(d) What Types of Expenses Are Included in the Administrative Expense Budget 6

18.3 METHODS USED FOR PREPARING THE ADMINISTRATIVE EXPENSE BUDGET 7

(a) Projecting the Level of Activity 7

(b) Projecting the Level of Resources Expected to Be Consumed to Support That Level of Activity 9

(c) Projecting the Factor Costs of Those Resources 10

(d) Gaining Agreement, Top-Down and Bottom-Up 10

18.4 FACTORS THAT IMPACT THE ADMINISTRATIVE EXPENSE BUDGET 11

18.5 UNIQUE ISSUES IMPACTING THE ADMINISTRATIVE EXPENSE BUDGET 12

18.6 TOOLS AND TECHNIQUES FOR MANAGING THE ADMINISTRATIVE EXPENSE BUDGET 13

(a) Budget Varience Analysis 13

(b) Administrative Charge-Back to the Operating Units 13

(c) Hybrid Transfer Costing 13

(d) Outsourcing Alternatives 14

(e) Performance Measures 14

(f) Activity-Based Costing (A-BC) 14

(g) Benchmarking 14

18.7 SUMMARY 14

18.1   INTRODUCTION.   The administrative expense budget is an important link with all other budgets, because it comprises activities that support other budgeted activities, and at the same time it provides some elements of control, and of independent perspective, on those other activities. Therefore, how management views administrative expenses says much about how management governs and leads the overall organization. In this sense, it is important to deal with what administrative expense includes and why it is important, before even beginning to address how it is budgeted. As a consequence, this chapter concentrates on the following subjects, namely:

- The role and scope of the administrative expense budget
- Methods used for preparing the administrative expense budget
- Factors that impact the administrative expense budget
- Unique issues impacting the administrative expense budget
- Tools and techniques for managing the administrative expense budget

18.2   THE ROLE AND SCOPE OF THE ADMINISTRATIVE EXPENSE BUDGET.   The surge of reengineering and other efforts to improve performance and productivity have increased management focus on administrative expenses. Administrative expenses are somewhat straightforward, but the value of the activities for which administrative expenses are incurred—that is, why administrative expenses are consumed by administrative activities—is not as straightforward. Therefore, the administrative expense budget is one of the more difficult budgets to manage because it is hard for many people to understand and agree to the value and purpose of administrative expenses. When a company can plan and conduct the activities that consume administrative expenses better than its competitors are able to, the company who is successful in doing so might develop through such competencies a competitive advantage.

(a)   Allocating Administrative Expenses from Those Who Incur Them to Those Who Use Them.   The difficulty of preparing and managing the administrative expense budget stems from two factors, namely: (1) the difficulty of allocation, and (2) the discretionary nature of the expenses. A "fashionable" company—which has hired the best people, read all the right books, and implemented the academics' and consultants' recommendations—might have empowered its people, established self-directed teams and pushed accountability into the organization, hence creating many departments, control units, budget units, strategic business units, service centers, and/or profit centers—each having a separate plan, budget, and/or P&L—of the overall administrative expense budget. Yet, it also might have selectively centralized some core functions that provide economies of scale for the overall organization. To hold individual revenue-producing units—the strategic business units (SBUs) or profit centers—accountable for all activities, however, the organization then might have attempted to assign or allocate these central service organizations (or overheads, as viewed by some SBU leaders). But how should the company allocate the costs, for example, of its corporate image marketing? Should the largest-revenue SBU shoulder most of the burden? But that might be inappropriate if that SBU relies less on the corporate image for achieving its mission than other, smaller units. If that is so, then should the smaller SBUs be assigned a larger share of this cost? If so, the economic effect might be larger than can be tolerated, and steps might have to be taken to affect the corporate image program, to change the way that costs are assigned, or to discourage new businesses. As can be seen, the dilemma of allocating the costs of the administrative expense budget can lead management into a vicious circle.

(b) Identifying the Value of Administrative Expenses. The discretionary nature of many of the activities that incur administrative expenses also can bedevil managers, because it is difficult for these activities to ascribe a quantitative value (an output) for the explicitly determined (input) cost budgeted. Managers are not always confident that the correct amounts are being spent. Is a larger legal department, for example, a good thing? For an organization that has incurred large regulatory penalties, or that has been sued for patent infringement, increasing legal expenses might be a good thing, but it might be too late. Therefore, it is often difficult to measure the value of corporate services and the right period of time for budgeting the expenditure compared to the period of time when the benefits will be realized.

The difficulty of measuring value might be attributed to, among other factors, the problem of measuring risk, which often is associated with low-probability occurrences but which can have very high costs per occurrence. Administrative organizations that monitor compliance with governmental or corporate policies on safety, environment, and labor issues are constantly battling for funding and for recognition of their value. Their value only becomes apparent when, for example, companies are faced with lawsuits or a loss of goodwill from their handling of a compliance matter, such as happened with the Exxon Valdez oil spill. But even in hindsight, it still might not be clear what level of additional investment—and, for that matter, what type of additional expenditure—might have mitigated or prevented problems such as this.

One way to deal with this value issue as it relates to the administrative expense budget is to categorize administrative activities, and the costs that they incur, as serving one of two purposes—namely, efficiency or effectiveness. For example, the purpose of a payroll department is to be efficient. The payroll department strives to process employee paychecks in the most cost-efficient manner. For an area focused on efficiency the question is, how much does it cost the company to do what needs to be done? Answering this question is relatively straightforward: management can conduct a market test, develop unit standards, or purchase available benchmark data to estimate the appropriate cost.

Alternatively, the purpose of another human resources activity—recruiting—is to be effective, not efficient. *Effectiveness* can be defined as the extent to which an activity supports or enables a predetermined objective or target to be met. The recruiting activity strives to identify, hire, and retain high-quality individuals. For an area focused on effectiveness, the question is, how do its activities benefit the organization? Answering this question is much more difficult than answering the efficiency question because areas that focus on effectiveness usually do not produce a tangible product, and thus there is less relevancy in performing external benchmarks, and there are few external data available. Rather, these areas tend to focus on the company's well-being related to its analysis of risks and objectives, and these areas are not as easily quantifiable. Value can be ascertained by assessing a company's tolerance for risk and how much it is willing to spend to be at a comfortable level of risk.

(c)   What Functions Are Included in the Administrative Expense Budget.   The administrative expense budget can be described by what it *does not include; in some ways, this is easier to describe than by starting with what it does include.* Typically, activities that touch either the organization's product or the organization's customer are usually considered part of core operations, and their expenses fall into operating—not administrative—expense budgets. These activities typically include customer service, distribution, manufacturing, research and development, and sales. Marketing and purchasing are usually considered operating expenses but can be found in some organizations' administrative expense budgets.

Thus, everything else—activities not part of the core operations—falls in the administrative expense budget. These activities often are shared by a number of internal, user organizations. Although organizations more frequently have been taking a process view of their businesses, few companies prepare budgets by process. In most cases, the administrative expense budget is still prepared on a functional or departmental basis. Exhibit 18.1 lists those areas that are most often part of the administrative expense budget and identifies whether their purpose is primarily efficiency or effectiveness.

| | Type of Focus | |
Department	Efficiency	Effectiveness
• Finance		
—Accounting	X	
—Fixed assets	X	
—Internal audit		X
—Tax		X
—Treasury		X
• General administration		
—Corporate executives		X
—Internal business development/strategy		X
—Internal consulting		X
—Policies and procedures		X
—Publication services and internal communications	X	
—Risk management		X
—Real estate and facility services	X	
—Secretaries, reproduction, and mailroom	X	
• Human resources		
—Benefits	X	
—Employee retiree administration	X	
—Payroll	X	
—Recruitment		X
—Training		X
• Insurance and risk management		X
• Information technology		
—IT development		X
—IT operations	X	
—Telecommunications		X
• Legal		X
• Public relations		
—Community and charitable activities		X
—Government and regulatory relations		X
—Industry, professional, and trade relations		X
—Investor relations	X	
—Media relations		X
• Purchasing	X	

Exhibit 18.1.   The primary purposes of typical administrative departments found in the administrative expense budget.

Exhibit 18.1, however, only shows the primary purpose at a high level; for example, within the purchasing function, ordering activities tend to be oriented toward efficiency, but vendor management activities tend to be oriented toward effectiveness. Furthermore, the purpose of an administrative activity can vary from one organization to another, and even for different relationships within an organization. A fast-food company, for example, might want to centralize the purchasing of ingredients, to ensure uniformity and to take advantage of scale, and thus might categorize the purchasing department as an administrative expense and might define its purpose as efficiency-focused. On the other hand, a chain of higher-priced restaurants might purchase locally, to emphasize freshness as well as regional tastes, and therefore might classify the purchasing department as an administrative expense focused more on effectiveness than on efficiency. Organizations also could have the same sizes of administrative expense budgets, but these budgets might include quite different levels of efficiency and effectiveness. And organizations might have similar levels of performance but at very different levels of administrative costs, as shown in Exhibit 18.2.

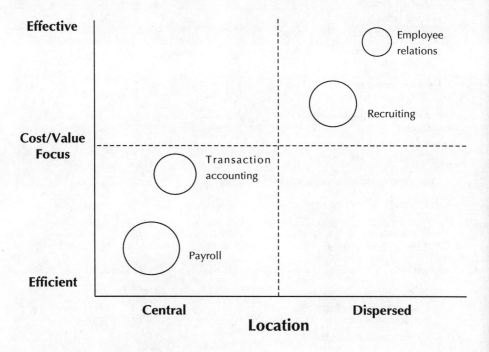

Exhibit 18.2.   Levels of administrative costs.

(d)   What Types of Expenses Are Included in the Administrative Expense Budget.   The majority of the administrative expenses typically include costs associated closely with human resources (namely, salary and benefits). There often is a large external services component, as many administrative activities (such as legal, business development, strategy, audit, and data processing operations and development) are often outsourced. There also might be some capital asset costs—in the form of depreciation expense, leasehold amortization, and the like—included in the administrative expense budget, particularly associated with information technology and real estate. Administrative expenses also can be associated with activities that are not easily understood or that might occur infrequently (such as expenses associated with litigation), and they often cannot be linked to specific products or services. Inasmuch as some administrative costs tend to be discretionary, their value and quality tend to be difficult to measure.

In contrast, operating budgets include both physical and human resource costs. Most operating costs are associated with specified and repetitive processes (such as production, sales, and distribution) and can be related to specific products or services. Examples of such operating expenses are raw materials, plant and equipment, and direct labor.

A typical administrative expense budget, structured for an administrative department, is illustrated in Exhibit 18.3.

Budget Year: 1996
Company Code: 19
Plant: QU
Owner: Alec Mundy
Cost Center: 421 MAIL SERVICES

Cost Element	Description	Annual
620000	SALARIES & WAGES	$1,956,000
623000	EMP ALLOWANCES	$11,000
624000	RELOCATION	$85,000
630000	OTHER MAT & SUPPLIES	$504,000
631000	TRAVEL & ENTERTAIN	$69,700
634000	POSTAGE	$8,000
640000	PURCHASED SERVICES	$82,000
640015	MAINTENANCE SERVICES	$0
641000	CONTRACT LABOR	$40,000
642000	PROF FEES & CONSULT	$6,000
644000	SOFTWARE	$3,000
	Controllable Totals	**$2,764,700**
621000	FRINGE BENEFITS	$731,544
622000	INCENTIVE COMPENSAT	$220,050
660000	DEPRECIATION	$400,633
661000	L/T OPER LEASE-EQUIP	$220,000
670900	ACT-OFFICE BLDG. & OT	$1,154,687
671803	R&D OVERHEAD (ADMIN.)	$402,356
672300	GEN. SERVICES	$91,468
	Non-controllable Totals	**$3,200,738**
	Cost Center Totals	**$5,965,438**

Exhibit 18.3. Typical administrative department expense budget.

18.3   METHODS USED FOR PREPARING THE ADMINISTRATIVE EXPENSE BUDGET.
After there is agreement on the roles and purposes of the administrative activities, as
discussed in the previous section, there are three basic steps to preparing the administrative expense budget, namely: (1) projecting the level of activity, (2) projecting
the level of resources expected to be consumed to support that level of activity, and
(3) projecting the factor costs of those resources. Each is discussed below. Also
important in preparing the administrative expense budget is how to gain "buy-in"
while maintaining a clear sense of direction, and this means combining what is often
identified, respectively, as the bottom-up and top-down approaches.

(a)   Projecting the Level of Activity.   Typically, a first step in preparing the administrative expense budget is to project the level of services to be provided, and hence
to project the level of expenses expected to be incurred to provide that level of services. Companies use a number of different methods to project administrative
expenses, and hence to develop a basis for applying costs to administrative activities.
Though these methods might be covered in previous chapters, this section will discuss briefly the applicability of these methods to the administrative expense budget.

- **Historical Basis (or ordinary incremental)**—Historical-basis budgeting takes
  into account the previous year's budget and the actual results. Budgeted levels
  of activity for the projected period are adjusted depending on the previous
  year's results and on the expectations for the projected period. Historical-basis
  budgeting does not usually consider the non-people costs; instead, it drives the
  budget to the number of people and the rates they are paid and then adds other
  costs through ratios.

- **Expense/Revenue Basis**—This method of budgeting determines the amount to
  be budgeted for the projected period based on some defined relationship
  between the particular administrative expense under consideration and revenue.
  For example, human resource departmental expenses, when using this method,
  might be considered to be equal to about 1% of sales; and this ratio might be
  considered to be valid for future periods. Similar to historical-basis budgeting,
  this method also is driven by people cost.

- **Zero Basis**—Zero-base budgeting is budgeting from the ground up, as though
  the budget were being prepared for the first time. When using this method,
  every proposed expenditure comes under review. Though zero-base budgeting
  requires more work than other forms of budgeting, it forces managers to better
  justify their outlays. Few firms adopt zero-base budgeting on an annual basis
  for all departments. When zero-base budgeting is undertaken, it typically is on
  a less regular basis, and only for a subset of responsibility centers at any one
  time.

- **Activity Basis**—Activity-based budgeting focuses on the activities that are projected to be used to support the production and sale of projected products and
  services, and then on estimating the costs of those activities. Activity-based
  budgeting can be valuable in the case of indirect—and administrative—costs.
  There are several ways to develop activity-based costs. In the accounting
  approach, for example, activity-based budgeting partitions indirect costs into separate but homogeneous activity cost pools. Management then uses cause-and-effect

criterion to identify the cost drivers for the separate cost pools. An organization then can apply these drivers to the costs of the services being provided (and, eventually, to the products themselves) in proportion to the volume of activity that a given service consumes. By assigning all resources to an activity, this method is more precise in that it considers more than just people-related costs.

Exhibit 18.4 compares the different methods.

Comparative Factor	Historical Basis	Expense-Revenue Basis	Zero Basis	Activity Basis
Simplicity	yes	yes	no	no
Level of Effort	no	no	yes	yes
Takes a Long Time	no	no	yes	yes
Enables Cost Management	yes	yes	yes	yes
Enable Cost-Benefit Analysis	no	yes	no	yes
Links Cost Drivers	no	no	no	yes
Supports Decision Making	no	no	yes	yes

Exhibit 18.4.   A comparison among budgeting methods.

The trade-offs among the various budgeting methods are between effort and value. Clearly, for organizations in which administrative expenses are not very important, simpler methods should be used. However, in many organizations, decisions about administrative expenses are visible and important, so more care might be taken with—and about—the methods used for budgeting such expenses.

In making its choice, an organization also should consider selecting a method that will provide a means to track performance in comparison to the desired outcomes on operational measures. Good budgeting techniques provide an ability to measure value received, and to track performance. Performance measures will vary by activity, and by the importance of any activity to the organization, but most organizations will at the least track (1) profitability, (2) customer satisfaction, (3) innovation, and (4) other internal measures relating to efficiency, quality, and time.

(b) Projecting the Level of Resources Expected to Be Consumed to Support That Level of Activity.   A second step in budgeting administrative expenses, once the level of activities is estimated, is to relate resources to activities. For example, processing payroll checks might lead to an estimate of the clerical and supervisory time that is required. The same might be done for each of the administrative activities. Relating resources to be consumed to the level of activity can be accomplished by using any of the methods described in the previous section. The reason for separating the steps in this description of the budgeting process is to suggest that separate analyses of activity levels and of resources consumed should be undertaken. For example, the level of activity might be the same as in the prior year, but the level of resources projected might be less due to the success of reengineering efforts.

(c) Projecting the Factor Costs of Those Resources.   The third step is to project the factor costs that are the unit costs of the resources to be consumed. For example, an increase in the costs of health care benefits would lead to a higher factor cost for benefits. On the other hand, better procedures and training might lead to a lower set of skills to support some activities than in the prior year. Again, this step can be combined with the previous ones, but it is useful to consider it separately; in this way, the budget can be developed separately for the level of activity, for the level of resources consumed by the activity, and for the factor costs (or unit costs) of those resources. Also, projecting factor costs might use other techniques, such as review of economic indicators (projected rates of inflation, for example) or review of changed business circumstances (such as the effects of changes in purchased services contracts, for example).

(d) Gaining Agreement, Top-Down and Bottom-Up.   The process for any of these methods could be top-down, bottom-up, or a hybrid. A typical hybrid approach entails guidelines provided from the top, numbers generated bottom-up and subject to top-level modification, and several iterations before a final budget is submitted. A blending of the top-down and bottom-up approaches is shown in Exhibit 18.5.

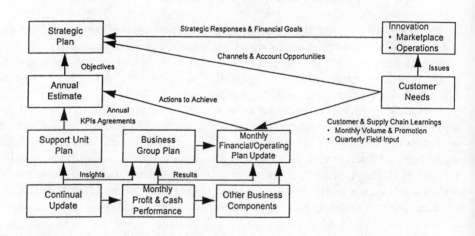

Exhibit 18.5.   A comparison of top-down and bottom-up approaches

The optimal approach for an organization depends on such characteristics as its governance and management styles, the extent of similarity—and of autonomy— among its business units, the competencies in its business units, and so forth. For highly diversified organizations, the optimal approach might be to have limited direction from the top. However, for less diversified organizations, or for organizations that are more operationally oriented (with a number of operating units that are not freestanding, for example), the optimal approach might be to have more direction from the top with regard to budgeting.

18.4   FACTORS THAT IMPACT THE ADMINISTRATIVE EXPENSE BUDGET.   The characteristics of an organization and its industry not only affect the approach it takes to preparing the administrative expense budget and the classification of the expenses (efficiency versus effectiveness), but also can affect the size of the administrative expense budget relative to other costs. Some of the key factors are presented below.

- Characteristics of the industry

    —**Service or Product Focus**—Service companies tend to have higher administrative expenses, due to such factors as higher turnover and higher training costs; also, labor reporting tends to be relatively more expensive than production reporting, but the costs tend to be less obvious.

    —**Diversified or Simple Organization Structure**—The diversified structure tends to have higher administrative expenses due to greater needs for coordination.

    —**Cyclical or Level Volumes**—Uneven flows of work tend to lead to higher administrative expenses, to have in place the resources for the peak periods of activity.

    —**Public or Private**—A public organization tends to have higher administrative expenses due to a variety of regulatory and reporting requirements.

    —**Regulated or Unregulated**—Regulated industries tend to have higher administrative expenses due to regulatory agency requirements.

- Maturity of the organization and the industry

    —**Start-up**—A start-up organization can have higher administrative expenses until it learns how to be efficient and until it becomes stable enough to satisfy investors.

    —**Growing**—A growing organization can have higher administrative expenses because it might not be focused on profits, and it might lose a sense of control on administrative expenses.

    —**Mature**—Mature organizations can have lower administrative expenses, if they have developed a profit focus.

- Organizational structure of company and operating philosophy

    —**Centralized or Decentralized**—Decentralized companies tend to have higher administrative expenses because a cost of decentralization often is to have redundant activities.

    —**Level of Technology**—The administrative expenses associated with less automated organizations tend to be higher.

18.5.   UNIQUE ISSUES IMPACTING THE ADMINISTRATIVE EXPENSE BUDGET.
Unique issues impact the administrative expense budget. Specifically, how does one
quantify the value associated with administrative activities?

Budgeting efficiency-oriented costs is relatively straightforward. One can develop
cost—and in some cases, time—standards for such process-oriented activities as
payroll, purchasing, and accounts payable, and might choose to use staffing ratios
for other activities such as secretarial, investor relations, and telecommunications.
And these standards can be compared and validated with available benchmarks.

Effectiveness-oriented costs, on the other hand, as discussed earlier, are much
more difficult to quantify for such reasons as the following:

- Activities that are oriented toward effectiveness often do not produce a tangible
  result and often do not produce any result in the same period in which the costs
  are incurred. For example, legal expenses are best spent to prevent legal problems; and if problems do occur, it might be years after the legal effort (to conduct a patent search, for example) was expended. In sum, these activities tend
  to focus on the company's well-being, which is not easily quantifiable.

- The degree of specialization of these effectiveness-oriented activities tends to
  be higher than for those administrative activities that are more oriented toward
  efficiency. It might be difficult for an executive who might have come from a
  sales background, for example, to assess the needs and performance of the public affairs department; yet those activities can help to influence legislators and
  regulators to understand the organization's point of view, and thus to prevent
  undesirable regulatory rulings. In the more extreme cases, a lack of understanding can lead to a lack of trust, which can over time cause inappropriate levels of
  support for these types of activities. Finally, the performance and effectiveness
  of these types of administrative activities depends much more on the quality of
  people in place than on the process that is followed.

- The factor costs of the kind of people who support these activities often is
  much higher than for the more efficiency-oriented activities. Legal, treasury,
  and business development/strategy personnel are often among the highest paid
  staff categories in a company. And, while the internal costs might be high, the
  costs of outsourcing these activities by using external groups that provide these
  services can be even higher.

- These roles often are shaped to, among other factors, prevent—or, if necessary,
  respond to—high-cost problems that have a low probability of occurring, yet
  management might fail to assess the value of these risks in a way that supports
  the budgeting of these activities correctly.

- The environment that drives these effectiveness-oriented costs is not the same
  as that which drives the other administrative areas or operations areas, and they
  might be driven by external (technological, governmental, and/or competitive)
  issues. For example, the costs of recruiting and of corporate advertising might
  be driven more by how much competitors spend than by the organization's
  strategy as such.

As noted earlier, the effectiveness orientation can be viewed as the degree to
which a predetermined objective or target is to be met, so the value of an activity's
effectiveness can be estimated by assessing an organization's tolerance for risk and

determining how much it is willing to spend to be at a comfortable level of risk to meet the predetermined objective or target. For example, when considering the legal department, does the organization want to avoid litigation at all costs due to potential damage to its image? Or will some litigation be acceptable, so long as the organization's position is clear and sustainable? Does the organization want all contracts written in an explicit, thorough, and detailed manner because contracting parties are perceived as untrustworthy? Or might the organization accept broader contracts that rely on trust between the contracting parties?

18.6   TOOLS AND TECHNIQUES FOR MANAGING THE ADMINISTRATIVE EXPENSE BUDGET.   There a number of tools and techniques that are useful in managing and controlling administrative expenses. These include

- Budget variance analysis
- Administrative charge-back to the operating units
- Hybrid transfer costing
- Outsourcing alternatives
- Performance measures
- Activity-based costing
- Benchmarking

Each is discussed below.

(a)   Budget Variance Analysis.   Variance analysis provides useful information for making decisions because it helps to provide insights into why the actual results differ from the planned performance. A variance is a performance gap between a benchmark—generally the budgeted amount—and the actual results, typically as reported in the accounting system for financial information, or in operating systems for non-financial information. The most important task in variance analysis is to understand why variances have occurred, and then to use that knowledge to promote learning and continuous improvement, and to enable better planning and better cost management. It is equally important to focus on positive variances as well as negative variances.

(b)   Administrative Charge-Back to the Operating Units.   Operating groups often are charged for the administrative services to remind profit-center managers that indirect costs exist and that profit-center earnings must be adequate to cover some share of these costs, as well as to provide for a return on invested capital and a fair return to creditors and investors. Organizations who do this believe that it will stimulate profit-center managers to put pressure on administrative managers to control the costs of the services that they provide.

(c)   Hybrid Transfer Costing.   Operating groups might be charged the budgeted expense instead of the actual expense, with the difference absorbed by the unit incurring the cost. Organizations who use budgeted costs as the basis for charging believe that this helps to motivate the manager of the support department to improve efficiency.

During the budget period, the support departments, not the user departments, bear the risk of any unfavorable cost variances because the user departments do not pay for any costs that exceed the budgeted costs.

The decision whether to allocate budgeted or actual costs affects the level of uncertainty that user departments face. Budgeted costs let the user departments know the costs in advance. Users then are better equipped to determine the amount of the service to request and, if the option exists, whether to use the internal department source or an external vendor.

Some organizations choose to recognize that it might not always be best to impose all of the risks of variances from budgeted amounts completely on the support departments or completely on the user departments.

(d)   Outsourcing Alternatives.   Exposing administrative cost centers to competitive forces of the marketplace is another way that some organizations use to force administrative areas to control their expenses. If operating units have a choice of buying services from an external party, then administrative units have the incentive of self-preservation to contain costs. This does, however, pose some risk of suboptimization of the centralized services if some operating units decide to outsource, leaving the remaining operating units with higher costs for these services.

(e)   Performance Measures.   Performance measures that are linked to compensation help motivate management in the right direction. However, it is critical to ensure that an organization's goals are aligned with how its incentive plan is designed. When this technique is used, performance measures should be considered that are both financial and non-financial measures of effectiveness or efficiency; and they should be monitored on an ongoing and systematic basis.

(f)   Activity-Based Costing (A-BC).   Activity-based costing can provide a mechanism for managing administrative expenses. If the administrative and user departments agree to a framework and agree to the level of work, it can provide an actual per-unit basis for charging back the costs with the associated services. But if the actual usage level is either above or below the targeted level, the actual per-unit charge-back might be different, and management will have to decide how any efficiency gains or losses will be treated.

(g)   Benchmarking.   Benchmark studies can provide information on the comparative cost efficiency of an organization. Benchmarking is the continual process of comparing products, services, and activities to objective indicators of performance. Benchmarks can be found inside or outside the organization.

18.7   SUMMARY.   The administrative expense budget is an important link with all other budgets because it comprises activities that support other budgeted activities and at the same time it provides some elements of control, and of independent perspective, on those other activities. The size of the administrative expense budget, what it includes, and how it is prepared can be unique to each organization for many reasons. However, the administrative expense budget primarily reflects how management views its support functions.

BUDGETING PAYROLL COSTS (New)

Leonard A. Haug, CPP

Digital Equipment Corporation in collaboration with the American Payroll Association

CONTENTS

18A.1 INTRODUCTION	**3**	
18A.2 OVERVIEW OF THE PAYROLL FUNCTION	**6**	
(a) Payroll Charter and Expectations	**6**	
(b) Suppliers and Customers	**6**	
(c) Systems Definition	**6**	
(i) Input	**6**	
(ii) Gross-to-Net	**7**	
(iii) Output	**8**	
(d) Business Definition	**8**	
(i) Data Capture Services	**8**	
(ii) Payment Processing Services	**9**	
(iii) Payroll Delivery Services	**9**	
(iv) Third-Party Payment and Reporting Services	**9**	
(v) Accounting and Reconciliation Services	**10**	
(vi) Customer Support Services	**10**	
(e) Understanding Your Payroll Is the First Step for Budgeting and Change	**11**	
18A.3 RELATIONSHIP WITH HUMAN RESOURCE FUNCTION	**12**	
18A.4 MAJOR COMPONENTS OF PAYROLL COSTS	**12**	
(a) Understanding Total Costs	**12**	
(b) Hardware and Data Center Costs	**12**	

(c) Software and Application Support Costs	**13**	
(d) Labor-Related Costs	**14**	
(e) Supplier Costs	**14**	
(i) Financial Institutions	**15**	
(ii) Federal and State Tax Administration Services	**15**	
(iii) Forms Providers	**15**	
18A.5 CONDITIONS AND FACTORS AFFECTING PAYROLL COSTS	**16**	
(a) Differentiators	**16**	
(b) Workload Drivers	**17**	
(c) Differentiators and Workload Drivers: Key to Understanding Costs	**17**	
(d) Expanded Explanations	**17**	
(i) Company Structure	**17**	
(ii) Decentralized/Centralized Operations	**18**	
(iii) Population Supported	**18**	
(iv) Tax Compliance and Reporting Requirements	**18**	
(v) Pay Frequency Alternatives	**19**	
(vi) Multiple Pay Programs	**19**	
(vii) Collective Bargaining Agreements	**19**	
(viii) Pay Media	**19**	
(ix) Level of Service Provided	**21**	
(x) Earnings Programs Offered	**21**	
(xi) Deduction Programs Offered	**21**	

(xii)   Time Collection/Reporting
        Methodologies   21
(xiii) Relationships with Other Internal
        Financial and Accounting
        Systems   22
(xiv)   Mergers and Acquisitions   22
(xv)   Industry- and Company-Unique
        Pay Practices   22

**18A.6   CHOICES AND DECISIONS:
          OUTSOURCING,
          ACQUISITION, AND
          DEVELOPMENT   22**

(a) Outsourcing   23
    (i)   Understanding the Plusses and
           the Minuses   23
    (ii)   Rationale   23
    (iii) Other Considerations—Costs
           and Benefits   23
    (iv)   Opportunities   24
    (v)   Outsourcing Does Not Mean
           Relinquishing Accountability   25
(b) Application Acquisition versus
    Development   25
    (i)   Legacy System/What to Do?   25
    (ii)   The Decision-Making Process   25
    (iii) Software Packages Will
           Require Modification   26
    (iv)   To Purchase or Not to Purchase:
           A Cross-Functional Decision   26

**18A.7   ORGANIZATIONAL FACTORS
          AFFECTING COST   27**

(a) Past Organizational Structures and
    Perceptions   27
(b) Changing Organizational Structures
    and Perceptions   27
(c) Coming of Age   27

**18A.8   TRADITIONAL AND
          CONTEMPORARY
          BUDGETING APPROACHES   27**

(a) Line Item (Traditional) Budgeting
    Approach   28
(b) Activity-Based Costing (Contemporary)
    Budgeting Approach   30
(c) Both Are Important   30

**18A.9   SMART BUDGETING
          (SPENDING MONEY TO
          SAVE MONEY)   32**

(a) Investing in Resources Required to
    Achieve Change   32
(b) Budgeting for Continuous
    Improvement   32
(c) The Importance of Strategic
    Planning   32

**18A.10 INNOVATIVE METHODS FOR
          RECOVERING COSTS
          INCURRED   33**

(a) Eliminating Elective Deduction
    Programs   33
(b) Charging for Child Support Payments 33
(c) Charging for Affidavits   33
(d) Charging for Copies of W-2s   33
(e) Charging for Rework   33
(f) Charging for Check versus Direct
    Deposit Transactions   34
(g) Charging for Nonstandard and
    Inefficient or Costly Practices   34

**18A.11 CYCLICAL PAYROLL EXPENSE
          PATTERNS IMPACTING
          BUDGETING AND
          FORECASTING   34**

**18A.12 USE OF TOTAL QUALITY
          MANAGEMENT   35**

(a) Overview of TQM   35
(b) Benchmarking   35
(c) Reengineering   37
(d) A delta t   37
(e) Six Sigma   40
(f) Continuous Improvement   41

**18A.13 PUTTING TECHNOLOGY TO
          WORK   45**

(a) Windows   45
(b) Desktop Integration   45
(c) Client/Server Environment   45
(d) Decision Support Systems   46
(e) Multimedia   46
(f) Document Image Processing   46
(g) Interactive Voice Response   46
(h) Check-Printing and Forms-Processing
    Technologies   48

**18A.14 BUDGETING TASKS AND
          CALENDAR   49**

18A.15 MANAGEMENT AND
     LEADERSHIP APPROACHES   50

18A.16 SUMMARY   51

SOURCES AND
SUGGESTED REFERENCES   51

ACKNOWLEDGMENTS   52

18A.1   INTRODUCTION. Finance organizations are placing significant emphasis on reducing transaction processing costs in the payroll function in order to shift resources and business focus to "business partnership" roles. Exhibits 18A.1 and 18A.2 illustrate this paradigm shift and highlight the need for companies to increase their payroll efficiencies. You will note on the latter exhibit that finance departments are being asked to reduce costs and improve performance. With transactions growing at twice the rate of business growth, and demand for services at a higher rate, this business decision has created pressures on chief financial officers to improve services at lower costs.

Because of the emphasis on reducing labor and costs associated with transaction systems, understanding the costs of such systems has become paramount to the payroll process. Benchmarking payroll costs with those of other companies, both within and outside one's industry, can help management understand the relative degree of opportunity that exists for their company. Consulting firms that provide benchmarking services can often help companies to accelerate the benchmarking process and obtain valuable information on comparative costs and best practices.

Exhibit 18A.3 illustrates the varying average cost per transaction for various accounting and related functions. Although the average payroll cost to process a check was estimated, in this comparative benchmark study, to be $2.77, actual costs

The Challenge Is Driving A "Paradigm Shift" In The Role of The Finance Function

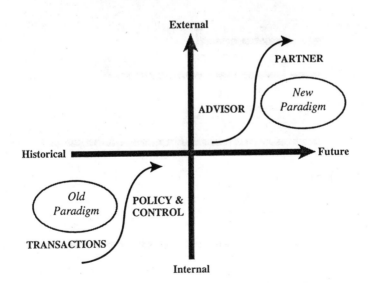

Finance Must Re-prioritize, Re-engineer And Reallocate Resources

Exhibit 18A.1.   Paradigm shifts. Reprinted with permission. © Gunn Partners, Inc.

Finance Is Being Asked To Significantly Reduce Costs At The Same Time It Seeks To Improve Performance

- Transactions are growing at twice the business growth rate

- Internal and external customer demand for service is higher

- Market and regulatory requirements are adding to business complexity

- Finance is being asked to limit or actually reduce costs

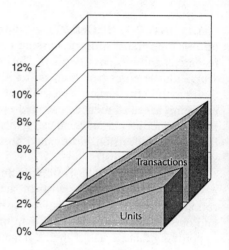

To Satisfy The CEO, Finance Must Deliver More, For Less

Exhibit 18A.2.   Paradigm shift effects. Reprinted with permission. © Gunn Partners, Inc.

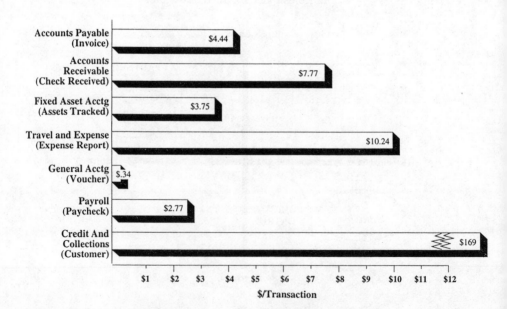

Exhibit 18A.3.   Average cost per transaction. Reprinted with permission. © 1991, A.T. Kearney, Inc. All rights reserved.

varied widely among participants. Other cost comparison studies report even higher costs per payment. Payroll expense data are often tracked by cost per payment or annual cost per employee paid, as shared by Digital Equipment Corporation in Exhibit 18A.4. Understanding payroll costs and the reasons behind variations in cost from one company to another can help companies improve their cost performance.

The best-practice companies are responding by consolidating multiple decentralized operations and by replacing narrow, "stovepipe" approaches with solutions that address the entire payroll delivery chain. In addition, best-practice companies are emphasizing standardization, simplification, reengineering, selective automation, effective use of technology, and partial to full outsourcing as ways to improve performance and reduce operating costs. Exhibit 18A.5 identifies three implementation stages typical of cost reduction efforts at successful companies. The primary driver of cost savings appears to be the stage of implementation to which the company has progressed; that is, the higher the implementation stage, the greater the savings.

Achievement of cost-effective payroll programs begins with an understanding of the business and its added-value services, customers and suppliers, current costs, and current performance levels. The use of total quality management (TQM) and activity-based costing (ABC) tools provides direction and assistance for understanding the business and for improving core competencies while reducing labor and costs associated with payroll, which ultimately should result in a more cost-effective payroll program.

Whatever your company's current status is, be assured that there are opportunities for higher performance and lower costs. This chapter focuses on helping the reader to achieve these objectives.

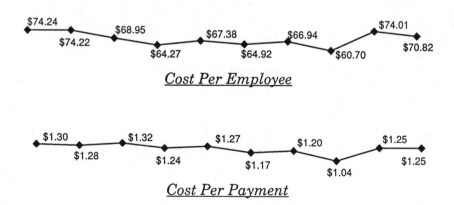

Cost Per Employee

Cost Per Payment

FY85 FY86 FY87 FY88 FY89 FY90 FY91 FY92 FY93 FY94

Exhibit 18A.4. Payroll cost performance. Reprinted with permission. © Digital Equipment Corporation—U.S. Payroll.

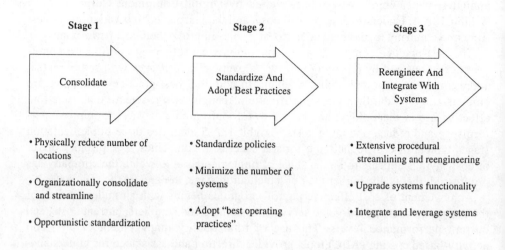

Exhibit 18A.5.   Stages of implementation. Reprinted with permission. © 1991, A.T. Kearney, Inc. All rights reserved.

18A.2   OVERVIEW OF THE PAYROLL FUNCTION

(a)   Payroll Charter and Expectations.   *Payroll* is generally defined as a tactical operational organization within accounting, finance, treasury, or human resources chartered with the critical responsibility of producing the company's payroll(s). Company expectations of performance are very high, with zero to little tolerance for anything less than 100% accuracy and timeliness.

(b)   Suppliers and Customers.   The definition of payroll must begin with the understanding that payroll is not a stand-alone function. Regardless of size, payroll depends on many suppliers, both internal and external, and delivers products and services to many different sets of customers, again both internal and external, as illustrated in Exhibit 18A.6. The definition of payroll from a process and cost perspective, therefore, must extend beyond payroll proper to include overlapping processes and costs incurred by payroll suppliers and customers.

(c)   Systems Definition.   To understand the function, payroll also must be defined from both a systems and a business perspective.

From a systems perspective, the payroll process is comprised of three components:

INPUT— — — — — —>GROSS-TO-NET— — — — —>OUTPUT

(i)   Input.   Input includes activities associated with the collection, validation, and approval of information essential to subsequent components of the payroll process.

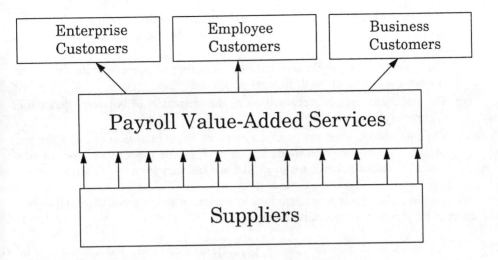

**Exhibit 18A.6.   Supplier/payroll/customer overview. Reprinted with permission. ©
Digital Equipment Corporation—U.S. Payroll.**

The payroll process begins with input changes made to the employee's record, which
may reside on an integrated human resource and payroll system or on a separate
human resource system that sends information to payroll for updating to its system.

The input process includes the following generic electronic and/or paper inputs:

- The collection and updating of data to the system, including employee profile
  and deduction data as well as file maintenance data from within the payroll
  business.
- The creation and/or receipt and storage of reference tables (e.g., tax, insurance,
  ledger, bank, and site data).
- The receipt and consolidation of time input data, supplementary compensation
  requests, and pay adjustments and exception payment and data initiated by payroll.
- The calculation of vacation accruals and updating of available vacation hours.
  This process may be done before the pay calculation process or after, depending on business rules (when an employee is credited with earned vacation
  hours).

(ii)   Gross-to-Net.   Gross-to-net includes activities associated with the calculation
of wage, salary, supplementary compensation, and adjustment payments, including:

- The calculation of gross pay using master file data and/or timecard, supplementary payment requests, and adjustments collected via the input process.
- The calculation of § 125 pretax deductions (e.g., deductions that are exempt
  from most federal and/or state and local taxes, such as 401k plans).

- The calculation of taxes to be withheld, including federal income withholding, Social Security and Medicare, state income withholding, and local withholding taxes (as applicable).
- The calculation of single and multiple child support garnishments, tax levies, and other wage attachments in legal-prioritized order.
- The calculation (if not precalculated by the originator) of voluntary deductions in company-prioritized order.
- The calculation of net pay, which represents the culmination of all of the preceding steps in the pay calculation process. (Some payrolls or types of payments are calculated on a net-to-gross basis and vary from this description).

(iii)   Output.   Output includes activities associated with the production and distribution of payments and reports, including:

- The creation of paycheck and/or pay deposit statements and applicable bank electronic funds transfer (EFT) file(s).
- The updating of current and historical online payment files and the creation of payroll reports for internal payroll administrative and compliance functions.
- The creation of informational output for payroll business customers and suppliers, including earnings extracts for groups such as labor collection and reporting systems (assuming labor allocation is performed outside of payroll), human resources, treasury, insurance providers, and financial institutions.
- The creation of payment requests to accounts payable and/or treasury for third-party trade payable checks or electronic funds transfer (EFT) payments to taxing agencies, courts, insurance providers, and other recipients, if not directly paid by payroll.

(d)   Business Definition.   From a business perspective, payroll includes the following generic types of activities:

- Data capture services
- Payment processing services
- Payroll delivery services
- Third-party payment and reporting services
- Accounting and reconciliation services
- Customer support services

(i)   Data Capture Services.   Data capture services include all activities associated with the processing and data entry of all forms and data related to employee record information. Data capture functions may be a shared and/or integrated function with human resources and/or other organizations. For many companies, time collection is the most labor-intensive activity of all front-end processes. The effort involved depends heavily on company time reporting policies (who and what is reported) and on the methods of reporting (how time is collected, validated, and processed).

Programs with paper timecards and centralized data collection and entry processes represent the most labor-intensive systems and often result in high levels of rework and additional labor costs.

(ii) Payment Processing Services. As companies increasingly move from fixed compensation programs to variable performance- and incentive-based compensation programs, and as companies consolidate multiple employee disbursement systems into single disbursement systems, the number of supplementary compensation programs with which payroll has to support and interface will continue to increase.

Activities within this service focus on the administration of such programs and require close coordination with each authorizing program office to ensure accurate and timely payment services. The degree of work to perform this function depends not only on volumes but on whether the linkages between originators and payroll are paper- or electronic-based.

(iii) Payroll Delivery Services. Delivery services include tasks associated with the preparation and controlled distribution of pay statements from point of production to point of employee receipt. Specific processes will vary depending on company demographics and method(s) of payment (check or direct deposit), as well as on the number of pay cycles, pay frequencies, and volumes of payments. The method of payment selected, the type of pay production technology used, and the mode of pay statement delivery will determine the overall cost of the function. There are numerous options available for performing this function and lowering overall costs.

(iv) Third-Party Payment and Reporting Services. Third-party payment and reporting services include both mandatory and voluntary activities:

• Tax Payment and Reporting Services

If not performed in an accurate and timely fashion, tax payment and reporting services may represent one of the highest areas of financial exposure and risk. This function includes activities associated with the monitoring of federal, state, and local tax regulations to ensure ongoing compliance; the authorization and issuance of employee- and company-paid taxes in adherence to tax payment schedules; and the creation and issuance of customized reports dictated by individual taxing agencies, including calendar year-end wage and tax reporting processes (e.g., W-2s and expatriate reporting).

• Attachment Payment and Reporting Services

This function includes all activities associated with the receipt, execution, payment, and reporting of various forms of wage attachments related to support orders and federal and state tax levies, as well as civil orders. Due to the lack of standardization regarding withholding, payment, and reporting, this function represents a significant labor effort for most companies. Recent revisions to the Family Support Act making employer-withheld child support mandatory has further increased, in some companies, the workload in this area.

- Voluntary Deduction Program Administration Services

Based on volumes, the number of deductions processed by a payroll organization today often exceeds the number of payments made by ten to one. Therefore, in today's environment, payroll organizations might more appropriately be viewed as "deduction agents" rather than "paymasters." The degree to which this is true will depend on a number of factors, including the number and nature of mandatory and elective deduction programs offered by the company.

The degree of work and cost involved for payroll will also depend on the role that the payroll organization plays in administering each program. From an overall company perspective, it is important to measure costs for an overall process, regardless of the unit performing a given task. However, the effort for payroll specifically will be smaller in companies in which deduction program ownership lies outside of payroll, for example, with human resources or benefits.

Conversely, the effort and therefore the cost for payroll will be greater to the degree that the role of payroll extends beyond merely withholding and reporting authorized deductions. For example, payroll costs will be higher if payroll is processing all enrollment, change, and stop forms or performing program compliance reporting functions.

Cost and quality can often be favorably impacted by moving those functions that go beyond deduction agency functions to human resources and/or benefits. With today's technology, benefit enrollment and change processes can often be placed directly with the customer (employee), as discussed later.

(v)   Accounting and Reconciliation Services.   Accounting and reconciliation services include activities associated with closing the books and reconciling balance sheet accounts, bank accounts, journal entries, labor distribution, employee receivables (tracking and collecting monies due the company), and internal balancing and controls. The number of resources required to perform the function is often an indicator of the quality and efficiency of total payroll operations. Fewer resources and account reconciliations with fewer variances and reconciling items might, for example, point to a well-controlled and clean front-end process, whereas a larger number of resources and a higher number of out-of-balance accounts might indicate an environment with problems.

(vi)   Customer Support Services.   Customer support services include services that provide customers with information, assistance in resolving problems, and support to meet changing system requirements and needs. Although some of these services can be automated, the majority are delivered through direct interaction with customers and suppliers. This value-added service, in many respects, is the most important and challenging of all services provided by the business and may in fact represent one of the most costly of all payroll services.

Performance of this function requires business experts and accessibility to data and information. Communication tools, ad hoc reporting capabilities, structured life cycle expertise (for system development programs), and good record retention and retrieval programs are essential elements for success in this area.

(e)   Understanding Your Payroll Is the First Step for Budgeting and Change.   Every payroll function will be defined differently and will include different types of responsibilities. An in-depth understanding of the payroll business is needed as a foundation for budgeting and change. Understanding of your payroll function can be enhanced by creating and documenting data and process models, inventories of suppliers and customers, and so on, as illustrated in Exhibit 18A.7.

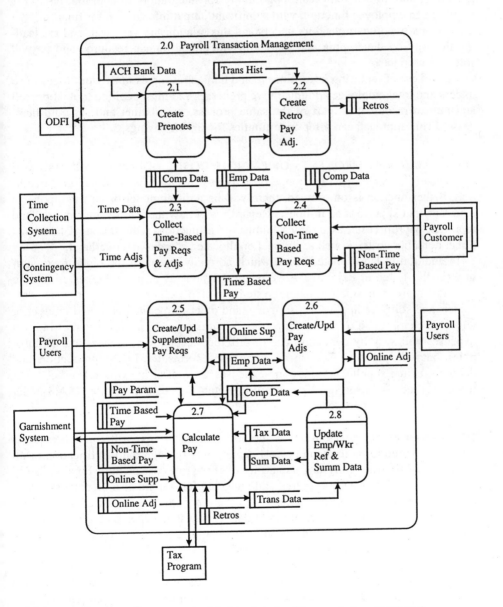

Exhibit 18A.7.   Payroll process model. Reprinted with permission. © Digital Equipment Corporation—U.S. Payroll.

18A.3   RELATIONSHIP WITH HUMAN RESOURCE FUNCTION.   In most companies, payroll reports through the finance organization. However, there is a trend
toward a reporting line within the human resource organization, and there is good
reason for this.

Human resources is a major supplier and customer of payroll data, and separate
systems and master files represent redundant warehouses, if not repetitive data entry
processes, and offer a significant opportunity for integration. In addition, payroll is
primarily an employee function, with significant output information for finance.

Third-party software vendors understand this relationship very well and are leading the way by developing and marketing integrated human resource and payroll
software products.

Regardless of reporting lines, finance and human resources must work together to
understand total employee administrative processes and must begin to look at payroll
and human resources as part of the same process, not distinct and separate businesses. This approach can offer opportunities for sizable savings.

18A.4   MAJOR COMPONENTS OF PAYROLL COSTS.   Direct payroll costs will
vary greatly depending on the range of activities included in the function. In addition, if the function is outsourced, there will be a different set of cost components
from one that is performed in-house. Regardless of how these costs are captured and
reported, payroll costs, as in any administrative function, will consist of labor and
direct nonlabor costs, as well as indirect or allocated charges and overhead.

In addition to labor-related costs, which normally represent the highest expenditure (as illustrated in Exhibit 18A.8), major components of payroll costs, in high to
low dollar order, normally include systems-related expenses (e.g., hardware, data
center, and software application support), and other (direct nonlabor and indirect or
allocated charges and overhead) expenses. What is reported as direct versus indirect
expenses will vary by company, due to different accounting practices and philosophies, but will include such costs as supplies and forms, third-party production, and
delivery-related supplier services and expenses, as well as banking related costs. A
more detailed listing of specific payroll cost items appears in section 18A.8 under
traditional budgeting approaches.

(a)   Understanding Total Costs.   It should be noted that payroll component costs
may be captured in more than one cost center; only through the identification of all
costs can a company fully understand its total payroll cost picture. Finally, "soft"
costs, though not normally captured and budgeted for, should also be understood, as
they may represent significant expense to the company. Examples of soft payroll
costs include company labor required to deliver pay statements to employees within
each paysite or labor required by employees and supervisors to collect, review,
approve, and deliver information to payroll.

(b)   Hardware and Data Center Costs.   The age and type of the hardware may be a
key factor affecting payroll costs. Exhibit 18A.9 provides a sample template for estimating annualized hardware-related costs. To calculate payroll processing costs, one
needs to (1) post the annual depreciation or lease cost of all categories (e.g., mainframe, midrange, and personal computer) of hardware; (2) calculate the percentage

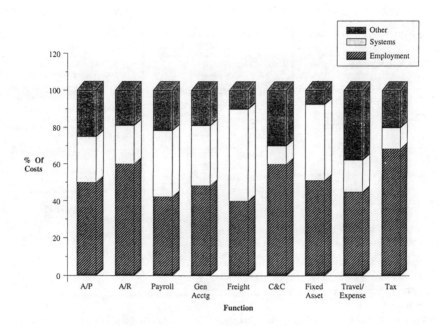

Exhibit 18A.8.   Cost breakdown by function. Reprinted with permission. © 1991, A.T. Kearney, Inc. All rights reserved.

of CPU cycles, input/output, and disk space utilization for the payroll application resident on each hardware platform; (3) add the calculated percentages and divide by the three (essentially, calculate the average of the three percentages); (4) multiply the result of your average calculation in the third step by the annual depreciation or lease cost of the appropriate hardware category; and (5) add the results of each hardware category for a total hardware cost estimate. It should be emphasized that the result will represent a "quick and dirty" estimate technique. Many companies use a systems cost allocation methodology for determining hardware-related costs for each application (e.g., payroll). Such methodologies may offer a more accurate estimate of cost.

More often than not, payroll is not supported by dedicated hardware. In today's environment, payroll often utilizes the capacity and expertise resident in a shared service center (SSC). Such use drives standardization and optimizes automated production processes. Costs for such services are often based on standardized cost allocation methodologies provided under a service agreement with rates set on a fiscal-year basis. Whether internally or externally provided, the business should clearly understand the rate structure and performance level provided under such an agreement.

(c)   Software and Application Support Costs.   Some companies use in-house developed software, whereas others use vendor-acquired software. Each approach involves different kinds of costs. In-house software requires ongoing maintenance

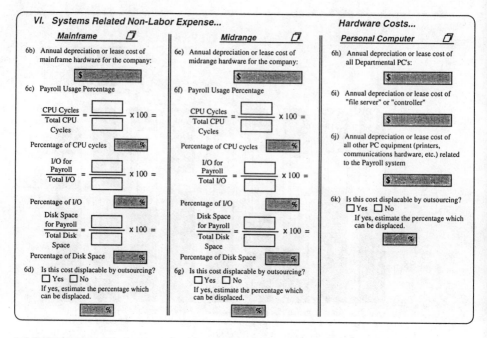

Exhibit 18A.9.   Hardware-related cost estimating. Reprinted with permission.
© Coopers & Lybrand L.L.P.

support. Software acquired from a third-party vendor requires special investment dollars (usually capitalized) at the time of acquisition and then involves annual license fees. Companies that purchase and then modify third-party software will continue to incur significant ongoing maintenance and enhancement costs as well.

The trend in payroll software is to move from in-house legacy systems, which require significant dollars to maintain and longer timeframes to introduce change, onto more flexible and table-driven vendor-acquired products. At the same time, mainframe systems are being replaced with lower cost PC-based architecture.

(d)   Labor-Related Costs.   Labor-related costs normally represent the largest single cost component of the payroll function and include labor, overtime, sick, vacation, personal allowance, and fringe benefit allocations. Because labor represents such a large portion of the average payroll budget, companies are well served by understanding and tracking the equivalent headcount required to support each payroll activity. This knowledge, in combination with volumes and anticipated changes in the business, helps to create a more accurate budget. This information is also helpful in identifying opportunities for labor and cost savings. Exhibit 18A.10 offers one type of mechanism for capturing headcount and labor-related costs by location and business function.

(e)   Supplier Costs.   Much of the payroll-related cost will be incurred on behalf of the business by suppliers.

Please allocate the General Office and field FTEs for each of the labor categories into the Sub–Processes.

General Office:	# of FTEs			Direct Labor / Contractor Costs
	Supervisor	Clerical	Contractor	
Total Number of General Office FTEs	——	——	——	$ ——
Data Capture	——	——	——	$ ——
Payment Processing	——	——	——	$ ——
Payment Production	——	——	——	$ ——
Tax Payments and Reporting	——	——	——	$ ——
Accounting & Reconciliation	——	——	——	$ ——
Customer Support Services	——	——	——	$ ——
Record Retention	——	——	——	$ ——

General Office:	# of FTEs			Direct Labor / Contractor Costs
	Supervisor	Clerical	Contractor	
Total Number of General Office FTEs	——	——	——	$——
Data Capture	——	——	——	$——
Payment Processing	——	——	——	$——
Payment Production	——	——	——	$——
Tax Payments and Reporting	——	——	——	$——
Accounting & Reconciliation	——	——	——	$——
Customer Support Services	——	——	——	$——
Record Retention	——	——	——	$——
Other (non–productive)	——	——	——	$——

Please allocate the FTEs for each of the labor categories:

	# of FTEs	Direct Labor / Contractor Costs
Human Resources	——	$__
Legal	——	$__
Information Systems	——	$__

2. Provide the non–labor and indirect costs for the Payroll process as identified in the scope. Use the following definitions when completing the table.

Direct Non–Labor cost – Includes all direct, non–labor costs charged to the process.

Contract Services cost – The outsourcing of all or part of a function to a third party.

Overhead cost – Costs associated with training, travel, telephone, facilities, office equipment, office supplies, etc.

	1993 Non–Labor Costs
Direct Non–Labor cost	
Contract Services cost	
Overhead cost	
TOTAL	

Exhibit 18A.10.   Labor resource table. Reprinted with permission. © 3D Consortium. All rights reserved.

(i)   Financial Institutions.   Financial institutions that provide payroll services to companies represent important suppliers and should be managed, like any other supplier, under a service agreement and regularly evaluated for performance, including cost of product. Payroll services normally provided by financial institutions include check processing and reconcilement services, automated clearing house (ACH) direct deposit credit, debit, and prenoting services, as well as an array of other administrative services. The cost of such services may be covered by offsetting balances maintained at the institution or may be based on per-transaction fees with varying rates based on volume. As in any vendor evaluation, requests for proposals (RFPs) should be used to compare services and prices, which can vary significantly from one financial institution to another.

(ii)   Federal and State Tax Administration Services.   Many companies choose third-party vendors to perform payroll tax payment and reporting functions associated with federal, state, local, and unemployment tax processes. Companies that select this option gain the expertise of the provider and do not have to maintain in-house resources to perform the function. Historically, the provider has been compensated via access to the funds in advance of scheduled payment due dates; therefore, this may or may not be a budgeted expense. Companies that choose this option retain ultimate liability and relinquish some direct control over the process. The provider is normally liable for errors it makes.

(iii)   Forms Providers.   Forms, including checks, direct deposit pay statements, time-cards, and W-2s, can represent substantial costs. These costs can be minimized by using laser printers whenever possible or by ordering multiple printed forms under a

single purchase order and taking advantage of volume discounts. Stock levels should be sufficient to meet short- to intermediate-term needs but should not be maintained at levels that would represent sizable waste in the event of form revisions.

18A.5   CONDITIONS AND FACTORS AFFECTING PAYROLL COSTS.   Many internal and external factors affect payroll costs; some are controllable and others are not. Factors that impact different levels of cost between companies are sometimes referred to as *cost differentiators*.

(a)   Differentiators.   Actual payroll costs may vary greatly from one company to another, due to classes of differentiators identified in Exhibit 18A.11. Differentiators may cause costs to go up or down.

Differentiators

Features and characteristics of an organization or its practices that distinguish one company from another when attempting to compare efficiency or effectiveness.

- *Questions/concerns you would immediately raise if someone said your "cost per invoice" was 25% below Company B's*

- *If automation is a key driver of cost, and Company A uses a Cray XMP supercomputer and Company B uses an Apple Macintosh, there is clearly a practice difference worth identifying*

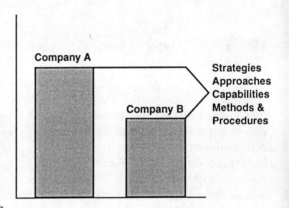

Exhibit 18A.11.   Classes of differentiators. Reprinted with permission. © 3D Consortium. All rights reserved.

In some cases differentiators are largely beyond the control of the business and are often due to the nature of the business or the industry in which the company operates. In other cases, positive or negative differentiators may be the result of company policies or practices. In many instances, these policies and practices can be changed and significant dollars saved in the process.

Examples of differentiators that tend to drive payroll costs up or down include the following:

CATEGORY	HIGHER COSTS	LOWER COSTS
• Employee Composition	Heavily Hourly	Predominately Exempt
• Labor Unions	Present	Absent
• Operations	Decentralized	Centralized

• Pay Programs	Multiple	Single
• Pay Frequency	More Frequent (e.g., weekly)	Less Frequent (e.g., biweekly, semi-monthly, etc.)
• Taxing Jurisdictions	Larger Number	Smaller Number
• Earnings Categories	Larger Number	Smaller Number
• Deduction Categories	Larger Number	Smaller Number
• Pay Media	Check	Direct Deposit
• Time Reporting Environment	Complex	Simple
• Degree of Automation	Low	High
• Use of Technology	Low	High
• Human Resource and Payroll Systems	Independent	Integrated
• Controls	Manual	Automated Validations
• Payroll Skill Set Focus	Maintenance	Development/Change

(b) Workload Drivers. In addition, costs are also affected by workload drivers. Examples of workload drivers include the following:

- Number of payees
- Number of out-of-cycle payments
- Number of pay adjustments
- Number of paysite locations
- Number of time capture systems
- Number of timecards processed
- Number of new hires, transfers, terminations, retirees
- Number of child support orders, federal and state levies, civil attachments, etc.
- Number of payroll bank accounts
- Number of direct deposit accounts offered per employee
- Number of payroll general ledger and subledger accounts

(c) Differentiators and Workload Drivers: Key to Understanding Costs. Differentiators and workload drivers must be fully understood if one is to identify opportunities for improvement and maximize efficiency and effectiveness. As illustrated in Exhibit 18A.12, this understanding can be facilitated by categorizing information into types of differentiators and workload drivers.

Understanding these conditions and factors is the first step toward reaching a high-service, low-cost operation. Factors unique to the industry, as well as historical (and often discretionary) choices made by a company, can have a significant impact on cost of product. It is in important to understand these factors as one company compares its costs with those of other companies and sets future spending plans.

(d) Expanded Explanations. Following are some of the factors that may drive costs up or down.

(i) Company Structure. Paying multiple legal entities significantly impacts costs, especially if each entity has different compensation and benefit programs with

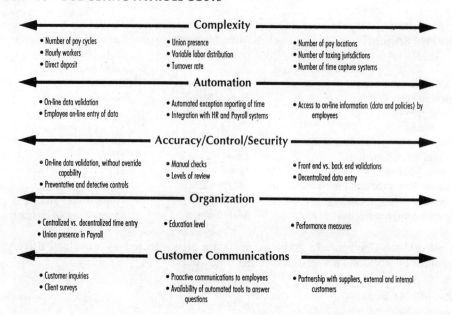

Exhibit 18A.12.   Types of differentiators and work drivers. Reprinted with permission. © 3D Consortium. All rights reserved.

different business rules and regulations, pay cycles, and so on. The degree to which these differences can be eliminated will determine whether any cost-saving opportunities exist. At a minimum, each legal entity will require separate tax and accounting processes.

(ii)   Decentralized/Centralized Operations.   Companies located in multiple states or regions have additional requirements when it comes to delivery of payroll services. Decentralized payroll operations to support each geographic or sub-business unit may involve redundant resources, systems, processes, and overhead expenses. Companies currently operating with multiple payroll operating units should consider consolidation. Given today's technology and networking capabilities, companies are combining the benefits of consolidated processing with the advantages of distributed input and output capabilities. Operating in a consolidated fashion presents problems only when input and output at the processing location are based on paper.

(iii)   Population Supported.   The size of the population being paid can drive the cost of the function up, especially in the absence of consolidation, standardization, and automation. However, employee population of and by itself is not the primary driver of expense.

(iv)   Tax Compliance and Reporting Requirements.   The number of taxing jurisdictions to which the payroll function is subject, at the federal, state, and local levels, certainly drives cost and potentially represents the highest level of financial exposure and risk. In today's environment, taxing jurisdictions are looking for every dollar they can generate and are quick to impose fines and penalties. Employers cannot afford to underspend in this area. At the same time, there are many opportunities to

lower costs in this area, including consolidated tax reporting under a single Employer Identification Number (E.I.N.); utilization of available software vendor products to permit downloading of payroll withheld taxes into customized tax paper and electronic payment and reporting formats; or outsourcing to third-party vendors.

(v)   Pay Frequency Alternatives.   Less frequent pay cycles can save dollars. Payroll costs, whether measured via cost of money or via cost of operation, can be minimized by selecting the least frequent pay cycle allowable by state law (or bargaining agreement, in the case of unions). The standard and most commonly used pay frequency within the United States is biweekly, followed by semi-monthly. Although states do not change pay frequency laws often, companies should monitor state pay frequency regulations periodically. For example, the Commonwealth of Massachusetts now permits biweekly pay cycles. Some states also provide exemptions to weekly state pay frequency laws through partitions and under certain conditions, when formally requested by employers.

(vi)   Multiple Pay Programs.   Consolidating multiple pay frequency programs also offers an opportunity for savings. For example, some employers maintain a separate executive payroll. Elimination of multiple pay cycles translates into fewer differences between employee sets (e.g., fewer unique policies, procedures, forms, and processes) and in turn reduces costs of production and administration.

In both these cases, companies need to understand their demographics and, within the framework of current state legal parameters, evaluate the financial, business, operational, and employee relations pros and cons of each viable option. As is true of other payroll-related decisions, cross-functional considerations are a necessary part of the decision-making process.

(vii)   Collective Bargaining Agreements.   There is no question that payrolls required to support bargaining units are more costly. The number of bargaining units and the differences between each bargaining agreement determine the degree of cost impact. Although companies may not be able to effect short-term change, the challenge exists to begin to influence administrative changes that provide win–win opportunities. Eliminating costly customized services that provide less value to the customer may provide a starting point for mutually supported change.

(viii)   Pay Media.   Finance management and decision makers often do not understand that payment via direct deposit offers an opportunity for savings. Check processing is more expensive, especially in low interest periods. Direct deposit operational savings match and often exceed the loss of float. Companies should complete a comparative cost analysis between the two payment methods. Hard and soft savings statistics often support claims that direct deposit is less expensive. One example of a soft savings is costs saved in employee time away from work for cashing checks. Best-practice companies have high participation direct deposit levels and are moving toward electronic pay delivery solutions to replace paper pay statements, representing even more savings. Exhibit 18A.13 presents one company's projected cost savings achievable via converting to direct deposit. You will see that in this illustration, savings exceeded costs by $616,732.80. This points out that direct

deposit can provide payroll savings to many companies, with the amount of savings directly linked to the percentage of direct participants.

At the same time, when considering the implementation or expansion of direct deposit programs, employers need to recognize that state pay media laws vary, and in most states employees must voluntarily agree to participate. Regional and nation-wide employers cannot, under most current state laws, impose compulsory direct deposit programs for salary and wage payments.

Direct Deposit Cost/Savings Analysis

	Cost/Savings	Our Company
I. Initial Investment		
1. Modifications to payroll system	$ _____	$0.00
II. Annual Costs		
2. A. Initial collection of authorization forms and input (includes paper cost for advices)	$ _____	$6,367.20
B. Annual add, stop, change file maintenance	$ _____	$5,068.80
3. Bank service charges @ _____ per item	$ _____	$67,200.00
4. Direct deposit campaign costs	$ _____	N/A
5. Lost float	$ _____	$218,736.00
6. 20% of investment (item I) (5 year amortization)	$ _____	N/A
TOTAL	$ _____	$297,372.00
III. Annual Savings		
7. Bank check processing charges @ _____ per item x number of items	$ _____	$353,472.00
8. Bank reconcilement maintenance @ per month	$ _____	$ incl. in #1
9. Bank reconcilement charges @ _____ per item x number of items	$ _____	$ incl. in #1
10. In-house reconcilement costs	$ _____	$1,584.00
11. Check storage and microfilming	$ _____	$ incl. in #1
12. Bank stop-payment charges @ $ _____ per stop x number of items	$ _____	$3,000.00
13. Check reissue costs _____ (cost per reissue x number of reissues)	$ _____	$15,000.00
14. Incremental check forms costs	$ _____	$12,280.80
15. Check distribution and handling costs	$ _____	$528,768.00
16. Check cashing service charge (if applicable)	$ _____	N/A
17. Employee lost time to cash checks (___ hours per employee x average pay per hour x # of employees) NOTE: Some companies prefer to exclude item 16 from analysis due to difficulty in estimating.	$ _____	N/A
TOTAL	$ _____	$914,104.80
IV. Net Addition to Profits		
A. 1st year	$ _____	$616,732.80
B. 2nd through 5th year (if depreciating initial investment)	$ _____	N/A
C. After fifth year (if depreciating initial investment)	$ _____	N/A

Modified from *The Payroll Manager's Guide to Successful Direct Deposit*, Sixth Edition.

Exhibit 18A.13.   Sample direct deposit cost savings. Reprinted with permission. © American Payroll Association.

(ix)   Level of Service Provided.   It is a traditional mindset within the payroll area that service means doing anything and everything that customers (anyone) ask for. Fortunately, this mindset is being challenged, and services and levels of performance provided are being adjusted and balanced with business need and cost considerations. The customer is being redefined to recognize that the internal customer (employee) is not equivalent to the customer that buys the company's products and services.

Companies are beginning to learn that the focus of internal administrative services should be on core competencies (for example, accuracy and timeliness) and that services and performance levels that go beyond might offer opportunities for cost savings. Companies with high direct deposit participation levels, for example, may be able to eliminate advance vacation pay options, as employees will have access to their funds while on vacation or away from the work site.

(x)   Earnings Programs Offered.   Over the years, companies have had a tendency to create new earnings categories "on demand," without giving proper attention to the costs associated with introducing and maintaining each new earnings category—not only for payroll, but for downstream suppliers and customers. Each earnings category, regardless of whether the software can accommodate the addition, involves ongoing administrative costs in the form of specialized processes, forms, policies, and procedures.

In addition, companies are rapidly moving from traditional fixed compensation programs to variable, performance-based programs. With this change, the number of earnings programs is increasing and becoming more complex. For these reasons, best-practice companies are moving to reduce or consolidate the number of earnings categories, to replace (in the case of those with in-house software) hard-coded earnings logic with table-driven menus and to place greater responsibility with business suppliers and customers for calculating such payments and storing historical data.

(xi)   Deduction Programs Offered.   Payroll has become more of a deduction than a disbursement agent. Though much of this is unavoidable, many best-practice companies are revising their roles in deduction administration and moving to eliminate discretionary deduction programs not essential to the business. Where elective deduction programs are offered, some companies are beginning to pass administrative costs on to employees or providers.

The number of deduction programs that payroll offers and the role that payroll plays in the process will impact cost. For example, if payroll is responsible for processing enrollment and changes to deduction programs, its costs will be higher.

Best-practice companies are also moving toward accountability and entry at the source. For example, the use of voice response systems and client server technology permits employees, supervisors, and/or suppliers (e.g, human resources, benefits, etc.) to initiate or change transactions without the involvement of payroll employees. In turn, payroll can then receive prevalidated data in a format that can be processed automatically.

(xii)   Time Collection/Reporting Methodologies.   Time collection and reporting processes can be two of the most labor-intensive and error-prone processes in the

payroll supply chain, especially if they are manual (paper-based). All processes in the creation, approval, and processing of time data should be fully understood. Companies are beginning to realize that time reporting programs often represent high cost and low value. As a result, best-practice companies are moving from mandatory reporting to exception reporting processes when possible, and reducing and/or eliminating the number of reporting categories.

Companies must begin to ask whether the need for reporting is based on current legal and business requirements or on historical precedent. Unessential time reporting practices should be discontinued and necessary reporting upgraded to smart clocks, voice, or terminal-entered processes available from multiple third-party vendors.

(xiii)   Relationships with Other Internal Financial and Accounting Systems.   Some organizations perform labor collection and reporting duties as well as other peripheral duties. Each of these functions should be reexamined to determine first, whether the function serves a valid business need; and second, if essential, where the function might best be performed. Often, companies find that tasks being performed are no longer needed or that such functions could better be performed elsewhere.

(xiv)   Mergers and Acquisitions.   In today's rapidly changing business climate, many companies are acquiring new businesses, establishing new business alliances, or looking to divest portions of their existing businesses. These situations ultimately involve decisions regarding the delivery of administrative functions, such as payroll services. Each of these opportunities should be closely examined prior to making any decision. Supporting new compensation and benefit programs that normally accompany acquisitions may represent significant complexity and cost. Added to the complexity is the fact that often such decisions have to be made quickly. The decision to operate under separate payroll systems, migrate to one system, or use a third-party service provider, on a temporary or permanent basis, should all be considered from legal, service, and cost perspectives prior to a final decision.

(xv)   Industry- and Company-Unique Pay Practices.   Additional practices unique to an industry or company can also drive costs higher and also should be considered. Whenever possible, these practices should be modified or eliminated to maximize service and minimize cost. Reviewing company compensation policies, for example, might identify pay practices that are not legally required and if eliminated would provide financial as well as operational savings. For example, some companies have determined that their overtime pay practices exceed those required by law (e.g., paying overtime for more than eight hours a day versus more than forty hours a week).

18A.6   CHOICES AND DECISIONS: OUTSOURCING, ACQUISITION, AND DEVELOPMENT.   No solution is permanent, and all companies sooner or later need to make decisions about whether to outsource payroll to a third-party processor, purchase an external software product, invest in the internal development of an in-house application, or manage a variety of these solutions. Each approach has its pros and cons and should be considered carefully during the budgeting process, as all choices will have financial implications.

(a)   Outsourcing.

(i)   Understanding the Plusses and the Minuses.   Outsourcing has become an emerging best in class practice, especially in areas of benefit administration (e.g., 401, pension, etc.). In payroll, companies are also looking at outsourcing all or portions of the payroll function. Cost is increasingly the motivating factor.

Size of company often determines the viability of outsourcing. The smaller the company, the more likely it is that outsourcing will provide a cost-effective solution. This is true because normally smaller companies have less need for customized solutions. Their needs can be more readily met via an outside service bureau with a generic set of products and services.

However, as depicted in Exhibit 18A.14, the gap between what larger companies need and what service providers can deliver at a competitive rate is closing, and some consultants now predict that, within two to three years, service providers will be able to offer viable products and services to this yet untapped market. Experts predict that this will happen as a result of several "enablers." First, as companies are consolidating and reengineering their internal payroll operations, they are also standardizing and simplifying their internal programs. Second, service providers are combining forces with payroll software vendors and are adopting or developing more flexible and functionally robust software applications.

At the same time, outsourcing, even for medium-sized and smaller companies, should not be viewed as a panacea. All companies that are evaluating the option of outsourcing should consider (1) how complex their needs are; (2) how much customization is anticipated (not only at the time of implementation, but also in the future); and (3) how much control is needed over the vendor's products and services. Unfortunately, companies sometimes discover, after they have outsourced payroll, that their service bureau is unable to support their unique needs for change at an affordable price and within the timeframe needed. As in carpentry, companies would do well to "measure twice and cut once."

(ii)   Rationale.   Companies considering outsourcing should clearly understand their rationale for outsourcing and should weigh both direct and indirect potential benefits and risks against the overall strategic objectives of the business. Some valid reasons may include the following:

- Rate of Change: The business must implement solutions faster than it can develop them internally.
- Resources: There is a shortage of dedicated business and/or technical resources and/or equipment.
- Expertise: The base knowledge is not available or is eroding.
- Expense: The function is too costly to establish or sustain.
- Exposure: Company performance in areas of compliance and cost avoidance has been unacceptable.

(iii)   Other Considerations—Costs and Benefits.   When determining if outsourcing is an effective alternative, consideration should also be given to the not-so-obvious

Outsourcing Will Become Increasingly Viable In The Next Few Years As Businesses Simplify And Vendors Gear Up

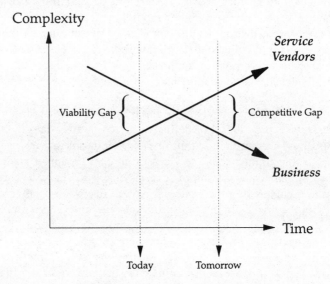

Exhibit 18A.14.   Service provider potential. Reprinted with permission. © Gunn Partners, Inc.

costs and benefits. Some services currently provided to employees may be lost as a result of outsourcing and other services may have to continue to be performed by the company. Decisions on these issues may have both financial and nonfinancial (e.g., employee relations) implications.

The business should also carefully evaluate whether there are low- or no-cost underutilized resources within the company that, if used, would make outsourcing an expensive alternative. Underutilized computer capacity and resources are a prime example.

(iv)   Opportunities.   Payroll outsourcing traditionally includes the processing of prevalidated input data (company and employee profile data, authorized deduction amounts, and timecard input), the gross-to-net (pay calculation) process, and the production of checks and standard payroll-related reports and general ledger interfaces. Supplementary services may be added at additional cost (e.g., the generation and distribution of W-2s, optional employee direct deposit account(s), tax filing services, unemployment reporting, etc.).

Even when companies outsource payroll, they will need to continue to maintain human resource and payroll professionals in-house to collect, validate, and process accurate input to the service provider and to act as a liaison to the provider. This is often the most costly portion of the process.

However, outsourcing does not have to be an all-or-nothing proposition. Instead of an all-inclusive package, companies can outsource portions of the function. Some of the specific payroll-related functions that lend themselves to outsourcing include:

- Tax administration (the payment and reporting of federal, state, and local income and unemployment payroll taxes)
- Pension payrolls
- Expatriate and/or foreign payrolls
- Subsidiary, division, or decentralized payrolls
- Deduction programs (e.g., U.S. Savings Bonds administration)
- Special employee payroll sets (e.g., hourly employees, executive payrolls, annuity payrolls, etc.)
- Pay statement production and distribution services
- W-2 production and distribution services

(v)   Outsourcing Does Not Mean Relinquishing Accountability.   Outsourcing does not mean relinquishing accountability for the outsourced function(s). Regardless of the magnitude of outsourcing being considered, companies must realize that outsourcing is often easier than bringing the function back in house. Therefore, the longer term implications and cost of outsourcing should be carefully considered in the evaluation and vendor selection process.

In considering the outsourcing of payroll, a detailed analysis of company requirements against the service provider's capabilities should be undertaken, including a cost comparison analysis. If positive, a detailed service agreement should be developed (including performance standards and measurements, fee schedules, software change conditions, contingency plans, cancellation rights, and responsibilities) to ensure that all aspects of the business are covered.

(b)   Application Acquisition versus Development.

(i)   Legacy System/What to Do?   In today's environment, larger companies are finding that legacy payroll systems do not meet today's more complex needs. More often than not, companies find themselves in a quandary over whether to continue to invest in their current systems or to purchase an outside vendor package. In either case, the cost of making major modifications to existing software or of purchasing an outside product is an expensive undertaking, often amounting, for medium to large companies, to hundreds of thousands of dollars.

Traditionally, payroll has not been the recipient of corporate investment dollars, and changes have normally been made in a reactive fashion, thereby increasing the complexity of such software and compounding the difficulty and cost of future changes. On the positive side, though, in-house solutions have traditionally been reliable. Their weakness is normally limited functionality and flexibility, along with high maintenance costs. In general, aged systems (those more than ten years old) are not equipped to support the more dynamic environment of today's business needs. Although the acquisition or development of software is a big-ticket item, software limitations if not addressed can be more costly or even catastrophic to a company.

(ii)   The Decision-Making Process.   Unfortunately, decisions are more often forced around a short-term crisis or change in business needs than around a solution arising

from a longer range tactical evaluation and plan. But ideally, this decision should be made only after the following steps have been completed:

- As a basis for planning, the current system should be well documented. Documentation should include business and technical documentation, data and process models, strengths and weaknesses, costs, and the like.
- Current and future business requirements should be inventoried. This process should include the participation of both business customers and suppliers.
- An opportunity evaluation should be completed to identify and justify the need for change. The scope of change and the cost of internal software development should be calculated.
- A request for proposal (RFP) should be prepared to define business requirements and then should be sent to selected (prescreened) vendors.

The quality of this work will determine the quality of vendor responses and often the quality of the final decisions made from the process. Quality should be emphasized on the front end, as it will reduce the cost and effort of downstream action items. Access to software products for on-site testing is not always possible, but is always preferable before entering into a purchase contract.

(iii) Software Packages Will Require Modification.   Once an employer decides to select an outside product, the decision-making process is not over. The purchaser will have to determine how much of the work will be contracted to the vendor and how much of the work will be performed in house. It should be noted that understanding, modifying, testing, and implementing a new software product is a significant effort, often requiring twenty-four to thirty-six months to complete, depending on the complexity of the business. Training, communications, and coordination with business suppliers and customers will also require substantial efforts. For these reasons, selection of the vendor and the vendor's product is a very critical step.

There should also be an agreement with the vendor on how much customization will be allowed for the vendor to continue to support the product. In some cases, overcustomization has forced the payroll organization to take ownership of software changes. This can ultimately lead to another legacy system.

(iv) To Purchase or Not to Purchase: A Cross-Functional Decision.   Finally, the decision to purchase is not only a finance or payroll decision, but a human resources decision as well. Payroll is a subprocess of the human resource process, regardless of reporting lines. It is inconceivable that human resources or payroll would make an architectural decision of this magnitude without the involvement of its business partner in today's business environment. Such an independent decision might very well cost the company even more money in future years.

In summary, short-term needs of twelve months or less can hardly ever be met via product acquisition. The key is to anticipate and make this investment decision well in advance of the need. This requires that the payroll professional understand the directions of the company, its business customers, and suppliers and that investment dollars to support this effort be included in the budget.

18A.7   ORGANIZATIONAL FACTORS AFFECTING COST.

(a)   Past Organizational Structures and Perceptions.   Traditionally, payroll organizational structures have been formed hierarchically with a manager, supervisor(s), and a staff of accounting and clerical personnel. Until recently, the payroll function has been viewed as a predominately clerical (transaction processing) function and has been staffed with hourly or nonexempt employees. As an overhead function that is perceived as simply being a "check-cutting" organization, payroll has not always received the resources and investment dollars it has deserved. As a result, its development and contributions to the company have been impeded.

In many companies today, payroll labor (and therefore costs) is greater than it needs to be due to these outdated perceptions.

(b)   Changing Organizational Structures and Perceptions.   Fortunately this is now changing. Today, best-in-class payroll organizations with low cost of products and high levels of customer satisfaction have the following organizational characteristics:

- Payroll departments are more likely to be staffed by professional (exempt) rather than clerical (hourly) jobs. Best-in-class payroll organizations are often staffed with 80–90% professionals instead of 80–90% clerical.
- Payroll professionals in these organizations bring with them a higher level of education than in the past. Employees with bachelor's degrees are now more common than those with high school diplomas. Master's degrees and professional certifications (e.g., Certified Payroll Professional) are increasingly common.
- Outdated organizational structures with multiple reporting levels are being replaced with teams of highly specialized single contributors, as illustrated in Exhibit 18A.15.

(c)   Coming of Age.   The focus of these new payroll organizations and jobs has shifted from status quo and maintenance to change and development and from transaction processing to financial control and accountability. Payroll professionals today have an opportunity to be viewed more as valued business partners and are now in a position to influence decisions and contribute to the success of the enterprise at a level never before possible.

In summary, how the payroll organization is viewed and how it is staffed and organized are key to the company's success. Decisions and actions taken on this matter will ultimately determine payroll and company costs.

18A.8   TRADITIONAL AND CONTEMPORARY BUDGETING APPROACHES.
Traditional budgeting approaches are based on understanding the business in accordance with established general ledger accounts and the company chart of accounts. Newer approaches focus on understanding the business from the perspective of its value-added services and its cost drivers. Referred to as activity-based costing (ABC) or activity-based management (ABM), these newer methods force business

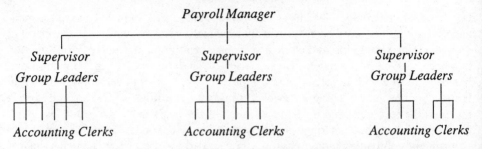

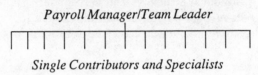

**Exhibit 18A.15.   Organizational structures contrasted. Reprinted with permission. ©
Digital Equipment Corporation—U.S. Payroll.**

owners to look more closely at their businesses. ABC captures cost by individual
value-added service and provides a structure for pricing products and services to
business customers. ABC has become increasingly more important as some companies begin to deliver financial services (including payroll) to their divisions and subsidiaries via shared service centers.

For some time into the future, businesses may have to use both traditional and
ABC processes and try to map one to the other. ABC not only allows companies to
understand costs of each component, it also provides the ability to track costs to specific customer sets. ABC, in turn, lays the groundwork for treating payroll and other
overhead functions like the businesses they truly are. The following subsections discuss the differences between these methods.

(a)   Line Item (Traditional) Budgeting Approach.   A traditional payroll department
budget consists of the following components, with dollars typically based on historical spending patterns adjusted for anticipated changes. In establishing spending levels by account, it is wise to document assumptions for each line item within the
budget:

- Labor and Benefits
    - Salaries
    - Overtime (seasonal, periodic, conversions)
    - Fringes (employment taxes and benefits)
    - Pension (defined benefit, defined contribution)

—Perquisites (parking, wellness, dependent care, education, others)
—Workers' compensation
—Consultants and contract labor

- Data Processing
  —Software-related support expenses
  —Hardware-related expenses
  —Outsourcing-related expenses
  —Licenses
  —Equipment rental and leases
  —Supplies
- Travel and Entertainment
  —Travel
  —Lodging
  —Meals
  —Car rentals
  —Entertainment
  —Other travel-related costs
- Capital Assets and Related Expenses (capitalized or expensed)
  —Equipment (machinery, transportation, installation, training)
  —Software
  —Furniture and fixtures
  —Leasehold improvements (permanent improvements or upkeep)
  —Maintenance and repairs
  —Depreciation
- Facilities
  —Office space/rent
  —Utilities
  —Maintenance and repairs
  —Storage and archives
- Communications
  —Telephones (line charges, instrument lease, maintenance)
  —Long distance (WATS, inbound 800 numbers, vendor costs)
  —Fax
  —Postage (post office box, stamps, postage meter, W-2s, certified)
  —Couriers (ground and air)
- Reproduction/Printing
  —Forms
  —Check and direct deposit statements

    —Employee communications (memos/stuffers)

    —Supplies (paper/toner/staples)

- Professional Associations and Publications
  —Trade association membership dues (American Payroll Association)
  —Trade and educational conferences
  —Trade publications

- Miscellaneous and Conditional Expenses
  —Audit-related costs
  —Legal and tax compliance-related liabilities and costs
  —"Corporate Services" allocations (i.e., mailroom support, human resource support, etc.)
  —Recruitment and relocation costs
  —System conversion and implementation costs
  —Contingencies (crisis management, change management, unknowns)
  —Banking-related costs

(b)   Activity-Based Costing (Contemporary) Budgeting Approach.   Although the traditional method provides a vehicle for planning and tracking payroll-related expenses, the traditional line item budgeting approach does not lead to maximum understanding of the business. As highlighted in Exhibit 18A.16, activity-based costing helps companies to gain added insight into the cost of current payroll operations. (Please refer to this exhibit again when reading section 18A.12b on benchmarking).

This knowledge can help the business to focus its attention on opportunities for reducing its costs. It can also provide an opportunity for influencing change in business practices, as well as serve as a pricing structure for allocating costs to business customers (e.g., divisions). As illustrated in Exhibit 18A.17, keeping the pricing metric simple facilitates both the administration and the communication of the ABC program. As reflected in the exhibit, costing based on numbers of employees paid and/or numbers of transactions processed is the simplest method. Tracking time and materials and pricing services by using other metrics on a selective basis might be appropriate as well.

Activity-based costing is essential for companies evaluating outsourcing, as it will provide a more accurate means of cost comparison. For a complete discussion on this subject, see chapter 27A in this supplement.

(c)   Both Are Important.   In reality, both methods are essential. The first method supports current accounting systems and is not likely to be replaced in the short term. The second method provides the knowledge essential to truly manage the business. It requires additional work to design, implement, and maintain. Because the value of activity-based costing is in the knowledge derived, it does not have to be precise, automated, or repetitive. A periodic ABC look at the business can provide the necessary information needed. At least initially, companies might want to keep the use of ABC as simple as possible.

ActivityBased Costing And Benchmarking Reveal Different Information... Both Are Important

Benchmarking........................Versus.....................Activity-Based Costing

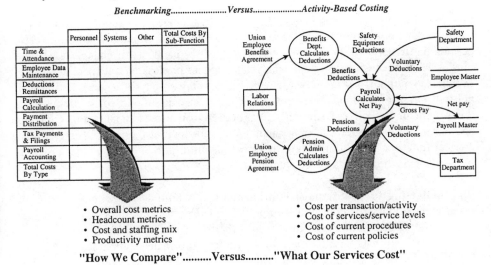

- Overall cost metrics
- Headcount metrics
- Cost and staffing mix
- Productivity metrics

- Cost per transaction/activity
- Cost of services/service levels
- Cost of current procedures
- Cost of current policies

"How We Compare"..........Versus.........."What Our Services Cost"

Exhibit 18A.16.   Benchmarking versus activity-based costing. Reprinted with permission. © Gunn Partners, Inc.

Payroll Added Value Service	Pricing Metric
✪Reference Management	Number of Employees
✪Salary & Wage Calculation	Number of Employees
✪Supplementary Compensation	Number of Employees
✪Payment Delivery	Number of Employees
✪Tax Payment & Reporting	Number of Employees
✪Deduction Administration	Number of Employees
✪Customer Support	
→Employee Inquiry	Number of Employees
→Pay Adjustment	Number of Transactions
→Customized Information	Time and Materials
→Tactical/Strategic Support	Time and Materials
✪Accounting	Number of Employees

Exhibit 18A.17.   Payroll service pricing model. Reprinted with permission. © Digital Equipment Corporation—U.S. Payroll.

18A.9   SMART BUDGETING (SPENDING MONEY TO SAVE MONEY).

(a)   Investing in Resources Required to Achieve Change.   Change (including cost savings) does not come without spending some money. Companies should invest in people, particularly those who can effectively act as catalysts of change (e.g., planning specialists, business systems analysts, data and process model specialists, etc.). In addition, support for the development and training of payroll department personnel will pay big dividends over the longer term, as will support for participation in the American Payroll Association's Certified Payroll Professional (CPP) education and certification program. Management should not look at the payroll function as a clerical function, but should begin to view it as an important professional organization critical to the success of the enterprise.

(b)   Budgeting for Continuous Improvement.   A sound budget should include investment dollars for continuous improvement. Investments today can mean success in the future. Waiting to invest until there is a "real" problem is one way to ensure that there will be a problem in the future. Too many companies find out too late that making major changes takes time.

(c)   The Importance of Strategic Planning.   Budgeting for payroll is not a single-cycle event with strictly short-term spending implications. A successful budgeting process should be built on a solid long-term business plan that considers the directions and needs of the enterprise.

Many have heard the saying, "You cannot do anything about yesterday—it's gone—but you can do something about today and tomorrow." Proper planning allows payroll to correct problems of the past and anticipate the future, thereby being in a proactive instead of reactive mode of operation.

Those responsible for payroll must always be looking to introduce and develop new models of and approaches to running the payroll function, to be more effective and, most of all, efficient in serving their customers. This is where strategic planning is beneficial. Strategic planning involves identifying and analyzing areas that are both internal and external to your organization. To succeed, the business must focus on:

- Its mission statement
- The company's long-range "strategic" issues
- Goals and objectives
- Communication

Strategic planning is the key to the success of the payroll department because it allows the business to stay focused on the future objectives. As part of the strategic planning process, the following questions should be asked:

- Where are we now?
- Where are we going in the longer term?
- Where should we be going?
- How will we get there?

Strategic planning will ensure success if focus is maintained on established goals and objectives that are measurable and quantifiable in real time, by evidence of performance, while permitting the business to stay focused on today and tomorrow.

18A.10 INNOVATIVE METHODS FOR RECOVERING COSTS INCURRED. Although some payroll-related costs are fixed, companies can take a number of avenues to reduce expenses. For example, companies can choose not to offer certain payroll services, or can charge suppliers, business customers, or even employees for certain types of activities. Decisions to use these options will require an evaluation of the financial returns against the legal, business, and employee relations implications. Some examples follow.

(a) Eliminating Elective Deduction Programs. Many companies are choosing to offer only those deductions required by law and eliminate elective deduction programs. Reducing the number of deduction programs offered can result in both systems and administrative cost savings associated with such programs.

(b) Charging for Child Support Payments. Most courts permit employers to deduct additional monies from employees' wages for each child support payment made, to cover the administrative costs associated with child support withholding, reporting, and payment processes. Courts designate the authorized amount that employers may withhold on each payment; amounts range from under $1.00 to as much as $5.00 per payment. Given the recent changes to the Family Support Act, which requires all child support payments to be employer-withheld, as well as the labor-intensive nature of this work, employer costs can be significant. Court-sanctioned cost recovery programs can offset some or all of this burden.

(c) Charging for Affidavits. As payroll professionals know, preparing affidavits can be a lengthy and costly process. Affidavits often necessitate the preparation of large amounts of data in customized reporting formats. Some companies have begun to charge attorneys for such requests on a C.O.D. basis. Reception has been good, as this represents a standard practice within the legal profession. Attorneys, in turn, pass these costs onto their clients.

(d) Charging for Copies of W-2s. The Internal Revenue Service (IRS) only requires employers to issue a W-2 once. The IRS permits employers to charge employees for duplicate copies, either of current or prior year W-2s. The current rate that employers can charge, as set by the IRS, is $7.50 per copy. This practice not only can help offset some costs, it can also help to discipline employees to take greater ownership of their personnel recordkeeping. As an alternative, employers do have the option to refer employees to the IRS for copies of previously issued W-2s.

(e) Charging for Rework. Payroll products and services can only be as good as the quality and timeliness of supplier input. If input is inaccurate and/or late, payroll can incur additional costs in reacting to these situations. Companies are beginning to realize the tremendous costs involved in rework. Adjustments, out-of-cycle payments, stop payments, and W-2Cs all represent avoidable cost. More important, companies are also beginning to realize that suppliers (even employees, supervisors, and managers) should be accountable for accurate and timely input.

In response, employers are beginning to quantify and communicate these costs to the sources of the errors and are implementing mechanisms for charging these sources for such errors. Although cross-charging a business supplier or cost center for incorrect input resulting in payroll rework may represent "internal money," it can change behavioral patterns and, in the longer term, provide real dollar savings to the company. Some companies may even wish to pass certain rework costs directly on to the employee. One example might be to charge the employee who receives, but loses or destroys, a paycheck and then requests an out-of-cycle payment to replace the lost or destroyed check. The administrative effort along with the bank charge can easily exceed $50.

(f)   Charging for Check versus Direct Deposit Transactions.   Compulsory direct deposit programs are prohibited in most states, but companies do have the option of passing on incremental costs to business customers serviced by payroll (e.g., divisions, subsidiaries, business units, etc.) who do not choose to support direct deposit programs offered by the company. Current data collected via a 1995 American Payroll Association pay media survey of U.S. industry suggests that the average savings per payment via direct deposit versus check can be $0.86 or more.

(g)   Charging for Nonstandard and Inefficient or Costly Practices.   Companies that provide payroll services to internal business units may want to influence more cost-effective behavior changes by establishing an "ideal" baseline cost for services and then charging business customers (e.g., divisions and/or subsidiaries) for incremental services that are unique or inefficient. For example, a business unit that insists on submitting timecard data in paper format when electronic reporting tools exist, or requires unique reports that no other customer requires, should be charged a premium for such practices and services. These tactics are not intended to make money, but rather to force business customers to think twice about the level of service they require.

In summary, there are many opportunities to reduce and or recover costs, and it is up to organizations to look for and implement the opportunities that will work within their business environment. In all cases, financial incentives must be quantified and evaluated against the impact on employees and should be assessed for their potential legal implications as well.

18A.11   CYCLICAL PAYROLL EXPENSE PATTERNS IMPACTING BUDGETING AND FORECASTING.   Although most payroll charges are constant, variations in spending patterns do occur and must be recognized in the budgeting and forecasting process.

Most notable are costs associated with single planned nonrecurring purchases of products or services, or infrequent but repetitive purchases of forms such as pay deposit and check statements or renewals of hardware and software licenses.

Disbursement patterns may also exist and must be considered. For example, some companies may process salary increases or issue large volumes of commission, bonus, or royalty payments during certain periods of the year. As a result, such companies may incur added costs during these timeframes.

Labor settlements and bargaining agreement renewals may also drive costs on a cyclical basis.

Finally, payroll spending patterns often peak in the first and fourth quarters of each calendar year, because of annual expenses related to the production, delivery, and administration of W-2s and related wage and tax reporting processes, including expatriate equalization (if applicable).

At the same time, preparations for the beginning of a new tax year affect workload and spending. These closing-out and starting-up activities associated with the tax year can represent significant costs in both labor and material and should be carefully considered in the budgeting process.

As in other areas of payroll, there are a number of opportunities for reducing the stress and cost related to cyclical workload patterns. For example, the use of temporary accounting resources during such times may be a good investment and can negate the need to carry additional full-time resources throughout the year to accommodate workload fluctuations.

In regard to year-end costs, as in all processes, front-end validations of supplier input, including accurate employee address information, can reduce the number of W-2Cs and W-2 reissues, which in turn can lower the amount of rework and costs associated with corrections.

Finally, investments made in timely and complete communications to employees can more than pay for themselves in the form of lower volumes of inquiries.

In summary, budgeting and forecasting cyclical and nonrecurring expenses, along with proper expense tracking processes, can eliminate the element of surprise and contribute to proper cash flow requirements and spending forecasts.

18A.12   USE OF TOTAL QUALITY MANAGEMENT.

(a)   **Overview of TQM.**   Total quality management (TQM) methods and tools are designed to improve business performance and improve customer satisfaction. TQM represents a shift in focus from inward considerations to customer (internal and external) satisfaction.

There are many different TQM methods and tools. No single method or tool can satisfy all needs. Many TQM methods and tools overlap each other and are often used in combination with each other. TQM can address multiple goals of productivity, quality, customer satisfaction, and economic benefits, as illustrated in Exhibit 18A.18. Exhibit 18A.19 emphasizes what TQM is and is not.

Following are some examples of TQM methods and tools being used by companies today.

(b)   **Benchmarking.**   Benchmarking involves learning from others and adopting their best practices to the benefit of your company. Exhibits 18A.20 and 18A.21 provide a visual history, brief description, and overview of the benchmarking process.

The twelve steps in a typical benchmarking process include:

Step 1.   Initiate project
Step 2.   Identify key processes to be benchmarked
Step 3.   Identify customer(s) for benchmarking

- **Productivity**
  - Cost and headcount metrics
  - Cost per product/transactions per employee

- **Quality**
  - Error rates
  - Cycle times

- **Customer satisfaction**
  - Customer surveys
  - Problem resolution reports

- **Economic benefit**
  - Direct contribution
  - Upstream and downstream contribution

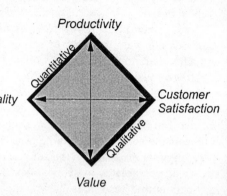

Exhibit 18A.18.   TQM goals. Reprinted with permission. © Gunn Partners, Inc.

 Total Quality Management - A Definition: Conformance to Standards

What it is...	...and isn't -
• A new way of thinking, being, acting and doing (change)	• Doing the same things differently
• Error rate analysis	• Getting it right the first time
• Customer driven	• Internally focused
• Changing the work itself	• Stressing people-work linkages
• Expensive (in the short and even intermediate term)	• Expensive over the long term
• A permanent change in the way work is done (continuous improvement)	• A temporary adjustment

Exhibit 18A.19.   TQM definition. Reprinted with permission. © Management Resource Group.

Step 4.   Select and prepare team
Step 5.   Identify type of benchmarking
Step 6.   Approach benchmarking partners
Step 7.   Collect data
Step 8.   Analyze data
Step 9.   Communicate findings
Step 10.   Develop action plan
Step 11.   Implement and monitor
Step 12.   Recalibrate.

When undertaking a benchmarking effort, it is important that participants understand their processes and have done their homework and that those who are identified as benchmarking partners be recognized leaders in the areas under comparison. The most successful benchmarking efforts focus on specific areas of interest rather than attempt to benchmark an entire function. For example, a focus on benchmarking payroll time reporting practices may be more fruitful than attempting to benchmark every aspect of payroll.

Benchmarking can lead to new insights and possibilities that can, in turn, lead to dramatic improvements. Any company that is not taking full advantage of benchmarking risks is losing its competitive edge. Unlike the early days of benchmarking, there are many new ways to keep pace with best-in-class practices. For example, many services and associations, such as the International Benchmarking Clearing House, provide access to benchmarking information never before available at reasonable costs.

(c)   Reengineering.   Reengineering represents an approach that looks at the business from fresh perspectives and evaluates the processes through which products and services are currently delivered to customers. It is not initially about automation, although automation may be a downstream action coming out of the reengineering process. Reengineering looks at the business as a total process, from supplier to customer, and in that sense is closely linked with the Six Sigma approach to understanding the business. Reengineering, in essence, draws upon all the other TQM methods and tools and translates learning into action plans. It addresses whether the work should be done, who should do the work, where the work should be performed, and how the work should be done.

Reengineering focuses on the business model, especially customer and the products that satisfy customer needs. With regard to each process, activity, and task, the reengineering process prompts the business to ask the question "Why?" Why is the business doing this? What is its purpose? What customer is this serving? Asking these fundamental questions is what distinguishes reengineering from incremental process improvement. Exhibit 18A.22 provides an overview of the various phases of the reengineering cycle.

(d)   A delta t.   A delta t, developed by Digital Equipment Corporation, provides a simple methodology for mapping current process steps and identifying nonvalue-added steps, with the focus on reducing total cycle time. Through the use of this tool,

Benchmarking Process Evolution

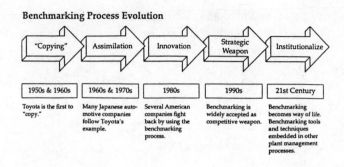

Benchmarking Continuum

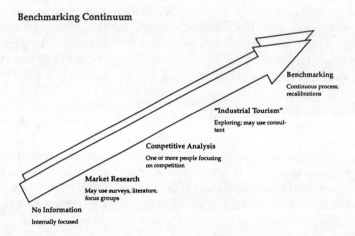

Exhibit 18A.20.   Benchmarking. Reprinted with permission. © EDS People Systems.

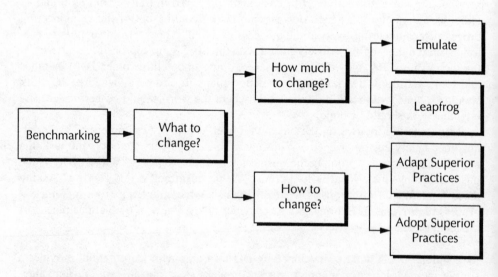

Exhibit 18A.21.   Benchmarking process. Reprinted with permission. © 3D Consortium. All rights reserved.

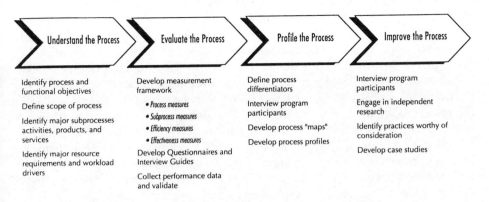

Understand the Process	Evaluate the Process	Profile the Process	Improve the Process
Identify process and functional objectives	Develop measurement framework	Define process differentiators	Interview program participants
Define scope of process	• *Process measures*	Interview program participants	Engage in independent research
Identify major subprocesses activities, products, and services	• *Subprocess measures*	Develop process "maps"	Identify practices worthy of consideration
	• *Efficiency measures*	Develop process profiles	
Identify major resource requirements and workload drivers	• *Effectiveness measures*		Develop case studies
	Develop Questionnaires and Interview Guides		
	Collect performance data and validate		

Exhibit 18A.22.   The reengineering cycle. Reprinted with permission. © 3D Consortium. All rights reserved.

the delta (difference or change) between current actual and theoretical process times can be identified and potentially eliminated.

Unlike most mapping tools, A delta t does not require extensive mapping knowledge and, more important, engages those responsible for the process in performing this work. As illustrated in Exhibit 18A.23, a number of steps have been eliminated from this time reporting process example. A delta t, by reducing the number of steps, often contributes to lower defect levels by eliminating additional opportunities for such defects from the process, which in turn translates into lower costs.

PAST:

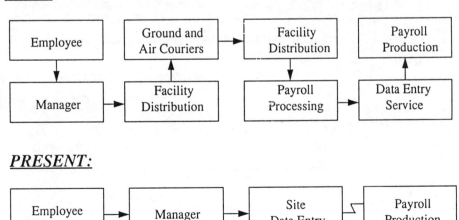

PRESENT:

Exhibit 18A.23.   A delta t reporting. Reprinted with permission. © Digital Equipment Corporation—U.S. Payroll.

(e) Six Sigma.   The Six Sigma program, as designed by Motorola Inc., focuses on reducing defects and provides both a methodology for measuring defect levels and a system for reaching a level of three defects or fewer per million opportunities. The Six Sigma program is designed around six steps, as outlined in Exhibit 18A.24.

Six Sigma was originally created for use in the manufacturing and engineering environment, but it can be applied to any business area. For example, Digital Equipment Corporation has implemented Six Sigma extensively within finance to improve its payroll performance. Digital Equipment Corporation is recognized as a best-in-class payroll organization and has reached levels of three defects or fewer per million opportunities via the Six Sigma program in a number of its payroll products and services. Exhibit 18A.25 illustrates steps 1 to 3 and 6 within the business unit of "Direct Deposit Timeliness" as applied by Digital Equipment Corporation.

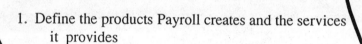

1. Define the products Payroll creates and the services it provides

2. Identify the customers of Payroll products and services and determine what the customers consider important.

3. Identify what Payroll needs from its suppliers to provide products and services that satisfy Payroll customers.

4. Define the current process for doing the work.

5. Make the process mistake-proof and eliminate wasted effort.

6. Ensure continuous improvement by measuring, analyzing, and controlling the improved process.

Exhibit 18A.24.   Six steps of the Six Sigma program. Reprinted with permission.
© Motorola, Inc.

In summary, Six Sigma is a powerful tool for defining and understanding the business from the customer's perspective and for focusing attention and energy on the opportunities for defects that represent the highest payback. It helps businesses to understand the entire pipeline from supplier to customer and provides a statistical tracking mechanism for understanding and tracking performance in areas important to the customer. Those interested in knowing more about the Six Sigma program may wish to contact Motorola Inc. directly.

(f) Continuous Improvement.   TQM tools do not deliver a final resolution on any process. They provide a means for catching up or momentarily taking the lead. Ongoing programs geared toward continuous or incremental improvement must always be in place. As quality improves, customers begin to expect higher levels of performance. All of these TQM tools must continue to be used and new ones applied to ensure ongoing success. Motorola Inc., for example, is setting new goals and designing new programs to reach three defects per billion opportunities. Other companies must continue to raise their sights as well.

Methods and tools are just methods and tools. They can be misused and can become product rather than a process for improvement. If they become an end in themselves, they are not fulfilling the purpose for which they were intended. They can provide valuable information, but learning can be misinterpreted and can lead to erroneous conclusions and incorrect actions if the users of these methods and tools are not careful. At the same time, these risks should not be used as justification for not employing TQM tools.

All methods and tools require investments, first to understand them, and second to apply them correctly. Investments can lead to exciting changes and add to the success of the business, or they can waste valuable time and resources. It is all up to the

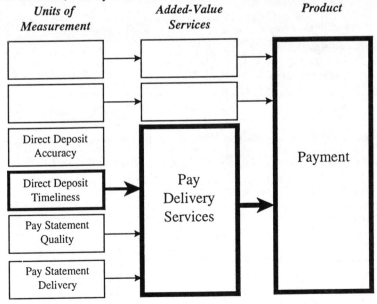

Exhibit 18A.25.   Digital Equipment Corporation's Six Sigma program. Reprinted with permission. © Digital Equipment Corporation—U.S. Payroll.

Six Sigma – Unit Definition

U. S. Payroll Six Sigma Program

2.5.4   Direct Deposit (Timeliness)

Product: Payments

**value–added
Service: Payment Delivery Services**

Customer Expectation:

Immediate access to pay by opening of banking hours on pay day (Thursday)

Measurement of:

Timeliness of weekly employee direct deposit pay delivery to all U. S. financial institutions (including DCU) as measured by notification on non receipt by employee, Receiving Financial Institution, or Originating Depository Financial Institution (Shawmut/Connecticut National Bank.)

Defects:

Late Deposit: Pay not deposited in employee account on opening of banking hours on payday (Thursday). NOTE: Effective Q2FY92, Payroll will begin to utilize a more conservative defect counting procedure. In the past, Payroll has only counted defects as individually reported by customers. In the future, we will begin to count the total number of depositors at a financial institution as individual defects if the problem is determined to be institution–wide even though not all customers may be aware of or impacted by the problem.

Opportunities for Defects: (in chronological order) = X

Entity	Opportunities
1. Payroll	X
2. Payroll Systems	X
3. Data Center	X
4. Shawmut/Connecticut National Bank	X
5. Federal Reserve Bank/ACH	X
6. Receiving Financial Institution	X
# Opportunities for Defects	6

Explanation of Defect Opportunities:

1. Payroll fails to begin or complete weekly production on time. Cut–off transmission time to ODFI missed.
2. Payroll Systems software changes result in production related defect(s) impacting direct deposit timeliness.
3. Data Center fails to perform data center services in an accurate and timely fashion in accordance with Service Agreement.
4. ODFI unable to process files in time to deliver to Federal Reserve Bank for Tuesday AM window.
5. Federal Reserve Bank experience operational problems which delay interregional routing and timely distribution to Receiving Financial Institutions.
6. Receiving Financial Institution (including DCU) does not receive transactions or receives but fails to post pay to employee account on time.

Data Source:

Transactions: Totals page from the final Deposit Statement Files

Defects: Bank Problem Logs maintained by Customer Service

Exhibit 18A.25.   (continued).

Six Sigma - Goal Worksheet

Direct Deposit Timeliness Goal Worksheet

Total Defects Per Million Opportunities (DPMO) as of FY94: .47

DPMO Performance Goal for Fiscal Year 95: < .47

Description of Specific Defect Area(s) to be Addressed:

Defect #4: ODFI unable to process files in time to deliver to Federal Reserve Bank for Tuesday AM window

---

Strategies to Achieve (FY95) DPMO Performance Goal:

1. Work with ODFI to assure that all procedures are documented and contingency plans are in place.

Exhibit 18A.25.   (continued).

Six Sigma-Historical Performance

Pay Statement Timeliness
Six Sigma Levels from FY90 to FY94

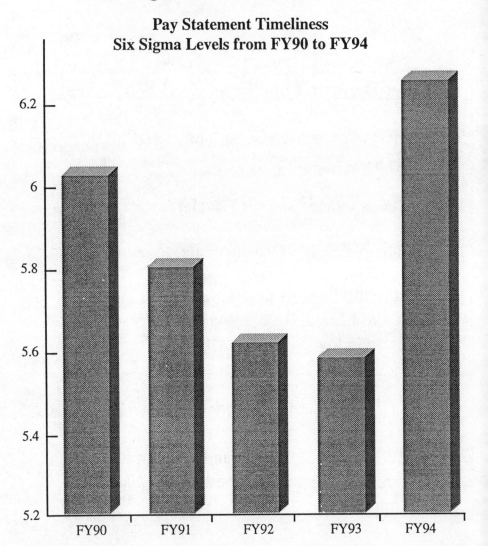

Exhibit 18A.25.   (continued).

user. For a further, in-depth discussion on TQM, refer to chapter 26A in this supplement.

18A.13   PUTTING TECHNOLOGY TO WORK.   The secret to the successful use of technology is in (1) selecting and applying technology appropriate to the need and (2) the proper training of users. Technology must pay for itself to be justified. The timing and sequencing of technology application is important to maximizing benefits. General capabilities can be enhanced or limited by the computing environment selected by the business. Specific tools, such as interactive voice response technology, can be used to eliminate manual and paper-based processes.

Following is an inventory of various technologies, along with brief descriptions, benefits, and possible applications within the payroll environment.

(a)   Windows.   Windows software allows the user to access multiple screens on one video display unit (VDU) and permits the user to view, update, and report on multiple applications and options at the same time. With Windows capabilities, the user can increase productivity and better service customers.

In today's environment, when access to information is the key to success, Windows enables the payroll user to increase the amount of data that can be seen simultaneously. Separate application options can be designed to handle different tasks, thereby allowing the user to perform multiple functions at the same time. Because many human resource and payroll systems are separate, Windows can be used to link both systems together on a single screen, thereby obviating the need to log in and out of separate systems. (Windows is a trademark of Microsoft Corporation.)

(b)   Desktop Integration.   Desktop integration uses a series of software and hardware tools that allow users to access and process information from their desks. These tools permit users to download data from a larger system (mainframe or other host system) to a desktop workstation on a personal computer (PC) platform. The user can work on the data at his or her personal workstation and then upload the changed data back to the host machine. This concept enables the business user to access all the applications and systems right from the desktop. With desktop-integrated tools, the payroll user is able to perform all job functions independently, without time-consuming and complex processes. Full integration of hardware and software can mean much greater productivity.

(c)   Client/Server Environment.   The client/server environment is a computing environment that provides access to information to different users with varying business needs while sharing the computer resources among multiple users spread across different organizations and locations. The distinguishing characteristic of a client-server environment is the distribution of tasks among multiple processors.

The client/server environment is software- rather than hardware-driven. It permits central storage of data (on the server) while allowing access to data at remote areas (or client workstations) and offers tremendous opportunities regarding where and how work is performed. For example, in a client/server environment, local sites may be responsible for entering timecard data into a system that resides elsewhere. At the same time, it can permit centralized production of gross-to-net processes for greater efficiency, lower cost, and higher levels of control. On the output side, it can permit local sites to receive pay information for local printing and distribution of pay statements. Client/server environments offer the best of both worlds, and are especially advantageous to businesses with multiple dispersed operating units.

(d)   Decision Support System.   Decision support systems are databases of information with preprogrammed access routines or user-defined queries that allow the business to access information in the time and format necessary. This permits the business to have access to up-to-date information without special programming efforts. In essence, decision support systems can automatically access raw data and apply such data to various formulas and analyses to permit users to draw conclusions and take appropriate actions. For example, in the payroll environment, decision support systems can be used to collect and validate supplier feeds to ensure data accuracy prior to the pay calculation process.

(e)   Multimedia.   Multimedia consists of a series of PC applications that allow a user to access multiple types of data and to research key business issues and create presentations. Multimedia tools are often on a CD-ROM application that can hold up to twenty times more information than can be held on a common 3.5-inch diskette. Multimedia also allows access to information stored on both video and compact cassette tapes. The benefit of multimedia is that it allows access to up-to-date information and speeds up the process of retrieving such information from many sources to produce charts, graphs, and other types of presentations. In the payroll function, some tax law service providers are replacing their paper products, often consisting of five or more volumes, with one CD, thus providing their payroll customers with an easier vehicle to access federal, state, and local payroll tax-related information.

(f)   Document Image Processing.   Document image processing—the storage and subsequent retrieval of document images in electronic format—is rapidly changing the records management industry. This new technology permits data to be condensed and then recreated in its original format as needed. It is particularly cost-effective for high-volume operations, but is steadily becoming affordable for lower-volume users as well. By changing the manner in which historical records and source documents are stored and accessed, companies can eliminate the more labor-intensive processes that most still use to store and retrieve paper documents. Document image processing, once in place, can reduce offsite storage costs and, more importantly, provide immediate access (via integrated desktop systems) to historical records. As a transaction processing system, there are many applications for the payroll function, including but not limited to W-2s, W-4s, timecards, special payment authorization forms, new hire and termination paperwork, benefit enrollment forms, and so on. Document image processing service providers are now beginning to make this a financially viable option for more and more companies.

(g)   Interactive Voice Response.   Interactive voice response (IVR) systems, as illustrated in Exhibit 18A.26, derive their name from the use of scripted voice prompts and responses to interact with callers who use a touch-tone telephone to enter requests for simple information or to initiate routine transactions. Unlike many other voice systems, IVR systems have a unique power to communicate directly with other computer systems to access payroll database information requested by callers. IVR systems have also kept pace with trends in computing and database management, and the current generation of systems is very proficient in interfacing to both mainframe systems and network-based systems. The shift, in recent years, has been toward accessing payroll information through a client/server architecture. Because client/server systems can be implemented on different databases, IVR systems are available with efficient access to the newly designed database systems.

IVR systems can handle many of the routine calls directed to a payroll department, resulting in a significant increase in payroll department productivity. In addition, in applications where employees or supervisors are entering information, a substantial reduction in errors can be anticipated because IVR systems check each entry as it is made. General paperwork handling and key entry tasks are also reduced when IVR systems are used to collect routine benefit enrollment information.

There are many payroll applications. For example, IVR systems can be used to provide employees with access to current or historical pay information; enroll in, change, or stop direct deposit; or request a copy of their current or historical W-2s, as presented in Exhibit 18A.27. The opportunities are almost limitless, and functionality can be customized to the specific needs of the business. The capability can be performed in-house or outsourced to a service provider. IVR systems in combination with automated call directors can provide cost-effective solutions to labor-intensive processes while improving overall customer service levels.

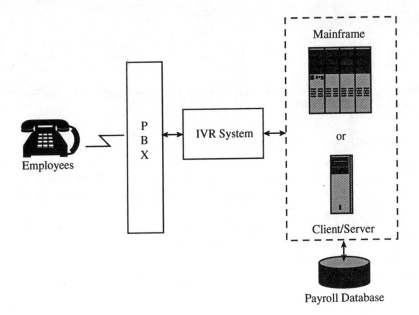

Exhibit 18A.26.   IVR system interfaces. Reprinted with permission. © TALX Corporation, 1995. All rights reserved.

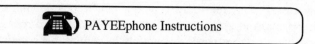

PAYEEphone Instructions

PAYEEphone is the Touch-Tone Phone system that allows you to enroll in Direct Deposit for both Payroll and Employee Expense, allows you to listen to your recent Payroll pay information, and provides you with current year W-2 assistance. This system is available 24 hrs. each day, seven days each week for your convenience.

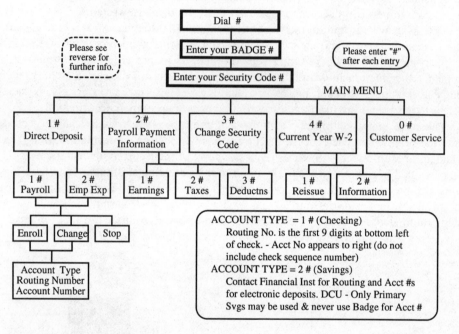

Exhibit 18A.27.   Payroll IVR system. Reprinted with permission. © Digital Equipment Corporation—U.S. Payroll.

(h)   Check-Printing and Forms-Processing Technologies.   The most commonly used check-printing technology involves the impact printer, which consists of physical characters that "impact" or strike the form through an ink ribbon. Impact printers come in many forms to support low- to high-volume operations and can be rented, leased, or purchased.

Laser printers, a newer technology, use heat and toner to create the print characters. As with impact printers, laser printers can be tailored to meet the unique needs and volumes of a business.

Impact printers cost less to implement and maintain than laser printers, but do not allow as much flexibility. The use of laser printing technology is ideally suited for higher volume businesses that process forms with frequent changes. Laser printing technology can also permit the use of barcoded zip codes to expedite delivery and obtain lower presorted zip code U.S. Postal rates, a savings that could be significant for employers that deliver pay statements to employees' homes via the U.S. Postal Service. Laser paycheck delivery vendor products also exist and permit companies to transmit pay data and print paychecks at remote sites in place of courier delivery services.

One cannot discuss printer technology without also discussing forms-construction and forms-processing equipment. Forms can consist of single or multipart forms (using carbon or noncarbon). Self-mailer forms can eliminate the need for separate envelopes and insertion processes and can be especially useful in large operations in which pay statements are sent via the U.S. Postal System to employees' homes. In addition, self-mailers offer greater security. Pressure and heat-sealing forms-processing equipment, as with printers, can be rented, leased, or purchased.

Companies wishing to maximize capabilities while minimizing costs should review all printer, forms, and forms-processing equipment options in a single evaluation. Companies would be wise to look at these needs across multiple disciplines (e.g., payroll, accounts payable, and other disbursement functions) rather than within a single discipline, such as payroll, and should be careful about purchasing equipment that might be better rented or leased—in today's rapidly changing environment, purchased equipment far too often becomes obsolete prior to full depreciation. In any case, a thorough financial evaluation and return on investment (ROI) should be completed in advance of any decision.

18A.14 BUDGETING TASKS AND CALENDAR. Although the budgeting schedule will vary based on each company's unique fiscal calendar, generic tasks to create a sound budget will be similar. Ideally, the process should not begin with budgeting dollars, but with a review of the following:

- Company documents (stated values, goals, directions, etc.)
- Business partner long-range plans and priorities, especially those of finance, human resources, benefits, and compensation
- External conditions and factors that may affect payroll (e.g., changes in federal or state wage or tax laws)
- Payroll charter, long-range plan, and current operational status
- Current and prior year payroll spending performance and analysis

From these items, which may represent the most time-consuming portion of the process, fiscal year business priorities can be set and an informed budget created. Confirmation of business priorities should be obtained from decision makers prior to creating the budget or as part of the budget review and approval process.

Next, rates for the coming budget period should be collected from all necessary sources, including but not limited to information surrounding future salary plans, fringe rates, occupancy rates, supplier pricing estimates, and so on, along with estimated volume information essential to the business (e.g., projected company employee population data). Using this information, budgets for individual line items can then be calculated.

Because labor usually represents the single largest cost for payroll functions, the initial focus should be placed on direct labor, fringe, and related labor cost projections. This job is made simpler if the salary planning calendar parallels the fiscal calendar. If it does not, a portion of the budget will be based on the salary plan and a portion on estimated salaries. Assumptions are always a key component of each expense line of the budget. Assumptions must be made and documented regarding anticipated turnover, increases or decreases in headcount, performance ratings, job level reclassifications and promotions, and salary increases, as well as estimated overtime usage.

A similar process should be followed for each expense category within the budget.

The final budget package should include not only the financials but also the text supporting the proposed spending levels. This information will be important later in the year to understand both positive and negative variances and to adjust future spending forecasts.

Building the budget on a month-by-month basis results in a more accurate plan than creating a fiscal year plan and then allocating the dollars by month and quarter. However, this process may take a little longer and may not be justified in some cases. In general, best-practice companies are reducing the number of expense reporting and forecasting cycles.

Time spent on the front end of the budgeting process pays off throughout the year with less time needed to reconcile actuals and understand differences between budgeted and actual dollars. The use of automated budgeting tools also facilitates the preparation and modification of budgets while providing good audit trails. These same tools can be used to translate line item budget dollars into activity-based costing budgets.

Although budgeting is important to payroll, like other overhead functions, it should not be the primary focus of the business. If done properly, only a small portion of payroll resources and time should be required for developing and managing the payroll budget.

18A.15   MANAGEMENT AND LEADERSHIP APPROACHES.

A high-performance, low-cost payroll function cannot be achieved overnight and can only be achieved with vision and commitment, and through empowered people. As companies work toward a more efficient and cost-effective program, they should consider the advice of Southwestern Bell Telephone Company and:

Do What's Right: That is to say, do not focus on workforce and expense reduction alone, but on quality; do not look to shift costs; wisely challenge top-down directions that are not cost-effective; and, finally, work to achieve an informed decision.

Actions Speak Louder Than Words: Work to create an environment that focuses on the big picture; do not always require "it" to be in writing; and of course, in the process, have fun!

View Yourself as a Corporate Trustee: Clearly understand the required levels of authority; determine who needs to know and understand who really cares; use experienced consultants; and, finally, develop a conservative business case for each project.

As learned by Digital Equipment Corporation's payroll organization in its ongoing evolution to higher payroll quality and lower cost, change cannot be dictated, but must begin from within the organization. The right attitudes are a prerequisite. Visions come before plans and actions. Those who wish to take on change must also accept accountability and risk. There is a logical and sequential order to change. The process must engage business customers and suppliers. When getting started, companies should begin small and build on success. Use structure as a process, not as an end product. Most importantly, invest in the people who are going to make you and your company successful!

18A.16   SUMMARY.   In summary, budgeting for payroll can be as limited or as limitless as companies want the process to be. Some may view the process as strictly an exercise to create a line item budget to ensure that anticipated costs can be covered over the coming year. Others will view the budgeting process as something more and will use it as a springboard to better understand the business, its customers, and its suppliers, and as a vehicle to seek out opportunities for improving performance and reducing costs.

Good budgeting can help to facilitate the implementation of business plans, enhance financial controls, and improve the overall decision-making process. Higher quality and lower cost are not mutually exclusive and can be achieved via the budgeting process.

If this chapter can help both sets of users described herein to see the possibilities, then the work put forth in this chapter will have been well worth the effort!

SOURCES AND SUGGESTED REFERENCES

American Payroll Association, *APA Guide to Payroll Practice and Management.* New York: American Payroll Association, 1995.

American Payroll Association, *Federal Payroll Tax Laws and Regulations.* American Payroll Association, 1995

American Payroll Association, *The Payroll Manager's Guide to Successful Direct Deposit,* 8th ed. American Payroll Association, 1995.

American Payroll Association, *The Payroll Source.* New York: American Payroll Association, 1995.

American Payroll Association Basic Guide to Payroll. Bureau of Business Practice/Prentice Hall, 1995.

Clermont, Paul, "Outsourcing Without Guilt," *Computerworld,* September 1991.

Gow, Brent, "Analyze Your Options," *PaytecH,* July/August 1994, at 30–32.

Kotter, John P., and James L. Heskett, *Corporate Culture and Performance.* New York: Free Press, 1992.

Quinn, James Brian, Thomas L. Doorley, and Penny C. Paquette, "Beyond Products: Services-Based Strategy," *Harvard Business Review* No. 90212 (March/April 1990).

Rhinesmith, Stephen H., *A Manager's Guide to Globalization.* Homewood, Ill.: Business One Irwin, 1993.

Tagliani, Bob, "Service Bureau or In-House Payroll Processing?" *PaytecH,* July/August 1994.

Watson, Gregory H., *The Benchmarking Workbook.* Cambridge, Mass.: Productivity Press, 1992.

ACKNOWLEDGMENTS.   The author would like to acknowledge the following companies and individuals for their contributions and their permission to use exhibits appearing in this document:

- Eileen Anderson, Editor, Paytech, American Payroll Association
- Nancy S. Bishop, Director, Editorial Services, A.T. Kearney, Inc.
- Matthew J. DeLuca, President, Management Resource Group, Inc.
- L. Robert Dillon, Vice President, Duke Engineering and Services, in behalf of the 3D Consortium (Digital Equipment Corporation, Duke Engineering and Services, Inc., and Deloitte & Touche) with the Center for Performance Management
- Robert A. Foster, Managing Associate, Coopers & Lybrand L.L.P.
- James A. Motter, Partner, Gunn Partners Inc.
- James Owen, Payroll Manager, Meijer, Inc.
- Michael E. Smith, Vice President, TALX Corporation
- Roger A. Smith, CPP, Business Planning Consultant, EDS People Systems
- Joseph L. Urban, Corporate Payroll Manager, Motorola Inc.

The author would also like to acknowledge the expertise, contributions, and assistance provided by the following companies and individuals in the preparation of this document:

- Kenneth Bourgeois, U.S. Payroll Production Control Staff Accountant, Digital Equipment Corporation
- Robert C. Cunningham, Manager, Compensation Processing and Human Resource Operations and Employee Services, Chevron Corporation
- Andrew E. Jones III, General Manager—Accounts Payable and Payroll, Southwestern Bell Telephone Co.
- Michael D. Jones, Director of Payroll Operations, NYNEX Corporation and President, American Payroll Association
- Mary Lou Koch-Hanners, CPP, Payroll Manager, Ross Products Division, Abbott Laboratories and President, American Payroll Association
- Anna R. Lipofsky, U.S. Payroll TQM Consultant, Digital Equipment Corporation
- Kenneth McGonagill, CPP, Director, Human Resources, Manheim Auctions, Cox Enterprises, Inc.
- William A. Minneman, Midwest Region Manager, The Hunter Group, Inc.
- Pamela Starr Nisetich, U.S. Payroll Senior Business Consultant, Digital Equipment Corporation
- William Price, National Account Manager, Automated Data Processing Inc.
- Michael P. O'Toole, Director, Education Division, American Payroll Association
- Robert Rachlin, Assistant Dean for Business Studies, UCCE, Hofstra University
- Kenneth Sawyer, Vice President and General Manager, Dun & Bradstreet Software

CHAPTER **18B**

BUDGETING THE PURCHASING DEPARTMENT AND THE PURCHASING PROCESS (New)

Thomas F. Norris

Coopers & Lybrand L.L.P.

CONTENTS

18B.1 DESCRIPTION AND DEFINITION OF THE PROCESS APPROACH 1

(a) The Purchasing Department 2
(b) The Procurement Process 3
(c) Implications of the Process Approach 6

18B.2 THE ROLE OF PROCESS MEASURES 6

(a) Supplier Capabilities and Process Requirements 6

18B.3 PROCESS MEASURES 7

(a) Production Capabilities 7
(b) Product Development Capabilities 7
(c) Cost Reduction Capabilitites 9

18B.4 CREATING THE PROCUREMENT PROCESS BUDGET 11

SOURCES AND SUGGESTED REFERENCES 13

18B.1 DESCRIPTION AND DEFINITION OF THE PROCESS APPROACH. Traditionally, management has used the budget as a tool to track, control, and forecast the financial effectiveness of the business. Typically, budgets are prepared in some hierarchical manner by departments and then aggregated along organizational lines to create the business unit's budget. Today, as a result of the use of such techniques as reengineering and right-sizing, and the use of cross-functional teams, there is an increased emphasis and need to manage and optimize along a process perspective as well as to use budgeting for control of the individual responsibilities, departments, and functions within the process. (To distinguish the purchasing department from the purchasing process, the term *procurement* will be used herein to identify the process perspective.) To be effective, an organization must control the spending of both the function and the process; or, in other words, the organization must consider

- Purchasing as defined by the activities of the purchasing department
- Purchasing as defined by the activities of the procurement process

(a)   The Purchasing Department.   The control of the purchasing departmental budget is a very important piece of the procurement process. The purchasing budget, to begin, will be influenced by the manner in which the business is organized. Many purchasing departments function both centrally and locally. For example, companies might buy key commodities or services centrally through long-term purchasing agreements, but the actual ordering and releasing might be executed locally, at the operating site. Additionally, there might be local purchasing departments that buy items and services such as capital equipment and maintenance for that particular site. Purchasing activities are sometimes intentionally delegated and distributed to other departments. This normally is a function of size, efficiency, and mission, and the level of special competencies required. Some examples are

- Advertising, purchased by the marketing department
- Research and development, purchased by medical doctors or scientific specialists
- Transportation, purchased by the logistics arm of the organization
- Outsourcing of IT (information technology) activities
- Travel and entertainment, purchased by authorized managers

Another common technique used by the purchasing department to delegate authority to the organization is via the procurement card, usually used for low-dollar and high-volume item purchases. This tool has enabled significant cost reductions through the elimination of several activities, such as the requisition, the purchase order (PO), the invoice, the check request, and the check itself. Some leading-edge companies, in support of programs called "JIT II Purchasing," further delegate purchasing by bringing key suppliers on-site and "hooking them up" to the company's information system. The suppliers then actually do the buying/planning of the material or service provided to the company. Whenever purchasing delegates responsibility, it is still responsible for oversight, as well as appropriate purchasing training and education.

The purchasing department also has an important role in providing both strategic and operating assistance to the organization. Strategically, purchasing is an integral partner in all make/buy decisions. Purchasing is involved in developing the budget for materials and services. This is a consistent role among the various business sectors, whether private, public, or nonprofit. A 1990 study by the National Association of Purchasing Managers (NAPM) concluded that the tasks or duties that purchasing managers perform are fairly similar in the private, public, and nonprofit sectors—"Purchasers across these sectors appear to 'speak the same language' and approach their jobs with reasonably the same duties and goals in mind." An article in the December 1996 issue of *Purchasing Today* concludes that manufacturing and service industries are facing similar struggles—"In many cases, service industry purchasers find themselves dealing with issues that manufacturing sector companies have already confronted, such as supplier reduction strategies and cost-price analysis."[1]

Purchasing is the department most involved in the selection and control of suppliers. Purchasing typically establishes the policies and procedures that govern the review, selection, and certification of suppliers. Many purchasing departments have focused on cost elimination through strategic partnerships. Successful partnerships have individually yielded cost reductions of 15% to 45% of the purchasing bill. Because only a handful of partnerships can be resourced and managed, each partnership is highly leverageable and could be worth 3% to 5% of the total annual buy dollars. Advanced organizations are building these targets into their purchasing budgets. A critical mass needs to be developed and dedicated to expand improvement efforts internally and, as appropriate, to extend them to the supplier's suppliers. Care must be taken that reductions are properly resourced and budgeted for implementation.

The purchasing department is well positioned to strongly influence the entire procurement process by its involvement in various supply chain activities. Purchasing typically is involved in both product and process development, as well as in other technical activities within the organization. In most organizations, purchasing has continual involvement with operational activities, such as stores, materials handling, production, quality, receiving, and shipping, as well as with administrative activities such as accounts payable and accounts receivable.

Whether purchasing departments function centrally, locally, or in a distributed model, or are in the private, public, or nonprofit sectors, departmental expenses can be identified and budgets combined or separated as needed to manage and control departmental spending.

(b)   The Procurement Process.   It is more difficult to identify and control the expenses of the procurement process. In many organizations, procurement is not recognized as a process, and therefore the complete set of its elements has not been identified. Additionally, expenses are more difficult to track because they are spread throughout the organization. However, there is a value in expanding the departmental focus of the typical budget process to include the entire procurement process. Particularly, this is responsive to management's need for continuous improvement.

To begin, it is useful to identify the elements of a process and determine the definition of a process. A *process* is a set of linked activities that take an input, transform it, and create an output. Ideally, the transformation that occurs in a process should add value to the input and should create an output that is more useful to, and effective for, the recipient. Exhibit 18B.1 describes a process and illustrates the movement from supplier to customer.

---

[1]Carolyn Pye, *Service-Industry Speaks Out,* Purchasing Today, December 1996.

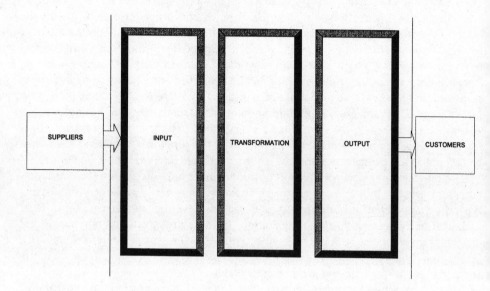

Exhibit 18B.1.   Illustration of the purchasing process. *Reprinted with permission.* **David K. Carr and Henry J. Johansson,** *Best Practices in Reengineering* **(McGraw-Hill, Inc. 1995).**

How does a process add value? Value can be created or added through improved product quality and/ or service, reduced cycle time, and reduced cost to the customer. Exhibit 18B.2 describes these value metrics in greater detail.

Exhibit 18B.2.   Metrics for adding value. *Reprinted with permission.* Johansson, McHugh, Pendlebury, and Wheeler, *Business Process Engineering* (John Wiley & Sons, Limited 1993).

The procurement process not only encompasses the internal organization but also includes external customers and suppliers. This process will vary by industry, by business unit, and by the nature of the product or service provided.

For most companies there are two major components of the procurement process, namely:

- The product development sub-process, which encompasses the make/buy selection and includes
  —Marketing
  —Design
  —Manufacturing

—Costing

—Engineering

—Supplier

—Customer

—Purchasing

—Accounting

- The ordering sub-process, which encompasses ordering, delivery, receipt, and payment of the requested goods or services, including

—Customer or requisitioner

—Purchasing

—Supplier

—Receiving

—Quality

—Materials handling

—Production

—Customer

—Accounts payable

(c)   Implications of the Process Approach.   The primary benefits of a process approach are that it is more holistic, reduces departmental sub-optimization, and provides a better identification of the total cost and benefit to the business unit.

The evolution of such techniques as benchmarking, and the use of best practices, has facilitated the ability to establish goals for continuous process improvement. Activity-based costing (A-BC) provides the information to understand what is spent, what is done, and what resources are required; it also is a useful tool for segregating value-adding from non-value-adding activities, rather than having to rely only on control through variances based on estimates and averages. Companies are just starting to recognize that the application of A-BC to the procurement process is the next tool required.

18B.2   THE ROLE OF PROCESS MEASURES.   A key to managing the procurement process is establishing key performance indicators (KPIs), or process measures. Key performance measures will support the enterprise in meeting its objectives. KPIs establish the visibility to monitor and control the process. Each company will have to establish the appropriate measures for its business. Measures should be both strategic and tactical, and should be focused on the goals of the business.

The importance of this focus is reinforced in *Reinventing the CFO*. The authors stress that "best practices derive appropriate business measures from business objectives rather than merely from financial reporting line items. These measures ask: Is what we want to achieve good enough? What key performance indicators must we focus on to meet our goals?"[2]

---

[2]Thomas Walther, Henry J. Johansson, John Dunleavy, & Elizabeth Hjelm, Reinventing the CFO 54 (1997).

To be effective, measures must be timely and should result in value-added and integrated support of the process. In the case of the procurement process measures inevitably will involve each supplier's ability to meet the needs of the process, and will be established as part of the budget process when the company typically sets business-specific improvement goals.

(a)   Supplier Capabilities and Process Requirements.   One of the most strategic aspects of the procurement process is the supplier base. The management of this critical asset requires some very difficult decisions both during the budget process and during operations. There are three very different classes of suppliers:

- **Strategic**—A provider with whom an open partnership has been established, and who provides goods or services that are critical to operations, are of high value, and are essential for competitive advantage.
- **Collaborative**—A provider with whom dealings are continual and trustworthy, and who provides goods or services that are important to operations, are of high value, and are required but not essential for competitive advantage.
- **Arms-length**—A provider with whom dealings are under market conditions, and from whom purchases are typically at spot or catalog prices, and who provides goods or services that are not of high value and are not essential to the core business.

The number of suppliers needed for each class is dependent upon a very specific understanding of procurement requirements and on the supplier's ability to meet these requirements. A supplier's classification should be based upon its ability to meet specific performance expectations in categories such as

- Production
- Product development
- Cost reduction

The individual category measures will vary by industry and the specific needs of the business. However, the number of suppliers per category should be reevaluated during the budget process and once established be continually reviewed and realigned based upon the supplier's performance.

18B.3   PROCESS MEASURES.   With an understanding of the industry, the business, process requirements, and suppliers' capabilities, specific process improvement goals and process improvement metrics can be established within each of the following categories:

- Production capabilities
- Product development capabilities
- Cost reduction capabilities

By addressing these measures at the time of budgeting the procurement process, the focus is on both planning and improvement.

(a) Production Capabilities. Measures also can be established during the budget process to plan and monitor—in other words, to control—each supplier's production capabilities: Such measures include the following:

- **Supplier Process Reliability**—or the ability of the process to constantly produce high-quality product. The processes must run when they are required, at the capable rate, and produce a quality product.
- **Supplier Certification Capability and Potential**—which is the ability of the supplier to produce quality output at start-up and throughout the production run, without rework.
- **Supplier Capacity Utilization**—which is the time the process is actually in operation compared to the total available time the process is available for operation.
- **Commodity Management**—or the right size supplier base as measured by the number of suppliers per materials category.
- **Inventory Management Capability**—or the ability to control and manage the days of inventory on hand for the total supply chain based on seasonally adjusted sales.
- **Technology**—measured by the systems used to control production, develop products, and communicate and share information.
- **Leveraging Purchasing Power**—which can be measured as the ability of the customer and the supplier to combine requirements resulting in preferential treatment.
- **Reserve Capacity**—or the amount of production capacity in excess of baseline capacity that is available to support incremental demand for promotions.
- **Supplier Lead Times**—which is the elapsed time from order placement to actual delivery.
- **Service Requirements (quantity and timeliness)**—which can be measured by the ability to deliver the requested quantities, on time, and as requested with the required accurate paperwork.
- **Quality Levels**—measured internally as incoming and production defects in parts per million and externally by amount of product returns, reclaims, and recalls.
- **Continuous Improvement Capability**—or the ability to make improvements year to year based upon mutually agreed targets and criteria.

These measures provide the necessary information for evaluating supplier's capabilities, identifying areas for improvement, providing the data for measuring performance, and establishing targets for continuous improvement.

(b) Product Development Capabilities. Product development capability is an area that many companies do not formally measure for either budgeting or monitoring purposes. This can be a critical part of the overall business process, and selected measurement often can lead to substantial improvements. Depending upon the business needs and goals, some possible areas in which useful measures can be developed are discussed below.

- **Renewal of Specifications**—The review and updating of all specifications could identify major opportunities. Cross-functional development teams are useful in this area and should include suppliers.
- **Qualified Materials**—It is important to review the requirements for materials specifications and establish performance-based specifications. Over-specifying can limit the supplier's ability to take full advantage of the commodity market because it can create the need for specialty materials or their equivalents.
- **Development Process and Budgets**—Reviewing opportunities to increase collaborative efforts by sharing technology and best practices could both improve time to market and reduce costs. When these areas are considered, it might lead to the development of a set of mutually agreed measures that will drive the desired cooperative behavior, such as joint

  —Specification development and review, early in the product development cycle
  —Process improvement
  —Product development
  —Cost reduction

- **The Number of Varieties**—Reevaluating the need for the number of varieties (such as flavors, widths, sizes, colors, and the like) might lead to highlighting products or supplies that are very close to each other, and hence might offer opportunities for rationalization.
- **Testing Requirements**—Reviewing the need and value of the various customer-specified quality tests might identify areas for cost reduction.
- **Lot Control Requirements**—Reviewing the extent to which suppliers are requested to maintain lot control and identification can identify improvement opportunities.
- **Labeling and Identification Requirements**—Reviewing the extent to which the supplier is required to label, mark, and identify specified information is another possible improvement area.

In summary, it can be seen that procurement budgeting is much more oriented toward operations improvement and control than it is to merely estimating the amount of goods to be procured.

(c) Cost Reduction Capabilities. Many of the factors that impact product development also impact operational costs and vice versa. Both areas should be reviewed as part of budgeting as both potential cost drivers and appropriate measures should be established. Some possibilities are as follows.

- **Customer Requirements and Procedures for Loading and Identification Information**—Review all of the requested loading information, such as bills of lading, packing lists, advance shipping notices (ASNs), bar codes, labels, load reports, and the like, and evaluate costs and benefits.
- **Procedures for Establishing and Communicating Forecast Information, Orders, and Changes to the Supplier**—Frequent and untimely changes to

quantities, varieties, and delivery dates create the need for excess capacity, and supplier inventories, and are a source of hidden costs. Reexamine the need and the costs avoided at the customer compared to the costs incurred and passed along by the supplier.

- **Communications**—Communications and the supporting technologies are enablers of all improvement opportunities. This is especially true in the area of information technology. Explore opportunities to jointly develop approaches to systems such as

  —Management of total supply inventory at the supplier, in-transit, and at the customer, considering

  —Consignment

  —Automatic replenishment

  —Direct vendor shipments to customers

  —Administrative systems, including:

  —Procurement cards

  —Monthly or consolidated invoicing

  —EDI, to share forecasts and transmit orders

  —EFT/ACH, for payment

  —Bar coding, to record receipts and track inventories

  —ASN, to schedule receiving

  —Pay-on-receipt, eliminating invoices

- **Quality Information**—Are there opportunities to share certificates of analysis and other quality information?
- **Sharing Business Plans**—Synchronize business plans, including business development, product development, and process development, with an emphasis on capital expenditures and cost reduction.
- **Sharing Technology**—Share both the plans and the current application of various technologies, such as process automation, information automation, and communications automation.
- **Materials and Capacity Utilization**—Assess opportunities to favorably impact a supplier's cost of underutilized capacity or to share/leverage energy.
- **Sourcing Arrangements**—Realign the supplier's shipping locations with the customer's producing plants.
- **Buffer Stock Requirements**—Variations between the standard and actual plant efficiency and scrap factors have an impact on run-out and replenishment orders placed by the plants. These variations should be mitigated by the plant's run strategy, plant safety stocks, and supplier buffer stocks. There might be an opportunity to improve the effectiveness and cost of how these factors are being used and balanced.

- **Various Ways Trucks Are Used, and How Material Is Loaded and Unloaded**—Review common routes and evaluate whether there are opportunities for cross-docking, mixed truckloads, or joint scheduling of back hauls. Review the quality and materials-handling characteristics to determine cost-effective ways to load and unload trucks, such as the use of dunnage, reusable pallets, disposable pallets, and so forth. Evaluate the use of requested containers and their usefulness in production.
- **Purchasing Leverage with the Suppliers of the Supplier**—There might be opportunities to combine volume and increase leverage for commodities, for energy, and for shared capacity with suppliers, or by commonly using such items as maintenance materials and spare parts.
- **Physical Assets**—Review and compare the locations, equipment, and information used by both companies. There might be opportunities to share facilities, equipment, offices, communications systems, and/or information systems.
- **Best-Practice Initiatives**—Evaluate each supplier's (and its suppliers') process improvement initiatives and such enablers as statistical process control (SPC), supplier certification production certification, and ISO certification.

Finally, the sharing and accuracy of cost information should be reviewed and confirmed during the budget process. Understanding costs will have an important bearing on each supplier's cost reduction capabilities. Some of the elements required to understand a supplier's costs are

- Breakdown of costs (labor, materials, and overhead)
- Service requirements (quantity and timeliness)
- Cycle times
- Quality levels
- Continuous improvement capabilities

As with product development, cost reduction capabilities being reviewed at the budget cycle can lead to substantial improvements beyond simply estimating future procurement expenditures.

18B.4   CREATING THE PROCUREMENT PROCESS BUDGET.   Today, many companies use a series of performance measures to manage and control the budget processes for procurement. These performance measures either supplement or replace traditional budgets. The steps involved are

- Defining the process
- Establishing appropriate business goals
- Identifying the requirements of the process
- Relating business goals to the process
- Establishing goals for the process
- Establishing metrics for the process
- Organizing those metrics into a meaningful process budget

Many techniques that support process management are available and in use today, such as the following:

- Business-process reengineering is a widely accepted and proven technique to define process and identify requirements.
- Benchmarking and best-practice techniques can identify opportunities for improvement.
- Activity-based costing and performance metrics can be used to identify and track causes and results.
- Management reporting can be used to organize and present the results.

All of these techniques are directly applicable to procurement. In addition, there are professional organizations that specialize in procurement. Two of the best are CAPS and NAPM. CAPS, the Center for Advanced Purchasing Studies, is jointly sponsored by Arizona State University and the National Association of Purchasing Managers. Both are important sources for purchasing benchmarking and performance data, and for the cost of the process, providing data such as

- Purchasing expense per purchasing dollar
- Annual purchasing dollar per purchasing employee (as full-time equivalents, or FTEs)
- Average invoices per employee in the accounts payable function
- Average receipts and inspections per employee involved
- Active suppliers per purchasing employee
- Company purchase dollars per active supplier

CAPS provides substantive research data; and its mission states that "CAPS strives to contribute competitive advantages to organizations by providing leading-edge research to support the evolution of strategic purchasing/supply management." This includes research that

- Identifies the leading edge of current practice and application
- Identifies the current state of procurement practice
- Benchmarks the current state of the practice

Local experience together with sources like CAPS and NAPM can be used to establish metrics to be used in budgeting. These metrics can be prioritized and further integrated with the strategic and tactical goals of the business units as well as with the key activities of the procurement process. Business-process reengineering (BPR) supported with benchmarking and activity-based costing can be used to identify areas for improvement. The goals of the business unit can be used to establish priorities. Together with an understanding of the process, and with the availability and the skill sets of resources and of performance categories, specific targets can be established. These measures when organized into a process framework can be used to predict the impact of planned continual improvement, and can provide for the management and control of a process-oriented purchasing/procurement budget.

SOURCES AND SUGGESTED REFERENCES

Carr, David K., and Johansson, Henry J., *Best Practices in Reengineering,* New York: McGraw-Hill, Inc., 1995.

Gumaer, Robert, "Synchronizing the Supply Chain," *APICS,* January 1997.

Harwick, Tom, "Optimal Decision-Making for the Supply Chain," *APICS,* January 1997.

Johansson, Henry J., McHugh, Patrick, Pendlebury, John A., and Wheeler III, William A., *Business Process Reengineering,* New York: John Wiley & Sons, Inc., 1993.

Kaplan, Robert S., *Measures for Manufacturing,* Cambridge Massachusetts: Harvard Business School Press, 1990.

Maskell, Brian H., *Performance Measurement for World Class Manufacturing,* Cambridge, Massachusetts, and Norwalk, Connecticut: Productivity Press Inc., 1991.

McNair, C.J., Mosconi, William, and Norris, Thomas, *Beyond the Bottom Line,* Homewood, Illinois: Dow Jones-Irwin, 1989.

McNair, C.J., Mosconi, William, and Norris, Thomas, *Meeting the Technology Challenge: Cost Accounting in a JIT Environment,* Montvale, New Jersey: National Association of Accountants, 1988.

Pye, Carolyn, "Service-Industry Speaks Out," *Purchasing Today,* December 1996.

Walther, Thomas, Johansson, Henry J., Dunleavy, John, and Hjelm, Elizabeth, *Reinventing the CFO,* New York: McGraw-Hill, Inc., 1997.

CHAPTER **20A**

LEASING (New)

Robert Dale Apgood

Canterbury Group

CONTENTS

20A.1 INTRODUCTION	1	(a) Relevant Information for Purchase Alternative	16
20A.2 OVERVIEW OF THE LEASING PROCESS	3	(b) Depreciation Calculation	17
		(c) Leasing Information	18
20A.3 POSSIBLE ADVANTAGES OF LEASING	6	**20A.8 FASB 13 CASE ILLUSTRATION**	20
		(a) Lessor Solution	20
20A.4 POSSIBLE DISADVANTAGES OF LEASING	6	(b) Lessee Solution	21
		(c) Conclusion	21
20A.5 TYPES OF LEASE SOURCES	7	**20A.9 NEGOTIATION OF LEASES**	21
20A.6 LEASE REPORTING	9	**20A.10 SELECTING A LESSOR**	22
(a) Basic Terminology	9		
(b) Technical Analysis	9	**20A.11 LEASE ANALYSIS TECHNIQUES**	22
(c) FASB 13	10		
(i) Four Tests of Substance	10	**20A.12 LEASE FORM**	28
(ii) Analysis of the Four Tests	10		
(iii) Present Value—How?	11	**20A.13 SUMMARY**	35
(d) Minimum Lease Payments	14		
(e) The 90 Percent Rule	15	**SOURCES AND SUGGESTED REFERENCES**	36
(f) Retrospect	16		
20A.7 LEASE VERSUS PURCHASE ANALYSIS	16		

20A.1 INTRODUCTION.   The budgetary process in today's business environment requires a dutiful coordination of a business strategic plan carefully supported by a capital budget (primarily a balance sheet planning tool) and an operating budget (typically an income statement planning tool) (see exhibit 20A.1).

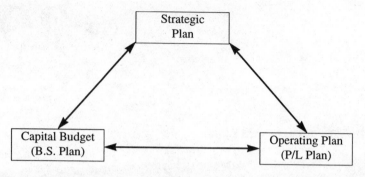

Exhibit 20A.1.   Coordination of planning tools.

Typically top management envisions a strategy and subsequently subordinates are required to project a capital plan (assets, liabilities, and equity) that will enable the company to march toward fulfillment of the strategy vision. Accordingly, a capital budget is prepared, complete with all necessary asset, liability, and equity elements, a process well covered in another chapter of this book. Frequently, however, the company prefers to avoid balance sheet implications by electing to lease assets. Thus, off-balance-sheet financing is selected, the balance sheet impact is minimized, and the operating budget is impacted. To graphically illustrate the financial statement impact, let us examine Exhibit 20A.2.

	OPERATING LEASE		CAPITAL LEASE	
	Balance Sheet	P/L	Balance Sheet	P/L
LESSEE	-0-	Rent expense	Fixed asset	Depreciation expense
			Accumulated depreciation	
			Debt:	Interest expense
			current	
			long-term	
LESSOR	Fixed asset	Depreciation expense		
	Accumulated depreciation		-0-	income
	Debt:	Interest expense		
	current	Rental income	(simplest of several possible	
	long-term		structures)	

Exhibit 20A.2.   The impact of leasing in financial statements.

From a budgetary viewpoint, it thus becomes evident that leases must be analyzed carefully, in order that the proper budgets become impacted. Occasionally, leasing transactions may be immaterial for a company, but since the mid-1980s, nearly 33% of all property, plant, and equipment acquired by U.S. companies have been acquired through operating and capital leases.[1]

---

[1]Annual statistics available from ELA (Equipment Leasing Association of America), Arlington, Virginia.

Thus the case is made. Budgeting is important and leasing is an increasingly material part thereof.

20A.2   OVERVIEW OF THE LEASING PROCESS.   A typical lease (usually called a single-inventor lease) involves four parties (exhibit 20A.3).

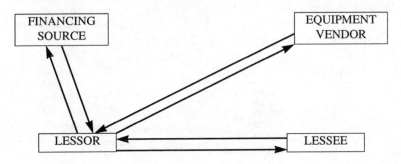

Exhibit 20A.3.   A typical lease.

Simple analysis suggests that, if the lessor retains title to the asset in question, the transaction is a rental or lease. If, however, the lessee eventually ends up with the asset, the lease in question begins to look like some kind of sale from the lessor to the lessee. In budgetary parlance, the transaction is either analyzed as part of the operating budget (if an operating lease) or the capital budget (if a capital lease). Because these two budgets are frequently prepared by different persons, require vastly differing analytical approaches, and dramatically alter balance sheet and income statement presentation, we must become skilled captains of the leasing ship as it sails the financial waters.

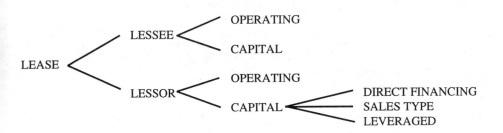

Exhibit 20A.4.   Lease analysis.

Internationally, two different approaches have been taken to properly classify leases on financial statements. The first and simplest approach is observed in the geographical region roughly approximated by southern Europe and is called the "form" approach to leasing. In these countries, if the lease contract stipulates or labels a lease as an operating lease, all analysis is finished. It *is* a rental. Lessor has balance sheet ownership and lessee is a renter. If, in contrast, the lease agreement calls the transaction a capital lease, it *is*. Lessor then accounts for the transaction as a sale and the lessee has balance sheet ownership. How simple! And how consistent! One party is always an owner and the other a nonowner.

But in the United States, as in many other countries, it matter not what a lease is called or labeled. Evidence must be gathered, measurements taken, and then the lease classified as either on- or off-balance sheet for both lessee and lessor. In other words, the substance of a lease dictates its financial statement classification. A short list of countries using each system is displayed in Exhibit 20A.5.

Countries Utilizing Form	Countries Utilizing Substance	Rules of Substance Found in:
France	U.S.	FASB 13, 91, 98, & IAS 17
Italy	U.K.	SSAP 21 & IAS 17
Spain	Canada	CICA 3065 & IAS 17
Portugal	Australia	ASAP 21 & IAS 17
Malta	New Zealand	IAS 17
	Holland	IAS 17
	etc. (approximately 50 additional countries)	IAS 17

Exhibit 20A.5.   International lease typology.

As long as both parties to the lease, lessee and lessor, are in the same country, lease treatment will normally be uniform. In the event, however, that a lease becomes bi-national, intriguing cross-border financial results are possible.

Case One:

1. Both the lessee and lessor are in France.
2. The lease document stipulates that the lease is an operating lease—therefore, it is.
3. Lessor assumes balance sheet ownership and is, therefore, entitled to the related income statement deductions for depreciation and interest expenses. Lessor also has balance sheet ramifications.
4. Lessee may not assume balance sheet ownership, but rather must account for the lease as a rental.
5. We have one owner and one nonowner.

	BALANCE SHEET	INCOME STATEMENT

LESSOR	Fixed asset
	Accumulated depreciation
	Debt:
	  current portion
	  long-term portion
		Depreciation expense
		Interest expense
		Rental income

LESSEE	No impact	Rental expense

Case Two:

1. Lessor is an Italian corporation and lessee is in the United States.
2. The lease document stipulates that the lease is an operating lease. For this lessor, it is.
3. Lessor assumes balance sheet ownership and takes the related income statement deductions for depreciation and interest expenses as well as all balance sheet ramifications.
4. Lessee must follow FASB 13 (U.S. rules). Let us assume that the present value of the minimum lease payments is greater than 90% of the fair value of the leased asset. According to U.S. rules, the lease is a capital lease, the lessee assumes balance sheet ownership also (not necessarily legal ownership), and we have a double-dip lease, or as it is frequently called, a *cross-border tax transfer*.
5. Both lessee and lessor must follow the accounting rules of their countries. Thus, each claims accounting ownership.

	BALANCE SHEET	INCOME STATEMENT

LESSOR	Fixed asset
	Accumulated depreciation
	Debt:
	   current portion
	   long-term portion
		Depreciation expense
		Interest expense
		Rental income

LESSEE	Fixed asset
	Accumulated depreciation
	Debt:
	   current portion
	   long-term portion
		Depreciation expense
		Interest expense

Case Three:

1. Lessor is a Spanish corporation and lessee is in the United States.
2. The lease document stipulates that the lease is a capital lease. For this lessor, it is.
3. Lessor accounts for the lease as a sale. It is no longer on the balance sheet.
4. Lessee must follow FASB 13. Let us assume that the present value of the minimum lease payments is less than 90% of the fair market value of the asset. According to U.S. rules, the lease is an operating lease. The lessee does not have balance sheet ownership and accounts for the transaction as a rental. In this case, neither lessee nor lessor claims balance sheet ownership. It is off the books for each and rightfully so. Lessee and lessor *must* each follow the generally accepted accounting principles of its own country. In the parlance of the leasing community, this is sometimes called a skinny-dip lease, since neither party has balance sheet coverage.

	BALANCE SHEET	INCOME STATEMENT
LESSOR	Nothing. This assumes the asset was sold and the resulting note receivable was also sold.	Income
LESSEE	Nothing	Rental expense

20A.3 POSSIBLE ADVANTAGES OF LEASING.

1. Shifts risk of obsolescence to lessor.
2. Shifts legal ownership and responsibility to lessor.
3. Provides off-balance-sheet financing.
4. Typically paid for from operating budget rather than capital budget.
5. Profitability ratios appear improved.
6. Liquidity ratios appear improved.
7. Solvency ratios appear improved.
8. Tax benefits (depreciation and interest expense) can be shifted to a party better able to utilize them.
9. Lower cash flow up front to obtain asset.
10. Flexibility increases (swaps, upgrades, roll-overs, take-outs, etc.).
11. Inflation hedge (can negotiate longer term and pay with cheaper dollars).
12. Approval can be accelerated.
13. Circumventing capital budget constraints.
14. Delaying sales tax payments (as high as 33% in some European countries).
15. Government reimbursement policies (overhead is frequently a limited or prescribed element for reimbursement; lease payments are not overhead and qualify for reimbursement).
16. Alternative minimum tax (AMT) may dictate no additional purchases.
17. Ownership may be unavailable (satellite usage).
18. Bundling (full-service leases) is facilitated.
19. Excessive usage of equipment by lessee would make ownership unwise.
20. Vendor control (nonperformance of equipment).
21. Finance source diversification.
22. Fewer restriction (bank covenants).
23. Lower cost (lessor may obtain economies of scale and pass through to lessee).

20A.4 POSSIBLE DISADVANTAGES OF LEASING.

1. Opportunity to gain from residual value is shifted to lessor.
2. Balance sheet analysis is hindered, as both asset and liability are disclosed only in footnotes.
3. Capital budgeting decisions are disguised and frequently not analyzed.
4. Tax benefits of ownership: depreciation and interest expense are not normally available to minimize cash flows.

5. Reimbursement policies may be hindered (utilities, for example, are often given a targeted ROA approval figure for rates. If leased, the assets are less and the targeted profitability can be reduced—rates lowered).

6. Higher cost (if lessee is not sophisticated in lease negotiations).

7. Lease versus buy analytical techniques are not universally known and applied.

8. Trends or fads may suggest that leasing is wise when it is only current.

20A.5   TYPES OF LEASE SOURCES.

Lessors

- Financial institutions (banks, savings & loans, finance companies, etc.)
- Captives (vendors and banks)
- Independents

In the United States, independent leasing companies have traditionally held the biggest share of the leasing business.[2] Banks entered the game in a big way in the late 1970s and early 1980s and built large portfolios, many of which were liquidated in the late 1980s and early 1990s as they experienced operating and regulatory difficulties. The current trend in the industry is the awakening and substantial growth of the "vendor" sector, who have discovered that leasing can be a tremendous marketing tool for expansion as well as a profit center.

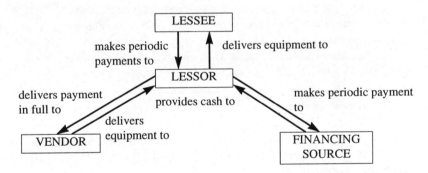

Exhibit 20A.6.   Typical independent lease company transaction (third-party lease).

Many entities have joined the leasing game. They include:

- **Independent leasing companies**—This is the traditional type of lease provider who originally would lease anything to anyone (Exhibit 20A.4). Increased competitive pressure has forced many of these companies to concentrate in niches, such as telecommunications or automobiles. The largest such player is Comdisco, an international participant in Chicago that specialized originally in the used IBM market.

---

[2]ELA statistics.

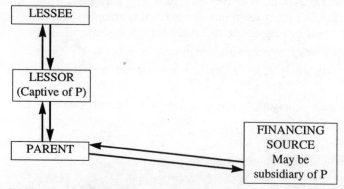

Exhibit 20A.7.   Typical captive lease transaction.

- **Captives**—This is the hot market of the early 1990s. Because they operate under the scrutiny of a parent, they are usually not as nimble and flexible as an independent, but they have tremendous clout becuase of this same parent relationship (exhibit 20A.5). Examples include GECC (General Electric) and ICC (IBM).

- **Brokers**—During the frothy and profitable "go-go" years of the 1980s, many experienced leasing professionals discovered that they could function as financial intermediaries, bringing together the necessary participants, thus functioning as a manager. Brokers come and go, but typically prefer to manage bigger deals, such as jumbo jets and large computer mainframes.

- **Banks**—In the United States, banks entered the leasing game after it was somewhat mature. By way of contrast, banks in Europe and the Middle East were primary developers, and hence currently enjoy a much larger market presence in those geographical regions. U.S. banks dramatically altered their position in the leasing arena during the last few years because of large credit losses and subsequent government tightening of regulations.

- **Insurance companies**—Two approaches have been taken in this industry. Several large firms, such as Metropolitan Life Insurance, formed leasing subsidiaries and aggressively funded deals. Others are content to purchase large individual leases or portfolios on the secondary market, much like the home mortgage market.

- **Finance companies**—Many of these players jumped into the arena, especially in the area of consumer leasing. Because they already were active here, they expanded their horizon to include operating leases and thereby assumed a risk they were not experienced in—residual risk!

- **Pension funds**—Usually these funds serve as a reservoir of lease portfolios and purchased leases from others. Needless to say, many questionable and some worthless paper found its way into the hands of these typically inexperienced participants.

- **Lease pools**—Functioning much like a mutual fund, many lease pools sold "shares" in future expected values to wealthy individuals and companies.

20A.6   LEASE REPORTING.

- FASB 13, 91, 98—Provide criteria for accrual (income statement, balance sheet) reporting.
- IRS Rev. Rul. 55-540, Rev. Proc. 75-21—Provide criteria for tax analysis of a lease.
- IAS 17 (International Accounting Standard 17)—Provides criteria for international lease reporting to the approximately 55 member nations who have adopted it.
- Internal reporting
  a. Lease versus buy
  b. Internal rate of return
  c. Net present value
  d. Breakeven
  e. Pricing
  f. Asset tracking
  g. Accounting
  h. Tax
  i. Billing and collections
  j. Portfolio management.

Software providers have developed an abundance of software application packages to assist in lease analysis and reporting.[3]

(a)   Basic Terminology.   The leasing industry is exceedingly creative, and accordingly a host of synonyms or near-synonyms has been created to describe operating and capital leases. These include the ones listed in exhibit 20A.8.

(b)   Technical Analysis.   Various national and international bodies have labored extensively to codify leasing rules. In the United States, the IRS and FASB have provided mandatory models.

The IRS was the first group in the United States to codify leasing rules, and these still exist. In 1955, Revenue Ruling 55-540 provided initial but very weak "nonguidelines" for lease classifications as either operating or capital. The IRS followed up this initial attempt with an improved but still weak definition of operating and capital in 1975 with Revenue Procedure 75-21. Since then, the IRS has given the lease definition and measurement process little additional attention. Because what it has produced is impractical and insufficient for satisfactory application, the IRS tends to rely upon the subsequent and much superior FASB 13 in its deliberations.

The FASB in 1975 issued FASB 13, which became effective in 1977. This is a much tighter document, which provides definitions and measurements for operating and capital lease classifications.

---

[3]Some of the major software dealers are: Decision Systems, Inc., Minneapolis, Minnesota; SSI, Norcross, Georgia; Better Programs, Denver, Colorado; McCue Systems, Inc., Burlingame, California; The LeMans Group, King of Prussia, Pennsylvania.

Operating Lease Synonyms	Capital Lease Synonyms
operating	capital
real	direct finance
true	finance
rental	installment sales contract
off balance sheet	deferred sales contract
off the books	open-end lease with a bargain purchase option
closed-end	$1.00 purchase option
open-end lease with fair market value purchase option	nominal purchase option
tax	peppercorn (British)
guideline	full payout
non-guideline	full payoff
walk away	sales type
	non-tax
	secured transaction

Exhibit 20A.8.   Basic terminology to describe operating and capital leases.

(c)   FASB 13.   FASB 13 contains the four criteria that must be observed if a lease is to be classified as a capital lease.

(i)   Four Tests of Substance.

  1. Will title pass from lessor to lessee?
  2. Does the lease contain a bargain purchase option?
  3. Is the lease life greater than or equal to 75% of the economic life?
  4. Is the present value of the minimum lease payments greater than or equal to 90% of the fair market value of the equipment?

If the answer to any of these questions is affirmative, the lease is a capital lease. If all four are negative, the lease is an operating lease.

Internationally, all of the previously mentioned lease codification numbers (CICA 3065 in Canada, FASB 13 in the United States, SSAP 21 in England, etc.) are substantially identical and are also substantially identical to IAS 17, issued by the International Accounting Standards Board in London. In other words, once the intricacies of FASB 13 are mastered, all others are virtually identical.

Therefore, these four tests must be carefully examined and mastered if the financial statements are to be properly stated *and* if the budgeting classifications of operating and capital assets are to be proper. An operating lease will be included in the operating "budget" and is usually approved by a department head. A capital lease, on the other hand, is in the capital budget and is typically approved by someone at a higher corporate level.

(ii)   Analysis of the Four Tests.   The first test is simple to control. If an operating lease is desired, do not provide for the transfer of title in the lease document. Simply state that the lease is a closed-end lease or a walk-away lease (i.e., no purchase

option is available to the lessee). Conversely, if a capital lease is desired, stipulate how and when title will pass (i.e., after 24 payments, after 60 months, etc.).

The second test is equally easy to control. If an operating lease is desired, avoid the inclusion of a bargain purchase option (B.P.O.) in the lease agreement. If the parties to the lease desire a capital lease, a B.P.O provision automatically qualifies the lease as a purchase.

The third test is quite easy to control once one term is mastered—*economic life.* As used in the leasing industry, and in contrast to accounting and tax usage, life of an asset in its "economic" sense is defined as the expected useful life. Fully deciphered, FASB and the leasing industry define *economic life* as the length of time the asset has usefulness to multiple, subsequent users, not just the present user. Thus, economic life assumes a measure much longer than book life and considerably longer than tax life—a long, long life. Thus, cars usually are given an economic life of 10 to 15 years, mainframe computers 12 to 15 years, and ordinary desks and chairs a life of 15 to 20. The budget analyst who is trying to convert a lease into a capital variety is probably wise not to try to qualify it with this third test. Lease lives are virtually always much less than 75% of the economic life. This third test will normally result in a rental situation.

Understanding and manipulating (not meant in its derogatory connotation) the budgetary journey of a lease from operating to capital usually involves a very mundane control of the fourth test—the present value of cash flows. This can easily be the point of departure where the budget novice errs, concluding that a lease is operating when in fact it should be capital and vice versa. In short, the forecasted balance sheet and income statement are in danger of being misbudgeted and malforecasted.

To shorten the fourth test, we observe the technical language of FASB 13.

$$(PV)(MLP's) \geq (90\%)(FMV)$$

If the present value of the minimum lease payments is greater than or equal to 90% of the FMV, a capital lease exists. Of course, the result is an operating lease if the 90% line of demarcation is not reached Now to understand the implications of the formula.

(iii)   Present Value—How?   FASB 13 dictates the alternative discounting rates to be utilized by the lessor and lessee.

Discount Rate to Be Utilized by Lessor	Lower of Discount Rate to Be Utilized by Lessee
The lessor must present-value the cash flows using the implicit rate in the lease.	The lessee must use the lower of: 1. The lessor's implicit rate in the lease, if known by the lessee. or 2. The incremental borrowing rate of the lessee.

Let us examine why FASB directed that the implicit rate is the only acceptable rate for the lessor. In order to establish its logic, let us pictorially examine the cash flows of the lessor in a leasing transaction (see Exhibits 20A.9 and 20A.10).

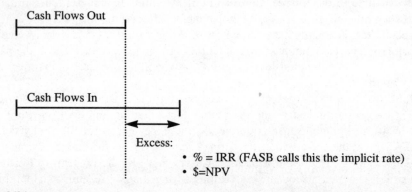

Exhibit 20A.9.

Lessor

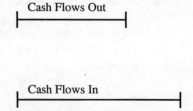

Exhibit 20A.10.

Possible cash flows out for the lessor include:

1. Equipment cost (broadly defined as historical cost of the equipment plus freight-in, installation, debugging, etc.).
2. Initial direct costs (referred to in FASB 13 and FASB 91 as I.D.C.s)
   A. Commissions paid by lessor to sales representative to obtain lease
   B. Lawyers' fees paid by lessor to structure document
   C. Credit investigation fees paid by lessor to ascertain creditworthiness of lessee
   D. Other costs.

Possible cash flows in for the lessor include:

1. Initial (at inception date of lease)
   A. Advance payments
   B. Refundable fees
   C. Nonrefundable fees.
2. Periodic (typically occur monthly in U.S. lease transactions but frequently quarterly or semiannually in European deals).

3. Terminal (at the end of the lease terrn)
   A. Fees (nonrefundable fees, pick-up fees, refurbishing fees, etc.)
   B. Sale (could either be to the lessee or to a third party)
   C. Re-lease (could either be to the lessee or to a third party)
   D. Lessee-guaranteed residual value (which automatically makes the lease a capital lease, as all risk has effectively been removed for the lessor)
   E. Third-party residual insurance (the lessor could buy an insurance policy at lease inception date providing for a stipulated terminal value).

Now let us quickly cast our gaze again at the top of Exhibit 20A.10, keeping in mind that we are examining it from the viewpoint of the lessor. It becomes clear that the lessor knows with precision each and every cash flow assumption (interpret this to mean budget or forecast) in the exhibit. Thus, the lessor can indeed calculate the implicit rate in the lease because the lessor knows all the data.

Next, let us remove our lessor hat and replace it with that of the lessee—think like a lessee. Look again at Exhibit 20A.10. The lessee rarely knows the equipment cost, never knows the commissions paid, the lawyers' fees, the credit investigation charges, and so on. In other words, the lessee does not know all cash flows out. Likewise, the lessee does not know all cash flows in. Some budgeted (estimated) flows in are known, such as the initial and the periodic flows, but the lessee would only know the terminal budgeted flows if the lessee holds a purchase or renewal option. In conclusion, the lessee would virtually never know all cash flows forecasted in a lease transaction. Thus, lessee could not possibly calculate the implicit rate inherent in the lease. The only other way for the lessee to know (notice FASB 13 did not use the words, "estimate the implicit rate"—it says "know it") the implicit rate would be to ask the lessor for it. Because the implicit rate is also the profitability rate inherent in the lease transaction, no lessor would or could divulge such detail to an outside party. In other words, the lessee normally cannot know the implicit rate. This brings us to the alternative discount rate posited by FASB for use by the lessee—the incremental, pretax, installment, secured, co-terminus borrowing rate—what rate would the lessee have to pay to borrow a like sum for a like period for a like transaction? A strong lessee might, therefore, select prime, whereas a weaker lessee would add several percentage points to the rate.

Lessor and lessee will each present value the budgeted cash flows, but each will use a different rate. If each uses a different rate, one set of cash flows could be above the magic 90% and the other below. Conclusion: it is possible, and indeed desirable, that the sophisticated lessor and lessee may structure the budgeted lease so that each gets the desired result, which could be:

1. Single-dip lease—on one set of books only
2. Double-dip lease—on both sets of books
3. Skinny dip lease—on neither set of books.

Enough of rates. Let's move on to MLPs, the second element in the formula of test number four.

(d) Minimum Lease Payments. FASB 13 directs lessors and lessees to present-value the minimum lease payments (MLPs). MLPs are not all but just some of the cash flows in the lease—the flows that can be predicted or budgeted with certainty.

LESSOR	LESSEE
1. Periodic payment in lease (usually monthly payment)	1. Periodic payment in lease (usually monthly payment)
2. Guaranteed residual payment	2. Lessee-guaranteed residual payments
3. Nonrenewal penalties	3. Nonrenewal penalties
4. *BUT* Fees, per FASB 91, are to be capitalized by lessor and amortized over the lease life, thus impacting future budget periods	4. Fees
5. Bargain purchase option	5. Bargain purchase option
6. *But not* executory costs	6. *But not* executory costs
7. Third-party residual insurance on the terminal value of the equipment	

Let's take a brief detour to discuss executory costs, after which we'll return to MLPs. Executory costs are defined in FASB 13 and 91 as cash flows out—operating costs paid by the lessee once a lease is in place. A logical way to picture these appears in Exhibit 20A.11.

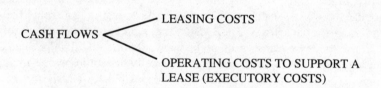

CASH FLOWS
— LEASING COSTS
— OPERATING COSTS TO SUPPORT A LEASE (EXECUTORY COSTS)

Exhibit 20A.11. Executory costs.

NET LEASE	FULL SERVICE LEASE OR BUNDLED LEASE
The lease pays only a: 1. Low net monthly payment (assume $500) PLUS 2. Executory (operating) costs (assume $300 per month)	The lessee pays a higher monthly payment to lessor who, in turn, pays the executory costs. New monthly payment would be approximately $500 + $300 = $800.

Exhibit 20A.12. Lessee executory costs.

Now assume:

$$(PV)(\$500) = 92\% \text{ of FV} = \text{capital lease}$$

Lessee may not desire a budgeted capital transaction, so the two parties negotiate a bundled lease resulting in the $800 monthly budgeted payment being allocated as shown in Exhibit 20A.13.

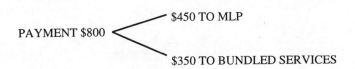

PAYMENT $800

$450 TO MLP

$350 TO BUNDLED SERVICES

Exhibit 20A.13.   Bundled lease.

Thus, the (PV)($450) < 90% FMV and the lessee gets an operating lease. Real-world evidence of this exists in the normal lease proposals of Xerox, IBM, and many other companies, wherein they push bundling. They want to provide a machine plus supplies, maintenance, insurance, training, and any other product and/or services.

If the lessee desires a budgeted capital lease, the agreement can bundle more cash flow into the monthly payment. If, however, the capital budget is all used up, bundle a lease so that less of the cash flow is attributed to the monthly payment and an operating lease is created.

Now let's return from our detour to the MLP discussion. Notice that FASB directed that executory costs not be included in the MLP to be present-valued. Also, notice that the minimum lease payments listed under lessor and lessee are *not* the same.

The result? If different budgeted cash flows are present-valued, it is possible to:

1. Single-dip a lease
2. Double-dip a lease
3. Skinny-dip a lease.

(e)   The 90 Percent Rule.   In all countries of the world that follow the rules of substance (not form countries), there is general agreement on the 90% rule. However, the lessee and lessor each must measure according to "known" information. Thus, the lessor and lessee end up with different comparison bases (90% of the fair market value).

Lessor — 90% of "the" FMV

Lessee — 90% of "a" FMV

Because the exact cost of the equipment is known to the lessor, the lessor can indeed make this calculation. The lessee, however, normally will not "know with precision" the FMV. Thus, an estimate must suffice. Conceptually, this means that the lessee will rely upon one of the following for the fair market value:

1. Written bid
2. Telephone quotation
3. Newspaper advertisement
4. Price list—wholesale
5. Price list—retail
6. Estimated cost
7. Other.

Conclusion: Rarely would the lessor and the lessee take 90% of the same cost.

(f) Retrospect.   Once again, let us examine the fourth test of substance.

$$(PV)(Minimum\ Lease\ Payments) \geq 90\%\ of\ the\ Fair\ Market\ Value$$

As we have seen, lessor and lessee will utilize different variables for three of the four test components. It is not only possible but probable that each can control the variables to obtain the desired type of lease and thereby shift impact from the operating budget to the capital budget or vice versa.

20A.7 LEASE VERSUS PURCHASE ANALYSIS.   Lease versus purchase analysis begins with the assumption that the investment analysis (capital budgeting) decision has been made in favor of acquiring a piece of equipment. The next step requires a financing decision—lease versus purchase analysis.

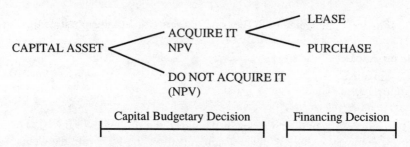

Exhibit 20A.14.   Lease versus purchase analysis.

Mega Corp. recently decided to obtain a computer with a retail value of $400,000. The company can either obtain a loan and purchase the computer, or it can be leased. Mega Corp. is in the 40% tax bracket.

(a)   Relevant Inforrnation for Purchase Alternative.   A bank loan must be obtained for the purchase price of $400,000 less a down payment of $100,000. The balance ($300,000) is to be financed over 36 months with monthly payments in arrears of $9,680, an implicit borrowing rate of about 10%. Sales tax is 6% and will be paid at the time of purchase. The bank requires a loan origination fee of 2% of the loan proceeds. Each monthly payment is composed of both principal and interest, the latter being tax deductible as follows:

Year 1	$25,939
Year 2	$16,492
Year 3	$ 6,055

Depreciation expense on the computer will be straight line for book purposes and Modified Accelerated Cost Recovery System (MACRS) with a five-year life for tax. The sales tax of $24,000 will be capitalized as part of the computer's depreciable base.

(b)   Depreciation Calculation.

Weighted Average Aftertax Cost of Capital of 12%.

Equipment cost	$400,000
Sales tax	24,000
Depreciable basis	$424,000

Year 1	$84,800	(20%)(424,000)
Year 2	135,680	(32%)(424,000)
Year 3	81,408	(19.2%)(424,000)
Year 4	48,760	(11.5%)(424,000)
Year 5	48,760	(11.5%)(424,000)
Year 6	24,592	(5.8%)(424,000)
	$424,000	

Operating costs (executory cost):

1. Repairs and maintenance = $1,000 per month for 72 months
2. Insurance = $400 per month for 72 months
3. Supplies = $700 per month for 72 months

Preset Value Factors:

Type of Flow	Rate	N	Factor
PV annuity	.83%	36 months	31.0093
PV annuity	1%	72 months	51.1504
PV annuity	1%	70 months	50.1685
PV annuity	.83%	72 months	54.0375
PV of 1	12%	3 years	0.7118
PV of 1	12%	2 years	0.7972
PV of 1	12%	1 year	0.8929
PV of 1	12%	4 years	0.6355
PV of 1	12%	5 years	0.5674
PV of 1	12%	6 years	0.5066

HP 12 C keystrokes for loan amortization:

300,000 CHS PV

g end
9,680 PMT
10 g 12 ÷
0 n

12 f amort	25,939	
X ⪥ Y	90,221	
RCL PV	209,779	
12 f amort	16,492	
X ⪥ Y	99,668	
RCL PV	110,111	
12 f amort	6,055	
X ⪥ Y	110,105	
RCL PV	7	(Rounding error)

(c) Leasing Information.   The lease would be for six years with monthly payments of $8,250 in advance. The first and last two payments are due at the lease inception date. A lease origination fee of $4,000 must be paid in advance. The lease contains a fair market value purchase option, but Mega Corp. does not plan on exercising the option.

Operating costs (executory costs) are:

1. Use tax of 6% on each monthly payment = $495
2. Insurance = $425 per month
3. Repairs and maintenance = $1,000 per month
4. Supplies = $600 per month.

Present Value of Purchase Alternative

	Cash Flow	x PV Factor	x Tax Factor	= Amount
Initial flows:				
Down payment	$100,000	1	N/A	$100,000
Sales tax	24,000	1	N/A	24,000
	6,000	1	1-0.4	3,600
Periodic flows:	9,680	31.0	N/A	300,080
Terminal flows:				
Repairs and				
maintenance	1,000	54.04	1-0.4	32,424
Insurance	400	54.04	1-0.4	12,970
Supplies	700	54.04	1-0.4	22,697

Tax shielded by:

Interest expense	(16,247)
Depreciation expense	(125,176)
Net present value of aftertax cash flows to purchase	$354,348

Present Value of Leasing Alternative

	Cash Flow	x PV Factor	x Tax Factor	= Amount
Initial flows:				
Advance payments (2)	$16,500	1	1-0.4	$9,900
	4,000	1	1-0.4	2,400
Periodic flows:				
Monthly payments (70)	8,250	50.17	1-0.4	248,342
Terminal flows:				
Use tax in advance (2)	990	1	1-0.4	594
Use tax	495	50.17	1-0.4	14,900
Insurance	425	50.17	1-0.4	12,793
Repairs and maintenance	1000	50.17	1-0.4	30,102
Supplies	600	50.17	1-0.4	18,061
Net present value of aftertax cash flows to lease				$310,001

Calculation of Tax Shielded by Interest Expense:

Year	Interest Expense	PV Factor	Tax Factor	Income Tax Shielded
1	$25,939	0.8929	0.4	$9,264
2	16,492	0.7972	0.4	5,259
3	6,055	0.7118	0.4	1,724
	$48,486			$16,247

Calculation of Tax Shielded by Depreciation Expense

Year	Interest Expense	PV Factor	Tax Factor	Income Tax Shielded
1	$84,800	0.8929	0.4	$30,287
2	135,680	0.7972	0.4	43,266
3	81,408	0.7118	0.4	23,178
4	48,760	0.6355	0.4	12,395
5	48,760	0.5674	0.4	11,067
6	24,592	0.5066	0.4	4,983
	$424,000			$125,176

20A.8   FASB 13 CASE ILLUSTRATION.

Lease provisions
Lease term: 60 months
List price of equipment: $140,000
Discount to lessor from vendor: $14,000
First and last two payments due at inception date
Nonrenewal penalty: $1,500
Estimated residual value: $19,000
Monthly payment, net of executory costs: $2,600.

(a)   Lessor Solution.

Step 1: Calculation of Implicit Rate

Keystrokes	Display	Explanation
f REG	0.00	Clears all registers
118,200 CHS g CFo	118,200	Enters initial cash flow
2,600 g CFj	2,600	Enters first cash flow
57 g Nj	57.00	Enters number of times first flow occurs
0 g CFj	0.00	Enters second cash flow
2 g Nj	2.00	Enters number of times second flow occurs
20,500 g CFj	20,500	Enters third cash flow
f IRR	1.16	Answer (the calculated monthly yield)
12X	13.94	IRR (the implicit rate)

Step 2: PV of MLPs

Keystrokes	Display	Explanation
f REG	0.00	Clears all registers
1.16 i	1.16	Enters monthly discount rate
7,800 g CFo	7,800.00	Enters initial cash flow
2,600 g CFj	2,600.00	Enters first cash flow
57 g Nj	57.00	Enters number of times first flow occurs
0 g CFj	0.00	Enters second cash flow
2 g Nj	2.00	Enters number of times second flow occurs
1,500 g CFj	1,500.00	Enters third cash flow
f NPV	116,540.57	Answer (the calculated net present value)

Step 3: Calculation of a Comparison Base

$126,000
x   0.9
$113,400

Conclusion: Capital lease, because the PV of the MLPs is more than 90% of the FMV.

(b)   Lessee Solution.

Step 1: PV of MLPs

Keystrokes	Display	Explanation
f REG	0.00	Clears all registers
10 g 12 ÷	0.83	Enters monthly discount rate
7,800 g CFo	7,800	Enters initial cash flow
2,600 g CFj	2,600	Enters first cash flow
57 g Nj	57.00	Enters number of times first flow occurs
0 g CFj	0.00	Enters second cash flow
2 g Nj	2.00	Enters number of times second flow occurs
1,500 g CFj	1,500	Enters third cash flow
f NPV	126,301.28	Answer (the calculated present value)

Step 2: Calculation of a Comparison Base

$$\begin{array}{r} \$140,000 \\ \underline{x \quad\quad 0.9} \\ \underline{\$126,000} \end{array}$$

Conclusion: Capital lease, because the PV of the MLPs is more than 90% of the FMV.

(c)   Conclusion.   For the lessor, the lease would be classified as a capital lease because $(PV)(MLP) \geq (90\%)(FMV)$. But for the lessee, the lease could be either operating or capital, depending on the choice of the PV rate. If the lease is being analyzed near the end of the year and if the lessee has extra cash available in the operating budget, an operating lease could be structured, keeping the deal off the books. If, however, the lessee has cash left in the capital budget, a direct finance lease could be structured, thereby putting the equipment on the books.

It becomes imperative that budget experts, both operating and capital, understand the principles dictated by FASB 13 in order to optimize plans and results.

20A.9   NEGOTIATION OF LEASES.   How do you negotiate a lease? Many factors must be considered, including, but not limited to:

1. Number of periodic payments
2. Number of advance payments
3. Stub payments (partial initial payments)
4. Nonrenewal penalties
5. Lease origination fees
6. Contingent payments
7. Excess usage or "beat up" fees
8. Deposits
9. Step up, step down, skip payment provisions
10. COLA or other escalation provisions
11. Tax indemnifications

12. Equipment subleasing rights
13. Usage restrictions
14. Late payment penalties
15. Leasehold improvement ownership rights
16. Lease assignment rights
17. Lessor subrogation rights
18. Executory cost provisions (insurance, supplies, repairs, taxes, etc.)
19. Warranties on equipment by vendor and/or lessor
20. Rollovers, upgrades, early outs, swaps
21. Renewal options
22. Purchase options
23. Residual value insurance
24. Equipment inspection provisions
25. Equipment maintenance provisions.

20A.10   SELECTING A LESSOR.   Lessor selection demands that the lessee consider:

- Financial condition of leasing company
- Flexibility
- Services offered
- Rate commitment
- Turnaround time
- Prior experience with similar equipment
- Geographic presence
- Financing sources
- Ultimate disposition of lease paper.

20A.11   LEASE ANALYSIS TECHNIQUES.   There are many types of returns which may be calculated for any lease transaction. These measures of performance are usually stated in some form of return on investment. Typical returns would be stated as the internal rate of return for a particular transaction or the "return" on a portfolio. The return on a portfolio would be some type of weighted average calculation. However, all quoted returns are based on cash flows, or, in other words, when cash changes hands. Some of the different titles for types of returns would be:

- Internal Rate of Return
- External Rate of Return
- Modified Rate of Return
- Street Rate or Stream Rate
- Return on Assets
- Return on Equity
- Average Return on Assets
- Yield

Because so many different names may be used, it would be easier to take a particular transaction and view the different types of return calculations from the lessee and lessor perspectives. For this example, the following assumptions will be utilized in developing different yield calculations:

1. Lease term: Four years with the first rental payment due at the end of the first year of the lease. For tax purposes, the lease is considered a true or guideline lease; that is, the lessor will be entitled to the tax benefits of tax depreciation, and the lessee will be entitled to expense the full amount of the payments made to the lessor.

2. At the conclusion of the lease term, the lessee will have the option of purchasing the equipment for its then fair market value, renewing the lease for the equipment at its then fair market value, or returning the equipment to the lessor and having no further involvement with the particular piece of equipment.

3. The lessor is a calendar year taxpayer in the 35% tax bracket.

4. The annual rental shall be $60,000 and the inception date of the lease transaction is December 31.

5. The purchase price or fair market value of the equipment is $200,000.

6. The expected fair market value of the equipment at the end of the lease term is $30,000, as estimated by the lessor at the inception of the lease arrangement.

7. The lessor will require a $5,000 refundable security deposit from the lessee. This amount will be held by the lessor throughout the term of the lease and returned to the lessee at the end of the lease term if there is no reason to use it for default reasons. The lessor will not pay the lessee any monies for the use of these funds.

8. A $ 1,000 nonrefundable commitment fee is to be received by the lessor from the lessee.

9. A $2,500 brokerage fee is to be paid by the lessor to a third party as compensation for its bringing this transaction to the lessor.

10. General and administrative costs have been allocated to the lease along with the initial direct costs of $4,000. First-year general and administrative costs are $3,000 and have a 5% inflation factor built in.

11. Tax benefits are assumed to result fully in tax savings.

The "interest" cost to the lessee is the first type of yield calculation to be performed. The lessee "cost" is calculated because a lease transaction does not contain a stated interest rate or cost of money, as a lease is a usage transaction and not a money-financing transaction. The lessor is providing the use of equipment and not the lending of money to the lessee to be used for whatever purpose it desires.

From the lessee's perspective, it is gaining the use of $200,000 of equipment for four years and at the end of four years it has a number of options which may be exercised at its discretion. If the lessee returns the equipment to the lessor at the end of the initial lease term, then it would have the use of $200,000 for four years at a cost of $60,000, payments in arrears for the four-year period. The "interest" cost of money would be 7.71 percent. If the lessee were to purchase the equipment at the end of the four-year term for the lessor's estimated fair market value of $30,000, the "interest" cost of money would be 12.29%. If the lessee were to renew the equipment lease at the end of the four-year term, it would not be possible to calculate an "interest" cost of money to the lessor, because the terms of the renewal are not yet known, even if the renewal amount of $30,000 were to be known.

Both the 7.71% and 12.29% calculations are pretax. From the perspective of the lessee, any aftertax calculations would be based on a number of assumptions and are really not relevant to an understanding of this transaction.

The remainder of the calculations in this chapter are from the lessor perspective and are done from both a pretax and aftertax perspective. The calculations are numerous and it can readily be seen why confusion often reigns when trying to compare yields in lease transactions. One must understand what elements of cash flow are included when arriving at a particular stated yield and whether the calculation is pretax or aftertax. To fully understand aftertax calculations, one must also understand the leverage or gearing of the lessor and whether the transactions have been funded on a pooled or match-funded basis, the pretax cost of debt to the lessor, and whether the rate is fixed throughout the transaction or is adjusted at times throughout the lease term in accordance with some borrowing agreement in place for the lessor. The corporate tax rate and the timing of when taxes are remitted enter into a fine tuning of any calculation, and the desired return on equity contributed funds plays perhaps the most important role of all these variables.

Pretax lessor calculations would be as follows:

1. *Stream or street rate.* This calculation only takes into account the cost of the equipment to the lessor and any noncancelable payment amounts. Because the residual amount is anticipated but not absolutely known (unknown to the lessee), it would be the same as making a $200,000 investment and receiving $60,000 per year in arrears for the use of this invested amount. This would be a return of 7.71% and compares with the same amount as calculated by the lessee previously.

2. *Stream rate including residual.* This calculation includes the expected, but unguaranteed, residual amount of $30,000. When the residual is included in the calculation, then the lessor yield would be 12.29% and would be equivalent to the similar calculation of the lessee as performed previously.

3. *Pretax payback.* Both the stream rate and stream rate with residual calculations would indicate a payback period of 3.33 years. This does not take into account any adjustment for the time value of money. A time-adjusted payback period could be calculated if one were to assume some hurdle rate or cost of funds to the lessor. For purposes of this chapter, this calculation is not performed, but could be readily accomplished if some hurdle rate were to be brought into focus.

4. *An all-inclusive pretax return on asset yield.* This amount would include all of the pretax cash flows and would be based on when the cash is expected to change hands. This would take into account all known and expected cash flows to be received by the lessor, but does not take into account the tax benefits to be received and utilized by the lessor. In our example, the cash flows would occur as follows:

Initial or inception:

($200,000)	Equipment cost
(2,500)	Brokerage fee
(4,000)	Initial direct costs
1,000	Nonrefundable fee
5,000	Refundable security deposit
($200,500)	Net outflow at inception

During the term of the transaction:

Three payments of $60,000 per year

At termination:

$60,000	Final payment amount
30,000	Purchase option amount
(5,000)	Security deposit refund
$85,000	Net termination inflow

When taking into account all of these cash flows and the timing of when they would occur, the yield to the lessor is 11.47%. This is close to the 12.29% amount previously calculated, but includes all cash flows. As must be noted, this is a lower value than the stream rate including the residual.

5. *Net, pretax yield.* This calculation takes into account all of the cash flows as shown in item 4 with the addition of the general and administrative costs. The following illustration shows the timing of the cash flows and results in a pretax yield to the lessor of 9.25%. The 9.25% value is calculated by determining the internal rate of return for the cash flow amounts for each year of the transaction.

	0	1	2	3	4
Rental payments	0	60,000	60,000	60,000	60,000
Commitment fee	1,000				
Initial direct costs	(4,000)	0	0	0	0
Brokerage fee	(2,500)				
G&A	0	(3,000)	(3,150)	(3,308)	(3,473)
Residual	0	0	0	0	30,000
Security deposit	(5,000)	0	0	0	(5,000)
Deduct: cost of equipment	(200,000)	0	0	0	0
TOTAL	(200,500)	57,000	56,850	56,692	81,527

f IRR = 9.25

6. *Net, aftertax yield.* This calculation takes into account the cash flows included in the previous calculations and then includes the impact of recovering the lessor's investment through tax depreciation. It is seen that this net, aftertax yield is 7.00%. Some analysts will arrive at the aftertax yield by multiplying the pretax yield of 9.25% by the reciprocal of the tax rate, or 65%. If this were done (9.25 times 0.65), the resultant yield would be 6.01%. As can be seen when calculating the internal rate of return for the final cash flows, the yield is 7.00%. The difference is due to the timing of the cash flows, which is not taken into account when performing the 6.01% calculation.

	0	1	2	3	4
Rental payments	0	60,000	60,000	60,000	60,000
Commitment fee	1,000	0	0	0	0
Initial direct costs	(4,000)	0	0	0	0
Brokerage fee	(2,500)	0	0	0	0
G&A	0	(3,000)	(3,150)	(3,308)	(3,473)
Depreciation	(40,000)	(64,000)	(38,400)	(23,040)	(34,560)
Residual	0	0	0	0	30,000
Pretax income	(45,500)	(7,000)	18,450	33,652	51,967
Taxes @ 35%	15,925	2,450	(6,458	(11,778)	(18,188)
A-T income	(29,575)	(4,550)	11,993	21,874	33,779
Add: depreciation	40,000	64,000	38,400	23,040	34,560
Security deposit	5,000	0	0	0	0
Deduct: cost of equipment	(200,000)	0	0	0	0
TOTAL	(184,575)	59,450	50,393	44,914	63,339

7. *Return on equity.* This final calculation is found by making assumptions as to the method of funding employed by the lessor which, in this example, assumes that the lessor wishes the lease. Also, the leverage employed by the lessor is 80% debt and 20% equity. The pretax interest cost on borrowed funds is 9% and the tax rate of the lessor throughout the life of the transaction will be 35%. The return on equity for the lessor based on the cash flows calculated in 6 and adjusted for the cost of debt and including the repayment of borrowed funds is 11.60%. This amount is found by deducting the aftertax cost of debt from the aftertax cost of capital as calculated in 6.00 or 7.00%. The aftertax cost of debt to the lessor is found by multiplying the pretax cost of debt times the quantity (one minus the tax rate or 0.65) times the 0.8 debt leverage factor. This is found to be 4.68%.

When this amount is deducted from aftertax cost of capital of 7.00%, the cost of equity is determined to be 2.32%. When this is divided by the 0.2 equity leverage factor, the return on equity to the lessor is determined as 11.60%.

Net Aftertax Cash Flows

0	1	2	3	4
(184,575)	59,450	50,393	44,914	63,339

80% Debt = 147,660
20% Equity = 36,915

Year One

147,660 x 0.09 = 13,289 x 0.65 =   8,638 A-T Return on Debt
36,915 x 11.60 =   4,282 A-T Return on Equity
                                          12,920
.8 x 9(.65) = 4.68   (59,450) CF
.2 x 11.60 = 2.32   46,530
              7.00   x .8
                                          37,224 Debt
                                          9,306 Equity

Year Two

147,660 - 37,224 = 110,436 x 0.09 = 9.939 x 0.65 =   6,461 A-T Return on Debt
36,915 - 9,306 = 27,609 x 0.1160 =   3,203 A-T Return on Equity
                                                        9,664
                                                       (50,393) CF
                                                        40,729
                                                         x .8
                                                        32,583 Debt
                                                        8,146 Equity

Year Three

110,436 - 32,583 = 77,853 x 0.09 = 7,007 x 0.65 =   4,554 A-T ROD
27,609 - 8,246 = 19,463 x 0.1160 =   2,258 A-T ROE
                                                       6,812
                                                      (44,914) CF
                                                       38,102
                                                        x .8
                                                       30,482 Debt
                                                       7,620 Equity

Year Four

77,853 - 30,482 = 47,371 x 0.09 = 4,263 x 0.65 =   2,771 ROD
                   [x]
19,463 - 7,620 = 11,843 x 0.1160 =   1,374 ROE
                   [y]   4,145
                                                      (63,339) CF
                                                       59,194
                                                        x .8

[x] 16 Δ due to rounding.   [x] 47,355 Debt
[y] 4 Δ due to rounding.   [y] 11,839 Equity

20A.12 LEASE FORM.

AGREEMENT NO. _____

EQUIPMENT LEASE

LESSOR: _____   LESSEE: _____

_____   _____
(STREET ADDRESS)   (STREET ADDRESS)

_____   _____
(CITY, STATE, AND ZIP)   (CITY, STATE, AND ZIP)

Description of Leased Equipment

NEW/USED	QUANTITY	MAKE and DESCRIPTION	SERIAL NO.

EQUIPMENT LOCATION: ❑ SAME AS ABOVE   ❑ OTHER: (address) _____

LEASE PAYMENT TERMS

MONTHS	AMOUNTS
TOTAL LEASE TERM # _____ MONTHS	MONTHLY RENTAL AMOUNT: _____
	PLUS USE TAX, IF ANY
ADVANCE RENTALS PAID # _____ MONTHS	TOTAL RENTALS PAID
	IN ADVANCE: _____
	RENTAL x # PAID

TERMS AND CONDITIONS OF LEASE

LESSEE HEREBY WARRANTS AND REPRESENTS THAT THE EQUIPMENT WILL BE USED FOR BUSINESS PURPOSES, AND NOT FOR PERSONAL, FAMILY, HOUSEHOLD, OR AGRICULTURAL PURPOSES. LESSEE ACKNOWLEDGES THAT LESSOR AND ITS ASSIGNS HAVE RELIED UPON THIS REPRESENTATION IN ENTERING INTO THIS LEASE.

1. LESSEE ACKNOWLEDGES THAT LESSOR IS NOT THE MANUFAC-TURER OF THE EQUIPMENT, NOR MANUFACTURER'S AGENT AND LESSEE REPRESENTS THAT LESSEE HAS SELECTED THE EQUIPMENT LEASED HEREUNDER BASED UPON LESSEE'S JUDGMENT

(Continued on next pages.)

THE UNDERSIGNED AGREE TO ALL THE TERMS AND CONDITIONS SET FORTH ABOVE AND ON THE REVERSE SIDE HEREOF, AND IN WITNESS

WHEREOF, HEREBY EXECUTES THIS LEASE AND CERTIFIES THAT THE UNDERSIGNED IS DULY AUTHORIZED TO EXECUTE SAME, ON BEHALF OF OR AS THE LESSEE AND THAT HE HAS RECEIVED AN EXECUTED COPY OF THIS LEASE.

Executed this _____ day of _____, 19__.

LESSOR: _____   LESSEE: _____

By: _____   BY: _____
                                                                                                TITLE

TITLE: _____   BY: _____
                                                                                                TITLE

PRIOR TO HAVING REQUESTED THE LEASE. THE EQUIPMENT LEASED HEREUNDER IS OF A DESIGN, SIZE, FITNESS, AND CAPACITY SELECTED BY LESSEE AND LESSEE IS SATISFIED THAT THE SAME IS SUITABLE AND FIT FOR ITS INTENDED PURPOSES. LESSEE FURTHER AGREES THAT LESSOR HAS MADE AND MAKES NO REPRESENTATIONS OR WARRANTIES OF WHATSOEVER NATURE, DIRECTLY OR INDIRECTLY, EXPRESSED OR IMPLIED, INCLUDING BUT NOT LIMITED TO ANY REPRESENTATIONS OR WARRANTIES WITH RESPECT TO SUITABILITY, DURABILITY, FITNESS FOR USE AND MERCHANTABILITY OF ANY SUCH EQUIPMENT, THE PURPOSES AND USES OF THE LESSEE, OR OTHERWISE. LESSEE SPECIFICALLY WAIVES ALL RIGHTS TO MAKE CLAIM AGAINST LESSOR HEREIN FOR BREACH OF ANY WARRANTY OF ANY KIND WHATSOEVER. LESSOR HEREBY PASSES TO LESSEE ALL WARRANTIES, IF ANY, RECEIVED BY LESSOR BY VIRTUE OF ITS OWNERSHIP OF THE EQUIPMENT. LESSOR SHALL NOT BE LIABLE TO LESSEE FOR ANY LOSS, DAMAGE, OR EXPENSE OF ANY KIND OR NATURE CAUSED DIRECTLY OR INDIRECTLY BY ANY EQUIPMENT LEASED HEREUNDER FOR THE USE OR MAINTENANCE THEREOF, OR FOR THE FAILURE OF OPERATIONS THEREOF, OR BY ANY INTERRUPTION OF SERVICE OR LOSS OF USE THEREOF OR FOR ANY LOSS OF BUSINESS OR ANY OTHER DAMAGE WHATSOEVER AND HOWSOEVER CAUSED. NO DEFECT OR UNFITNESS OF THE EQUIPMENT SHALL RELIEVE LESSEE OF THE OBLIGATION TO PAY RENT, OR ANY OTHER OBLIGATION UNDER THIS AGREEMENT OR ITS ASSIGNEE.

1. LEASE: Lessor hereby leases to Lessee and Lessee hereby hires and takes from Lessor the personal property described above and on any attached supplemental "schedule A" (hereinafter, with all replacement parts, additions, repairs, and accessories incorporated therein and/or affixed thereto, referred to as "Equipment").

2. TERM AND RENT: This Lease is non-cancelable for the term stated above and shall commence upon the Date of Acceptance of the equipment and shall continue for the period specified as the "term" stated

above. If one or more advance rentals are payable, the total amount of such advance rentals shall be set forth in the Advance Rental Payment(s) section above and shall be due upon acceptance by the Lessor of this lease. Advance rentals, when received by Lessor, shall be applied to the first rent payment for the Equipment and the balance of the advance rental shall be applied to the final rental payment or payments for said Equipment. In no event shall any advance rent or any other rent payments be refunded to Lessee.

3. Equipment is and shall at all times remain, the property of Lessor, and Lessee shall have no right, title, or interest therein, except as herein set forth, and no right to purchase or otherwise acquire title to or ownership of any of the equipment. If Lessor supplies Lessee with labels indicating that the equipment is owned by Lessor, Lessee shall affix such labels to and keep them in a prominent place on the equipment. Lessee hereby authorizes Lessor to insert in this lease the serial numbers and other identification data of equipment when determined by Lessor. Lessor is hereby appointed by Lessee as its true and lawful attorney in respect to being hereby authorized by Lessee, at Lessee's expense, to cause this lease, or any statement or other instrument in respect of this lease showing the interest of Lessor in the equipment, including Uniform Commercial Code Financing Statements, to be filed or recorded and refiled and re-recorded, and grants Lessor the right to execute Lessee's name thereto. Lessee agrees to execute and deliver any statement or instrument requested by Lessor for such purpose, and agrees to pay or reimburse Lessor for any searches, filings, recordings, or stamp fees or taxes arising from the filing or recording any such instrument or statement.

4. Lessee, at Lessee's own cost and expense, shall keep the equipment in good repair, condition, and working order and shall furnish all parts, mechanism, devices, and servicing required therefor and shall not materially alter the equipment without the consent of Lessor.

5. Lessee hereby assumes and shall bear the entire risk of loss for the theft, loss, damage, or destruction of the equipment, from any and every cause whatsoever. No such loss or damage shall impair any obligation of Lessee under this Agreement which shall continue in full force and effect. In the event of such loss or damage and irrespective of, but applying full credit for payment from any insurance coverage, Lessee shall, at its own cost and expense at the option of Lessor: (a) place the same in good repair, condition, and working order; or (b) replace the same with similar equipment of equal value; or (c) pay all the sums due and owing under this Agreement, computed from the date of such loss or damage, in which case this Agreement shall terminate, except for Lessee's duties under paragraph 9, as of the date such payment is received by Lessor.

6. Lessor shall have no tort liability to Lessee related to the equipment, and Lessee shall indemnify, defend, and hold Lessor harmless against any liabilities, claims, actions, and expenses, including court costs and legal expenses incurred by or asserted against Lessor in any way relating to the manufacture, purchase, ownership, delivery, lease, possession, use, operation, condition, return, or other disposition of the equipment by Lessor or Lessee or otherwise related to this lease, including any claim alleging latent or other defect under the doctrine of strict liability or otherwise; any other claim under the doctrine of strict liability; and any claim for patent, trademark, service mark, or copyright infringement. Each party shall give the other notice of any event covered hereby promptly following learning thereof.

7. Lessee shall keep the equipment insured against all risks of loss or damage from every cause whatsoever. Lessee shall maintain (a) actual cash value all risk insurance on the equipment, naming Lessor as <u>LOSS PAYEE</u> and (b) single limit public liability and property damage insurance of not less than $300,000 per occurrence, or such greater or lesser amount as Lessor may from time to time request on notice to Lessee, naming Lessee as Named Insured and Lessor as <u>ADDITIONAL INSURED</u> and Lessee shall be liable for all deductible portions of all required insurance. All said insurance shall be in form and amount and with companies satisfactory to Lessor. All insurance for loss or damage shall provide that losses, if any, shall be payable to Lessor, and all such liability insurance shall be in the joint names of Lessor and Lessee. Lessee shall pay the premiums therefor and deliver to Lessor the policies of insurance or duplicates thereof, or other evidence satisfactory to Lessor of such insurance coverage. Each insurer shall agree, by endorsement upon the policy or policies issued by it or by independent instrument furnished to Lessor, that it will give Lessor <u>10 DAYS</u> written notice prior to the effective date of any alteration or cancellation of such policy. The proceeds of such insurance payable as a result of loss of or damage to the equipment shall be applied at the option of Lessor, as set out in paragraph 6. Lessee hereby irrevocably appoints Lessor as Lessee's attorney-in-fact to make claim for, receive payment of, and execute and endorse all documents, checks, or drafts received in payment for loss or damage under any said insurance policies. In case of the failure of Lessee to procure or maintain said insurance or to comply with any other provision of this Agreement, Lessor shall have the right but shall not be obligated, to effect such insurance or compliance on behalf of Lessee. In that event, all money spent by and expenses of Lessor shall have the right but shall not be obligated, to effect such insurance or compliance on behalf of Lessee. In that event, all money spent by and expenses of Lessor in effecting such insurance or compliance shall be deemed to be additional rent, and shall be paid by Lessee to Lessor with the next monthly payment of rent.

8. Lessee shall pay directly, or to Lessor, all license fees, registration fees, assessments, and taxes which may now or hereafter be imposed upon the ownership, sale (if authorized), possession, or use of the equipment, excepting only those based on Lessor's income, and shall keep the equipment free and clear of all levies, liens, or encumbrances arising therefrom. Lessee shall make all filings as to and pay when due all property taxes on the equipment, on behalf of Lessor, with all appropriate governmental agencies, except where Lessor is notified by the taxing jurisdiction that Lessor must pay the tax direct, and within not more than 60 days after the due date of such filing to send Lessor a confirmation of such filing. If Lessee fails to pay any said fees, assessments, or taxes, Lessor shall have the right, but not the obligation, to pay the same and such amount, including penalties and costs, which shall be repayable to Lessor with the next installment of rent and if not so paid shall be the same as failure to pay any installment of rent due hereunder. Lessor shall not be responsible for contesting any valuation of or tax imposed on the equipment, but may do so strictly as an accommodation to Lessee and shall not be liable or accountable to Lessee therefor.

9. Time is of the essence in this agreement and no waiver by Lessor of any breach or default shall constitute a wavier of any additional or subsequent breach or default by Lessor nor shall it be a wavier of any of Lessor's rights. If any rental payment shall be unpaid for more than TEN (10) DAYS after the due date thereof. Lessor shall have the right to add and collect a reasonable late charge of <u>five percent (5%)</u> or a lesser amount if established by any state or federal statute applicable thereto, plus interest at the maximum rate permitted by law together with any other expense necessarily incurred by reason of such non-payment and Lessor may exercise any one or more of the remedies set forth in paragraph 12.

10. An event of default shall occur if: (a) Lessee fails to pay when due any installment of rent; (b) Lessee shall fail to perform or observe any covenant, condition, or agreement to be performed or observed by it hereunder; (c) Lessee ceases doing business as a going concern, makes an assignment for the benefit of creditors, admits in writing its inability to pay its debts as they become due, files a voluntary petition in bankruptcy, is adjudicated a bankrupt or an insolvent, files a petition seeking for itself any reorganization, arrangement, composition readjustment, liquidation, dissolution, or similar arrangement under any present or future statute, law, or regulation or files an answer admitting the material allegations of a petition filed against it in any such proceeding, consents to or acquiesces in the appointment of a trustee, receiver, or liquidator of it or all or any substantial part of its assets or properties, or if it or its shareholders shall take any action looking to its dissolution or liquidation; (d) within 60 days after the appointment without Lessee's consent or acquiescence of any trustee, receiver, or liquidator of it or of all or any substantial part of its assets and properties, such appointment shall not

be vacated, or (e) Lessee attempts to remove, sell, transfer, encumber, part with possession, or sublet the equipment or any item thereof.

11. Upon Lessee's default, the rights and duties of the parties shall be as set forth in this paragraph: (a) Acceleration: Lessor may revoke Lessee's privilege of paying the total rent installments and, upon Lessor's demand, the portion of the total rent then remaining unpaid plus all other sums due and unpaid shall promptly be paid to Lessor. (b) Retaking: at Lessor's option, Lessor may demand and Lessee must promptly deliver the equipment to Lessor. If Lessee does not so deliver, Lessee shall make the equipment available for retaking and authorizes Lessor, its employees, and nominees to enter the premises of the Lessee and other premises (insofar as Lessee can permit) for the purpose of retaking. Lessor shall not be obligated to give notice or to obtain legal process for retaking. In the event of retaking, Lessee expressly waives all rights to possession and all claims of injuries suffered through or loss caused by retaking. (c) Disposition: Lessor may sell or release the equipment and Lessee agrees to pay any deficiency resulting from the sale or releasing of the equipment. To the extent of Lessee's liability, all proceeds of the sale or releasing, or both, less all expenses incurred in retaking the goods, all expenses incurred in the enforcement of this lease, all damages that Lessor shall have sustained by reason of Lessee's default, including those incurred by obtaining a deficiency judgment and a reasonable attorney fee, shall be credited to Lessee as and when received by Lessor. Sums in excess of Lessee's liability shall belong to Lessor. (d) Unpaid Rent: The provisions of this paragraph shall not prejudice Lessor's right to recover or prove damages for unpaid rent accrued prior to default. Lessor may seek to enforce the terms of this Agreement through any court of competent jurisdiction and Lessor may seek relief other than as specified in this Agreement to the extent such relief is not inconsistent with the terms of this Agreement. Lessee agrees to pay reasonable attorney's fees and court costs incurred by Lessor in the enforcement of the terms of this Agreement. In any instance where Lessee and Lessor have entered into more than one contract, Lessee's default under any one contract shall be a default under all contracts and Lessor shall be entitled to enforce appropriate remedies for Lessee's default under each such contract.

12. Lessee shall not sell, assign, sublet, pledge, mortgage, or otherwise encumber or suffer a lien upon or against any interest in this agreement or the equipment or remove the equipment from the place of installation set forth herein, unless Lessee obtains the written consent of Lessor which consent shall not be unreasonably withheld. Lessee's interest herein is not assignable or transferable by operation of the law. Lessee agrees not to waive its right to use and possess the equipment in favor of any party other than Lessor and further agrees not to abandon the equipment to any party other than Lessor. Lessor may inspect the equipment

during normal business hours and enter the premises where the equipment may be located for such purpose. Lessee shall comply with all laws, regulations, and orders relating to this Agreement and the use, operation, or maintenance of the equipment.

13. All rights of Lessor hereunder and to the equipment may be assigned, pledged, or otherwise disposed of, in whole or in part, without notice to Lessee, but subject to the rights of Lessee hereunder. Lessee shall acknowledge receipt of any notice of assignment in writing and shall thereafter pay any amounts designated in such notice as directed therein. If Lessor assigns this lease or any interest herein, no default by Lessor hereunder or under any other agreement between Lessor and Lessee shall excuse performance by Lessee of any provision hereof. In the event of such default by Lessor, Lessee shall pursue any rights on account thereof solely against Lessor and shall pay the full amount of the assigned rental payments to the assignee. No such assignee shall be obligated to perform any duty, covenant, or condition required to be performed by Lessor under the terms of this lease.

14. This Agreement cannot be canceled or terminated by Lessee on or after the date the equipment is delivered to and accepted by Lessee. If Lessee cancels or terminates this Agreement prior to delivery or acceptance of the equipment, Lessee shall pay to Lessor (a) the value (at cost) of all equipment ordered or purchased by Lessor prior to Lessee's termination or cancellation, (b) all of Lessor's out-of-pocket expenses, and (c) a sum equal to 1% of the total rents for the lease term as liquidated damages, the exact sum of which would be extremely difficult to determine, to reasonably compensate Lessor for credit review, document preparation, ordering equipment, and other administrative expenses.

15. Upon expiration of the lease term, Lessee will immediately retum the equipment in as good a condition as received, less normal wear, tear, and depreciation, to Lessor's branch office which is nearest to the place of installation or to such other reasonable place as is designated by Lessor. The equipment shall be carefully crated, shipped freight prepaid, and properly insured. Should Lessee not return the equipment at the end of the lease term, Lessee shall continue to pay rent to Lessor in the sum and on the due dates set out in this Agreement as a month-to-month lease term until returned by Lessee or demand therefor is made by Lessor.

16. This Lease Agreement consisting of the foregoing and the reverse side hereof, correctly sets forth the entire agreement between Lessor and Lessee. No agreements or understandings shall be binding on either of the parties hereto unless set forth in writing signed by the parties. The term "Lessee" as used herein shall mean and include any and all Lessees who sign hereunder, each of whom shall be jointly and severally bound thereby. No representations, warranties, or promises, guarantees, or

agreements, oral or written, express or implied, have been made by either party hereto with respect to this lease or the equipment other than set forth herein. No agent or employee of the supplier is authorized to bind Lessor to this or to waive or alter any terms or conditions printed herein or add any provision hereto. This Lease Agreement is binding upon the legal representatives and successors in interest of the Lessee. Lessee shall provide Lessor with such interim or annual financial statements as Lessor may reasonably request. In addition, Lessee warrants that the application, statements, and financial reports submitted by it to the Lessor are material inducements to the granting of this lease and that any material misrepresentations shall constitute a default hereunder. If any portion of this contract is deemed invalid, it shall not affect the balance of this Agreement.

DELIVERY AND ACCEPTANCE NOTICE

The undersigned Lessee hereby acknowledges receipt of the equipment described below or on any attached schedule (the "Equipment") fully installed and in good working condition, and Lessee hereby accepts the Equipment after full inspection thereof as satisfactory for all purposes of the above-referenced lease executed by Lessee with the Lessor. Lessee certifies that Lessor has fully and satisfactorily performed all covenants and conditions to be performed by Lessor under the Lease and has delivered the Equipment selected solely by Lessee in accordance with Lessee's directions.

LESSEE AGREES THAT THE LESSOR HAS MADE AND MAKES NO REPRESENTATIONS OR WARRANTIES OF ANY KIND OR NATURE, DIRECTLY OR INDIRECTLY, EXPRESS OR IMPLIED, AS TO ANY MATTER WHATSOEVER, INCLUDING THE SUITABILITY OF SUCH EQUIPMENT, ITS DURABILITY, ITS FITNESS FOR ANY PARTICULAR PURPOSE, ITS MERCHANTABILITY, ITS CONDITION, AND/OR ITS QUALITY, AND AS BETWEEN LESSEE AND LESSOR OR LESSOR'S ASSIGNEE, LESSEE LEASES THE EQUIPMENT "AS IS" AND LESSEE AFFIRMS THAT IT HAS NO DEFENSES OR COUNTECLAIMS AGAINST LESSOR IN CONNECTION WITH THE LEASE.

———————————————————
(Lessee)

Date Equipment Accepted: —————— By: ————————————————

20A.13 SUMMARY.   Leasing over the past several decades has become a very complicated topic, one that affects the budgetary process in a multitude of ways. The Financial Accounting Standards Board has specified the treatment of leases on balance sheets, income statements, and cash flow statements. Additionally, internal analysis, such as lease versus purchase, pushes the treatment of leasing well beyond GAAP considerations. In today's international financial milieu, the managerial expert must cross the financial Rubicon and extend the frontiers of leasing, budgeting, and finance well into heretofore uncharted domains.

SOURCES AND SUGGESTED REFERENCES

Allison, "New Rules Increase Exposure of Lessors to Tax on Rents that Will Not Be Received Until Later," *Journal of Taxation,* Vol. 64, at 8 (1986).

Amembal, Halladay, and Isom, *The Handbook of Equipment Leasing*, Publishers Press, 1988.

Amembal and Halladay, *A Guide to Accounting for Leases*, Publishers Press, 1992.

Auerback, "A Transactional Approach to Lease Analysis," 13 *Hofstra Law Review* 309 (1985).

Carson, Roger L., "Leasing, Asset Lives and Uncertainty: A Practitioner's Comments," *Financial Management*, Summer 1987.

Carter and Wight, "New Tax Law Makes Major Changes to the Foreign Tax Credit Limitation," *Journal of Taxation*, Vol. 66 at 140 (1987).

Delessio and Shenkman, "Improvement to Leased Property: Maximizing the Tax Benefits Regardless of Who Makes Them," *Taxation for Accountants*, Vol. 33, at 256 (1984).

Financial Accounting Standards Board, *Financial Accounting Standards Board Statement No. 13*, "Accounting for Leases" (November 1976).

Knight, Ray, and Lee G. Knight, "True Leases Versus Disguised Installment and Sales/Purchases," *The Tax Adviser*, March 1987.

Naughton, "International Leverage and Facility Leasing in the United States," *NYU Institute of Federal Taxation*, Vol. 44, ch. 47 (1986).

Rosen, Howard, *Leasing Law in the European Community*, Euromoney Books, 1991.

Shulman and Cox, *Leasing for Profit*, AMA, 1987.

Weisner and Massoglia, "Sec. 467 Rental Agreements: Lessors and Lessees Must Watch Their Step," *Tax Advisor*, Vol. 16 at 392 (1985).

UNDERSTANDING FOREIGN EXCHANGE TRANSACTIONS (New)

Françoise Spares-Kemp

Credit Suisse

CONTENTS

23A.1 FOREIGN EXCHANGE RATES	**1**	**23A.2 IMPACT OF FOREIGN EXCHANGE ON OPERATING EXPOSURE MANAGEMENT** **8**
(a) Exchange Rate	1	
(i) Spot Rate	1	**SOURCES AND**
(b) Forward Operations	2	**SUGGESTED REFERENCES** **11**
(c) Swap Operations	3	
(d) Derivatives Operations	4	
(e) Forecasting and Foreign Exchange Risk	5	

23A.1 FOREIGN EXCHANGE RATES. As multinational companies become involved with payables and receivables denominated in many different currencies, product and service shipments across national borders, and subsidiaries operating in different political jurisdictions, they face an additional set of problems than the firm with a purely domestic operation. The basic issues—budget control, cash management, intracompany transfers, and capital budgeting—face all multinational companies. These companies have responded by becoming increasingly sophisticated in international finance and foreign exchange. This chapter attempts to give a summary description of these topics.

(a) Exchange Rate. The *exchange rate* is the price for which a currency can be bought or sold in terms of another currency. Most of the time the value of the exchange rate is decided by free market forces, but occasionally there is central bank intervention in an attempt to ensure that currencies do not depreciate or appreciate excessively.

(i) Spot Rate. A *spot foreign exchange deal* is one made for settlement in two working days. Under normal conditions, a spot deal done on Monday is settled on Wednesday.

A *working day* is defined as one in which both banks are open for business in both settlement countries; except that if the deal is done against the U.S. dollar, if the first of the two days is a holiday in the United States, but not in the other settlement country, that day is also counted as a working day. *Direct quotation* of foreign exchange rates takes the form of variable amounts of domestic currency against a fixed amount of foreign currency. *Indirect quotation,* conversely, takes the form of fixed amounts of domestic currency against varying amounts of foreign currency. In the United States, both types of quotations are used. For domestic business, as well as on the commodity exchanges, U.S. terms are used, that is, direct quotation (e.g., DM 1 = US $0.6800). For international business and increasingly for domestic business too, U.S. banks use European terms or reciprocal indirect quotation (e.g., US $1 = DM 1.4706). Whatever system is used, when two cross-border interests wish to transact foreign currency business, one of them will have to apply an indirect quotation when dealing in the other's currency.

A foreign exchange rate is called a *cross-rate* when the national currency is not party to the transaction. A Paris bank buying or selling Deutschemarks against the U.S. dollar is using a cross-rate. A New York bank buying or selling Deutschemarks against French francs is also using a cross-rate.

Example: Customer wants to buy DM 10,000,000 against French francs. Because all currencies are quoted against the dollar, we have to work it out with the respective dollar rates, which at the moment may be:

$$\text{\$/DM} = 1.4750 - 1.4760$$
$$\text{\$/FF} = 5.1280 - 5.1305$$

We get our selling rate for DM against French francs with this calculation:

$$\text{\$/DM} = 1.4750 - 1.4760$$
$$\text{divided by}$$
$$\text{\$/FF} = 5.1280 - 5.1305$$
$$\frac{\text{Sell Ffr } 5.1305}{\text{Buy DM } 1.4750} = \text{Ffr } 3.4783$$

(b) Forward Operations. A *forward exchange contract* is an agreement between a bank and another party to exchange one currency for another at some future date. The rate at which the exchange is to be made, the delivery date, and the amounts involved are fixed at the time of agreement. Such a contract is distinguished from a foreign exchange futures contract in that a *futures contract* is a contract between two parties for the exchange of a certain amount of foreign currency at a future date, with the date and the amount usually standardized.

Theoretically, the forward (or futures) price for a currency can be identical to the spot price. Almost always, however, the forward (futures) price in practice is either higher (premium) or lower (discount) than the spot price. Suppose a quoted currency is more expensive in the future than it is now in terms of the base currency; the quoted currency is thus said to be at a premium in the forward market, relative to the base currency. Conversely, the base currency may be said to stand at a discount relative to the quoted currency.

Taking the U.S. dollar as the base currency and the French franc as the quoted currency, we have a spot rate of US $ 1 = Ffr 5.1120. The dollar buys fewer French francs in one year than it does today and thus the dollar is at a discount to the French franc. Conversely, the French franc is at a premium to the U.S. dollar.

The size of the dollar discount or French franc premium is the difference between 5.1300 and 5.1120, that is, 1.80 centimes. This is normally quoted as 180 points. To arrive at the forward price, the French franc premium or dollar discount must be subtracted from the spot. The spot rate might be quoted as 5.1300/50 and the one-year discount at 180/130. In other words, if the trader is buying U.S dollars forward, he or she will charge a discount of 180 points, but if he or she is selling, he or she will give away only a 130-point discount.

A price of 180/130 indicates a premium for the quoted currency (the French franc) in the forward market and a discount for the base currency (the U.S. dollar). However, a price of 130/180 would indicate a discount for the quoted and a premium for the base. In summary,

$$\text{High/Low} = \text{Subtract points}$$
$$\text{Low/High} = \text{Add points}$$

The use of points in forward quotations is convenient because the points tend to move much less quickly than the spots, and because it is the points that are relevant in the forward and swap markets.

The forward swap points (discount or premium) always tend to be equal to the interest differential in the Euromarket. When the markets are not disturbed by monetary or political unrest, the bulk of activity in the forward market originates from money market activities and (to a lesser extent) commercial operations. Interest rate levels in the Euromarket for the various currencies will be the determinant of forward points or swap points.

(c) Swap Operations. In general, a *swap* is an exchange of one currency for another on one day matched by a reverse exchange on a later day. Swaps have two basic uses:

1. To switch a deal from one currency to another, and back again, on a hedged basis.
2. To move a given currency deal forward or backward in time.

The formula to derive swap (or forward) points is:

$$\text{Swap points} = \text{Spot rate} \times (\text{currency interest rate} - \text{U.S. interest rate}) \times \text{no. of days/365}$$

Example:

$$\frac{12 \text{ months}}{\text{U.S. interest rate}} = \frac{\text{Bid}}{6.75} - \frac{\text{Offer}}{7.00}$$

$$\text{French interest rate} = 6.50 - 6.75$$

$$\text{Swap points} = 1.5300 \times (0.25) \times \frac{365}{365}$$

Swap points = 129 points premium for the French franc

The forward premium (or discount) on a currency relative to the dollar, expressed as a percentage of the spot rate, will tend to (about) equal the differential between interest rates available in that currency and dollar interest rates.

(d)   Derivatives Operations.   *Derivatives* is a term usually applied to futures, options, and interest rate and currency swaps. These are markets that are "derived" from other markets. They are all additional instruments to be used by a multinational for hedging and, when appropriate, for profit. To hedge is to reduce risk. A hedger transfers risk by temporarily offsetting a position in a cash market with a related position in a futures market.

Options have become a very useful tool in foreign exchange markets. They allow us the luxury of a one-way bet. We can bet that a rate will go up and make a profit from that—but if it comes down we don't lose. They are particularly useful for hedging cash flows when we feel uncertain about the future. They can also be used to take leveraged positions.

A *currency option* is an agreement between two parties. One party grants the other the right to buy or sell a currency under certain conditions. The counterparty pays a premium for the privilege of being able to buy or sell the instrument without committing to do so. There are two basic types of options: puts and calls. A *call option* gives the buyer the right to buy or "call" a specified amount of the underlying currency at the specified price during a specified period. The price at which the instrument may be bought is the *exercise price* or the *strike price*. The last day on which the option may be called or exercised is called the *expiry date* or the *maturity date*. A *put option* gives the buyer the right to sell or put to the writer a specified amount of the underlying currency at the strike price until the expiry date. Under an American option, the holder of the option has the right to exercise at any time before maturity. Under a European option, the holder may exercise it only at the time of expiration.

The growth of options contracts since the early 1980s has stimulated the development of new products and techniques for managing foreign exchange assets and liabilities. One recent development combines the features of the forward contract and option contract. Terms such as "break forward," "participating forward,"or "FOX" (forward with option exit) refer to forward contracts with an option to break out of the contract at a future date. In this case, the forward exchange rate includes an option premium for the right to break the forward contract. The incentive for such a contract comes from the desire of customers to have the insurance provided by a forward contract when the exchange rate moves against them and yet not to lose the potential for profit available with favorable exchange rate movements. The break-forward contract has several good features that do not exist with an option. For one thing, an option requires an up-front premium payment. Corporate treasurers may not have a budget for option premiums or may not have management approval for using options. The break-forward hides the option premium in the forward rate. Because the price at which the forward contract is broken is fixed in advance, the break-forward may be treated as a simple forward contract for tax and accounting purposes, whether the contract is broken or not.

One of the more difficult problems in hedging foreign exchange risk arises in bidding on contracts. The bidder submits a proposal to perform some task to a firm or government agency seeking to award a contract to the successful bidder. As there may be many other bidders, the bidding firms face the foreign exchange risk associated with the contract only if they, in fact, are awarded the contract. Suppose a particular bidder assesses only a 20 percent chance of winning the contract. Should it buy a forward contract or option today to hedge the foreign exchange risk it faces in the event it is the successful bidder? If substantial foreign exchange risk is involved for the successful bidder, then both the bidders and the contract awarder face a dilemma. The bids will not be as competitive with the outstanding foreign exchange risk as they would be if the exchange rate uncertainty were hedged.

One approach to this problem is the "Scout" contract. Midland Bank developed the Scout (share currency option under tender) as an option that is sold to the contract awarder, which then sells it to the successful bidder. The awarding agency now receives more competitive and, perhaps, a greater number of bids, because the bidders know that the foreign exchange hedge is arranged.

Over time, we are seeing a proliferation of new financial market products aimed at dealing with future transactions involving foreign exchange. If there is a corporate interest in customizing an option or forward arrangement to a specific type of transaction, an innovative bank will step in and offer a product.

(e)   Forecasting and Foreign Exchange Risk.   International business involves foreign exchange risk, because the value of transactions in different currencies will be sensitive to exchange rate changes. The appropriate strategy for the corporate treasurer and the individual speculator is at least partly determined by expectations of the future path of the exchange rate. As a result, exchange rate forecasts are an important part of the decision-making process of international investors.

One problem we encounter when trying to evaluate the effect of exchange rate changes on a multinational company arises in determining the appropriate concept of exposure to foreign exchange risk. Understanding exchange exposure is complicated by the multiplicity of definitions and interpretations of what constitutes foreign exchange risk for the company. For example, anticipated foreign exchange rate movements represent no risk, as they can be embodied in the corporate budget. (As an example, most of the impact of the devaluation of the Mexican peso can be anticipated and reflected in the company budget.) However, unanticipated currency changes are a source of risk, because they cannot be incorporated into the budgeting process.

The distinction between economic and financial risk is also important in understanding foreign exchange exposures. *Economic risk or exposure* is the danger that budgeted business expenses could become uncompetitive because the real purchasing power of a currency has risen to a point where competitors with costs in other currencies could gain a significant advantage.

All other exposure or risk is financial and can lead to losses realized in cash or unrealized losses, which show up in companies' balance sheets. Economic exposure management is part of the wider subjective corporate planning task, which includes estimating future cash flows over an arbitrary time horizon, using economic analysis. The finance and budgeting, marketing, production, and sourcing departments must all be involved in this process. These departments must all take a hard look at whether a sustained real rise, or drop, of a currency against the currencies of competitors will—adversely or positively—affect the company's competitive costs and, therefore, its sales, profit margins, and market share, which in turn will reduce or increase the return on the capital and revenue investment previously sunk in its present commercial activity. This forces the corporation to focus continuously on the specific nature of the business of each individual overseas subsidiary and allows no sweeping generalizations.

Furthermore, focusing on economic exposure is consistent with the overall corporate goal of maximizing cash flows or profits over time. In considering strategies for hedging budgeted cash flows, a company's options include changing foreign currency product prices and entering into foreign exchange contracts.

An exchange rate change will affect the U.S. company's dollar-denominated cash flows through two channels. First, changes in the foreign exchange rate will affect the dollar value of all relevant foreign currency denominated cash flows directly. For example, for a U.S. dollar-based company, the dollar value of future sales denominated in a foreign currency will decline when that currency depreciates against the U.S. dollar. Secondly, actions taken in response to changes in the exchange rate can affect the foreign currency value of these cash flows. These actions could take the form of changes in sales volume or sales prices. Foreign currency values of future sales would increase if (1) prices are raised to compensate for depreciation of the currency or (2) sales rise because of increased competitive advantage in the foreign market. In these instances, there is an automatic hedging mechanism which partially or totally eliminates the exposure. The combined impact of these two factors determines the ultimate overall impact of exchange rate changes on the dollar-denominated value of cash flows. When the two effects do not offset each other, the affected flows are said to be "exposed" to the particular foreign currency involved.

Forward market hedges are appropriate only when foreign currency prices cannot be changed immediately following a change in the exchange rate between the particular currency and the dollar. The forward market hedge thus provides protection against losses that occur between the time of the exchange rate change and the compensating price changes.

Prices changing to compensate for exchange rate changes is also a big marketing issue, and pricing policy considers many factors in addition to exchange rate movements. Volatility of exchange rate movements is another major consideration in pricing changes. If a depreciation currency begins to appreciate after prices have increased, the market share for that product could be threatened (or enhanced). Thus, exchange rate changes are financial in nature and frequently bear little relation in the short term to the local business environment. Trying to change prices as fast as exchange rates change is not advisable, and, in reality, raising prices that quickly is impossible. Forward market hedges can provide protection against losses while pricing decisions are evaluated and implemented. The ideal hedge considers the time each entity needs to effect these changes; only in this way can the maturity of the hedge be structured to maximize its benefits.

Having defined economic exchange exposure or risk, we can go on to identify others. *Transaction exchange exposure or risk* refers to gains and losses that arise from the settlement of transactions whose terms are stated in a foreign currency. Foreign exchange transactions may include:

1. Purchasing or selling on credit goods or services in foreign currencies
2. Borrowing or lending funds denominated in foreign currencies
3. Being a party to an unperformed forward foreign exchange contract
4. Acquiring assets or incurring liabilities denominated in foreign currencies.

Translation exposure (risk), often referred to as *accounting* or *FASB* (Financial Accounting Standards Board) *exposure (risk),* arises from the need to report consolidated worldwide operations according to predetermined accounting rules. Assets, liabilities, revenues, and expenses originally measured to a foreign currency must be restated in terms of a home currency to be consolidated with home currency accounts.

Whether a company focuses on accounting or economic exposure, stock market analysts seem to focus on the economic consequences of foreign exchange rate changes. Apparently this market reaction has been triggered by concerns over fluctuating exchange rates, volatile inflation rates, taxation of foreign source earnings, and the widespread political instability that has given rise to these conditions. An integral part of a company's attempts to adjust to this volatile financial environment is the increased emphasis it places on forecasting foreign exchange rate movements. Volumes of literature discuss the causes of these movements. To summarize, the main factors that make currencies move and influence the demand and supply of each currency in the market are:

1. Relative price levels
2. Relative inflation rates
3. Relative interest rates
4. Relative changes in money supply
5. Investment or portfolio preferences of big international investors
6. Bandwagon effect (if a currency seems to be on the way up, speculators may exaggerate the trend by buying in the hope of a quick profit)
7. Intervention by central banks
8. Political changes and stability.

Regression analysis models are at the basis of many forecasting services, but the most impressive results have recently been obtained by market analysts called "chartists," who simply track price movements. Finally, some forecasters concentrate on so-called psychology gleaned from the attitudes and statements of people with the greatest direct influence on the supply and demand of currencies, such as the monetary authorities of the major reserve currencies and those responsible for administering huge portfolios such as mutual funds and pension funds.

All three methods can be used simultaneously, and this way the many aspects of foreign exchange forecasting are all addressed. It has already been concluded, after years of effort, that accurate forecasting is probably impossible. All companies' foreign exchange managers are unavoidably in the business of forecasting, but they should restrict their efforts in this endeavor to the greatest extent possible. There are several organizations that provide some form of foreign exchange advisory service:

1. Morgan Guaranty Trust Company
2. Citibank
3. MMS
4. IDEA.

The ability to anticipate and prepare for events is critical to a company's remaining competitive in today's world.

23A.2 IMPACT OF FOREIGN EXCHANGE ON OPERATING EXPOSURE MANAGEMENT.

An unexpected change in foreign exchange rates affects a company's levels, depending on the time horizon under review. The goal of operating exposure management is to anticipate and influence the effect of unexpected changes in foreign exchange rates on a firm's future cash flows—rather than just keeping one's fingers crossed!

To illustrate the impact of operating exposure, here is an example: Parfumeries S.A. is the wholly owned French subsidiary of Perfumes U.S.A., a U.S.-based multinational firm. The required rate of return after taxes to Perfumes U.S.A. is 20% from Parfumeries S.A.

Parfumeries S.A. manufactures in France from French material and labor. Fifty percent of production is sold in France and the other half is sold in the European Union. All sales are invoiced in French francs, and accounts receivable are equal to 25% of annual sales.

In this example, we assume that on January 1, 1996, before any business has begun, the French franc unexpectedly drops 20% in value, from FF 5.13/$ to FF 6.1550/$.

Parfumeries S.A.
Beginning Balance Sheet and Expected Cash Flows

Balance Sheet, December 31, 1995

Cash	FF 2,000,000	A/P	1,000,000
A/R	4,000,000	S/T Bank Loan	2,000,000
Inv.	3,000,000	L/T Debt	2,000,000
Net P&E	5,000,000	Comm. St.	2,000,000
		Ret. Earn.	7,000,000
Total	FF 14,000,000		
		Total	FF 14,000,000

Case 1. *Expected Cash Flow, No Devaluation, 1996*

Sales (500,000 units @ FF. 25/unit)	FF 12,500,000
Direct costs (500,000 units @ FF. 20/unit)	10,000,000
Cash operating fixed expenses	1,500,000

Depreciation	250,000
Pretax profit	FF 750,000
Income tax expense (50%)	375,000
Profit after tax	FF 375,000
Add back depr.	625,000
Cash flow from operation in FF.	FF 1,000,000

Existing exchange rate: FF 5.13 = $1.00

Cash flow from operations in U.S. dollars = $195,000

Cash flow from operations in francs = FF 1,000,000

New exchange rate: FF. 6.1550 = $1

Cash flow from operations in U.S. dollars = US $162,500

Parfumeries S.A. has experienced a shortfall of US $32,500 in its French franc cash flow.

However, we now assume that sales in France double following the devaluation, because French-made perfume is now more competitive with foreign imports. Furthermore, export volume doubles. The sales price is kept constant in French franc terms because management of Perfumeries S.A. has not had any change in its local French operating costs.

Case 2. *Expected Cash Flow, Volume Increases*

Sales (1,000,000 units @ 41 FF 25/unit)	FF 25,000,000
Direct costs (1,000,000 units @ FF 20/unit)	20,000,000
Cash oper. final expenses	1,500,000
Depreciation	250,000
Pretax profit	FF 3,250,000
Income tax expense (50%)	1,625,000
Profit after tax	FF 1,625,000
Add back depreciation	250,000
Cash flow from oper. in FF	FF 1,875,000

New exchange rate: FF 6.1550 = US $1.00

Cash flow from operations in U.S. dollars = $305,000

Projected cash flows for five years:

Year	Item	Francs	Dollars @ FF 6.1550
1	Cash flow from operations	FF 1,875,000	
	less new investment in working capital	− 4,000,000	
		FF −2,125,000	$−345,000

2	Cash flow from operations	1,875,000	305,000
3	Cash flow from operations	1,875,000	305,000
4	Cash flow from operations	1,875,000	305,000
5	Cash flow from operations	1,875,000	305,000
	Incremental working capital recapture	4,000,000	650,000

Case 3. *Expected Cash Flow, Sales Price Increase*

Sales (500,000 @ FF 30/unit)	FF 15,000,000
Direct costs (500,000 @ 20/unit)	10,000,000
Cash operating final expenses	1,500,000
Depreciation	250,000
Pretax profit	FF 3,250,000
Income tax expense (50%)	1,625,000
Profit after tax	FF 1,625,000
Add back depreciation	250,000
Cash flow from operations in FF	FF 1,875,000

New exchange rate: FF 6.1550 = $1.00

Cash flow operations in U.S. dollars = $305,000

Projected cash flows for five years:

Year	Item	Francs	Dollars @ FF 6.1550
1	Cash flow from operations	FF 1,875,000	
	less new investment in working	− 600,000	
	capital	FF 1,275,000	$207,000
2	Cash flow from operations	1,875,000	305,000
3	Cash flow from operations	1,875,000	305,000
4	Cash flow from operations	1,875,000	305,000
5	Cash flow from operations	1,875,000	305,000
	Incremental working capital recaptured last year	600,000	97,500

The key to this improvement is in the operating leverage. If costs are incurred in francs and do not increase after a devaluation, an increase in the sales price will lead to sharply higher profits.

If a company's operations are well diversified internationally, management is prepositioned both to recognize disequilibrium when it occurs and to react to maintain competitiveness and profitability.

In summary, multinational companies must obtain information in a form valid for internal evaluation and control of their subsidiaries. Comparison of results with operating budgets is the dominant criterion for performance evaluation of foreign subsidiaries. Performance relative to budget in an international context involves decisions about which exchange rate to use in the budgeting process and which to use in the assessment of results. Use of a forecasted exchange rate in budgeting and the end-of-period actual rate in assessment is most common.

SOURCES AND SUGGESTED REFERENCES

Choi, Frederick D.S., "International Data Sources for Empirical Research in Financial Management," *Financial Management,* Summer 1988, at 80–98.

Holland, John, *International Financial Management.* New York and Oxford, U.K.: Basil Blackwell, 1986.

Lessard, Donald R., "Global Competition and Corporate Finance in 1990's," *Journal of Applied Corporate Finance,* Vol. 3, No. 4, Winter 1991, at 59–72.

Lessard, Donald R., *International Financial Management 2d ed., Theory and Application.* New York: John Wiley & Sons, 1987.

Lessard, Donald R., and Peter Lorange, "Currency Changes and Management Control: Resolving the Centralization/Decentralization Dilemma," *Accounting Review,* July 1977, at 628–37.

Lessard, Donald R., and David Sharp, "Measuring the Performance of Operations Subject to Fluctuating Exchange Rates," *Midland Corporate Finance Journal,* Fall 1984, at 18–30.

Mueller, Gerhard G., Helen Gernon, and Gary Meek, *Accounting: An International Perspective.* Homewood, Ill.: Richard D. Irvin, 1987.

Persen, William, and Van Lessif, *Evaluating the Performance of Overseas Operations.* New York: Financial Executives Research Foundation, 1980.

Robbins, Sidney M., and Robert B. Stobaugh, "The Best Measuring Stick for Foreign Subsidiaries," *Harvard Business Review,* September/October 1973, at 80–88.

Shapiro, Alan C., "The Evaluation and Control of Foreign Affiliates," *Midland Corporate Finance Journal,* Spring 1984, at 13–25.

Walmsley, Julian, *A Dictionary of International Finance.* New York: Macmillan/John Wiley & Sons, 1986.

Walmsley, Julian, *The Foreign Exchange and Money Markets Guide.* New York: John Wiley & Sons, 1992.

Walmsley, Julian, *Global Investing.* London: Macmillan, 1991.

Weetman, Pauline, and Sidney J. Gray, "International Financial Analysis and Comparative Corporate Performance: The Impact of U.K. vs. U.S. Accounting Principles on Earnings,"*Journal of International Financial Management and Accounting,* Vol. 2, Nos. 2 and 3, Summer & Autumn 1990, at 111–30.

CHAPTER 24

BUDGETING PROPERTY AND LIABILITY INSURANCE REQUIREMENTS

Ronald K. Tucker
Hagedorn & Company

Vicki L. Tucker
Good Samaritan Hospital

CONTENTS

24.1	INTRODUCTION	1	24.6	SELF-INSURANCE ALTERNATIVES (NEW TITLE)		2
24.2	THE ROLE RISK MANAGEMENT PLAYS IN THE BUDGETING PROCESS	2	24.8	KEY INSURANCE COVERAGES		3
24.3	TYPES OF INSURANCE MECHANISMS	2		(b) Casualty Coverages		3
	(c) Self-Funded Plans	2				

24.1 INTRODUCTION

Page 24 · 2, add at end of section:

This analysis summarizes the principal insurance coverages and programs available and purchased by most middle-market buyers as the center of their risk management program. Self-insurance alternatives are not usually considered until the firm accumulates earnings that are large enough to sustain significant losses and still not seriously diminish the value of the enterprise.

Common terms are defined as follows.

- Middle-market firms: Generally, firms under $100 million in gross sales producing net incomes of $5 million or less.
- Self-insurance: Absorption of some risk on behalf of the firm. Insurance above

a retention (deductible) is purchased. There is a finance plan, which also involves risk financing and loss prevention/reduction, in the risk retention/deductible area.

- Twenty-four-hour coverage: A concept of combined efforts in various areas of medical reimbursement. The three most common casualty coverages are workers compensation (medical component), no-fault automobile coverage, and employee health plan (sickness and accident). Twenty-four-hour coverage attempts to manage medical exposures more economically. As of this writing, this coverage is available in a few states.
- TPA (third party administrator): An outside vendor (usually a claims administrator) hired to help administer the self-insurance portion (retention/deductible) of a risk management program.

What does this mean to effective budgeting? Budgeting of property and liability losses, coverages, and ultimate costs are not static. Many premiums are not flat charges, but variable costs depending on sales, payroll, units, employees, values, or other fluctuating variables. A budgeter needs to be aware of these variables in order to plan effectively.

In addition, property and casualty losses cost much more than the actual loss and involve asset replacement or indemnification of injured third parties. This hidden cost of loss resembles an iceberg: the cost of the actual loss is the visible iceberg, and the less identifiable costs are buried beneath the water. The hidden costs are usually three to four times the actual loss cost—a truly significant amount.

24.2   THE ROLE RISK MANAGEMENT PLAYS IN THE BUDGETING PROCESS

Page 24 · 2, replace first sentence of third paragraph with:

Identification of risk exposures is the first step in the risk management process.

Page 24 · 3, replace first sentence of first paragraph with:

Usually, most firms use insurance as a risk control solution (transfer).

24.3   TYPES OF INSURANCE MECHANISMS

(c)   Self-Funded Plans

Page 24 · 3 , replace last sentence of paragraph with:

Examples are workers' compensation and general liability.

24.6   TPAS AND OTHER SERVICE PROVIDERS

Page 24 · 5, replace heading 24.6 and first paragraph of section with:

24.6   SELF-INSURANCE ALTERNATIVES (New Title).   As a firm grows, the likelihood of fortuitous losses becomes more certain. This factor is due to the increase of similar exposure units. Obviously, the larger the pool of similar exposure units, the smaller the outcome variations. This statistical concept has been called the *law of*

large numbers and forms the basis for the insurance industry's rate structure and outcome predictability. By combining large groups of similar exposure units, an insurer,
with the aid of an actuary, can readily predict the losses for this group.

Large firms begin to accumulate group status and predictability as they grow.
This predictability becomes the basis for self-insurance plans. As discussed in the
introduction to this chapter, self-insurance suggests a plan of risk financing based on
risk/reward scenarios and other factors. Largely, a self-insurance program evolves in
several ways beginning with small retentions (deductibles).

Good exposure candidates for self funding are small predictable losses high in
frequency but low in severity. Workers compensation exposures are excellent candidates, as the most frequent losses tend to be small medical claims with no lost time.
A catastrophe exposure exists, but severe large losses are rare in most industries. An
industry- and individual-loss assessment is urgent before considering even the most
basic self-insurance plan.

A key element for any level of self-insurance is the separation of losses from
administrative services. An insurance premium contains two elements, losses and
expenses (sales, administrative, profit, claims adjustment, taxes licenses, and fees).
Generally, a premium allocates approximately 65–75% for losses and 35–25% for
expenses. By separating these elements, the insured controls them and can improve
ultimate costs.

The most basic self-insurance plans are known as *retro plans*. Here, the ultimate
premium is a result of ultimate losses plus expenses. The firm's worst case scenario
is capped at a pre-negotiated threshold, with the majority of self-funding in the most
predictable small loss area. Often, it takes five to seven years before all losses are
paid and ultimate costs determined. This fact is critical to the budget process; proper
forecasts of ultimate costs are a must. Retro plans are the more efficient net cost
plans but represent significant challenges to budgeters. A list of plans from the least
aggressive to the most aggressive self-insurance programs follows.

- Retention, sliding scale dividend, or loss divisor plan
- Incurred loss retro
- Paid-loss retro/deductible plan
- Fronted program
- Captive on self-insurance program

A brief outline of the services needed to administer an aggressive self-insurance program follows. The intent of this analysis is to help management become familiar
with the terms and functions of TPAs (third party administrators) available to assist
in the administration of a self funded plan.

24.8 KEY INSURANCE COVERAGES

(b) Casualty Coverages

Page 24 · 11, delete last paragraph.

CHAPTER 26

BRACKET BUDGETING

Michael W. Curran

Decision Sciences Corporation

CONTENTS

**26.4 DEVELOPING A TACTICAL
BUDGETING MODEL**   2

(e)   Tracking and Feedback
Mechanism   2

**26.6 CONSOLIDATING INCOME
STATEMENTS**   3

26.4 DEVELOPING A TACTICAL BUDGETING MODEL

(e)   Tracking and Feedback Mechanism

Page 26 • 20, replace Exhibit 26.15 with:

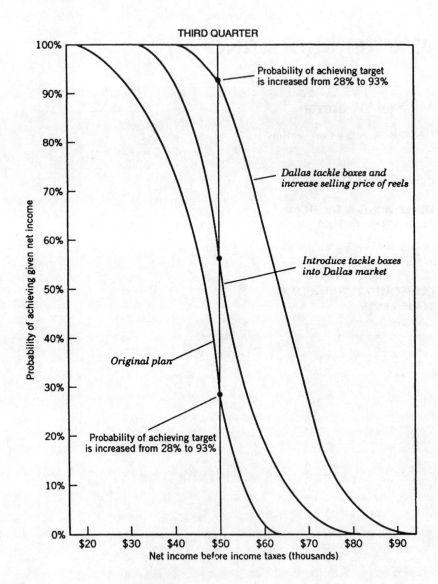

Exhibit 26.15   Fishing Supplies Company—income profiles of third quarter.

That is what TQM is really all about: empowering employees to improve the process and creating a culture that encourages error-free performance. The exact chronology of TQM is probably less important than the factors that combined to cause it to come on the scene. Key among these factors are two major changes in the international and domestic industry environment: (1) the end of the Cold War, with the result that a major part of industry found that its primary customer was no longer the U.S. government, and (2) the recognition that quality of products and quality of management performance were essential for the new customer base (the public consumer).

(b) Why TQM Was Developed. During that period of time, many publications and spokespersons expounded the values of excellence: *In Search of Excellence,* by Tom Peters; *Quality is Free,* by Philip Crosby; and *Iacocca,* by Lee Iacocca; as well as books more specifically related to quality by Deming, Juran, Feigenbaum, and others less well known. This proliferation of information and insight, combined with visible support by the United States demonstrated with its announcement of the Baldridge Award for Quality Excellence, demanded a "program." This program became known as TQM.

(c) TQM the Acronym. One of the confusing areas of the business culture is the use of acronyms and their meaning. For the purpose of simplicity within this chapter, *TQM* means Total Quality Management (continuous improvement of the management process toward the goal of perfection). If we consider that the management process consists of strategic activities and operational activities (implementation of strategies), TQM focuses primarily on the operational activities.

It is also worth noting that TQM is today's acronym. Other acronyms that existed in the past addressed many of the same issues and techniques (total quality control, quality circles, self-managed teams), and there will be new ones in the future. However, the principles remain the same, and the goal continues to be essential to success.

(d) How TQM Relates to the Budgeting System. In many ways, the relationship of TQM to the budgeting system is introduced in chapter 27A on activity-based budgeting, in particular section 27A.2, titled "Traditional Budgeting Does Not Support Excellence." TQM is about creating excellence. TQM deals with the development of operating processes, review and continuous improvement of these processes (by utilization of employee-empowered teams), and identification of cost reductions and waste. A major factor in the identification of waste and potential cost reduction is the budget and its related dollar distribution. One of the tools TQM also uses to measure continuous improvement looks very similar to the "Actual vs. Budget" performance reports used in financial tracking.

(e) Key Individual Contributors to TQM. A chronological review of TQM begins with F.W. Taylor.

(i) Taylor. Taylor really had a negative impact on what has ultimately developed into what we now call TQM. In the early 1900s, he developed and implemented the Management Control System, which separated the planning function from the

CHAPTER **26A**

BUDGETING FOR TOTAL QUALITY MANAGEMENT (New)

Ronald A. Follett

RF Group, Inc.

CONTENTS

26A.1 INTRODUCTION 2

(a) Brief History of TQM 2
(b) Why TQM Was Developed 3
(c) TQM the Acronym 3
(d) How TQM Relates to the Budgeting System 3
(e) Key Individual Contributors to TQM 3
   (i) Taylor 3
   (ii) Deming 4
   (iii) Juran 4
   (iv) Crosby 4
   (v) Others 4
   (vi) Summary of Inputs 4

26A.2 DEFINITIONS AND CONCEPTS 5

(a) The Unique Language 5
(b) Defining the Elements 5
(c) Understanding the Elements 5
(d) Benchmarking Relationship to Budgeting and TQM 6
(e) The Core Processes 6
(f) The New Paradigms 7

26A.3 APPLYING QUALITY CONCEPTS 7

(a) Product versus Process 7

(b) Manufacturing versus Nonmanufacturing Processes 9

26A.4 FOCUSING ON THE CUSTOMER 10

(a) How to Identify the Customer 10
(b) How to Understand Customer Expectations 10
(c) The Use of Benchmarking to Understand Customer Expectations 10

26A.5 TQM MODEL 11

(a) Basis for the Model 11
(b) Characteristics of the Model 11
   (i) Audit 11
   (ii) TQM Program Management 12
   (iii) Mission/Vision Statement 13
   (iv) The Infrastructure 13
   (v) Core Processes 13
   (vi) Benchmarking 14
   (vii) Continuous Improvement 15
   (viii) Performance Measurement 15
   (ix) Performance Reporting 15

26A.6 PHASES OF IMPLEMENTATION 17

(a) Phase I—Preparation 17

(b) Phase II—Initial Implementation   17

(c) Phase III—Transition   18

(d) Phase IV—Growth   18

(e) Phase V—Internal
Institutionalization   18

(f) Phase VI—External
Institutionalization   19

26A.7 BUDGETING FOR TQM   19

(a) Management Commitment   19

(b) Manpower and Time Commitment   20

(c) Maintenance Cost Commitment   20

(d) Impact on the Budgeting Process   21

26A.8 RETURN ON INVESTMENT   21

(a) Assessment of Impact on
Bottom Line   21

(b) Risks and Pitfalls   23

**26A.9 INDUSTRY EXAMPLES AND
STRATEGIES**   24

(a) Manufacturing   24

(b) Construction Industry   25

(c) Health Care Industry   26

26A.10 SUMMARY   28

**SOURCES AND
SUGGESTED REFERENCES**   28

26A.1 INTRODUCTION.   The purpose of this chapter is to provide a basic foundation for an understanding of Total Quality Management (TQM) and the model for the development of a budgeting system which reflects implementation and maintenance costs and tracks benefits.

TQM came on the scene more than a decade ago as the great elixir for a struggling industrial atmosphere. Most of the known, and many other not-so-well-known, experts got into the game and developed books and programs for every need. For those who fit TQM to their business and worked at it, the results were reflected in growth and profits for the business. The initial successes within the industrial environment prompted other types of a organizations to get into TQM and adapt the programs to their functions and infrastructure. Soon schools, hospitals, government, nonprofit service organizations, and others were working their continuous improvement activities with their empowered employee teams. Through all of this, though, little had been developed or implemented related to the budgeting impacts on the organization. This chapter puts this into perspective.

(a) Brief History of TQM.   Although the TQM acronym is relatively new, the principles and concepts have been around and in practice much longer. Dr. Juran, many years ago, noted in his *Quality Manual:*

> A key dimension of the management *process* is the establishment and maintenance of a work *climate* that encourages and makes it possible for *workers* to behave in ways that contribute to effective individuals and organizational performance. Only management can create the conditions which enable workers to control the process over which they preside and participate with management in projects that seek to achieve breakthrough to new quality levels.[1]

---

[1]Juran, J.M., *Quality Control Handbook* 4th ed. (McGraw Hill, 1988).

26.6 CONSOLIDATING INCOME STATEMENTS

Page 26 • 23, replace Exhibit 26.17 with:

ANNUAL EARNINGS PER SHARE			PROBABILITY OF ACHIEVING TARGET
LOWEST $1.10	TARGET $1.27	HIGHEST $1.45	72%

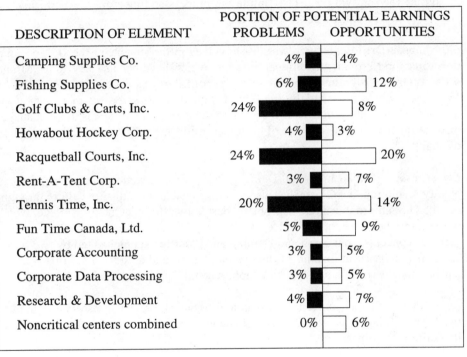

DESCRIPTION OF ELEMENT	PORTION OF POTENTIAL EARNINGS	
	PROBLEMS	OPPORTUNITIES
Camping Supplies Co.	4%	4%
Fishing Supplies Co.	6%	12%
Golf Clubs & Carts, Inc.	24%	8%
Howabout Hockey Corp.	4%	3%
Racquetball Courts, Inc.	24%	20%
Rent-A-Tent Corp.	3%	7%
Tennis Time, Inc.	20%	14%
Fun Time Canada, Ltd.	5%	9%
Corporate Accounting	3%	5%
Corporate Data Processing	3%	5%
Research & Development	4%	7%
Noncritical centers combined	0%	6%

Exhibit 26.17.   The Fun Time Company—results of computer simulation of next fiscal year.

execution functions. This resulted in the creation of the specialist and the proliferation of organizations. Although many good things came out of this movement, responsibility and accountability for problems were lost by this decentralization. This approach is in direct contrast to TQM, which emphasizes employee responsibility and accountability for problem identification and resolution.

(ii)   Deming.   Dr. W. Edwards Deming had been on the quality scene for a number of years; however, his prominence developed in the 1950s, when he went to Japan to support the U.S. occupation program. His contribution became critical to all future quality practices. Although his philosophies and total contribution were far-reaching, the basics rely on two concepts: Define the process and measure the performance, with emphasis on statistical process control.

(iii)   Juran.   Dr. Joseph Juran was also involved in the support of the U.S. occupation force, and provided additional concepts which have become key to TQM and other quality programs. One of Juran's contributions has been *The Quality Handbook,* which is essentially the bible for quality. However, his major contribution to the TQM philosophy was insight into the application of teams in the management of quality, and the concept of customer needs and satisfaction in the definition of quality.

(iv)   Crosby.   Unlike Juran and Deming, Philip Crosby came along after the Japan quality revolution, but Crosby has also had his impact on the quality culture throughout the U.S. environment. He is probably best known for his Quality College, which was established to educate and train industry in quality concepts. The training includes concepts from Juran and Deming and is further supplemented by two major areas of emphasis: utilization of quality motivation and a cultural set that requires performance perfection and rejects a "good-enough" philosophy.

(v)   Others.   Several other individuals and organizations have also contributed to the TQM culture. However, the basic elements expounded in all of the various quality definitions emphasize:

- Utilize employee-empowered teams
- Define and measure the process
- Create a culture that drives continuous improvement to excellence

(vi)   Summary of Inputs.   All of the identified quality "gurus" summarized their quality programs by listing a number of points. Although each listing was different in context, they all essentially emphasize the same basic issues:

- Build a management commitment to continuous improvement for the future
- Create empowerment and teamwork
- Continuously measure the process quality indicators
- Continuously emphasize excellence as the only goal
- Expand training in quality skills

All of their program elements focus on the three basic elements of culture, process, and people, which are the basis of any effective TQM program.

26A.2   DEFINITIONS AND CONCEPTS.

(a)   **The Unique Language.**   The language of TQM is not unique in its words, but in their definition and implications within the environment and culture. The following defines some of the common terms used in TQM.

> *TQM*—A system designed to involve all employees in the improvement of the work process. Total Quality Management involves all employees in improving work effectiveness and output, focuses on customer needs, emphasizes improvement of every company process, and concentrates on process, not end result
>
> *Standard*—Perfection; no-fault performance
>
> *Quality*—Meeting customer requirements and expectations. These requirements generally take on the parameters of timeliness/schedule, performance within resource allocation (manpower and dollar budget), and customer satisfaction
>
> *Product*—Any output item or information provided to or used by others
>
> *Customer*—The receiver of any output or product
>
> *Empowerment*—Allocation of accountability and responsibility for decisions and changes
>
> *Core processes*—Processes that are essential to the operation's attaining its goals and objectives
>
> *Teams*—Employee groups selected and empowered for resolution of a specific issue or problem. Three types of teams are generally formed in the TQM environment: problem-solving teams (selected for a specific problem), task teams (selected to accomplish a specific task), and standing teams (requires specific knowledge in area of involvement).

(b)   **Defining the Elements.**   As noted earlier in this chapter, key individual contributors (Juran, Deming, Crosby) stressed three common elements within each of their quality process definitions: culture, process, and people.

> *Culture*—The working environment of the organization, starting with the management message. The end product is not an element of TQM, but is an indicator of the final process output step
>
> *Process*—The continuous series of steps or activities by which anything is done
>
> *People*—The employees, who are the most important resource and provide members for the empowered teams.

(c)   **Understanding the Elements.**   Although there are only three significant elements, understanding them is critical to a successful TQM program or process. They are further significant to the budgeting process because this is where the expense (investment) occurs, and where the waste and cost reduction are identified.

The *culture* is the environment, the work ethic, the standards, the expectations, and the clear message that exists within the organization for its people. In a TQM program, this culture must clearly state and reinforce the requirement for perfection as the ultimate goal. This must be reinforced by the rewards and recognition program as well as by the performance example of management. It must be clear that continuous improvement in every action and activity is everyone's responsibility.

The *process* of performing any activity is a series of discrete steps or actions that link together to provide an outcome. The approach that TQM utilizes in analyzing these processes is to look separately at each step's inputs and outputs. The aim is to assure perfection at each step in the process. It follows that if each step in the process is done to perfection, the process will be perfect. The concept that requires effort and diligence is the definition of each step in the process.

The *people* are the medium that holds it all together and makes it all happen. The people need to be a part of the changing culture.

- They are the active team members who solve the problems
- They search for continuous improvement opportunities
- They define and evaluate the processes
- They are experts in the execution of the process; that's what they do
- They want to be the best they can be and to be respected for it

(d) Benchmarking Relationship to Budgeting and TQM. A *benchmark,* in its original context, was a reference point used to establish the attitude or base position in a topographical survey. The term has since migrated into business, where it has come to signify a reference point or standard for a process or operation performance. Benchmarking is the continuous, ongoing process of measuring performance against these benchmarks. These benchmarks or standards are key in the development of a budget, because they define the anticipated or planned parameters of operation and resource needs. Development of the budget within the TQM environment drives "budgeting for perfection" based on benchmarks for error-free performance. The difference in dollars between the perfection budget and the operating budget identifies the cost of poor quality and the opportunity for improvement.

(e) The Core Processes. Knowing and understanding the core processes is essential to defining the operation and identifying opportunities for improvement and cost saving. The *core processes* define activities critical to the daily operation. Although they generally fall into five basic functional categories (the market, the product, the delivery system, the resource base [financial and manpower], and the planning), they diagram the specific implementation processes defined in the mission and the strategic plan. Exhibit 26A.1 illustrates the Core Process family tree by listing the critical functions and the corresponding core processes.

Mission/Vision

Critical Functions	Core Processes
Market	market definition market analysis sales strategy advertising and public relations
Product	product definition product development product control services (internal and external)
Delivery System	resource needs direct needs support needs capital needs

Resource Base	financial
	manpower
	  obtain
	  manage
	  develop

Planning	past performance review growth goals resource availability and needs organizational inputs

Exhibit 26A.1.   Core process family tree.

(f) **The New Paradigms.**   Industry and organizations are often based on one paradigm: "That's the way we have always done it." To successfully implement TQM and an aggressive budget, the paradigms must be put on the shelf. The new paradigms should be:

- Operational problems can best be recognized and solved by the employees involved in the process, not management
- Continuous improvement is the responsibility of all employees
- Self-empowered employee teams are an effective problem-solving tool
- Processes must be measured if consistency in performance is to be attained
- Excellence is the only acceptable goal

26A.3 APPLYING QUALITY CONCEPTS.

(a) **Product versus Process.**   The application of quality concepts to a product rather than a process differs considerably. However, from a wider viewpoint, there are similarities. Because TQM is focused on the process, it is important to understand how basic quality concepts apply.

- Product quality is based on performance as measured against end product performance standards
- Process quality is based on the outputs of each step as measured against a defined benchmark for that step

The marked difference is that product quality is measured on the end item, whereas the process is measured against the established benchmarks for each of the individual steps. This is true whether the end item is a hard item or a service product output. Those of us involved in the product manufacturing industry are all aware of the process control charts present on the factory floor; those charts graphically indicate the results of that step in the process as measured against upper and lower control limits. This is generally referred to as *Total Quality Control*. When these methods are applied to a management process, it becomes TQM. We are also aware that product quality generally refers to the resultant end product of a factory process. However, very few, if any, have ever seen similar process control charts for operational processes such as purchasing, the planning process, service performance, or other operational processes. These operational process controls are the ones that TQM measures and identifies as opportunities for improvement and cost savings. An example of a process control chart is shown in Exhibit 26A.2.

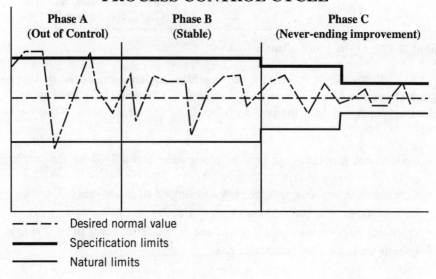

Exhibit 26A.2.   Process control chart.

(b) Manufacturing versus Nonmanufacturing Processes. Manufacturing processes are generally considered to define the movement of a product through assembly, test, and shipment. These process steps tend to be tangible, with a product that can be viewed as it progresses. Other characteristics of the manufacturing process are that it tends to be very machine-intensive, with people in a support role. Manufacturing is also a repetitive process in which a product that is designed is repeatedly produced in some defined volume.

The product of a nonmanufacturing process generally is less tangible, such as advice, counsel, service, or products that develop through a natural process that does not involve people. Nonmanufacturing by its nature is defined in its entirety by a series of steps, and is almost totally people-intensive. See Exhibit 26A.3 for an example of the purchasing function. The basic differences in characteristics are:

PURCHASING PROCEDURE

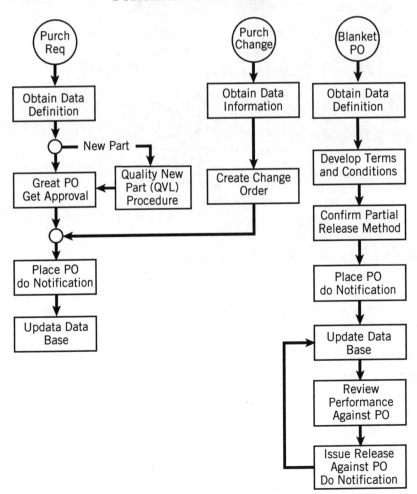

Exhibit 26A.3.   Flowchart.

- The nonmanufacturing processes are not repetitive in detail
- They tend not to be machine-intensive, but more people-intensive
- The output is generally unique to a specific situation

26A.4   FOCUSING ON THE CUSTOMER.

(a) **How to Identify the Customer.**   To address the issue of the customer, it is first necessary to clearly identify and define that entity. The generic definition used is the end user of the product. The customer within the end-product environment is the person or function to which the end product is delivered. The customer within the process-sensitive environment is the next person or function in the process. One way to simplify this definition is to isolate a particular function or step in the process and determine the inputs to and the outputs from that entity. The inputs are provided by suppliers and the outputs are provided to customers, as shown in Exhibit 26A.4.

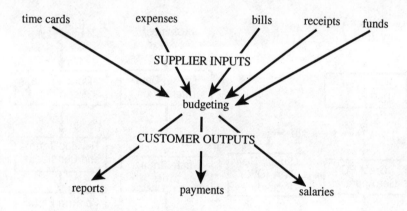

Exhibit 26A.4.   Customer/Supplier relationship.

(b) **How to Understand Customer Expectations.**   The best answer to this question is to ask the customer. Several tools and techniques can be used to obtain this information:

- Direct interface with agreed-to and documented output
- Regular review of this output with the customer
- Periodic customer survey
- Mutual definition of benchmarks
- Evaluation of customer complaints and returns

The emphasis should be on the effort to obtain information.

(c) **The Use of Benchmarking to Understand Customer Expectations.**   By definition, benchmarks are derived from the best, world-class performance. The customer determines whether performance is the best by acceptance or rejection of it. Therefore, the benchmarks are customer-driven and describe customer expectations and acceptance.

26A.5   TQM MODEL.

(a)   Basis for the Model.   Three assumptions form the basis of this model and its related implementation plan:

1. It is essential for management to understand, accept, and support the program.
2. TQM is not an automatic fit in all operations. The program must be made to fit the industry and the specific organization.
3. The program must be adapted to identified policies, processes, and problem areas.

(b)   Characteristics of the Model.

(i)   Audit.   The first activity necessary in implementation of the TQM program is the audit. This involves two distinct types of review and analysis: one that is used to evaluate the human elements of the organization, and another that is used to evaluate performance and business stability of the organization.

The employee audit involves a series of interviews with a cross-section of the employee and management base. There are several reasons for this activity, but the major goal is to determine the personality of the organization. Properly executed, it will identify:

- Leadership goals as related to commitment to continuous improvement
- Skills, attitudes, and commitment of key personnel
- Evaluation of "right people in correct position"
- Current status and depth of planning efforts
- Identification of issues that prevent people from performing their jobs

The interviews and the resultant audit report should focus on who they are, what they do, how they do it, and what opportunities for improvement exist. Exhibit 26A.5 is an example of an employee audit checklist.

The following items should be addressed in the interview.

Personnel attributes:
    Name
    Education (primary, secondary, other)
    Work experlence (last three positions or last ten years)
    Related skills

Organizational attributes
    Position in the organization
    Reports to / number of reports
    Primary involvement

Goals and plans
        Personal goals
        Plans within the organization/company
        Present activities in support of goals (education, skills training, etc.)

What items or issues prevent excellence in performance?
        What is being done on individual basis?
        What organizational changes would you make?
        What policies and procedures should be changed?

General comments regarding position, organization, personnel interfaces, etc.

Exhibit 26A.5.   Employee audit checklist.

The business audit involves the review and analysis of business characteristics and the effectiveness of the organization. This involves three types of business indicators: financial, organizational, and performance against industry benchmarks. Examples of these audit items are listed in Exhibit 26A.6.

Financial indicators
        Income
        Budgeting and management of financial resources
        Cash flow
        Outstanding financial liabilities

Organizational
        Management levels
        Levels of authority
        Accountability delegation
        Communication

Performance
        Schedule conformance
        Budget performance
        Customer satisfaction
        Other strategic goals

Exhibit 26A.6.   Business audit items.

This audit provides critical information on organizational effectiveness and ability to take on the challenges of a TQM program.

(ii)   TQM Program Management.   The TQM program management for a specific operation is established outside of the normal management structure. It is essential that this not become another management program, but that it be identified from its inception as an employee empowerment action. Therefore, management of the program is by a steering committee with membership from all employee levels. The chairperson is the TQM coordinator and becomes the primary interface to management and the outside world. The steering committee has the responsibility of defining the mission statement for the program, defining the policies and procedures for operation, and managing the overall TQM program.

(iii)   Mission/Vision Statement.   The mission/vision statement establishes a focus for the program and also provides a visible indicator on which the organization can focus. The mission/vision statement essentially defines the organization's focus on excellence. It is brief, inspiring, clear, and challenging, is about excellence, and provides a constant challenge.

(iv)   The Infrastructure.   A key part of the continuous improvement process is the empowered employee teams. These are groups of employees that analyze, evaluate, and develop solutions for the problems that impede perfectly performing processes. These teams are selected by the steering committee based on their involvement and knowledge of the process. They are selected from all levels of the employee strata and are given the power to work as a team in resolving the issues and developing a solution.

(v)   Core Processes.   TQM is about continuous improvement of the operational processes; therefore, it is necessary that those processes be identified. The most important processes are those that define the essential or *core* activities of the organization. These are generally identified in the critical goals reflected in the strategic plan and are classified as the core processes. From this base, the initial opportunities are selected for empowered employee teams to develop improvements.

- *Developing Core Processes*

The determination and definition of the core processes are initiated wth an analysis of the mission and goals of the organization, which are developed as part of the strategic plan activity. The strategic plan will define the product, the market, and the strategy.

In developing the core processes, it is necessary to work the sequence from the top down. It starts with the mission statement, which defines the reason for existence and the vision of future goals. If this does not exist, it must be created. Evaluation and review of the mission and visions will allow the organization to define the product, the market, the delivery system, the resources (financial and manpower), and the planning process. In each of these critical functional categories, there are a number of activities and processes that must occur to support the mission and vision. These processes provide the listing which, when prioritized, identifies the core processes.

- *Determination of Core Processes*

The *core processes* are defined as those activities critical to the success of the strategy implementation. Although this process of determining the core processes sounds easy, experience has demonstrated that it is one of the more difficult activities. The major reason seems to be that people and organizations do not often try to think about what they actually do for a living. One of the more effective methods seems to be the combination of brainstorming and workshop session with key employees. Exhibit 26A.7 illustrates examples of core processes by types of industry.

Industry	Core processes
Manufacturing	Design product
	Market and sell
	Procure materials and services
	Provide competent staff
	Manage financial solvency
	Plan for future
Construction	Estimate jobs
	Buy out materials and services
	Manage projects
	Provide competent manpower
	Manage financial solvency
	Plan for future
Health Care	Determine population market
	Educate market
	Service market
	Support regulations (state and federal)
	Provide competent staff
	Maintain financial solvency
	Plan for future

Exhibit 26A.7.   Examples of core processes.

- *Mapping the Process* (see Exhibit 26A.3)

Mapping of the core processes will result in a pictorial representation (process flowchart) of the steps involved. Accurately accomplishing this generally involves interviews and brainstorming sessions with the people who actively participate in the process. As each step is developed, four parameters must evolve: what is done, who does it, how it is done, and when it is done.

(vi)   Benchmarking.   The benchmarking of each core process is an essential part of the TQM model, in that it defines the numerical goal for that process activity based on the performance of top-of-the-class operation, or the best process capability. The benchmark establishes the standard of performance for excellence, creates the baseline against which the process improvements will be measured, and becomes the barometer of success, as shown in Exhibits 26A.8 and 26A.9

Competition
Process capability studies
Previous performance
Industry studies

Exhibit 26A.8.   Sources of benchmarks.

Industry	Process	Benchmarks
Manufacturing	Product design	Time to market Conformance to product cost
	Marketing/sales	Cost of sales % of market
	Procurement	Materials cost vs. goal Materials availability to manufacturing
Construction	Job estimating	Capture rate Estimate vs. budget vs. completion cost
	Buy out of materials	Availability vs. need Cost vs. budget
	Project management	Scope (# of jobs) % completion to budget and schedule
Health Care	Service the market	Cost per client % market serviced Customer satisfaction index

Exhibit 26A.9.   Examples of benchmarks.

(vii)   Continuous Improvement.   The continuous improvement activity is the ongoing process of identifying areas for improvement (reaching for the benchmark), evaluating, modifying, and changing the processes. Within the TQM environment, the continuous improvement process involves:

- Identifying opportunities for improvement
- Selecting and establishing of self-empowerment teams
- Evaluating information and data
- Developing solutions and a schedule of plans for improvement
- Implementing the changes and measuring resultant performance

This entire activity is coordinated by the steering committee and conducted in conformance with the policies and procedures.

(viii)   Performance Measurement.   The performance measurement activity is the ongoing activity of determining actual process performance. This measurement is indexed not only to the benchmarks, but also to previous performance, to ensure that changes are creating positive gains. The other important purpose of the process measurement is to provide positive reinforcement and demonstration of the TQM process. The importance of this activity cannot be overemphasized.

(ix)   Performance Reporting.   As with any good program, it is essential that activities and progress be reported to the organization and the employees on a regular basis. Many pieces of information can be reported; however, at a minimum, continuous update should be provided on:

- Active projects

- Teams and participants
- Schedule of activities
- Copies of proceedings
- Policies and procedures
- Numerical charting and reporting of improvement numerics
- Future opportunities for improvement

In addition to the text reports and information, a number of visual charting techniques are useful in communicating process performance and improvements, as shown in Exhibit 26A.10.

Balance Sheet
(based on construction company core activities)

Activity	Benchmark	Performance	
		Plan	Actual
Estimate	Estimate vs. completion cost	90%	75%
	Material cost vs. budget	100%	80%
	Capture rate	60%	70%
Management	Change order acceptance		
	> $100,000 impact	< 45 days	52 days
	< $100,000 impact	< 30 days	28 days
	< $50,000 impact	< 15 days	17 days
	< $10,000 impact	< 5 days	7 days
	performance to schedule (% of all jobs)		
	weekly performance	+/− 10%	18%
	completion performance	100%	75%
	performance to budget (% of all jobs)		
	weekly performance	+/− 15%	20%
	completion performance	100%	60%
Customer Satisfaction			
	based on job completion survey	95%	98%
	based on contract litigation	1%	1/2%

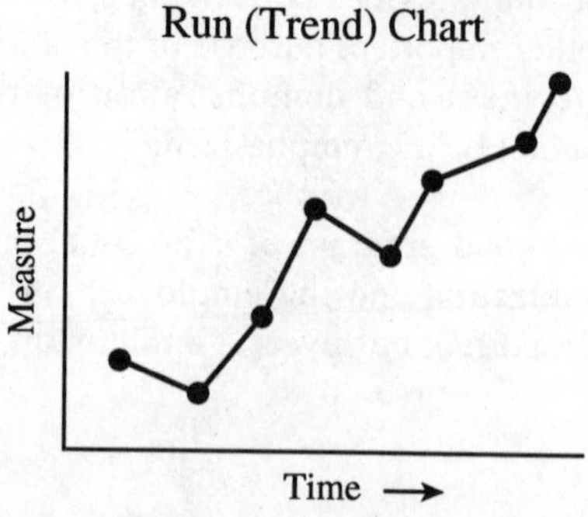

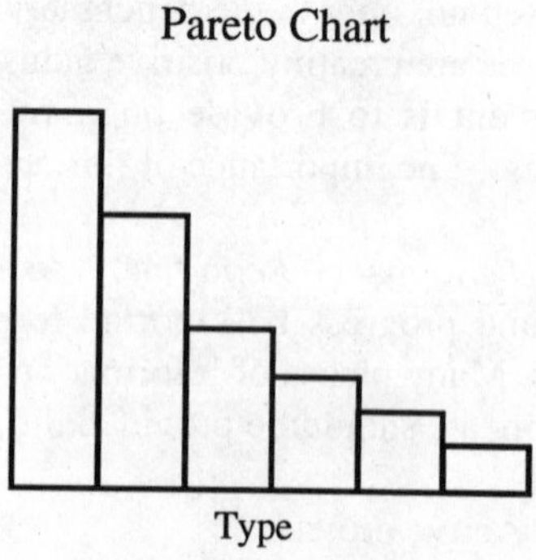

Exhibit 26A.10.   Visual charting.

26A.6 PHASES OF IMPLEMENTATION. TQM is not a process that occurs instantly. The time-consuming part of the program is changing the mindset of the participants and the culture of the company. Experience has shown that from initiation to integration will probably take two years. However, by utilizing the model defined in this chapter, progress and improvement will be occurring during that entire time. To better define the implementation, we have identified six separate phases.

(a) Phase I—Preparation. If TQM is to be effective and successful, the organization and its management must be ready to accept it and must be organizationally structured to implement it. The purpose of the preparation phase is to evaluate and align the company for this TQM implementation. Three separate, but linked, activities occur during the preparation phase, which essentially includes items (i) through (vi) in the model.

1. *Awareness* presentations are focused on providing senior management and employees with an understanding of quality concepts, principles, and commitment. Although this first phase really occurs prior to actual implementation, it is a critical decision point where management decides to commit to involvement. It also provides an opportunity to establish initial baselines of the operation.
2. *Audits* are conducted to evaluate the organization, people, and processes used to manage the company and to help establish basic core processes and benchmarks.
3. *Alignment* and adjustments within the operation may be needed to assure compatibility and effectiveness with the program.

(b) Phase II—Initial Implementation. Once the organization and its management are properly prepared, the implementation is planned and initiated. This is the beginning of the activities which become the repetitive continuous improvement process and involves items (vii) through (ix) of the model. Phase II has one major goal—to demonstrate the tools and techniques that will take the organization toward excellence. Several activities occur during this phase:

1. Employees are trained
2. Cross-functional teams are built
3. Problem-solving techniques are demonstrated
4. Visibility into organization occurs (who does what)
5. New communication loops between groups grow
6. Meeting effectiveness and reporting are developed
7. Process deviation analysis and root cause analysis are introduced.

This phase normally requires outside assistance, but it is the first step in developing acceptance and credibility within the organization and the employees.

(c)   Phase III—Transition.   At this point in the implementation, the basics of empowerment, process development, and evaluation and problem-solving have been demonstrated. The level of credibility and acceptance has risen, but there are still many skeptics. It is necessary for the organization to take charge and make quality a part of everyone's job and performance goals. During this phase, credibility and acceptance become critical. This phase includes all of the activities of phase II, but there are significant differences.

1. The steering committee takes over control of the program.
   - Training
   - Solution implementation
   - Team discipline
   - Measurement and evaluation
   - Employee motivation
2. Policies and procedures for TQM are modified and expanded.
3. Activity must result in considerable growth in credibility, acceptance, employee involvement, and positive management reinforcement.

Management and the steering committee need to be cautious with their involvement. They must have a role of guiding, not directing. They must be sure they truly understand the process. They should call on some outside assistance in auditing and critiquing progress and outputs.

(d)   Phase IV—Growth.   The goal of this phase is to spread the problem-solving, employee empowerment, and culture change through the organization. The new activities occurring deal with the continued change in the way management thinks and works in the process of doing their jobs.

1. A high level of visibility for communication and public relations.
2. A high level of employee involvement.
3. Many documented successes.
4. A problem identification system that reflects process variation.
5. A defined system of process control and measurement.
6. A policy with related benchmarks.

At this point, TQM and its measured outputs should be solidly in the management culture of the organization and acceptance should be high.

(e)   Phase V—Internal Institutionalization.   The goal is simply to make TQM total and complete across the organization. This has occurred when employee empowerment and problem-solving techniques are in place and natural, and when the numerical output of the measurement system becomes a management tool by which success is gauged. The new activities that become a part of this phase are:

1. Define and document all critical processes.

2. Define aggressive benchmarks for all critical processes.
3. Develop and utilize a measurement and reporting system for all critical processes.
4. Define a TQM function in management.

The activities in this phase are to assure the permanence and staying power of Total Quality Management.

(f) Phase VI—External Institutionalization.   As the organization takes control of its internal processes, it becomes obvious that external influences continue to affect the search for excellence. The goal of this phase is to develop a program that supports and interfaces with these outside influences. The program to be developed must have a degree of similarity to and synergism with the one the organization has implemented. Therefore, it is obvious that the model followed in development of the organization's successful and in-place TQM program is appropriate, because it will naturally be compatible and has already been tested.

26A.7 BUDGETING FOR TQM.   All smart managers know that poor quality costs money in lost customers and profits. However, quality improvement and Total Quality Management are not free. It does not make sense to address continuous quality improvement unless it will have a positive effect on the bottom line. The budgeting-for-quality activity provides a clear picture of the costs of TQM and points to the areas of profit and cost savings.

(a) Management Commitment.   Management's commitment to TQM involves more than a decision to introduce a new program. It involves an open and active commitment to employee empowerment, culture change, and the financial support necessary to sustain the efforts. The commitment also involves a proactive change in the strategic plan to include TQM as a management tool.

Experience has shown that TQM programs have not been successful with internally initiated and directed programs. Implicit in this is the expense of a consultant or consulting organization. The major reason for this is that organizations have difficulty in creating the self-assessment and culture change without outside help. The amount of effort involved for the consultant and the duration of tenure will vary depending on the needs and desires of the management staff. The details of the management commitment and approximate costs are tabulated in Exhibit 26A.11. They essentially track Phases I and II of Exhibit 26A.6.

Awareness and planning activities (see Exhibit 26A.11) include those needed for the staff to attain a basic knowledge of TQM, possible support needed, and the development of an initial plan and budget. Those total costs are cash expenses plus the cost of committed employee hours directly involved in the program (manhours per person or mh/person).

Activity	Cash Expenses/Manpower	
Awareness education Books Seminars Direct presentation	$3,000 to $5,000	40mh/person
Management training (consultant)	$2,000	16 mh/person
Employee audit (10% to 15% of employees)	$2,000 to $3,000	1 mh/person
Infrastructure Organization Policies and procedures	$2,000 to $3,000	24 mh/person
Core process development and benchmarking	$5,000	24 mh/person

Exhibit 26A.11.   Awareness and planning costs.

The scheduled time span of this activity should be approximately three months, with the costs spread evenly over that period.

(b) Manpower and Time Commitment.   The manpower and time commitment becomes more intense as the program implementation occurs. The primary reason for this is that the employees are brought in and become the major resource of the program. Initial implementation of the program involves activities (see Exhibits 26A.12 and 26A.13) that introduce the program to the employees and begin to involve them in the continuous improvement process. The consulting activity is still very much involved in process, because implementation is most difficult and requires an ongoing learning process and continuous reinforcement of the culture changes necessary. The consultant will be directly involved in the problem-solving teams during the first cycle and then will proceed to detach during the transition phase to a point where it assumes the role of an advisor only. These activities and events are those related in Phases II and III of Exhibit 26A.6. Those costs again reflect cash and manpower commitments with an even spread over a period of three to four months.

Activity	Cash Expenses/Manpower	
Team selection and training	$2,000	16 mh/person
Team meetings (continuous improvement) assume five teams	$5,000 to $6,000	15 mh/person
Solution implementation	$1,000	8 mh/person
Employee motivation	$2,000	

Exhibit 26A.12.   Implementation costs.

(c) Maintenance Cost Commitment.   The initial costs of the TQM program are incurred during the initial phases, which tend to occur over the first six months of the program. However, there are no free lunches—as with any worthwhile effort, there are ongoing maintenance costs, primarily for the manpower commitment and the cost of positive reinforcement. The efforts and costs related essentially address the items in Phases III, IV, V, VI and will become a part of the regular operating budget.

Activity	Cash Expenses/Manpower	
Continued training and motivation		16 mh/person
Team meetings (eight teams/yr)		15 mh/person
Solution implementation	$5,000/yr.	8 mh/person
Employee motivation	$2,000/yr.	
Consultant audit and assistance	$5,000/yr.	

Exhibit 26A.13.   Sustaining costs.

(d)   Impact on the Budgeting Process.   The manpower and cash estimates previously identified provide a scope of the commitment necessary in the implementation of a TQM program. In addition, it is necessary that the organization recognize the time span necessary for solid implementation. The impact on the expense budget is the management commitment over the first three months, the manpower commitment over the next three to four months, and the ongoing maintenance commitment as a built-in operating expense within the operating budget (see Exhibit 26A.14). This obviously implies that initial funding will be an out-of-budget expense. However, the ongoing budget expense after the implementation phase is very predictable and controllable. It is the expense of involving new employees on new teams, the motivation, and the periodic need for outside assistance.

Management commitment	$18,000	over 4 mos
Manpower commitment*	$11,000	over 4 mos
Maintenance commitment*	$12,000	per annum

*Manpower and cost commitments are related to the organization and its size.

Exhibit 26A.14.   Budget impact summary.

26A.8   RETURN ON INVESTMENT.

(a)   Assessment of Impact on Bottom Line.   The impact on the bottom line is more difficult to identify, because it generally involves cost avoidance or reductions in operating expenses as well as the effect of new opportunities for revenue. Part of the reason that this is difficult to quantify is the fact that organizations and companies do not generally have a good measure of their detailed operating costs within the processes. However, when this level of measurement has been put in place, it has been demonstrated that the bottom line impact has more than offset TQM program costs. There are many examples of bottom line improvements which were the result of TQM-type programs that used employee-empowered teams to improve process efficiency and effectiveness (see Exhibit 26A.15).

Organization	Team Goal	Result
Construction	Improve performance to budget and schedule	Performance to budget and schedule from 40% to 60% resulted in $300,000 added annual profit
Brokerage Company	Reduce turnaround on reports	Turnaround from 7 to 3 days
Construction	Reduce equipment downtime	Developed maintenance program and reduced average down time from 16 hrs. per. mo. to 2 hrs. per mo.
Manufacturing	On time, in budget procurement	Purchasing system improved; on time from 60% to 90%, in budget from 40% to 80%
Health Care Service	Improve vendor communication	Reduced forms from 3 to 1 Developed mutually acceptable standards of performance
Construction	Small tool replacement costs 2% of total revenue	Instituted tool control system which reduced cost to 1% ($50,000 savings)

Exhibit 26A.15.   Examples of TQM impact.

Many of these operational improvements are included within factors utilized in the budgeting process, such as productivity, efficiency, or general administrative (G&A) items, that translate into dollars and reflect directly to the bottom line. However, an analysis of these budgeting factors can provide a baseline from which cost savings and cost avoidance can be measured. Some examples of these subtle savings are:

1. Missing a schedule causes additional manpower costs, facilities cost, administrative support, and possible utility and occupancy costs. All of these are generally accounted for in the budgeting process by including them in the standard factors or in (often accepted) overruns.
2. A budget overrun obviously has a direct impact on profitability, which can additionally have an impact on competitiveness and ability to obtain business.
3. Equipment down time not only impacts the productivity and efficiency factors, but can affect manpower allocation, schedules, and eventually budget overruns.
4. Although materials cost is typically the smaller part of product or service costs, the impact of materials cost variances and availability is felt across all the other product cost areas.
5. The everpresent paperwork and its need to grow is accepted as part of company growth; however, experience shows that there is seldom a plan to throw out the old, obsolete, and unnecessary. Paperwork takes time to generate and review, and time is money.

The examples in Exhibit 26A.15 show some of the changes and improvements that resulted in cost reductions and efficiencies in daily operations, and the savings that may result.

(b) Risks and Pitfalls. As with anything new and threatening, there are several risks. This is particularly true with a change that occurs within the cultural environment and that affects the "comfort zone." TQM requires scrutiny and evaluation of everything being done, and strongly says that the status quo is not acceptable. This upsets the balance and results in an immediate defensive reaction by those involved. The development of, and linkage to, a TQM budget is an essential step to tie the unknown to a known. The other necessary action is to recognize and address known risks and pitfalls. Although there are several classic risks and pitfalls that all programs have exhibited, continuous evaluation and review must be an active part of the implementation and maintenance plan. Typical problems are:

1. *Expectation.* We live in a world where instant gratification is not soon enough. TQM will not result in immediate, recognizable financial returns. Effective and stable integration of a TQM philosophy will take two years or more. People are reluctant to accept a change to their normal lifestyles, and that is what TQM does.

2. *Control.* It is absolutely necessary that program and employee control be defined and planned, particularly during the initial phases of the program. Although TQM involves employee involvement, the level of empowerment must be defined and planned. There are several areas that should not be included in open employee empowerment. Generally, areas of open involvement should be limited to operational processes. Those tasks related to mission development, strategic planning, budget, organization, and manpower planning and evaluation, should be left to management and staff.

3. *Commitment.* Once the decision has been made to implement and support a TQM program, management must be diligent in their commitment toward its success. This requires visible, open support and recognition of the people and the ultimate results. Lack of commitment is the number one cause of failure of most programs.

4. *Linkage to Budget.* "Good for You" programs do not survive if they are not linked to traditional operational values. Therefore, creating a budget that integrates TQM provides a level of understanding and acceptance into the existing culture. This level of acceptance, comfort, and understanding is essential for success. Without this linkage, it becomes someone else's program that is a threat to others' position and control.

This list contains the basic pitfalls and risks. There will be others peculiar to each specific situation, but they will essentially be a subset of those noted.

26A.9   INDUSTRY EXAMPLES AND STRATEGIES.

(a) Manufacturing. The ABC Manufacturing Company provides products to the consumer market for use in telecommunications applications. This company had been very successful for eight years with total annual revenue of $60 million. However, their flagship products were no longer the latest technology, and new products were continually late to market. In addition, ABC was having difficulty being competitive due to an inefficient and costly manufacturing operation. Management made a strategic decision to implement TQM and assigned three members of the senior staff to implement a program.

The following are the parameters of the program developed:

Budget for first two years	$150,000
Total employment to be involved	400
First year	200
Second year	200
Source of training	Outside consultant
Measure of success	Improved employee attitude
	Reduced manufacturing costs
	Improved productivity
	Improved scheduling and performance to schedule

Twenty-five employees were initially trained, who were formed into the steering committee (ten members) and three problem teams of five each. The following is a summary of a problems evaluated by one of the teams.

One problem identified was the large materials premium costs:

Audit input (annual)	Gross income	$60,000,000
	Gross margin	30%
	Product cost (70%)	$42,000,000
	Materials cost (30% of product cost)	$12,600,000
	Material needing premium (5%)	$630,000
	Average premium (50%)	$315,000

Therefore, there was an opportunity to reduce premium costs on materials by $315,000. The team made two changes in the materials release and procurement process that reduced the premium costs by 50%, with an annual savings of approximately $160,000. The two changes involved:

- Creation of a proactive system of identifying material lead times
- Clear identification of long lead items on the materials lists.

The other two initial problems identified were:

- Product-to-market time
- Manufacturing repair cost and reduction in process defects.

The total projected savings from these three problems and the related process improvements were in excess of $500,000.

(b) Construction Industry.   The Do Good Construction Company is a subcontractor in the commercial building portion of the construction industry. Its areas of involvement are structural fireproofing, facade design, and construction and internal drywall installation. This company has an employee core of eighty people and utilizes union manpower for direct construction labor. The company is fifteen years old and into the second generation of ownership. Recent gross revenue has been flat at $30 million for the last three years. The new generation of management has determined that there is considerable waste which must be eliminated. As a result, a three-person executive committee has enlisted a consultant to assist in the development of a plan.
    The following are the parameters of the program proposed:

Budget for first year	$30,000
Budget reserve for next two years	$30,000
Total employees to be involved	80
First year	50
Next two years	30 (nonresident in home office area)
Source of training and assistance	Outside consultant
Measure of success	Improved employee attitude
	Reduced operating costs
	Improved competitiveness

Twenty one people were initially trained and formed into the steering committee (five members) and three problem teams of five each. One of the problems addressed by a team was that of excessive down time of the equipment used in spraycoating fireproofing on the structures and in coating materials utilized on facades.
    Here is a summary of the problem details:

Average spray system usage	2 full-time
Manpower involved per system	4-person team
Hourly rate	$30
Average equipment down time	6 hours per week (1 unit)
Sum of down-time cost	$120 per hour (1 unit)
	=$1440 (2 units, 1 week)
Annually	$75,000

This identified an opportunity of $75,000 in cost reduction for this portion of the business. The team made three changes in the utilization of this equipment and associated manpower, which reduced initial down time to two hours per week and to zero down time after six months. These changes resulted in a saving to the company of more than $50,000 in the first year. The changes made were:

- Weekly preventative maintenance program
- Formal on-the-job training for operators
- Major maintenance recall to the shop.

The other two problems identified were:

- Proper documentation of change orders
- Control and maintenance of small tools (value of less than $500).

The total identified annual cost savings from these three problems was $150,000.

(c)   **Health Care Industry.**   Northwest Home Care is a nonprofit organization that services the elder clients of a specific geographic area that has approximately 9,000 potential clients. This organization has 150 highly motivated, well-qualified employees, one-half of whom are directly involved in planning and managing the necessary client services. These services are procured from outside suppliers. Ninety percent of Northwest's revenue comes from state and federal reimbursement (at a standard rate) for its services. An internal audit found that actual client cost was $220 per month and state/federal reimbursement rate was $200. An internal committee was formed to look into the problem, and they came to the following conclusions:

1. Procedures were lacking, and those that did exist were inadequate.
2. Client tracking was very primitive.
3. Employee training was lacking in the task management and administrative areas.
4. Client managers were overloaded.
5. Vendor communication was lacking.
6. There was little or no understanding of the total process and, with the exception of the financial area, no performance tracking.

In addition to some specific short-term administrative changes, the committee recommended that a TQM program be initiated, and strongly suggested that the identified area of revenue be addressed as a problem area.

The following are the parameters of the program proposed:

Total employees to be involved	150
First year	90
Second year	60
Source of training and assistance	Outside consultant
Measure of success	Employee expertise in management
	Revenue differential reduction
	Process development
	Performance tracking
	Client satisfaction

(Note: the outside consultant used was available from a nonprofit service group which provided service at a special low rate for other nonprofits).

Thirty people were trained in the initial phase and formed into the steering committee (eight members), and four problem solving teams of five each. One of the problems addressed by a team was the billing process and the collection of data to support it.

A summary of the problem details follows:

Total revenue	$8,000,000
Federal and state reimbursement (90%)	$7,200,000
Active clients	3,000
Average reimbursement per client	$200 per month
Average cost of services per client	$220 per month

The audit of this information indicated that growth was not possible without additional outside funding. It further showed that the 10% differential was an unacceptable problem. The team made three basic changes which immediately resulted in a reduction of $18 per month, and recommended changes which would result in an additional $2 per month. As a result, the costs would be in control.

- Create an accurate client tracking system which would assure that client services were accurately billed to the state. The present system was not a real-time system based on daily inputs.
- Develop a vendor reporting system for providing accurate numbers on services provided, and develop an audit path for that input.
- Create a statistical performance tracking system on major vendors.

These changes immediately pointed out that the billing was inconsistent, and generally understated state billing versus vendor invoicing.

Additional needs were:

- Improved client manager training
- Better definition of service requirements to the vendors, to eliminate unnecessary tasks and reduce charges
- Identification and definition of key or core processes

The ultimate result of these changes was a more cost-effective, higher quality service, as well as a more efficient operation.

These three examples of TQM implementation and the resulting changes are based on actual cases, numbers and names changed. They are intended to show the types of problems and activities that develop in a TQM program implementation, and that, although the changes may appear small on the surface, they become significant in the overall picture.

26A.10 SUMMARY. Once management has made the decision to implement TQM, they have made a commitment to change the way the operation will do business in the future. They will develop and encourage employee empowerment, they will visibly support the concepts and elements of TQM, and they will boost credibility by adding TQM into their strategy and its supporting budgets. The critical steps involved in developing a TQM organization are:

1. Audit the organization and business elements to establish a baseline.
2. Evaluate the industry and competition to determine appropriate operating benchmarks.
3. Scope the proposed TQM program, with its parameters and implementation schedule.
4. Develop the budget to support necessary actions and activities.
5. Organize and activate the program and measure the gains.

Phil Crosby wrote *Quality Is Free,* but that is really not a correct assessment of the picture. Good quality actually adds to the bottom line, and often can mean the difference between success and failure.

SOURCES AND SUGGESTED REFERENCES

Adair, Charlene B., *Breakthrough Process Redesign: New Pathways to Customer Value.* New York: AMACOM, 1994.

Baldrige Winners on World-Class Quality, The Conference Board Report No. 990. New York: Conference Board, 1992.

Barry, Thomas J., *Management Excellence Through Quality.* Milwaukee, Wis.: ASQC Quality Press, 1991.

Berry, Thomas H., *Managing the Total Quality Transformation.* New York: McGraw-Hill, 1991.

Bogan, Christopher E., and English, Michael J., *Benchmarking for Best Practices.* New York: McGraw-Hill, 1991.

Brocka, Bruce, *Quality Management: Implementing the Best Ideas of the Masters.* Homewood, Ill.: Business One Irwin, 1992.

Carter, Carla C., *Human Resources Management and the Total Quality Imperative.* New York: AMACOM, 1994.

Cortada, James W., *TQM for Sales and Marketing Management.* New York: McGraw-Hill, 1993

Creating a Customer-Focused Organization, The Conference Board Report No. 1030. New York: Conference Board, 1993.

Crosby, Philip, *Let's Talk Quality.* New York: McGraw-Hill, 1989.

Crosby, Philip, *Quality is Free: The Art of Making Quality Certain.* New York: McGraw-Hill, 1979.

Crosby, Philip, *Quality Without Tears: The Art of Hassle-Free Management.* New York: McGraw-Hill, 1984.

Deming, W. Edwards, *Out of the Crisis.* Cambridge, Mass.: Massachusetts Institute of Technology, Center for Advanced Engineering Study, 1986.

Deming, W. Edwards, *Quality, Productivity and Competitive Position.* Cambridge, Mass.: Massachusetts Institute of Technology, Center for Advanced Engineering Study, 1982.

Environmental TQM, 2d ed. New York: McGraw-Hill: Executive Enterprises Publications, 1994.

Gevirtz, Charles D., *Developing New Products With TQM.* New York: McGraw-Hill, 1994.

Hiam, Alexander, *Does Quality Work? A Review of Relevant Studies,* The Conference Board No. 1043. New York: Conference Board, 1993.

Hoffherr, Glen D., *Breakthrough Thinking in Total Quality Management.* Englewood Cliffs, N.J.: PTR Prentice Hall, 1994.

Hutchins, Greg, *Standard Manual of Quality Auditing: A Step-by-Step Workbook With Procedures and Checklists.* Englewood Cliffs, N.J.: PTR Prentice Hall, 1992.

Johnson, Richard S., *TQM: Leadership for the Quality Transformation,* ASQC Total Quality Management Series vol. 1. Milwaukee, Wis.: ASQC Quality Press, 1993.

Johnson, Richard S., *TQM: Management Processes for Quality Operations,* ASQC Total Quality Management Series vol. 2. Milwaukee, Wis.: ASQC Quality Press, 1993.

Juran J.M., *Managerial Breakthrough.* New York: McGraw-Hill, 1964.

Juran, J.M., *Quality Control Handbook,* 4th ed. New York: McGraw-Hill, 1988.

Katzenbach, Jon R., and Smith, Douglas K., *The Wisdom of Teams.* Boston, Mass.: Harvard Business School Press, 1993.

Mahoney, Francis Xavier, *The TQM Trilogy: Using ISO 9000, The Deming Prize, and the Baldrige Award to Establish a System for Total Quality Management.* New York: AMACOM, 1994.

Maintaining the Total Quality Advantage, The Conference Board Report No. 979. New York: Conference Board, 1991.

Managing Globally: Key Perspectives, The Conference Board Report No. 972. New York: Conference Board, 1991.

Milakovich, Michael E., "Total Quality Management for Public Sector Productivity Improvement," *Public Productivity & Management Review,* Vol. 14, No. 1, Fall 1990.

Miller, William C., *Quantum Quality: Quality Improvement Through Innovation, Learning, and Creativity.* White Plains, N.Y.: Quality Resources, 1993.

Oakland, John S., *Total Quality Management: The Management of Change Through Process Improvement,* 2d ed. Boston, Mass.: Butterworth-Heinemann, 1993.

Organizational Transformation in Health Care: A Work in Progress, 1st ed. San Franciso: Jossey-Bass Publishers, 1994.

Petrone, Joe, *Building the High Performance Sales Force.* New York: AMACOM, 1994.

Pfau, Bruce N., *Innovative Reward and Recognition Strategies in TQM,* The Conference Board Report No. 1051. New York: Conference Board, 1993.

Profiting From Total Quality, The Conference Board Report No. 1048, New York: Conference Board, 1993.

The Quality Roadmap: How to Get Your Company on the Quality Track—And Keep It There. New York: AMACOM, 1994.

Rabbitt, John T., *The ISO 9000 Book: A Global Competitor's Guide to Compliance and Certification,* 2d ed., White Plains, N.Y.: Quality Resources, 1994.

Roberts, Harry V., *Quality Is Personal: A Foundation for Total Quality Management.* New York: Free Press, 1993.

Rust, R., Zahorik, A., and Keiningham, T., *Return on Quality.* Chicago, Ill.: Probus, 1994.

Sashkin, Marshall, *Putting Total Quality Management to Work: What TQM Means, How to Use It, and How to Sustain It Over the Long Run*. San Francisco: Berrett-Koehler, 1993.

Schmidt, Warren H., *TQManager: A Practical Guide for Managing in a Total Quality Organization*. San Franciso: Jossey-Bass, 1993.

Snyder, Neil H., *Vision, Values, and Courage: Leadership for Quality Management*. New York: Free Press, 1994.

Spendolini, Michael, *The Benchmarking Book*. New York: AMACOM, 1992.

Talley, Dorsey J., *Total Quality Management: Performance and Cost Measures: The Strategy for Economic Survival*. Milwaukee, Wis.: ASQC Quality Press, 1991.

Tenner, Arthur R., and DeToro, Irving J., *Three Steps to Continuous Improvement*. Reading, Mass.: Addison-Wesley, 1994.

Total Quality Management for Law Firms. New York: Practising Law Institute, 1992.

Total Quality Management in Higher Education, New directions for institutional research no. 71. San Francisco: Jossey-Bass, 1991.

Walker, Joseph V., *TQM in Action: One Firm's Journey Toward Quality and Excellence*. Chicago, Ill.: American Bar Association, 1994.

CHAPTER 27

PROGRAM BUDGETING: PLANNING, PROGRAMMING, BUDGETING

William B. Iwaskow

CONTENTS

27.3 HISTORY   1

(b) Federal Government
    (vi) Carter Administration   1
    (vii) Federal Phase-Out
        (Renumbered)   1
(c) Utilization Overview   2

**27.7   INSTALLATION
        CONSIDERATIONS**   2

(a) Information System
        (iii) Management's Needs   2

**27.8   SUMMARY AND
        CONCLUSIONS**   2

27.3 HISTORY

Page 27•7, add after second paragraph of section:

The most extensive use of PB ever embarked upon was by the U.S. federal government. The scope and scale of its application has never been matched by any other budgetary technique for a single organizational entity (other than the traditional line-item approach). PB became an official budget approach utilized throughout the federal government by the mid-60s, which was well documented. It is presented here in considerable detail, therefore, and in much of its original nomenclature.

(b)   Federal Government

Page 27•9, add new subsection (vi) at end of subsection (v):

(vi)   Carter Administration (New).   President Carter introduced zero base budgeting (ZBB) to the federal government in the mid-1970s following his experience with it as the governor of Georgia. ZBB was, among other things, an organizational departure from PB in that it developed budgets from the "bottom-up" rather than PB's

"top-down" approach. This hierarchical direction distinction is fading in budgeting and planning systems with the growing horizontal, global type of organizations in the twenty-first century era of global capitalism.

Page 27•10, change subsection numbering for Federal Phase-Out from "(vi)" to "(vii)".

(vii)   Federal Phase-Out

Page 27•10, delete last two sentences of fourth item bulleted list.

Page 27•10, add at end of ninth item of bulleted list:

More tailoring was necessary with a much lesser emphasis on format and procedures.

10. President Carter's introduction of ZBB and its lack of success gave further impetus to the bureaucracy and legislative entities to ease back to the old, comfortable, politically more manipulative standby: line-item budgeting.

(c)   Utilization Overview

Page 27•11, add at end of second paragraph in section:

, or insufficiently integrated into political environments.

Cynical economists and budgetary analysts have felt that for the public and government sectors, in particular, with their inherent significant political dynamics, only the line-item type of budgeting is feasible. They feel the bureaucrats and politicians do not want to relinquish their easier control of allocating resources via the line-item approach or discipline themselves in reviewing the consequences of their budgetary decisions.

27.7   INSTALLATION CONSIDERATIONS

(a)   Information System

(iii)   Management's Needs

Page 27•33, add at end of paragraph:

With the widespread availability of mini-computers and micro-computers and more sophisticated software programs, there is increasing potential for building dynamic, multi-factor models for analysis and resource allocation.

27.8   SUMMARY AND CONCLUSIONS

Page 27•38, replace last sentence of seventh paragraph with :

Many budget areas are now forecast beyond one year.

The concepts, approaches and spirit of PB endure therefore, albeit under other labels and forms. No other budgetary approach has provided the futurity and comprehensiveness for resource allocations, especially for public sector organizations.

Page 27•39, add new paragraph after third item in list:

> While PB history is a great teacher, many are destined to repeat the lessons. It is clear that more and more we need to think of budgets longer than one year and the consequences, especially as we enter the twenty-first century. Information, ideas, technology, and money flow easily and quickly across borders, and businesses and jobs go where they can best be performed. Global economic forces are making cataclysmic, fast-paced changes. They have a variety of threats, instabilities, and opportunities that must be addressed in shorter timeframes with ever greater consequences. This demands more from public and private sector organizations as they redefine their goals and roles and allocate their resources. Futurity and its importance in budgets and current decision-making grows. PB is a strategic tool that can provide guidance through these uncharted and opportunistic seas. The traditional line-item budget cannot serve all of these critical needs.

ACTIVITY-BASED BUDGETING (New)

James A. Brimson
ABM Institute

John J. Antos
Antos Enterprises, Inc.

CONTENTS

27A.1 INTRODUCTION 2

27A.2 TRADITIONAL BUDGETING DOES NOT SUPPORT EXCELLENCE 3

27A.3 ACTIVITY-BASED BUDGETING DEFINITIONS 5

(a) Principles of ABB 6
(b) Requirements for Successful ABB Budgeting 6
(c) Process Management Approach 6
(d) Culture Encourages Sustaining Benefits 7
(e) Commitment to Excellence 8

27A.4 ACTIVITY-BASED BUDGETING PROCESS 8

27A.5 LINKING STRATEGY AND BUDGETING 8

(a) Principles of Strategic Management 8
(b) Customer Surveys 9

(c) Core Competency Analysis 10
(d) Benchmarking 11
(e) Quality Function Deployment 11
(f) Reverse Engineering 12

27A.6 TRANSLATE STRATEGY TO ACTIVITIES 13

(a) Identify Activity Targets by Bill of Activities 13
(b) Strategic Management Tools and Targets 14
(c) Match Resource to Goals 14

27A.7 DETERMINE WORKLOAD 14

(a) Workload of Service-Determined Activities or Business Processes 14
(b) Explode Bill of Activities 14
(c) Workload for Non-Service-Related Activities 15
(d) Workload for Special Projects 15

27A.8 ABB CALENDAR 15

---

* This material has been adapted from *Activity-Based Management for Service Industries, Government Entities, and Not-for-Profit Organizations* by James A. Brimson and John J. Antos, NY (John Wiley & Sons, Inc. 1994).

27A.9   CREATE PLANNING
GUIDELINES   16

27A.10 IDENTIFY INTERDEPART-
MENTAL PROJECTS   16

(a) Activity-Based Budgeting for
Procuring Supplies   16
(b) ABB Example of Target Cost   16
(c) Creative Thinking Approaches   17
(d) Brainstorming   17
(e) Storyboarding   18
(f) Value Management   18
(g) Task Level Analysis   19

27A.11 IMPROVEMENT PROCESS   19

(a) Ranking Budget Requests   19
(b) Impact of Projects   19

27A.12 FINALIZING THE BUDGET   19

(a) Budget Review Panels   20
(b) Budgeting Options   20
(c) Steps in Implementing ABB   20
(d) Initial Project   20

27A.13 PERFORMANCE
REPORTING   20

(a) Data Capture   20
(b) Activity-Based Budget Report   21
(c) Business Process Reporting   22

27A.14 SUMMARY   22

SOURCES AND
SUGGESTED REFERENCES   22

27A.1   INTRODUCTION.   The purposes of this chapter are to:

- Discuss problems with traditional budgeting
- Define activity-based budgeting (ABB)
- Discuss the ABB process.

A budget is a financial expression of a plan. Traditional budgeting focuses on planning resources for an organizational unit. Each year managers look at history and any significant changes and create an annual budget. The budgeting process starts with the senior executive announcing budget goals. These may consist of revenue and profit goals as well as goals for new services.

Many managers respond by looking at last year's numbers and increasing their budget for the year based on inflation and/or the amount of the increase in revenues (see Exhibit 27A.1). For example, if revenues increase 10%, then the various department managers might increase the budgets for their departments by 10%.

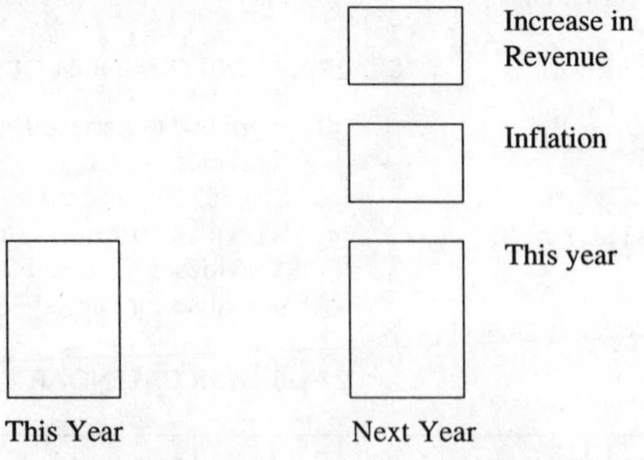

Exhibit 27A.1.   Manager's response to next year's forecast.

The problem with this approach is that last year's inefficiencies are incorporated into this year's budget. Often little attention is paid to improvements in each department. Finally, little incentive is incorporated into the budgeting process for continuous improvement. Changing workload for each department often is not considered.

Senior managers, during budgeting, often make arbitrary cuts across the board. A potentially negative consequence is that the better-managed departments may have already cut the majority of waste and now may have to cut into necessary resources. Instead, other, less-efficient departments should make more radical reductions to bring them to the same level of efficiency as the better-managed departments.

Budgets in this environment often become wrestling matches in which those who are the best presenters are given larger budgets. The theory goes that the best at presenting the reasons for the larger budget deserves the larger budget.

Once the budget is agreed on, it is often cast in concrete for the year.

27A.2 TRADITIONAL BUDGETING DOES NOT SUPPORT EXCELLENCE.

First, the budgeting process should highlight cost reduction and the elimination of wasteful activities and tasks. Traditional budgeting does not make visible what the organization does. Instead, managers look at their history of spending and simply increase last year's budget and/or actuals based on inflation and/or increases in revenue.

Second, budgeting should be a formal mechanism for reducing workload to the minimal level to support enterprise objectives. Excess workload due to poor structuring of activities and business process drives up cost and does not improve customer satisfaction. The budgeting process itself should give insight into how to reduce workload and how to set workload reduction goals.

Third, budgeting should consider all costs as variable; yet budgeting often formalizes the laissez-faire attitude toward occupancy and equipment costs. Most are familiar with the concept of fixed and variable costs. The problem with this classification is a psychological one. The term *fixed costs* seems to imply that these costs cannot be eliminated because they are fixed. Yet we all know that buildings and equipment can be put to alternative use, sold, demolished, or leased. Many assets are often dedicated to specific activities. By making these assets more flexible, the total capital base of an enterprise can be lowered. Even property taxes and property insurance can be reduced. A budget based on variable and fixed costs often focuses attention on the variable costs and implies that the fixed costs are not controllable.

A better classification would be utilized and unutilized capacity. This classification simply shows that some assets are being used and some are not. It does not present the psychological barrier to change that the term *fixed costs* does. Unutilized capacity can be saved for future growth, eliminated, used for other purposes, or consolidated with another division.

An important goal of budgeting should be to improve each process on a continuous basis. Traditional budgeting, as it is commonly practiced, seems to focus on simply repeating history. Activity budgeting sets improvement targets by activity/business process. Thus, this approach is something everyone can understand and use to work toward improvement. However, traditional budgeting sets goals like "reduce costs" by a specific percentage, without giving employees insights on how to achieve those targets.

Activity budgeting works to synchronize activities and thus improve business processes. Traditional budgeting may take the approach of "every department for itself." Managers pay lip service to coordinating between departments; however, managers will almost certainly respond in a way that will maximize their own department's performance. The inevitable consequence is to lower the performance of the organization as a whole.

Activity budgeting sets business process improvement goals, which requires the joint efforts of employees from a variety of departments. Because the goal is to improve the business process, old barriers between departments begin to crumble.

Traditional budgeting does not formally consider external and internal suppliers and customers. However, activity budgeting requires asking the internal and external suppliers and customers to describe their needs and their respective workload requirements.

Too often, the focus in traditional budgeting is to control the result. For example, consider the organization that closes its financial books in 4 to 15 days. Each month managers focus on information that is 34 to 45 days old.

It makes more sense to control the *process,* rather than to try to control the *result* through financial statements. The Japanese have unsophisticated accounting systems compared to U.S. companies of a similar size. If the secret was a more sophisticated accounting system, then U.S. companies should be superior. Yet that is not necessarily the case.

Activity budgeting and activity management focus on controlling the process. Only by controlling the process can results improve.

In a similar vein, traditional budgeting tends to focus on the effects rather than the causes. For example, it often requires a long time to hire new employees or introduce a new service. In reality, organizations should focus on the causes of these long lead times. In Japan, managers come to meetings asking their peers for suggestions to solve their problems. In the United States, our individualistic attitudes often makes managers consider a request for help as a sign of weakness. So managers make up excuses to explain the reasons they were over budget, rather than concentrating their efforts on how to improve operations.

Because activity budgeting focuses on the root cause of problems, everyone can work to identify how to reduce or eliminate them. Only by eliminating the "root cause" of the problem can the cost be permanently eliminated.

Activity budgeting requires that customers be asked for their requirements. Only by asking the customer can an organization understand whether it has properly applied resources to meet the customer's needs (e.g., do the patrons of the U.S. Postal Service want two- to three-day delivery, or do they want consistent delivery within some stated time period?). By asking the customer, the workload connected with the activities necessary to please the customer can better be determined.

Activity budgeting focuses on output, not on input. It focuses on what work is done, how the work is performed, and how much work is done. The required resources are only a consequence of the activities. The problem with traditional budgeting is that it lacks ownership. Even if the department manager "owns" the budget, seldom do the individual employees in that department own the budget. Activity budgeting asks each person to look at the activities he or she performs and set performance targets for those activities in the context of customer requirements and organizational objectives.

Activity budgeting allows people to be empowered to manage their activities properly. If something is wrong, if there is a better way to perform the activity or business process, or if a quality issue arises, the employee(s) who performs the activity or business process should make the necessary improvements or corrections without requiring management approval. (This assumes that the employee is not changing the service or the quality provided to the customer, and is improving the service or business process at a lower cost.)

Senior management needs to remember that people will not work themselves out of a job. People will contribute ideas to improve operations only if they understand that improvement in value-added activities allows the transfer of resources to growth-enabling activities.

Under activity budgeting, mistakes are acceptable, but repetition of mistakes is unacceptable. An executive told Sam Walton of a $10 million mistake and submitted his resignation. Walton told the executive he couldn't resign because the company had just spent $10 million training him. People need to know they can make mistakes, but they must learn from those mistakes and not repeat them.

Activity budgeting uses a common language—the language of the activities or business processes that everyone is performing. Traditional budgeting uses terms that the accountants are familiar with. This Tower of Babel makes communication more difficult and encourages specialization at the expense of cooperation.

Activity budgeting looks for consistency of the output. This means that the activity should be performed in a consistent way over time. Continuous improvement must be encouraged, but the activity should only be performed in accordance with current best practice. Success depends on finding the best possible way to perform an activity or business process and consistently looking for ways to improve it, while performing the activity/business process in a consistent manner.

Activity budgeting requires setting activity or business process targets as the minimum level of performance rather than the absolute level. These activity or business process targets should identify the minimum level of performance necessary to support organizational objectives. Managers should not try to exceed these minimum levels. Instead, they should look at ways to reduce waste and non-value-added portions of various activities.

27A.3 ACTIVITY-BASED BUDGETING DEFINITIONS. Activity-based budgeting

(ABB) is the process of planning and controlling the expected activities of the organization to derive a cost-effective budget that meets forecast workload and agreed strategic goals.

An **ABB** is a quantitative expression of the expected activities of the organization, reflecting management forecast of workload and financial and nonfinancial requirements to meet agreed strategic goals and planned changes to improve performance.

The three key elements of an ABB include:

- Type of work to be done
- Quantity of work to be done
- Cost of work to be done.

(a)   Principles of ABB.   ABB must reflect what is done, that is, the activities or business processes, not cost elements. Resources required (cost elements) must be derived from the expected activities or business processes and workload. *Workload* is simply the number of units of an activity that are required. For example, in the human resource department, the workload for the activity "hire employees" might be to hire 25 employees. The cost elements to perform that activity might be the wages and benefits of the recruiter, travel, advertising, testing, supplies, and occupancy costs for the space occupied by the recruiter and for interviewing. If a hiring freeze occurs, then the workload for this activity would be zero.

Budgets must be based on the future workload in order to meet:

- Customer requirements
- Organizational/departmental goals and strategies
- New/changed services and service mix
- Changes in business processes
- Improvements in efficiency and effectiveness
- Quality, flexibility, and cycle time goals
- Changes in service levels.

The final budget must reflect the changes in resource cost levels and foreign exchange fluctuations. However, it is better to initially budget using constant cost and foreign exchange rates to facilitate comparisons, and then to add inflation and foreign exchange adjustments at the conclusion of the budgeting process.

As part of the activity budgeting process, it is important to highlight continuous improvement. Each department should identify the activities or business processes to be improved, the amount of improvement, and how it plans to achieve its improvement targets.

(b)   Requirements for Successful ABB Budgeting.   The organization must be committed to excellence. If the organization does not have this commitment, then resources will be wasted on data analysis activities that will never be implemented. Changing is not easy. It is easier to study the problem than to make the difficult decisions required to improve.

(c)   Process Management Approach.   The organization must use a process management approach to improvement. This requires defining each activity as part of a repeatable, robust business process that can be continuously improved and the variability removed. Activities defined this way can use various techniques to decrease time, improve quality, and reduce the cost of those activities.

Process management is crucial to excellence, because high levels of performance are possible only when activities are done to best practices, the unused capacity is minimal, the best practices are continually made better, and the activities are executed perfectly. Activity definitions must support process management. Activities must be in the form of verb plus a noun. There must be a physical output. Two-stage definitions of drivers are usually not adequate. For example, the activity "pay employee" is compatible with process management. To define an activity as "supplies handling" and the output measure as the "number of service production runs" would not be compatible activity definitions. Two-stage activity definitions might be used in assigning costs to a service, but it does not help in improving operations. A better way to define this sample activity would be "move supplies," with the output measure defined as the "number of moves."

One of the first steps that an activity manager may have to take is to review activity definitions to make sure that they are compatible with a process approach.

(d) Culture Encourages Sustaining Benefits.   The organization culture should encourage sustaining benefits. These benefits should not be something that lasts for only a short while, after which everyone goes back to the old way. These benefits should change the way the people in the organization think and act. Often this means changing the way the employees are compensated, so that they share in the productivity improvement.

Organizations must overcome the cultural barriers shown in Exhibit 27A.2. Next to these barriers are actions the organization must take in order to overcome these cultural barriers.

Cultural barriers	Actions
Departmental structure often interferes with departments interacting, in order to minimize total enterprise cost.	Change information systems so the organization can see total cost of business processes rather than just the costs in a specific department.
Policies and procedures provide guidelines for employee behavior. These were often set up to ensure consistency and to make it easy for employees to handle specific situations.	Empower employees to handle various situations to ensure customer satisfaction. Use policies to set general guidelines and train, support, and empower employees to satisfy the customer.
Suggestion programs usually require the approval of management to implement change. This slows the change process.	Suggestion programs are only for changes to the service or for capital requests. Changes to efficiency should be made by employees without management approval.
Measurement systems tend to focus on the department level.	Abolish micromanagement. Give managers/employees the tools, authority, and responsibility to do their jobs. Make them responsible for outputs and a budget level of resources to do their work.
Specialization assumes that lowest cost is achievable through economies of scale.	Today flexibility is critical. People must be cross-trained for a variety of tasks. First, as slack or heavy periods occur, employees can help out in other departments. Second, they need to understand how what they do affects other departments and how what other departments do affects them.

Exhibit 27A.2.   Cultural barriers.

(e)   Commitment to Excellence.   Many organizations take a short-term approach to improving operations. Costs are easy to control—simply stop spending money. This approach is similar to a crash diet. The problem with crash diets is that the dieter usually regains what he or she lost and often gains even more weight. If an organization is committed to excellence, then its goal is to change the way it does business. This is similar to changing eating habits. For example, organizations must start compensating people based on business process performance rather than the traditional actual versus budget of cost elements that most organizations have historically used.

27A.4   ACTIVITY-BASED BUDGETING PROCESS.   The activity-based budgeting process begins with the customer. The organization must determine who the customer is and what the customer wants. It must look to its competitors. Competition consists of both direct competitors and alternate services that might compete with the organization's services.

Then the organization must develop a strategy to meet customer needs. A restaurant must decide whether to be a five-star restaurant, with crystal and linen tablecloths, or to provide good food in a clean environment with less sophisticated decor but with good value to the customer.

Next, the organization should forecast workload. Management and sales determine what sales levels will be, and managers need to estimate their workloads as a result of these sales levels. Often the sales forecast includes new services and new markets, as well as any changes in strategy.

Planning guidelines must be articulated to each manager to establish the specific activity-level targets within a business process context. Eventually, every activity manager should have targets for improving his or her respective value-added activities and eliminating non-value-added activities.

Next, interdepartmental projects should be identified. Because these projects will affect the workload, as well as the activities in several departments, they must be coordinated and done prior to each manager improving his or her own activities.

At this point in the budgeting process, specific activity-level projects can be identified. These are projects to improve operations at the individual activity level. However, improvement should always be within organizational objectives, a business process context, and a customer satisfaction context.

Activity-based investment analysis consists of defining improvement projects, evaluating those projects, and then using committees to select projects that will meet the organization's goals and meet customers' needs.

The final step is to determine the activities and workload for the coming year.

27A.5   LINKING STRATEGY AND BUDGETING.   One of the problems with traditional budgeting is that a clear link between the enterprise's strategy and budgeting often does not exist. Therefore, operating managers do not know how to incorporate strategy into their budgets.

(a)   Principles of Strategic Management.   There are a variety of seminars and books available on the subject of strategic management. This chapter does not discuss those techniques, but simply assumes that a strategic plan exists. The role of senior management is to set performance targets based on the strategic plans. The performance targets might be for sales, number of new services and/or markets, cycle time, cost, quality, or customer service levels. The role of the activity manager is to achieve or exceed those targets.

Strategic objectives and performance targets must be translated into activity-level targets. Activity managers must ensure that service requirements are a direct derivative of customer needs.

The translation process starts with customer requirements and an analysis of competitive strategies. Then strategic objectives are set. The price for services allowable by the market are determined and time, quality, and cost targets are determined. Then these targets are translated into activity-level targets.

There are several important strategic management tools to assist with this process. The key ones include:

- Customer surveys
- Core competency analysis
- Benchmarking
- Quality function deployment
- Reverse engineering.

(b) Customer Surveys.   One of the first steps in the strategic management process is to perform a customer survey. The customer survey can be done in person, by telephone, or by direct mail. The survey asks a variety of questions, but the focus is on the factors that are important to the customer, a ranking of those factors by the customer, and, finally, the customer's perception of the organization's performance regarding those factors.

Based on this survey, the organization needs to start with the factors most important to the customer and determine whether it is satisfying the customer on those factors of performance. Activity or business process and investment preference must be given to those activities or business processes that the customer feels are most important. Especially in the case where satisfaction levels are not satisfactory to the customer, the organization needs to change, improve, or increase resources and effectiveness of those activities or business processes.

For example, if an organization determines that it needs to allow nurses to spend more time with patients and less time doing paperwork, then it could create an activity budget in the following way:

For the activity "complete medical charts":

Total cost	Salaries	Depreciation	Supplies	Phone	Occupancy
$24,410	22,000	400	900	150	960

The assumptions are that a person would be hired to "complete medical charts." The employee's salary and benefits would be $22,000 per year. Depreciation on his or her desk and computer would be $400. Supplies connected with filling out the charts are estimated to be $900. Because this person would be communicating with other departments, a phone would be necessary for inter-hospital calls. The fully loaded cost of hospital space (including depreciation, heat, electricity, building maintenance, and janitorial cost based on the number of square feet occupied) equals $960.

Hiring this person will enable 10 nurses to spend 10% of their time comforting, informing, and answering questions for patients. A nurse earns $36,000 annually, including benefits.

For the activity "communicate with patients":

Total cost	Salaries	Depreciation	Supplies	Phone	Occupancy
$46,320	36,000	1,000	2,000	320	7,000

The following assumptions were made. Annual salaries and benefits for 10 nurses at $36,000 per nurse equals $360,000. Because they will spend 10% of their time on this activity, the salary portion of this activity cost equals $36,000. There would be some depreciation on the desk for the portion of time performing this activity. Some educational literature would be given to the patients, which would total approximately $2,000. Nurses would need a phone line for tracking down answers to patient questions, and a reasonable percentage of the total phone cost was estimated at $320. Because the nurses spent some time sitting at a desk for this activity, 10% of their total occupancy costs was apportioned, which amounted to $7,000.

Now senior management can look at the customer survey and performance as it relates to nurses communicating and comforting patients—a high-priority item in the eyes of the customer. Then they can determine if it is worth spending a total of $70,730 ($24,410 plus $46,320) to improve customer satisfaction in this area.

(c)   Core Competency Analysis.   An organization starts by asking what activities or business processes are critical to its industry. These activities or business processes become the *core competencies* of that industry. Then the organizations can ask themselves which activities or business processes they perform well. They need to compare themselves with external benchmarks and determine where there is a core competency gap. Then the organizations can set budget targets in terms of cost, quality, and time.

Industry	Core competency
Banking	Accuracy, fast turnaround, full service
Insurance	Low rates, knowledgeable representatives, fast claims handling
Hospitals	Friendly nurses, full service, high success rate
Airlines	On-time, convenient departures, reasonable fares
Fast food	Quality, service, cleanliness
IRS	Rules that are easy to comply with, fairness, easy access
Fund-raisers	Good cause, large percentage of funds directly to cause

An auto dealer decided that a core competency of the repair shop was to provide quality repairs the first time. A further analysis revealed an opportunity to improve performance by conducting auto repair training seminars for the mechanics. Four seminars for 20 mechanics who earn $14 per hour were planned. Each seminar was to be five hours long with $500 in training supplies. A consultant will charge $3,000 per training session.

For the activity "train mechanics":

Total cost	Salaries	Supplies	Phone	Consultant
$18,100	5,600	500	0	12,000

(d) Benchmarking. The benchmarking process compares performance to other organizations, either internally or externally. Benchmarks may measure:

- Activities
- Business processes
- Time
- New service introduction
- Customer service
- Quality
- Cost.

Comparisons should be made, where possible, across divisions, with competitors, and with the best organizations in the world. For example, one telephone company can process a request for new phone service within 43 seconds. This is a speed few other organizations can duplicate, and would serve as a great benchmark for the activity "process new customers' credit requests."

One association felt it was important to answer the phone after only two rings. This would be a high-quality service to the members, and would avoid lost sales of books and seminars because people tired of waiting for someone to answer the phone. The association's operators were currently answering the phone on the third or fourth ring. It decided to increase the number of telephone operators by three. Telephone operators could be hired for $18,000 per year. They would need a desk, a PC, a phone, and supplies for order taking. Fully loaded occupancy costs were running $10 per square foot. Each operator would need 64 square feet of space.
For the activity "answer phones":

Total cost	Salaries	Depreciation	Supplies	Phone	Occupancy
$60,120	54,000	2,000	1,200	1,000	1,920

(e) Quality Function Deployment. Quality function deployment (QFD) is a concept originating in the quality field, and is applicable to activity budgeting. In QFD, the organization compares the customers' requirements with the activities or business processes necessary to meet those requirements. For each activity or business process, a comparison is also made with the competition to determine how the organization is doing against the competition. Also, a correlation is made between activities to show which activities have a strong positive or strong negative correlation with meeting customer requirements. Some activities will have no correlation with each other. Finally, a correlation is made between various activities and customer requirements. Thus the organization can determine which activities are critical to greatest customer satisfaction. Customer requirements are ranked as part of this analysis.

Although a complete explanation of this technique can be found in a number of quality books and seminars, a simple example will be discussed here. An airline is looking to increase market share by better satisfying its customers. Using QFD, the airline determines that quick turnaround time is important in order to have on-time departures. One way to improve in this area is to have two jetbridges to load passengers instead of only one. There are two activities—"move jetbridge" and "maintain jetbridge"—connected with this second jetbridge.

The airline determines that 10 percent of a ticketing agent's time is needed to handle this second jetbridge. A ticketing agent earns $32,000 per year. Two hundred ticketing agents will be affected. This means that salaries with benefits dedicated to the activity "move jetbridge" would be $640,000 (200 x 10% x $32,000). An additional 100 jetbridges would have to be purchased, at the rate of $10,000 per jetbridge. Therefore, the depreciation on $1,000,000 (100 x $10,000) using a five-year life would be $200,000 per year. The annual cost of maintenance labor is $100,000 on these jetbridges and is $50,000 on maintenance parts. Occupancy costs are $20,000 for the maintenance space needed for these jetbridges. For the activities "move jetbridge" and "maintain jetbridge":

Activity	Activity cost	Salaries	Depreciation	Parts	Occupancy
Move jetbridge	640,000	640,000			
Maintain jetbridge	370,000	100,000	200,000	50,000	20,000
Total cost	1,010,000	740,000	200,000	50,000	20,000

(f) Reverse Engineering.   Reverse engineering involves studying a competitor's services. At first glance, one would think that reverse engineering is a concept that applies only to products. However, applying reverse engineering to a service and seeing how competitors perform the service is a very useful tool.

For example, consider a company that has a regulatory affairs department that must file with the FDA to get regulatory approval. The company's managers studied the process of filing for regulatory approval. The objective was to determine how to perform the process more effectively.

Using reverse engineering principles, they started by asking the customer, in this case the FDA, the testing requirements in order to get this new product approved. Then, based on the FDA comments, they improved how they designed their products and their testing procedures in order to get approval more quickly.

For the activity, "improve the FDA approval process," the following activity costs are determined:

Regulatory personnel with salaries of $50,000 will spend 10% of their time on this project. They will have travel costs amounting to $3,000. Supplies are expected to run $600. A seminar on this topic will cost $1,700. A 10% share of their office occupancy cost is running $2,000 per year. For the activity "improve FDA approval process":

Total cost	Salaries	Travel	Supplies	Seminar	Occupancy
$12,300	5,000	3,000	600	1,700	2,000

27A.6 TRANSLATE STRATEGY TO ACTIVITIES. Strategy must be translated to an activity level to identify necessary changes. An example of a translating procedure follows:

Steps	Example
Define mission statement with enterprise goals	Dominate the market and diversify where advantage can be applied
Establish critical success factors	Grow market share; increase new service sales as percent of total sales
Establish service targets	Increase market share: Service 1 by 7%; Service 2 by 8%; discontinue Service 3
Establish service level targets	Service 1: increase sales 5%; decrease cost 8%; deliver in 2 hours

(a) Identify Activity Targets by Bill of Activities. The next step is to identify activity targets for each service.

For example: the mission might be to dominate the consumer loan business in Dallas; the critical success factor might be to grow market share; the service target might be to grow auto loan revenue by 7%; and the service level targets might be to increase auto loan sales by 5% and decrease cost by 8%.

Bill of Activities

Activity description	Cost/ output $	Units of output	Cost of service $	Target activity reduction %	Target activity reduction $	Target cost of service $
Take application	100	1	100	<5%>	<5>	95
Order reports	50	3	150	<10%>	<15>	135
Review loans	200	1	200	<7%>	<14>	186
Complete paperwork	25	4	100	<30%>	<30>	70
Disburse funds	250	1	250			250
TOTALS			800	<8%>	<64>	736

This table shows that the employees have established cost reduction targets for four of the five activities. The total reduction of $64 is an 8% reduction from last year's bill of activity cost.

Once these strategic management tools are employed, then cost, time, and quality targets can be set by the employees for each activity. The following is an example of cost, time, and quality targets.

(b)   Strategic Management Tools and Targets.

Tool	Activity	Cost	Time	Quality
Customer survey	Communicate with patients	C: 46,320 T: 40,000	C: 10 minutes T: 30 minutes	C: 80% satisfaction T: 90%
Core competency	Train mechanics	C: 18,100 T: 22,000	C: 20 hours T: 24 hours	C: 9% redos T: 5% redos
Bench-marking	Answer phone	C: 60,120 T:	C: 4 rings T: 2 rings	C: T:
Quality function deployment	Move & maintain jetbridge	C: 1,010, 000 T: 900,000	C: 45 minutes T: 30 minutes	C: 85% T: 90% on time
Reverse engineering	Obtain FDA approval	C: 12,300 T: 10,000	C: 5 years T: 2 years	C: 75% T: 80% approval
		C = Current T = Target		

(c)   Match Resource to Goals.   Next, match resources to goals. Goals should be set to be achievable. Resources should be oriented toward goals. Identify improvements to business processes as well as activities.

27A.7   DETERMINE WORKLOAD.   There are three major steps in determining activity or business process workload. These include:

1. Forecast service-determined activities or business processes.
2. Forecast non-service-related activities or business processes.
3. Forecast special projects.

(a)   Workload of Service-Determined Activities or Business Processes.   The first step in forecasting total organization workload is to forecast workload for service-determined activities:

- Identify activities for new services
- Identify planned changes to services
- Create/update a bill of activities for each service line
- Forecast services by service lines rather than individual services, in most cases
- Explode bill of activities to determine activity quantity for each service line.

(b)   Explode Bill of Activities.   To explode a bill of activities, simply list each service line and the forecasted quantity of that service line. List the units of each activity used by each service line. Then multiply units of service times the units of each activity to calculate the activity quantity volume by service. Then sum the total activity quantities.

Service	Units of Service	Bill of activity units required for each service	Activity quantities
Mortgages	5,000	Order report 3	15,000
Auto loans	1,800	Order report 1	1,800
Personal loans	1,000	Order report 1	1,000
		Total Reports	17,800

(c)   Workload for Non-Service-Related Activities.   The second step is to forecast workload of non-service-related activities. Non-service-related activities are those performed by support departments such as MIS, human resources, security, and accounting.

Activity Class	Activity Measures
General management	# of employee
Financial reporting	# of financial reports
Corporate advertising	# of TV advertisements
	# of promotions
Marketing	# of trade shows
	# of market surveys
Research	# of new services
Facilities	# of square feet

(d)   Workload for Special Projects.   The third step is to forecast workload for special projects. Examples of special projects include:

- Install activity-based management
- Install activity-based budgeting
- Install new computer system
- Expand office.

Then the organization needs to set up a calendar for each special project, with the activities and tasks listed by time period.

27A.8   ABB CALENDAR.

Brief senior management	*
Select team	**
Select departments/services	**
Review activity definitions	****
Review strategic plan	****
Explode Bill of Activities	****
Start improvement projects	***

Each * equals a week

27A.9   CREATE PLANNING GUIDELINES.   An organization should identify activity or business process-level projects with the goal of continuous improvement. Look at the budgeted workload and divide it into mandatory, discretionary, and optional units for each activity or business process. This split helps to decide what portion of value-added activities to eliminate. For example, an organization might determine that it needs only one quote to purchase supplies. The workload to obtain quotes is the minimum mandatory work. Discretionary work occurs when the purchasing agent believes a lower price is obtainable through two quotes. For optional work, the agent feels better by getting three or four quotes, some of which are from noncertified vendors.

27A.10   IDENTIFY INTERDEPARTMENTAL PROJECTS.   The organization should look at its business processes to eliminate duplicate activities and synchronize the remaining ones. Consider the following business process to "procure supplies."

How do we handle??
Projects

(a) · Activity-Based Budget for Procuring Supplies.

Activity		Labor	Technology	Facility	Utilities	Supplies	Travel	Other	Total
LY	P	89088		7827	1293	1075	4000	162	103445
TY	Q								
LY	I	101479		8915	1472	1225	4000	175	117266
TY	P								
LY	A	108404	190299	9524	1573	1308	4000	187	315295
TY	P								
LY	S	29211		2568	424	353	5562	50	38168
TY	S								
LY	M	65545		5871	938	578	200	111	73243
TY	A								

PQ = Prepare Quotes; IP = Issue Purchase Order; AP = Administer P.O.; SS = Source supplies; MA = Manage Area; LY = Last year; TY = This Year

should be Available

   After reviewing last year's total costs for each activity, the next step is to calculate last year's unit cost for each activity. For example, the activity "prepare quotes" cost $103,445. Last year, 2,000 quotes were prepared. By dividing annual quotes into total cost, the unit cost for this activity is $51.72 per quote.

Activities	Workload measures	Volume	Total cost $	Unit cost $	Target cost $
Prepare quotes	Quotes	2,000	103,445	51.72	50.00
Issue P.O.	P.O.	5,679	117,265	20.65	19.65
Administer P.O.	P.O.	5,679	315,295	55.52	53.00
Source supplies	New suppliers	100	38,167	381.68	375.00
Manage area	staff	28	72,243	2,580	2,200

(b)   ABB Example of Target Cost.   The organization has set a target of $50 per quote. This is a reduction of $1.72 from last year's cost of $51.72 per quote. The improvement process for 2,000 quotes at $1.72 per quote results in a savings of $3,440. Managers feel that they can reduce supplies by $440 by keeping more information on the computer and less on paper. Travel could be reduced $1,000 by having more vendors come to the organization's offices. Because quotes will be kept on the computer, there will be a reduction in the filing activity, saving $2,000 for part-time employee wages and benefits.

(c)   Creative Thinking Approaches.   Continuous improvement requires innovative approaches to streamlining the way an activity is done. Although creativity is a very personal trait, studies have shown that certain environments and methods are better suited to drawing out creative ideas. Some of the more effective methods are:

1. Challenging assumptions about:
   - people
   - supplies
   - business processes
   - location
   - capital
   - automation
   - activities.
2. Viewing activities or business processes based on new assumptions.
3. Perceiving patterns from other:
   - divisions
   - offices
   - services
   - departments.
4. Making connections with other organizations.
5. Establishing networks between suppliers, supplier's suppliers, you, customers, and end users.
6. Exploiting failures (e.g., the glue for Post-It-Notes was too weak).
7. Performing activity or business process backward and from the middle.
8. Using idea triggers (e.g., a new idea for each of Baskin & Robbins 31 flavors).
9. Creating superheroes.
10. Imagining you are the service, activity, or business process.

(d)   Brainstorming.   Brainstorming techniques are fairly common today. They consist of:

1. Suspending judgment until all ideas are on the table.
2. Emphasizing quantity of ideas without worrying about quality.
3. Stimulating a freewheeling session, with wild ideas encouraged.
4. Involving people from throughout the organization.
5. Reminding people that wild ideas often will fertilize the thinking process.

(e)   Storyboarding.   Storyboarding is a creativity tool that consists of using colored index cards to show business processes, activities, and tasks. The first step is to define the department mission statement. For a hotel, the department mission for the maids might be: "to keep rooms clean in order to delight customers at a minimum cost."

ACTIVITIES

	Stock cart	Clean rooms	Empty carts
T	Stack towels	Empty trash	Dispose garbage
A	Stack linens	Change bedsheets	Separate linens/towels
S	Stack toiletries	Clean bathroom	Store cart/vacuum
K	Stack stationery	Restock toiletries	
S	Stack cleaning supplies	Replace towels	
		Dust room	
		Vacuum room	
		Refill stationery	

(f)   Value Management.   Value management is an organized way of thinking. It is an objective appraisal of functions performed by services and procedures. The focus is on necessary functions for the lowest cost. It increases reliability and productivity. Costs are decreased. Value management challenges everything an organization does.
   It starts by gathering information such as:

- The purpose and use of each service
- The operating and performance issues
- The physical and environmental requirements.

   For example, fresh fish must be kept cold. Jewelry must be kept in a secure environment. What types of support requirements are there? What problems exist? Which and how many liaison personnel are required? What are the economic issues?
   These requirements are translated into required functionality of the service. Begin by determining the worth of each portion of the service. Then calculate the value improvement potential. What part of the service does the customer want? Which parts add cost? Which part is the customer willing to pay for?
   Begin using creativity. Ask the customers to value different features. Ask suppliers for ideas. Use cross-functional teams and brainstorming. Use reverse engineering techniques and look at the competitor's services. Benchmark in other industries. Find the best customer service, warehousing, and order fulfillment organization. Eliminate part of the service. How can the organization create more commonality of services and support services as well as common reports and forms?
   Evaluate whether it would be better to buy a portion of the service from outside (e.g., catering/training/maintenance for airlines; check processing and MIS for banks; body work for car dealers; janitorial, engineering, waste collection for cities) or to perform those services and support services in-house. Analyze customer trade-off of cost and features. Calculate value versus cost to produce various portions of the service. Eliminate functions, procedures, and reports. Simplify procedures,

business processes, and functions. Use alternate supplies, specifications, and methods. Shorten the service operation cycle with cross-training of departments.

(g) **Task Level Analysis.** Sometimes it is useful to analyze the tasks of an activity in order to determine the improvement potential. For example, the activity "pay vendor invoice" has the following tasks:

Task	Total	Non-value-added	Value-added	Best practice
Receive P.O. (PO)	.50	.50		
Locate receiver (R)	.50	.50		
Get vendor invoice (I)	.50	.50		
Match PO, R, I	2.00	2.00		
Enter data	4.50		4.50	2.00
Determine errors	2.50	2.50		
Expedite payment	1.25	1.25		
Make payment: computer	3.00		3.00	2.75
Make payment: manual	1.00	1.00		
Document file	3.00	1.50	1.50	1.25
	18.75	9.75	9.00	6.00

27A.11 IMPROVEMENT PROCESS. The improvement process starts with creative thinking to determine solutions. An investment proposal is then prepared. Management selects the projects that have the highest priority in meeting customer needs. The solution is implemented and incorporated into the activity budget.

(a) **Ranking Budget Requests.** After all the budget requests have been made, they are ranked. One convenient way to rank them is through a rating system in which management looks at the budget requests in comparison with the customer needs. Another useful tool is to classify them according to whether they support the current level of service or whether they are at the minimum or intermediate. "Current" implies that this is the cost of activities as they are presently performed. "Minimum" implies that this is the minimum level of service for an activity. "Intermediate" implies that this is not a final solution.

(b) **Impact of Projects.** Then the organization should look at the impact of these projects in terms of the change in workload, but also in terms of the changes in activity or business process cost.

27A.12 FINALIZING THE BUDGET. Budget proposals are created for the most promising projects. They should be reviewed and the highest priority projects selected. An implementation plan should be conceived. An activity impact report should be generated to include its cost impact, assuming no inflation or foreign currency issues. This allows for comparisons with previous activity or business process performance. Finally, inflation and foreign currency should be incorporated into the budget.

(a)   Budget Review Panels.   Budget review panels should consist of cross-functional teams whose purpose is to question and review the budget. A review panel might consist of the directors, support departments such as human resources, administration, quality, finance, and operations.

(b)   Budgeting Options.   An organization has two options for activity budgeting. First, budget and report by activities. Second, budget by activities and convert the activity budget into a traditional cost element budget. In this second approach, the organization plans on an activity or business process basis. Managers would use activity costs per unit to determine cost elements. Then they would summarize by cost elements. This second approach is only temporary until the organization better understands how to manage by activities, and usually lasts for only a year.

(c)   Steps in Implementing ABB.

Activities/tasks	Months			
	1	2	3	4
Train and educate	**			
Perform strategic analysis	****			
Forecast workload	******			
Establish planning guidelines		****		
Propose interdepartmental improvement		****		
Propose activity improvement			********	
Select improvement options			*******	
Finalize budget				***

Each * equals one week.

(d)   Initial Project.   A steering group of three to five members should be created. A series of panels with five to six members from different departments should be created to discuss cross-departmental issues. Each budgeting unit should have a budgeting manager, which could be someone other than the department manager. There would be 10 to 20 budgeting units per in-house coordinator or per consultant.

27A.13   PERFORMANCE REPORTING.   Remember that the most effective reports are those that do not have to be made. Therefore, introduce proactive control rather than reactive cost monitoring wherever possible. Activity-based budgeting encourages this approach.

Emphasis should be made to control the process so that output is consistent. Also, make sure resources can be shifted when workload varies—workload seldom stays the same throughout the year. Plan and budget for using those slack times to improve the organization.

(a)   Data Capture.   There are three methods for data capture within an ongoing system. First, there is *dedicated resources*. Set up cost centers and define workload measures at the activity or business process level. Second, there is *shared resources,* in which an organization does time reporting by activity. Third, use a *surrogate* in which actual outputs are used at a standard activity cost. Actual costs would be compared to total department earned cost in this approach. Total actual cost could also be compared to best practices earned value.

(b)   Activity-Based Budget Report.

Department Total			Activity Analysis			
Expense	Budget $	Actual $	Issue P.O.	Certify vendor	Expedite order	Other
Wages	180,000	180,00				
Supplies	40,000	38,000				
Space	30,000	30,000				
Equipment	18,000	18,000				
Travel	22,000	20,000				
Other	10,000	8,000				
Total	200,000	194,000				
Output measure			# of P.O.	# of certification	# of orders	
Charge rate			$50	$2,000	$10	$9,000
Budgeted volume			3,000	20	100	1
Budgeted value	200,000		$150,000	$40,000	$1,000	$9,000
Actual volume			2,700	18	90	1
Earned value		181,000	$135,000	$36,000	$900	$9,100
Earned value variance		13,000				

In this example, the organization budgeted the activity "issue purchase orders" at $50 per purchase order. It budgeted 3,000 purchase orders. This yielded a budgeted value for the "issue purchase order" activity of $150,000. The same activity budgeting process was followed for the remaining activities, including an "other" or miscellaneous category of activities. This yielded a total activity budget for this department of $200,000, which was backflushed back into expense categories.

The actual expenses for the period were $194,000. Compared to the original budget of $200,000, this looks very good. However, when the earned value is calculated, the department is shown to have an earned value variance of $13,000. Earned value is calculated for each activity by multiplying the actual volume for each activity by that activity's charge rate. For the "issue purchase order" activity, the actual volume of 2,700 purchase orders when multiplied by the charge rate of $50 yields $135,000. The same calculation is made for all activities and the answers added for each department. This earned value total of $181,000 is compared to actual expenses of $194,000 to yield an earned value variance of a negative $13,000. This is a different picture than simply comparing actual with budget, which yielded a favorable variance of $6,000. Managers can now use this as a planning tool as well as a means to operate the organization more efficiently.

(c)   **Business Process Reporting.**   In business process reporting, activity cost could be shown for each department, as well as for each business process that delivers a service. This is an exercise for organizations that are more advanced in ABB techniques.

27A.14   SUMMARY.   Activity-based budgeting gives managers the tools they need to make better decisions about running their organization. This budgeting technique spends most of the time on improvement rather than filling out forms, which is often the case with traditional budgeting. This technique gives managers a method to improve activities as well as business processes.

SOURCES AND SUGGESTED REFERENCES

Antos, John J., "Activity-Based Management for Service, Not-for-Profit, and Government Organizations, " *Journal of Cost Management,* Vol. 6, No. 2, 1992.

Brimson, James A., and Antos, John J., *Activity-Based Management,* New York, John Wiley & Sons, Inc., 1994.

Brimson, James A., *Activity Accounting,* New York, John Wiley & Sons, Inc., 1991.

Brimson, James A., *Activity-Based Investment Management,* New York, American Management Association, 1989.

CHAPTER 28

COMPUTER APPLICATIONS IN BUDGETING

Donald R. Moscato

Thomas Pollina
Iona College

CONTENTS

28.4 **MICROCOMPUTER OVERVIEW AND NEEDS ASSESSMENT** 1

(a) Software 2
(b) Memory 2
(c) Speed 2
(d) Peripherals 2

28.5 **BUDGETING APPLICATIONS AND THEIR RELATIONSHIP TO OTHER CORPORATE SYSTEMS** 2

(c) Fixed Versus Variable Cost in the Budget Model 2

28.6 **THE MICRO TO MAINFRAME LINK** 3

28.4 MICROCOMPUTER OVERVIEW AND NEEDS ASSESSMENT

(a) Software

Page 28•6, add after second sentence:

Because we are most interested in budgeting, we should also consider possible extensions to consolidations, spreadsheet analysis, and graphics capability.

(b)   Memory

Page 28•6, replace remainder of section after seventh sentence with:

For example, programs, databases, and spreadsheets developed for Microsoft's Windows 95 Office when transferred to the Office 97 platform require significantly more memory. Of course, the more RAM, the greater will be the system cost. However, since the cost of increased RAM has been dropping significantly for quite some time, it is usually a prudent idea to use a multiple of the amount of RAM that your current needs justify. There is also another reason to have abundant RAM in your system. Cache programs convert unused RAM into a storage area for frequently used data. The effect of this is greatly increased speed of the computer application.

(c)   Speed

Page 28•6, replace first two sentences of section with:

The speed of a microcomputer is determined, for the most part, by its microprocessor chip. Early PCs used relatively slow processor chips compared to those available today. New generations of chips appear every eighteen months. This phenomenon causes the user to decide whether to purchase an upgrade chip or to trade in the entire system for an entirely new model.

(d)   Peripherals

Page 28•6, add after "frequency" in last sentence of first paragraph:

, printing speed in pages per minute (ppm),

Page 28•6, replace last two sentences in second paragraph with:

What size screen? Today, a seventeen-inch screen is often found in an office environment, while a fifteen-inch screen is normal for the home computer. What should the resolution be for your needs? Will you be doing much with graphics? Is there a need for video?

Page 28•6, add after "capability" in third paragraph, line two:

(Will you be using the Internet?)

28.5   BUDGETING APPLICATIONS AND THEIR RELATIONSHIP TO OTHER CORPORATE SYSTEMS

(c)   Fixed Versus Variable Cost in the Budget Model

Page 28•12, Exhibit 28.6, delete row one from diagram and renumber so that row two is one, three is two, and so forth. In so doing, the explanation that follows will match the exhibit.

28.6   THE MICRO TO MAINFRAME LINK

Page 28•15, replace second paragraph with:

Many organizations are recognizing that the prime role for the mainframe can be one of a central data repository and as a central switch, which is capable of distributing relevant sections of an overall database to the appropriate organizational entities on a timely basis. Issues of security, integrity of the data, and timeliness are solved through a cooperative sharing of the corporate data resource. The initial period of microcomputer use featured stand-alone machines doing relatively independent and/or unsophisticated applications. This period soon gave way to micros, which had to be linked to the mainframe. Using local area networks, client/server computing, the Internet, and corporate intranets, there has been an endlessly evolving array of platforms for positioning corporate data for the budgeting application.

FUZZY LOGIC APPLIED TO BUDGETING: AN INTUITIVE APPROACH TO COPING WITH UNCERTAINTY (New)

Donald R. Moscato

Iona College

CONTENTS

28A.1	CURRENT BUDGETING ENVIRONMENT	1	28A.5 BASIC ELEMENTS OF FUZZY MODELING — 3
28A.2	THE POTENTIAL OF FUZZY LOGIC IN BUDGETING	1	28A.6 EXAMPLE OF FUZZY LOGIC MODELING IN THE OPERATING BUDGET APPLICATION — 7
28A.3	THE NEED FOR INNOVATIVE THINKING	2	28A.7 FUTURE ISSUES — 20
28A.4	LIMITATIONS OF CURRENT APPROACHES	2	SOURCES AND SUGGESTED REFERENCES — 20

28A.1 CURRENT BUDGETING ENVIRONMENT. One of the most ubiquitous tasks in organizations is the preparation of the operating budget. It is a tool to make concrete the operating plan for the coming year. Budgeting has undergone an evolution from the manual method of preparation to the spreadsheet format of today.

Most budgeting logic is fairly well understood. Managers know the key business drivers. The challenge is to estimate the values of these key variables. The method the manager uses to derive these estimates is the focus of fuzzy number modeling.

The current state of budgeting makes use of best case, worst case, and most likely operations scenarios. From this exercise in sensitivity analysis, the decision maker must settle on a final set of estimates which becomes the foundation of the operating budget. Fuzzy number modeling can improve budgeting effectiveness and efficiency.

28A.2 THE POTENTIAL OF FUZZY LOGIC IN BUDGETING. In the mid-sixties researchers led by Lofti Zadeh developed an extension of set theory known as *fuzzy sets.* Fuzzy logic can be thought of as approximate reasoning. Since so much of business is characterized by vague statements of belief, confidence, or feeling, our analytical tools are more accurate when they are adapted to this reality.

Fuzzy modeling recognizes the inherent imprecision of management communications in the decision-making process. Traditional tools of analysis require a precision that creates arbitrary future estimates with no allowance for variability.

Fuzzy sets and fuzzy logic have many practical applications: refocusing cameras, automotive anti-lock brake systems, intelligent appliances, and business machines. Chips that were designed with traditional logic circuits have been augmented to include fuzzy logic analytical reasoning capability. Applications, as well as research, have been wide-ranging in the defense business and across continents.

Fuzzy logic found its way into business modeling applications as soon as spreadsheet modeling systems could handle the methodology of fuzzy numbers and their requisite operators.

28A.3   THE NEED FOR INNOVATIVE THINKING.   Business decision makers use both intuitive and analytical resources to make critical decisions. Some managers are comfortable with spreadsheets and others shy away from "managing by the numbers". Whether intuitive or analytical, most people would concede that graphical representations are more appealing than a simple column or table of numbers. Both spreadsheets and graphs assume that the numbers or graphs represent what is really believed as being a true representation of a manager's confidence level in the thing being measured. Today's spreadsheet tools assume that the use of numbers in the cells properly depict the underlying uncertainty of the events and things that are being measured.

Fuzzy modeling attempts to measure, in a more meaningful and accurate way, the underlying uncertainty present in most business decision-making. This chapter illustrates the application of fuzzy modeling concepts to the operational budgeting activity. The vehicle that will be used is the spreadsheet format. Millions of analysts are familiar with the basic format of the spreadsheet, and it has become a de facto form of business communication. Fuzzy modeling combines the familiarity and discipline of spreadsheet modeling with the intuitive expressiveness of today's manager. This combination can be a dynamic and innovative way to think about budgeting.

28A.4   LIMITATIONS OF CURRENT APPROACHES.   Current approaches rely almost exclusively on single value estimates. The implication of this approach is that any uncertainty surrounding the business must either be suppressed, or else several alternative estimates must be run through the budgeting logic. Each scenario introduces possible values of key variables. The decision maker must select a set of plausible values and see how their inclusion in the budget affects the results. After this process is finished a priority must be developed regarding the scenarios in order to help the decision maker resolve the inherent uncertainty surrounding the estimates. Alternatively, the decision maker could run just a single budget scenario and wrestle with the uncertainty in her head without the aid of trying out other plausible scenarios. In either case, uncertainty must be addressed either explicitly in the model or implicitly in the analyst's head.

Analysts use risk analysis to address the issue of capturing uncertainty. In this approach, the decision maker estimates a probability distribution for each input variable that is not treated as being certain. The shape of the probability distribution reflects the likelihood of that variable's values occurring. Software for the microcomputer such as @Risk® and Crystal Ball® can be used to build budgeting models using risk analysis. Inherent in this approach is the idea of randomness surrounding the uncertain input values.

Regardless of which spreadsheet-based approach used to prepare your budget, the decision maker must find an effective and comfortable way to capture the uncertainty present in the estimation process. The fuzzy modeling approach is presented as an alternative to the limitations of the traditional methods of dealing with capturing a decision maker's confidence level with numbers used in the budget model.

28A.5   BASIC ELEMENTS OF FUZZY MODELING.

A good starting-off point in understanding the basic concepts is to relate them to familiar surroundings, namely spreadsheet modeling using Lotus 1-2-3® or Microsoft's Excel®. In both of these modeling systems a number is represented as a single value which is used throughout the model. In our framework, this is called a *crisp number*. What would happen if the decision maker was not sure of a particular estimate? For example, he might say that sales will be around one hundred units. He is a little unclear about its eventual value. In this case we can introduce the notion of a *fuzzy* or vague number. This fuzziness is due to a general feeling or uncertainty about a given estimate. Rather than representing this belief with a single value, we can introduce a set of points over a plausible range. Each point represents a specific value along with a degree of belief in that particular value occurring. These numbers are approximate values tempered by one's degree of belief. The more uncertain one is, the wider is the range. The less belief in a value, the lower will be the belief value. This belief measure is how confidence level in a value is represented.

We represent a fuzzy number as a set of points expressed as coordinates. Each possible value has a paired degree of belief. For example, let's say that a scale of zero to one (0.0–1.0) is used to depict the strength of belief in a particular value occurring. Next year's sales estimate is required for the budget. Your best thinking states that the actual sales should be between 85 and 100 units. Your strongest belief is that 90 units will be sold. You can assign this value (90 units) a belief of 1.0. Since both 85 and 100 are possible but not very likely, you assign them both a belief of 0.0.

The visual representation of a belief system is defined by the concept of a membership function in fuzzy modeling. This can be presented graphically by a belief graph (Exhibit 28A.1).

The X (horizontal) axis represents the range of possible sales in units. The Y (vertical) axis depicts the degree of belief in possible values. This belief graph has three points: the highest belief or confidence (a sales value of 90 units), the maximum value of belief (1.0), and the minimum value of belief (0.0). Any value in this range can represent the degree of belief in a given value occurring.

To illustrate further how to represent a belief system we can use this sales estimate example to express several different perceptions.

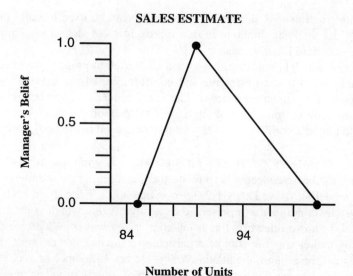

Exhibit 28A.1.   Triangular belief graph.

In the first case (Exhibit 28A.2) we have a belief graph that looks like a church steeple. This graph expresses much confidence in the sales estimate of 90. Confidence drops off rapidly on either side of 90.

If a manager was very confident in a range of values around 90, the belief graph would have a trapezoid shape (Exhibit 28A.3). The range or width of the plateau would follow the belief or confidence in a wider range of values occurring.

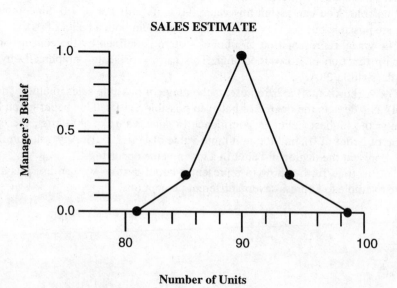

Exhibit 28A.2.   Steeple belief graph.

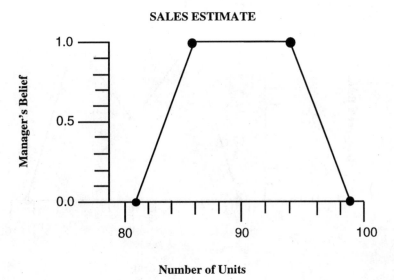

Exhibit 28A.3.   Trapezoid belief graph.

Many times estimates are characterized by vague language. "We should offer around fifty thousand dollars for the equipment bid" would be an example. This type of feeling is often captured with a tent-shaped belief graph. Exhibit 28A.4 has five coordinate points. The middle three have beliefs of 0.75, 1.0, and 0.75. In this way we can communicate the vague or fuzzy statement "around" with a specifically tailored belief graph.

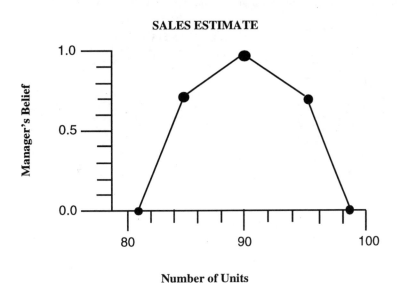

Exhibit 28A.4.   Tent-shaped belief graph.

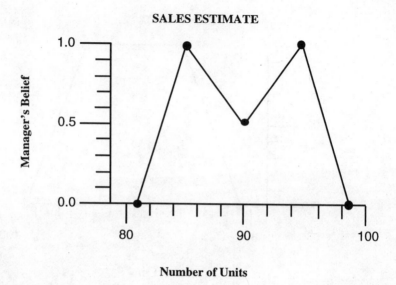

Exhibit 28A.5.   Twin-peaked belief graph.

If the manager believes that two values have the highest confidence within a range, the belief graph would have two peaks. In Exhibit 28A.5, the two values 85 and 95 are illustrated as having the highest belief measures. The sales estimate 90 has only a 0.5 degree of confidence.

In the last two variations of belief graphs, the graphs are cropped or cut off at a sales estimate of 96. Exhibit 28A.6 has a highest degree of belief of 1.0 for a range of values. Exhibit 28A.7 has a lower degree of confidence expressed for the same range of values; only 0.75. However, the both graphs communicate a reasonable degree of belief over a wide range of values.

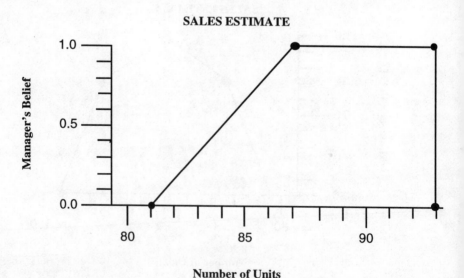

Exhibit 28A.6.   Modified belief graph (belief of 1.0 at maximum).

SALES ESTIMATE

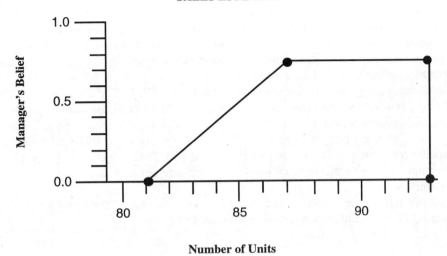

Number of Units

Exhibit 28A.7.   Modified belief graph (belief of 0.75 at maximum).

Exhibits 28A.1 through 28A.7 characterize the manager's feelings or degree of confidence that certain values can occur for sales. Estimates, no longer represented as certainty, can be portrayed consistent with the manager's true belief system. The shape of the graph can be tailored to one's expressed feelings.

Once the belief graphs have been defined for the selected key business drivers, you can then simulate the budget and compute the resulting target variables as you did under Lotus 1-2-3 or Excel. The major difference is that, instead of an answer expressed as a crisp certain number, your results will be expressed as a fuzzy number. This resultant fuzzy number has its own belief graph which is also derived with a series of coordinate points. Each point represents a value for the target variable along with its associated confidence level. The important point to appreciate is that the degrees of belief of the input assumptions are logically carried through to the degrees of belief of the criterion variables. You now have a measure of confidence in the eventual outcome variables, which is, after all, the reason you constructed the spreadsheet model in the first place.

When the fuzzy numbers are printed in a spreadsheet cell they are depicted as a single number. The single number that is printed in the cell is called the *centroid value* of the fuzzy number. It can be thought of as the center of gravity or the critical mass of the fuzzy number. All calculations in the spreadsheet model are done using the rules of fuzzy number arithmetic, which have been validated over 30 years of research.

28A.6   EXAMPLE OF FUZZY LOGIC MODELING IN THE OPERATING BUDGET APPLICATION.   An operating budget for a condominium demonstrates fuzzy modeling in budgeting. The general manager developed the operating budget using his best estimates. However, he believes that there is greater uncertainty surrounding some factors than with others.There is a very high confidence for the revenue side, so he will concentrate on the expense side. This area is made up of six cost categories:

building maintenance, grounds maintenance, pool maintenance, utilities, general and administrative, and planned capital expenses. He has decided that his estimates for building maintenance, grounds maintenance, and pool maintenance are fairly certain. He wants to explore the ramifications of uncertainty to a selected group of variables. The greatest degree of uncertainty is present in the sewer, water, electricity, telephone, insurance, and painting estimates.

All spreadsheets in this chapter were created in FUZICALC®, a product of FUZI-WARE, Inc. According to the vendor it is the world's first fuzzy number modeling tool. All models were run in a Microsoft Windows® environment. The spreadsheet for the operating budget appears in Exhibit 28A.8. In the traditional budgeting process the manager expects expenses to total $531,980, which matches expected revenue. What are the implications of uncertainty surrounding some of the key assumptions?

Since the manager feels less comfortable with several of the variables, he will employ fuzzy numbers to express his belief system.

Sewer Estimate	Low	$38,160	0.0
	Best	$42,400	1.0
	High	$46,640	0.0
Water estimate	Low	$34,800	0.0
	Best	$38,700	1.0
	High	$42,500	0.0
Electricity estimate	Low	$36,000	0.0
	Best	$40,000	1.0
	High	$44,000	0.0
Telephone estimate	Low	$6,750	0.0
	Best	$7,500	1.0
	High	$8,250	0.0
Insurance estimate	Low	$135,000	0.0
	Best	$150,000	1.0
	High	$165,000	0.0
Painting estimate	Low	$13,500	0.0
	Best	$15,000	1.0
	High	$16,500	0.0

Each three-point estimate results in a belief graph. Exhibits 28A.9 to 28A.12 illustrate the manager's belief graphs for electricity, water, telephone, and painting. Each graph has a belief scale from 0 to 1. Values close to 1 represent the greatest belief. The horizontal axes depict the scales of the estimated variables. Note the symmetric nature of each estimate.

199X Operating Budget

REVENUES

Regular Residential Dues	$515,550
Restaurant Lease	$12,180
Late Payment Interest	$500
Late Payment Charges	$1,000
Interest Income	$250
Miscellaneous	$2,500
TOTAL REVENUES	$531,980

OPERATING EXPENSES

BUILDING MAINTENANCE

Locksmith	$200
Electrical	$2,000
Plumbing	$1,800
Supplies & Equipment	$8,000
HVAC	$1,000
Interior Pest Control	$3,500
Termite Treatment Bond	$600
Elevator Maintenance	$12,000
Fire Protection System	$8,000
TOTAL BUILDING MAINT.	$37,100

GROUNDS MAINTENANCE

Supplies	$2,500
Signage	$500
Parking Lot	$1,200
Repairs	$1,500
Bulldozing	$3,000
TOTAL GROUNDS MAINT.	$8,700

POOL MAINTENANCE

Chemicals	$7,500
Supplies	$500
Equipment Maint. & Rep.	$5,000
TOTAL POOL MAINT.	$13,000

UTILITIES

Electricity	$40,000
Sewer	$42,400
Water	$38,650
Trash Removal	$6,700
Cable TV	$14,400
Telephone Equip. Maint.	$7,500
TOTAL UTILITIES	$149,650

GENERAL & ADMINISTRATIVE

Management Services	$97,850
Bank Charges	$200
Postage	$2,500
Office Supplies & Dupl.	$1,750
Office Telephone	$700
Insurance	$150,000
Legal Services	$5,000
Audit Expense	$5,500
Other Prof. Services	$1,200
Annual Meeting Expense	$500
Board Travel	$3,000
Board Meeting Expense	$3,500
Tax & Licenses	$500
Bad Debt Expense	$4,000
Pager Service	$1,200
Other	$250
TOTAL G & A	$277,650

General Capital Reserves	$4,405
Restaurant Property Tax	$2,750
HOA Personal Prop. Tax	$975
Contingency Reserves	$16,750
TOTAL OTHER EXPENSE	$24,880

TOTAL OPERATING EXP.	$510,980

PLANNED CAPITAL EXPENSES

Pool Furniture	$3,000
Landscape	$3,000
Exterior Painting	$15,000

TOTAL CAPITAL EXPENSES	$21,000

TOTAL OPERATING AND CAPITAL EXPENSES	$531,980

Exhibit 28A.8.   Traditional spreadsheet operating budget.

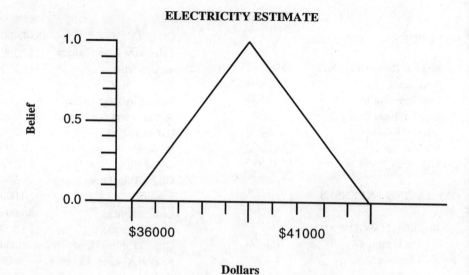

Exhibit 28A.9.   Manager's belief graph for electricity estimate.

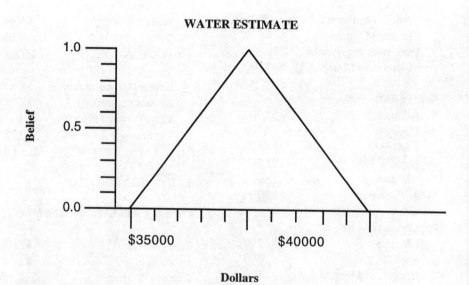

Exhibit 28A.10.   Manager's belief graph for water estimate.

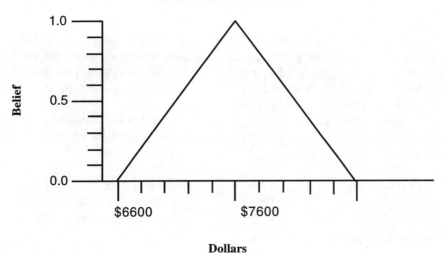

Exhibit 28A.11.   Manager's belief graph for telephone estimate.

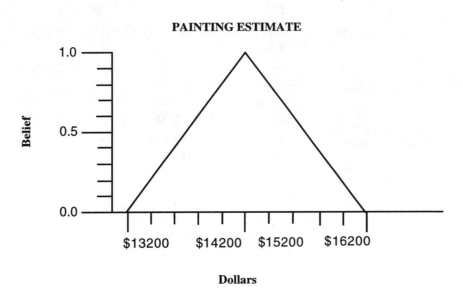

Exhibit 28A.12.   Manager's belief graph for painting estimate.

Exhibit 28A.13 depicts the spreadsheet model with the entries in Column E for the belief graphs' centroid values. For example, the centroid value for the insurance estimate is $150,000.

In this first budget spreadsheet, each selected input variable has a belief graph associated with it. These graphs are all symmetric around the best estimate value. Note that aside from the graphs there is no change in the results. This is due to the fact that the centroid values are the same as the original crisp estimates from Exhibit 28A.8. We will use this spreadsheet as our starting point.

The general manager reviews his estimates and adjusts the belief graph to reflect his degree of confidence in each key variable. The adjusted belief estimates are as follows:

Sewer estimate	Low	$38,160	0.0
	Best	$42,400	1.0
	High	$46,640	0.0
Water estimate	Low	$34,800	0.0
	Best	$39,986	1.0
	High	$42,510	0.0
Electricity estimate	Low	$36,000	0.0
	Best	$40,000	1.0
	High	$44,000	0.0
Telephone estimate	Low	$6,750	0.0
	Best	$7,500	1.0
	High	$8,250	0.0
Insurance estimate	Low	$135,000	0.0
	Best	$159,936	1.0
	High	$165,000	0.0
Painting estimate	Low	$13,500	0.0
	Best	$15,000	1.0
	High	$16,500	0.0.

199X Operating Budget

REVENUES

Regular Residential Dues	$515,550
Restaurant Lease	$12,180
Late Payment Interest	$500
Late Payment Charges	$1,000
Interest Income	$250
Miscellaneous	$2,500
TOTAL REVENUES	**$531,980**

OPERATING EXPENSES

BUILDING MAINTENANCE

Locksmith	$200
Electrical	$2,000
Plumbing	$1,800
Supplies & Equipment	$8,000
HVAC	$1,000
Interior Pest Control	$3,500
Termite Treatment Bond	$600
Elevator Maintenance	$12,000
Fire Protection System	$8,000
TOTAL BUILDING MAINT.	$37,100

GROUNDS MAINTENANCE

Supplies	$2,500
Signage	$500
Parking Lot	$1,200
Repairs	$1,500
Bulldozing	$3,000
TOTAL GROUNDS MAINT.	$8,700

POOL MAINTENANCE

Chemicals	$7,500
Supplies	$500
Equipment Maint. & Rep.	$5,000
TOTAL POOL MAINT.	$13,000

UTILITIES

Electricity	► $40,000
Sewer	► $42,400
Water	► $38,650
Trash Removal	$6,700
Cable TV	$14,400
Telephone Equip. Maint. ►	$7,500
TOTAL UTILITIES	$149,650

SEWER ESTIMATE

(Belief vs. Dollars: triangular fuzzy number with peak between $38000 and $43000)

WATER ESTIMATE

(Belief vs. Dollars: triangular fuzzy number with peak between $35000 and $40000)

ELECTRICITY ESTIMATE

(Belief vs. Dollars: triangular fuzzy number with peak between $36000 and $41000)

TELEPHONE ESTIMATE

(Belief vs. Dollars: triangular fuzzy number with peak between $6600 and $7600)

Exhibit 28A.13.   Fuzzy number spreadsheet for initial budget.

199X Operating Budget

GENERAL & ADMINISTRATIVE

Management Services	$97,850
Bank Charges	$200
Postage	$2,500
Office Supplies & Dupl.	$1,750
Office Telephone	$700
Insurance	►$150,000
Legal Services	$5,000
Audit Expense	$5,500
Other Prof. Services	$1,200
Annual Meeting Expense	$500
Board Travel	$3,000
Board Meeting Expense	$3,500
Tax & Licenses	$500
Bad Debt Expense	$4,000
Pager Service	$1,200
Other	$250
TOTAL G & A	$277,650

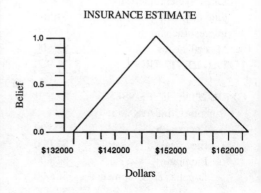

General Capital Reserves	$4,405
Restaurant Property Tax	$2,750
HOA Personal Prop. Tax	$975
Contingency Reserves	$16,750
TOTAL OTHER EXPENSE	$24,880

TOTAL OPERATING EXP. $510,980

PLANNED CAPITAL EXPENSES

Pool Furniture	$3,000
Landscape	$3,000
Exterior Painting	►$15,000

TOTAL CAPITAL EXPENSES $21,000

TOTAL OPERATING AND CAPITAL EXPENSES $531,980

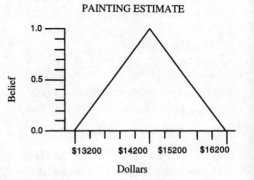

Exhibit 28A.13.   *(Continued)*

Changes were made only to the belief graphs for water and insurance. The estimates for the other variables in the budget were still acceptable. The results of the new assumptions on the budget are seen in Exhibit 28A.14.

The general manager is most interested in the final belief graph, the total operating and capital expenses. The centroid value for this critical variable is $536,887, which is greater than his revenue estimate of $531,980. This analysis means that there is a very strong belief that, with this set of belief assumptions for the input variables, there will be a negative result for the year. Upon closer review, he notes that this imbalance was due to a change in the total operating expense section. The capital expense section was not adversely impacted by the changes.

After reviewing these results with one of his subordinates who pointed out the possibility of an increase in the sewer rates next year by the municipal agency, the general manager felt he had to make one more revision of the budget. In order to account for this increased uncertainty, a new belief graph was constructed to reflect the current assessment of the plausible increase.

Sewer estimate	Low	$38,160	0.0
	Best	$46,552	1.0
	High	$46,552	1.0

He reran the budget with the modified sewer estimate. Exhibit 28A.15 shows the results.

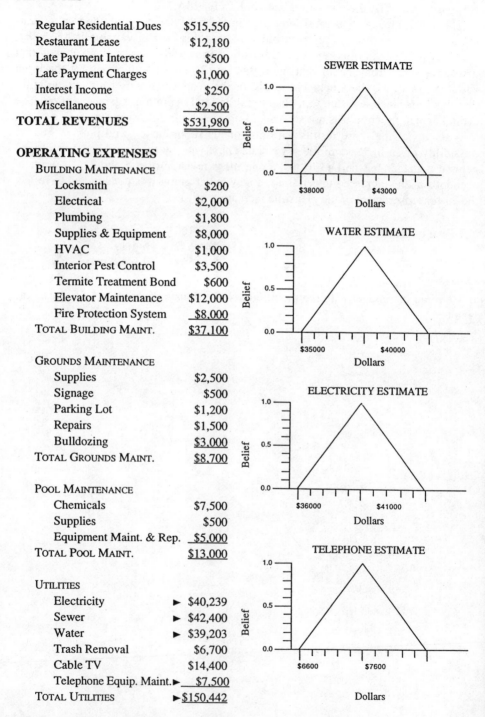

199X Operating Budget

REVENUES

Regular Residential Dues	$515,550
Restaurant Lease	$12,180
Late Payment Interest	$500
Late Payment Charges	$1,000
Interest Income	$250
Miscellaneous	$2,500
TOTAL REVENUES	**$531,980**

OPERATING EXPENSES

BUILDING MAINTENANCE

Locksmith	$200
Electrical	$2,000
Plumbing	$1,800
Supplies & Equipment	$8,000
HVAC	$1,000
Interior Pest Control	$3,500
Termite Treatment Bond	$600
Elevator Maintenance	$12,000
Fire Protection System	$8,000
TOTAL BUILDING MAINT.	$37,100

GROUNDS MAINTENANCE

Supplies	$2,500
Signage	$500
Parking Lot	$1,200
Repairs	$1,500
Bulldozing	$3,000
TOTAL GROUNDS MAINT.	$8,700

POOL MAINTENANCE

Chemicals	$7,500
Supplies	$500
Equipment Maint. & Rep.	$5,000
TOTAL POOL MAINT.	$13,000

UTILITIES

Electricity	► $40,239
Sewer	► $42,400
Water	► $39,203
Trash Removal	$6,700
Cable TV	$14,400
Telephone Equip. Maint. ►	$7,500
TOTAL UTILITIES	►$150,442

Exhibit 28A.14.   Modified fuzzy number spreadsheet for budget.

199X Operating Budget

GENERAL & ADMINISTRATIVE

Management Services	$97,850
Bank Charges	$200
Postage	$2,500
Office Supplies & Dupl.	$1,750
Office Telephone	$700
Insurance	►$154,116
Legal Services	$5,000
Audit Expense	$5,500
Other Prof. Services	$1,200
Annual Meeting Expense	$500
Board Travel	$3,000
Board Meeting Expense	$3,500
Tax & Licenses	$500
Bad Debt Expense	$4,000
Pager Service	$1,200
Other	$250
TOTAL G & A	►$281,766

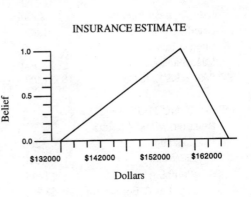

General Capital Reserves	$4,405
Restaurant Property Tax	$2,750
HOA Personal Prop. Tax	$975
Contingency Reserves	$16,750
TOTAL OTHER EXPENSE	$24,880

TOTAL OPERATING EXP.   ►$515,887

PLANNED CAPITAL EXPENSES

Pool Furniture	$3,000
Landscape	$3,000
Exterior Painting	►$15,000

TOTAL CAPITAL EXPENSES   ►$21,000

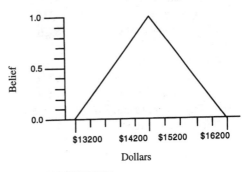

TOTAL OPERATING AND CAPITAL EXPENSES   ►$536,887

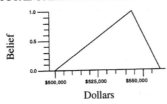

Exhibit 28A.14.   *(Continued)*

199X Operating Budget

REVENUES

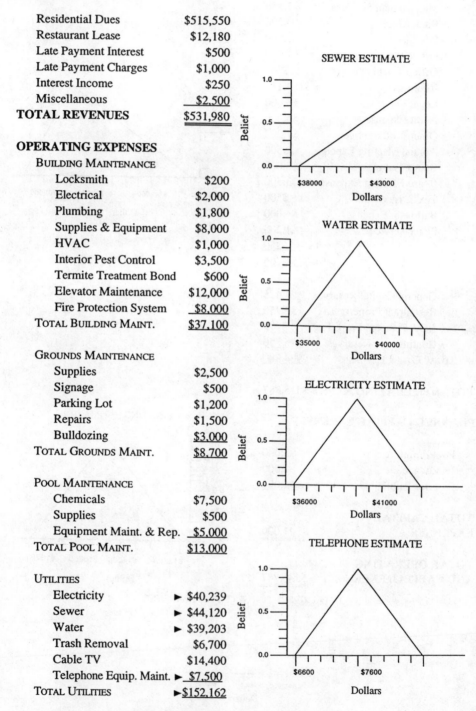

Residential Dues	$515,550
Restaurant Lease	$12,180
Late Payment Interest	$500
Late Payment Charges	$1,000
Interest Income	$250
Miscellaneous	$2,500
TOTAL REVENUES	**$531,980**

OPERATING EXPENSES

BUILDING MAINTENANCE

Locksmith	$200
Electrical	$2,000
Plumbing	$1,800
Supplies & Equipment	$8,000
HVAC	$1,000
Interior Pest Control	$3,500
Termite Treatment Bond	$600
Elevator Maintenance	$12,000
Fire Protection System	$8,000
TOTAL BUILDING MAINT.	$37,100

GROUNDS MAINTENANCE

Supplies	$2,500
Signage	$500
Parking Lot	$1,200
Repairs	$1,500
Bulldozing	$3,000
TOTAL GROUNDS MAINT.	$8,700

POOL MAINTENANCE

Chemicals	$7,500
Supplies	$500
Equipment Maint. & Rep.	$5,000
TOTAL POOL MAINT.	$13,000

UTILITIES

Electricity	► $40,239
Sewer	► $44,120
Water	► $39,203
Trash Removal	$6,700
Cable TV	$14,400
Telephone Equip. Maint.	► $7,500
TOTAL UTILITIES	►$152,162

SEWER ESTIMATE

WATER ESTIMATE

ELECTRICITY ESTIMATE

TELEPHONE ESTIMATE

Exhibit 28A.15.   Final fuzzy number spreadsheet for budget.

199X Operating Budget

GENERAL & ADMINISTRATIVE

Management Services	$97,850
Bank Charges	$200
Postage	$2,500
Office Supplies & Dupl.	$1,750
Office Telephone	$700
Insurance	►$154,116
Legal Services	$5,000
Audit Expense	$5,500
Other Prof. Services	$1,200
Annual Meeting Expense	$500
Board Travel	$3,000
Board Meeting Expense	$3,500
Tax & Licenses	$500
Bad Debt Expense	$4,000
Pager Service	$1,200
Other	$250
TOTAL G & A	►$281,766

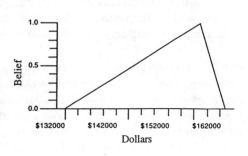

General Capital Reserves	$4,405
Restaurant Property Tax	$2,750
HOA Personal Prop. Tax	$975
Contingency Reserves	$16,750
TOTAL OTHER EXPENSE	$24,880

TOTAL OPERATING EXP. ►$517,607

PLANNED CAPITAL EXPENSES

Pool Furniture	$3,000
Landscape	$3,000
Exterior Painting	►$15,000

TOTAL CAPITAL EXPENSES ►$21,000

TOTAL OPERATING AND CAPITAL EXPENSES ►$538,607

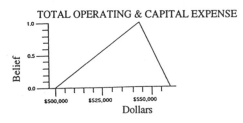

Exhibit 28A.15.   *(Continued)*

A review of the model results shows that the total operating expenses belief graph has changed to reflect the impact of the new input assumption. Its centroid value is now $517,607, approximately a $2,000 increase. Since he is finished with the analysis of the expense side, he will now have to explore alternative ways of bringing his expenses in line with his limited revenues. That process is beyond the scope of this chapter.

The general manager has utilized fuzzy number modeling to better understand the implications of uncertainty of the key business driver variables in his operating budget. He would continue to alter his belief graphs to explore any additional changes in his assumptions until he was content with the final analysis.

28A.7 FUTURE ISSUES.   It would be unrealistic to expect a new tool like fuzzy modeling to be accepted into mainstream budgeting without experiencing the traditional learning curve. Just as with traditional spreadsheet modeling of budgets with Lotus 1-2-3 and Excel, it will take a period of time before mainstream corporate business becomes comfortable with fuzzy numbers. Perhaps the front-line innovators can use the tool informally to develop their budgets. As the number of beneficial applications of fuzzy logic get publicized, the general level of comfort with the tool will increase.

There will always be the tension between the analytical and intuitive camps when it comes to decision-making areas like budgeting. Fuzzy number techniques can be used to bridge this gap. The use of belief graphs recognizes that there is a wealth of knowledge in the intuitive mind of the decision maker. It is a vehicle to convey her confidence level with the estimates that are used in the budget. It is a methodology to unite, in a synergistic way, both the intuitive and analytical approaches to decision-making. This is precisely its unique contribution to budgeting.

SOURCES AND SUGGESTED REFERENCES

Burnette, David, "MATLIB Adopts Fuzzy Logic Approach," *Advanced Systems,* March 1995.

Engler, Calvin, *Managerial Accounting,* 3d ed., Homewood, Ill.: Richard D. Irwin, 1993.

FUZIWARE®,Inc., *FUZICALC User's Guide Ver. 1.5,* FUZIWARE®, Inc., 1994.

Kosko, Bart, *Fuzzy Thinking: The New Science of Fuzzy Logic,* New York: Hyperion, 1993.

McNeil, Daniel and P. Freiberger, *Fuzzy Logic: The Discovery of a Revolutionary Computer Technology,* New York: Simon and Schuster, 1993.

Yager, Ronald, S. Ovchinnikov, R. Tong, and H.T. Nguyen, eds., *Fuzzy Sets and Applications: Selected Papers of Lofti Zadeh,* New York: John Wiley & Sons, 1987.

CHAPTER 29

THE BEHAVIORAL ASPECTS OF BUDGETING (Revised)

Gyan Chandra

Miami University (Ohio)

CONTENTS

29.1 INTRODUCTION	**2**	
(a) Objectives of Budgeting	2	
(b) Stages in Budgeting	3	
(c) Budgeting Approaches	3	
29.2 THE BEHAVIORAL ASSUMPTIONS	**5**	
(a) The Traditional View of Human Behavior	5	
(b) Budgeting and the Traditional Management Environment	6	
(c) The Modern View of Human Behavior	7	
29.3 HUMAN MOTIVATION	**8**	
(a) The Needs Hierarchy Theory	9	
(b) The Two-Factor Theory (New)	9	
(c) The Expectancy Theory	10	
(d) The X, Y, and Z Theories	10	
29.4 BUDGETS AND MOTIVATION	**11**	

(a) Budgets as Pressure Devices	**11**	
(b) Role Conflict	**12**	
29.5 BUDGETS AND PARTICIPATION	**13**	
(a) The Nature of Participation	**14**	
(b) The Significance of Participation	**15**	
(c) The Group Dynamics	**16**	
(d) Organization Culture and Leadership	**16**	
(e) Standards and Aspirations	**17**	
(f) Participation and Slack	**17**	
(g) Performance Reports and Rewards	**18**	
(h) The Role of Budget Staff	**20**	
29.6 CONCLUSION	**20**	
29.7 THE BEHAVIORAL LESSONS OF BUDGETING	**21**	
SOURCES AND SUGGESTED REFERENCES	**22**	

29.1   INTRODUCTION.   *The Wall Street Journal* carried the following article on its front page recently:

Budget Seeks to Raise U.S. Living Standards
And Reduce Inequality

With the nation at peace and the economy expanding, President Clinton's new budget gives him a chance to attack some underlying, long-run economic problems: a disappointingly slow rise of living standards and a widening gap between the well-off and the poor.[1]

The article emphasizes two points. First, budgeting is a very useful exercise in fiscal management. Even the mighty federal government uses it and has a separate office in charge of collecting data and preparing the annual budget that the President presents to the Congress. Secondly, the act of balancing resources with the demands on those resources is very difficult. That is where budgeting plays an important role.

One hears about budgets and budgeting every day both in business and in government circles. Both governments and businesses use them. One of the major 1996 general election campaign issues raised by both the Republican and Democratic parties was the need to run the nation's government on a balanced budget basis. There is even talk of a constitutional amendment that will mandate balanced budgets for the government.

Budgets are an expression of management's plans and expectations about the future. They institutionalize organization goals. Budgets make everyone aware of the resources, the demands on those resources, and the limitations. Budgetary limitations are faced by corporate managers all the time. Budgets affect programs, people and their behavior. They involve people at every step of the game and thus impact and are impacted by human behavior.

The purpose of this chapter is to review and learn about the interaction between budgets and people. We will proceed with a review of the relevant literature in management, social-psychology, organizational behavior, and other related areas and draw lessons for budgeting. A considerable amount of research has been conducted in the last 60 years or so on different questions dealing with the behavioral aspects of budgeting. Although it will not be possible to deal with all of the issues in one chapter, an attempt will be made to review the major ones here. A detailed list of readings is provided at the end of the chapter for pursuing the subject in depth.

(a)   Objectives of Budgeting.   A *budget* is a quantitative plan of action covering a period, normally a year or so, and is prepared for an organization as a whole or for its subunits, and *budgeting* is the process of preparing and implementing a budget. It is now universally considered as a necessary management tool. *Management* means managing limited resources to attain specific goals with efficiency and making decisions about the uncertain future. Successful managers try to attain the organization

---

[1]David Wessel, "Budget Seeks to Raise U.S. Living Standards and Reduce Inequality," *The Wall Street Journal,* February 7, 1997, p. A1.

objectives with the given amount of resources by planning and performing effectively. Their other principal functions include organizing, decision-making, staffing, communicating, motivating, leading, controlling, and evaluating performance. Today's managers operate in a complex economic, social, political, and technological environment that is largely beyond their control. The markets are now global, and the environment is all high-tech. In fact, social scientists call it the information age. The rate of technological change is dazzling, and the competition is absolutely fierce. And yet successful managers continue to expand the economic horizons by their skillful management of business affairs every day and are taking corporations to greater heights.

Social scientists have perceived the role of a business organization/firm in a variety of ways. In the old days, a firm was considered simply a way of organizing business activities for profit. It was a convenient way of assembling land, labor, capital, and entrepreneurial skills for a common objective—profit for the investors. With the passage of time, the role of the firm expanded. It is now considered as a way to carry out economic activity for social good, to provide goods and services to the consumers, to provide employment to the populace, and to provide a reasonable return on investment to the investors. The role of the firm continues to evolve. With the advent of high technology, the modern firm is increasingly viewed as a *technology delivery system* to the society.

Management uses budgets as an instrument to carry out its plans and policies through the lower echelons of an organization. Budgets serve several *objectives:* planning and coordinating activities, communicating and authorizing goals and actions, motivating people, implementing plans, and controlling and evaluating performance. Whether the organization is a profit-oriented firm or a not-for-profit organization, a small corporation or a large multinational conglomerate, budgets are universally used to carry out management plans and are increasingly used as an instrument to motivate people.

(b) Stages in Budgeting. To accomplish the objectives of budgeting, a budget generally moves through four stages: setting goals, implementing plans, evaluating incentives, and monitoring progress. Each stage involves people—the *budgeter or budgeteer* (one who prepares the budget or, as is the practice in many organizations, the budget committee) and the *budgetee* (for whom and for whose department the budget is prepared). To the extent the budget committee and its members are cognizant of human behavior, they succeed. To begin with, the goals are set and a budget is prepared (computer software can help) and sold, that is, gaining willing acceptance from the participants. Selling of the budget requires knowing the participants, reasonableness of the goals, avoidance of surprises, clarity of priorities, and willingness to negotiate. These steps ensure participation, commitment, and goal congruency. Second, plans have to be implemented through effective communication and by ensuring cooperation and coordination among all parties. Third, an incentive system is designed to motivate people and favorably influence their level of aspirations and anxiety in a positive manner. Finally, progress is monitored at the appropriate levels of authority.

(c) Budgeting Approaches. There are at least three types of budgets: *imposed or authoritative budgets, consultative budgets,* and *participative budgets.* As the term implies an *imposed or authoritative budget* is a plan handed down by the top management or the budget committee of an organization to the middle and lower-level management. It is also known as the "top-down" approach since all the decisions are made by the top management without consulting the lower echelons of an organization. The approach has some obvious advantages. It is a less expensive approach and saves time since not too many people are involved in budget preparation. Another advantage of the approach is the broad (company-wide) perspective it brings to budgeting, as the top management is less likely to suffer from narrow departmental considerations and politics.

Imposed budgets also have some serious flaws. Such budgets are an antithesis of divisionalization and delegation principles. People closer to work have a better feel of the situation and hence could be more realistic in preparing budgets than are people several layers away from the scene. Second, because of the lack of involvement in setting quantitative plans for the future, the lower-level management does not always feel totally committed to the top-management goals and policies. The budgetary goals are often taken as the goals of the top management and not of all the members of the organization. Such budgets fail to motivate employees. *Stretch budgets* are often used to motivate employees (associates). Here the management tries to push the organization to its limits. Each succeeding year sets targets higher than the previous year's targets. Some successful corporations like General Electric and Boeing have followed such budgeting.

In *consultative budgets* top managers ask their subordinates to discuss their ideas and goals, but no joint decisions are made. The senior management solicits ideas from the junior management, but the final budgets are those of the senior management. Consultative budgets are an improvement over the imposed budgets, as the junior management is led to believe that it has a say in the budgets. A variation of the approach is known as *pseudo consultation/participation* wherein the junior managers are given the impression that their input will be used in the final budgets although the top management has no such intentions. Such budgets often give rise to employee frustration and demoralization.

The third type of budget is called *participative budgets* because all levels of management are involved in developing them. Generally, the information emanates from the lower levels of management and reaches the top. For that reason, this approach is also known as "bottom-up" approach. The principal advantage of the approach lies in the attainability of the budgetary goals. Because the budgets are prepared on the basis of information provided by the people affected by the budgets, people feel concerned and involved. They develop a sense of commitment that is lacking in the imposed budgets. Participative budgets are also more realistic as they are based on the information provided by the people who are close to the scene of action where things are happening.

The participative budgets are not completely free from problems. They are expensive and time consuming. The old adage that work and expense grow with the number of people involved holds true here. Participation involves people, and they all want to feel important by participating in the budgeting process and thus adding to the time and resources spent on preparing budgets. Additionally, managers at lower levels may take a rather narrow view of their activities and ignore the effect of their activities on other departments or divisions of the firm. Finally, in their desire to protect their pet projects and look successful at the end (as people like to be achievers rather than losers), the participants may be prompted to inflate or deflate their estimates (build slacks and cushions). Rather than containing realistic estimates, budgets may end up being based on figures as managers *wish* to see them rather than as they *should* see them.

Negotiated budgets are essentially an extension of participative budgets. Under this approach, budgets are prepared by a process of give-and-take that may not produce plans liked by everyone but that are the best under the circumstances. The top management sets the broad goals and the constraints, and the lower-and middle-level managers arrive at the final figures through active participation. If either level of management does not feel satisfied with the other's expectations or plans, negotiations proceed to hammer out a consensus. No doubt such an approach could take time, and several rounds of negotiations may have to take place before the master budget is finalized.

29.2   THE BEHAVIORAL ASSUMPTIONS.   Budgets represent corporate quantitative plans of the people, prepared by the people, and prepared for the people. Those plans cannot accomplish much by themselves. It is how they influence people's behavior that distinguishes successful budgets from unsuccessful ones. In carrying out their activities, the accountants and budgeters utilize a frame of reference that is essentially their view of the nature of the firm and its participants. It follows, therefore, that they should operate with an understanding of human behavior and how people behave given certain incentives and rewards. Their model of the firm and operation should have some implicit or explicit assumptions about human behavior in an organizational setting. The relationship of an individual with his/her peers and others at work has been a fascinating subject of research for sociologists, psychologists, and other behavioral scientists for a long time. Numerous social psychologists have contributed to our understanding in this area. What follows is a review of some of the major contributions in the field.[2]

(a)   The Traditional View of Human Behavior.   The traditional view of human behavior is based on what is considered as the classical economic theory of the firm and organizational behavior. The names of Henry Fayol, Frederick Taylor, Frank and Lilian Gilbreth, and Henry Gantt are most prominent among those who are associated with the traditional view. This view is based on the premise that the principal objective of a firm is profit maximization, and all business activities should be directed toward that goal. This goal could be divided into subgoals, and the latter are assumed to be of additive nature. If every segment of a firm attempts to maximize its profit, the profit of the firm as a whole would also be maximized (shades of Adam Smith's Principles of Economics).

Another premise of the traditional view is that human beings are primarily economic and are motivated primarily by economic forces. The traditionalists assume that people are inefficient and wasteful. They are lazy and do not want to work

---

[2]A very good overview of the issues discussed in this section can be found in Edwin A. Caplan, "Behavioral Assumptions of Management Accounting," *The Accounting Review,* July 1966, pp. 496–509.

unless forced by the economic needs. Since work is unpleasant and leisure is pleasant, the employer has to devise ways to get work done in time and within the estimated cost. Henry Fayol described how management should be carried out in the fourteen *universal principles of management.* They included division of work, authority, discipline, unit of command, unity of direction, subordination of individual interest to the general interest, remuneration, centralization, scaler chain, order, equity, stability and tenure of personnel, initiative, and esprit de corps.[3] Frederick Taylor and his followers of the *scientific management* school focused their attention on the measurement and structure of work itself. People were considered as rational, economic beings and mere extensions of the machines they worked on. It was argued that they would act in their own best interest and ultimately in the best interest of the firm, if the workers understood correct work procedures and were assured of a fair reward. Accordingly, time and motion studies were conducted to devise efficient ways of doing work.[4]

The third premise of the traditional view deals with the behavior of management itself. The essence of management control is authority. The flow of authority is downward. The role of a manager is to maximize profit of the firm, and in order to do that, he/she should control wasteful and lazy behavior of the employees. The role of the accounting and budgeting system is to provide information that helps managers in controlling subordinates by pinpointing inadequate and unsatisfactory performance.

(b)   Budgeting and the Traditional Management Environment.   The traditional view of human behavior is characterized by authoritative management, and, as discussed earlier, budgets are imposed from the top. It is somewhat akin to military lines of command. If the traditional behavioral assumptions were to hold true, budgets would be a grand success. However, the experience shows that when budgets are imposed, the employees responsible for implementing budgets behave *dysfunctionally.* Dysfunctional behavior is defined as a situation wherein the subordinates' conduct does not optimize the performance of the firm or when the goals of subunits do not mesh with the goals of the firm. The actions of the subordinates are in divergence with the overall interests of the organization. Dysfunctional behavior could lead to *goal incongruence,* a condition that results when the goals of the subunits are not in accord with those of the firm. As long as employees are evaluated and rewarded only for achieving their narrow departmental goals, goal incongruency is likely to occur. Employees have a tendency to protect their personal and departmental interests first and then the long-run interests of the firm as a whole.

Another aspect of dysfunctional behavior is *gamesmanship, manipulation, and falsification of information* by the employees. Given the pressure on the subordinates to meet the budgets, they devise their own ways to beat the system. For example, when production exceeds budget target, they report less than the actual production for at least two reasons. One, in the future when the actual output is below the budget, they could use the unreported past output to make up for the shortage. Past excess production serves as a cushion for the future. Second, they are afraid of reporting excess

---

[3]See Robert Kreitner, *Management,* 3rd ed., Boston ma: Houghton Mifflin, 1986, p. 51.
[4]*Ibid.,* pp. 50–57.

production, as that level could become the standard in future.[5] Centrally planned economies like that of the former USSR and other East European countries provided good illustrations of such a phenomenon. A variation of the abuse can be traced in the tendency to average income (smoothing income) out in the corporate world. The budget participants have learned that a steady upward trend in corporate income is generally viewed more favorably than the fluctuating income.

Finally, the authoritarian management style tends to encourage *short-run performance over the long-run performance*. In their eagerness to meet the budgets, managers develop a myopic view of the firm's future. In a budget-constrained environment, managers are often evaluated on the basis of their budgetary performance. Consciously or unconsciously, the emphasis shifts from long-run profitability and effectiveness to immediate performance. Such an environment could discourage paying attention to the critical success factors of business—like customer service, employee training, and product innovation—and foster tension and mistrust among subordinates and managers.[6]

(c) The Modern View of Human Behavior. The modern view of human behavior is an amalgam of diverse theories and assumptions relating to organizational behavior, economics, and other social disciplines. The long list of social scientists who have contributed to our understanding of the modern organizational behavior and management practices includes, among others, Chester Barnard, Richard Cyert, Frederick Herzberg, James March, Abraham Maslow, Douglas McGregor, Herbert Simon, and Victor Vroom. The modern view of human behavior essentially started with the writings of Barnard and gained much popularity with the research of Cyert, March, and Simon. Their ideas are premised on the decision-making model of the firm.

Under the modern view, organizations are simply coalitions of individuals who join hands and pool their resources to accomplish certain common goals. As such, organizations do not have *goals*. They are legal fictions and are mindless. Only individuals have goals. The commonly understood organization goals are really the goals of the dominant members of the coalition running an organization. They change with the changes in socio-economic environment and the desires and capabilities of the participants. Today's organizations are a *complex* amalgam of people and resources and can hardly have a single goal like profit maximization. They are likely to operate with multiple goals like earning a reasonable return on investment, maintaining a market share, achieving leadership in research and development, developing a reputation for customer service, maintaining name recognition in the marketplace, and so on.

People join an organization and stay in it as long as they feel their participation will help them attain their own personal goals. As a result, the participants tend to emphasize the attainment of local (subunit) and personal goals more than the organization-wide goals, and if the two sets of goals do not mesh with each other, goal incongruency arises. It follows that organization goals are not always additive, and

[5]See Mohamed Onsi, "Factor Analysis of Behavioral Variables Affecting Budgetary Slack," *The Accounting Review,* July 1973, pp. 535–548.

[6]See Anthony G. Hopwood, "Leadership Climate and the Use of Accounting Data in Performance Evaluation," *The Accounting Review,* July 1974, pp. 485–495.

the maximization of subunit profits does not always lead to maximization of profit of the firm. In fact, survival of the organization becomes the first priority. If the organization survives, the participants then have an opportunity to attain their own goals. It seems that earning a satisfactory or reasonable return on investment rather than maximizing profit is a more realistic goal in today's economy.

In contrast to the traditional view of human behavior, the modern view is that people are motivated by a wide variety of sociopsychological needs and drives in addition to their economic needs. The relative strength of these needs and drives varies from person to person and from time to time. People have limited knowledge of the uncertain environment they face and are not always rational and consistent in their priorities and preferences. They join an organization with the assumption that the membership will help them in meeting their personal needs. The intensity of their efforts in an organization is a function of how they perceive the operation of the reward system in that organization. Whether they gain when the organization gains (gain sharing) has become a frequently asked question. The higher and faster the reward for the efforts, the more intensive are the efforts of the participants, as higher and faster rewards could lead them to meet their personal needs more fully and promptly. However, the reward is not always economic. It could be in sociopsychological terms also. Because people's needs are diverse, so should be the reward structure.

Management style is another area where the modern view of organizational behavior differs from the traditional view. The traditional view holds the authority of the management as given, and it can be imposed on the subordinates (or associates, as most firms like to call them), and the responsibility is assumed by the subordinates. In contrast, the modern view recognizes the fact that the responsibility is assigned from above, and the authority is accepted from below. The management's function is to *make decisions and influence* the behavior of others who will either implement those decisions or will be affected by those decisions. Management's responsibility is to create a conducive environment in which subordinates feel they are part of the system, and when they work to attain the organization goals they are also attaining their own personal goals. Realization of self-interest is, probably, the most effective inducement. Successful managers attempt to work out a fine balance between the inducement they offer to the subordinates (associates) and the contribution expected of them. Because of goal complexity and the balancing of inducement and effort, *management control* has acquired added significance in the modern firm. Budgets have been used by management to influence and motivate employee behavior. Budgets communicate and provide feedback to help the managers and employees attain their personal goals. One view is that the budget staff and the accountants are no longer the passive spectators they used to be. They are active participants in the budgeting process.

29.3   HUMAN MOTIVATION.   The word *motivation* originated from the Latin word *movere,* meaning to move or to drive (i.e., a need or desire that causes a person to act). It refers to the psychological process that gives human behavior a direction and purpose. Four theories or groups of theories about human motivation have received much coverage in recent years: needs hierarchy theory, two-factor theory, expectancy theory, and X, Y, and Z theories. These theories are premised on the foundation of a constructive reward (compensation system) in an organization. The four theories or theory groups are briefly reviewed below.

(a)   The Needs Hierarchy Theory.   In 1943, Maslow, a psychologist, proposed that all human needs can be grouped in a hierarchy of five levels: physiological needs, safety (security) needs, love (social) needs, esteem needs, and self-actualization needs. Since a human bieng is a perpetually wanting animal, as soon as one need is satisfied he/she feels the next need. The five needs essentially form a pyramid. At the bottom of the pyramid are the most basic physiological needs of food and shelter. They enable a person to survive. Once those needs are satisfied, the person gets concerned about his/her safety from the elements and other threats. At the third level of hierarchy Maslow stacked up social needs—the need for love, belonging, and friendship. A person satisfied with the social needs enters the fourth stage of self-esteem needs. Much of self-esteem comes from self-confidence, status, and respect from peers. The final and the highest level of needs is characterized as self-actualization or self-realization needs. These needs relate to creativity, continued self-development, and self-realization of one's true potential. A person at that level has warmth and sympathy for others. He/she is open and trusting, and could be rather unconventional in his/her ways. As a manager, the person would be willing to try new ways of doing things because he/she feels secure within him/herself.[7]

Although Maslow's theory of human needs has been questioned for its rigid hierarchy and the very idea of arranging needs into levels, it does have some important implications for today's management process. It is difficult to imagine that people move from one level of needs to the next level only when one type of needs is fully satisfied. People feel most of those needs somewhat concurrently. Nevertheless, the important lesson managers can learn is that satisfied needs cannot motivate people and may even lead them to complacency. For instance, a poorly paid individual could be motivated to work harder for more money, but the well-paid worker may not be. Likewise, one unemployment benefit scheme could fulfill the safety needs of an individual, but the second unemployment benefit scheme will not motivate a fully employed worker to work any harder (shades of diminishing returns). Effective management requires the manager to anticipate employees' emerging needs and devise ways to motivate them while satisfying their needs.

(b)   The Two-Factor Theory (New).   Frederick Herzberg's studies showed that two groups of factors—hygiene and satisfier—affect human behavior. *Hygiene factors* relate to the job environment. They include working conditions, base pay, organization policies, interpersonal relationships, and supervisors' behavior. A poor job environment inhibits employees' performance. But the improvement in environment by itself cannot motivate employees. It only creates the potential for improvement. The *satisfier factors* relate to job content and how employees feel about their job and work. They include achievement, recognition, responsibility, and perceived opportunity for growth. Presence of poor satisfier factors retards employee satisfaction and

---

[7]See A. H. Maslow, "A Theory of Human Motivation," *Psychological Review,* July, 1943, pp. 370–396; and Kreitner, *op. cit.,* pp. 381–391.

their performance. Satisfier factors can motivate employees to higher levels of performance, provided the hygiene factors are also present.[8]

(c)   **The Expectancy Theory.**   Victor Vroom explained human behavior in terms of an individual's goals, expectations of achieving those goals (outcomes), and the utility he/she places on those outcomes in the form of satisfying his/her personal needs. The theory assumes that an individual can rationally determine which outcomes he/she prefers and will make a realistic estimate (probability) of the outcomes.[9]

The expectancy theory uses two terms: expectancy and valence. *Expectancy* refers to the person's perception of the probability that certain outcomes will occur due to his/her particular behavior, and *valence* refers to the value or utility of those outcomes to that person. Valences could be of intrinsic or extrinsic nature. Intrinsic valence is the satisfaction one derives from the work itself or from successfully completing a task. The latter generates self-esteem and confidence in the person. The extrinsic valence comes from the outside world. These are rewards and recognitions received in the form of bonuses, promotions, increased pay, etc. Motivation, under the theory, is simply a mathematical function of expectancy and valence. Motivation requires the presence of both factors at a high level. For instance, if a manager has a high expectancy of receiving a promotion and places a high value on it, he/she will be highly motivated to work hard. On the other hand, if a manager has low expectancy of receiving a promotion but values it highly, he/she will have low motivation. The other extreme will be when a manager has low expectancy of receiving a promotion and places a low value on it, so that he/she will be hardly motivated to work for the promotion. To be effective, an employee is most motivated when he/she has high level of expectancy and a reasonable probability of achieving the goal.

What is important in the expectancy theory is the perception of the employees (associates) and not of the managers. People are motivated by their own expectations and how they perceive the reward. The effectiveness of the managers depends on how well they understand employees' perception of their expectations and valences. Such perceptions vary from employee to employee, and knowing what inspires each individual employee is a formidable challenge that managers face if they desire to motivate the employees.

Additionally, managers should make sure that employees are well trained in the jobs they are assigned to perform, that rewards are carefully selected to meet employee needs, and that employees understand the reward system and have confidence in the fair and equitable administration of rewards to them. From the employees' point of view, the theory can work only if the employees have a desire for the reward. They should believe that their efforts can lead to good performance and that different levels of performance can lead to differences in the reward.

(d)   **The X, Y, and Z Theories.**   Douglas McGregor and others have stressed the need for understanding the relationship between motivation and management

---

[8]See Frederick Herzberg, "One More Time: How Do You Motivate Employees?," *Harvard Business Review,* January–February, 1968, pp. 53–62.

[9]See Victor Vroom, *Work and Motivation,* New York: John Wiley & Sons, 1964; and R. Wayne Mondy, Arthur Sharplin, Robert E. Holmes, and Edwin B. Flippo, *Management Concepts and Practices,* 3rd ed., Boston, MA: Allyn & Bacon, 1986, pp. 282–302.

philosophies. He characterized the practices of management based on traditional assumptions of human behavior as *theory X.*[10]

Under the traditional model of organizational behavior, it is assumed that human beings dislike work, are motivated solely by their economic needs, and believe that authority is usually imposed from the top. One form of imposing such an authority can be found in the practice of imposed budgets. In contrast to theory X, McGregor characterized theory Y with the democratic and participative management environment. *Theory Y* is identified with the modern view of human behavior. This theory assumes that people like work and are willing to assume responsibility and make commitments if the rewards are commensurate with the expected effort.[11] Employees can be motivated to work for organizational goals if their higher order needs can be correctly perceived and satisfied. Managers can be very effective if they can create an accomplishment-oriented environment at the place of work. *Participation* is of key importance in the success of a modern complex organization.

A recent entry in the field of motivation and management philosophies is labeled as *theory Z.* This theory is essentially based on the Japanese style of corporate management. William Ouchi observed that the Japanese corporate environment is characterized by a high degree of mutual responsibility, consideration, and loyalty between the employees and their organizations. The oft-quoted Japanese practice of lifetime employment has fostered a strong sense of loyalty and commitment among the workers. To the extent possible, employee layoffs are avoided in Japan and the employees are expected to develop a feeling of being part of the corporate family. The Japanese companies are also known for *collective decision-making* and *total care of their employees.* Consequently, they experience low absenteeism and employee turnover, and have high employee morale. These and many other such practices have created a massive cadre of highly motivated and dedicated managers and workers in Japan. This theory also emphasizes success through commitment, mutual respect, and participation. The well-publicized idea of *quality circles* is but one example of the many successful management practices in Japan.[12]

29.4   BUDGETS AND MOTIVATION.   Budgeting as it affects the motivation of managers and subordinates has received much attention of the researchers in the last three decades or so. The modern theorists have emphasized *participation* of the employees in the budgeting process to increase its effectiveness. They have reached this conclusion on the basis of observing human behavior in a variety of working conditions.[13]

(a)   Budgets as Pressure Devices.   One of the most popular impressions about budgets is that they can be used to pressure employees to produce more or meet the

---

[10]See Douglas McGregor, *The Human Side of Enterprise,* New York: McGraw-Hill, 1960; and Mondy, et al., *op. cit.,* pp. 281–284.

[11]Douglas McGregor, *op. cit.,* p. 49.

[12]See William G. Ouchi, *Theory Z: How American Business Can Meet the Japanese Challenge,* Reading, MA: Addison-Wesley, 1981; and Mondy, et al., op. cit., pp. 300–304.

[13]See Chris Argyris, *The Impact of Budgets on People,* New York: Financial Executives Research Foundation, 1952, and Chris Argyris, "Human Problems with Budgets," *Harvard Business Review,* January–February, 1953, pp. 97–110, for many of the comments made in this section of the chapter.

ever-rising targets. Managers have been known to use budgets to blame employees for not working hard enough and, hence, not reaching their true potential. The traditional behavioral assumptions imply that if each employee maximizes output and minimizes costs, the firm as a whole will be able to attain its objective of profit maximization or earning the target profit. This often leads managers to think first of setting targets (imposed budgets) and then of enforcing them rigidly. If the targets are not met, the subordinates are to be blamed for the failure. The reward and, especially, the punishment are meted out on the basis of meeting the budgets, and little effort is made to understand the reasons for failure.

In one of the most widely quoted studies of manufacturing plants, Chris Argyris found that the foremen and the workers felt that the budgets were used as pressure devices. Management essentially assumed that the workers were lazy and inefficient and that they lacked self-motivation. Managers had to motivate them, and the finance people (budget staff) believed that budgets would be able to help in motivating the employees.[14] Such feelings do not remain hidden for long. They travel through the organization and reach all levels of the workplace. Once the workers learn, they get irritated and feel alienated from the management.

The management exerts pressure in a variety of ways, ranging from pep talk and red-marking the missed targets to threats and reprimands. What happens when the pressure continues? There is a limit to the degree of pressure one can stand. Workers absorb it initially and then start looking for others with similar experience. They start forming support groups as a defensive device. Once the process starts, it does not end even after the original cause is removed. The groups continue to exist even when the management attempts to eliminate the budget-caused tension by introducing participative budgeting. The employees become suspicious of company moves and wonder whether the management will not devise new ways of putting pressure on them.

How unproductive the budgetary pressure can become can be imagined by the fact that the process does not stop at the workers' level. Caught between the employees and the management, the supervisors also start feeling the ill effects of the budgetary pressure. Argyris observed the supervisors handle the pressure in a number of ways. First, interdepartmental strife may occur as the supervisors try to blame each other for the missed targets. Second, the supervisors may internalize the pressure and become tense. Unfortunately, the problem does not end here. Constant tension creates frustration in the supervisors, which spills over on their work and employees. They may no longer operate efficiently, and the output declines. In short, budgets become counterproductive.

(b)   Role Conflict.   Conflict between the operating personnel and the budget staff is another disturbing effect of the budget pressure. When budgets are used as a pressure device, conflict between line and staff people is almost inevitable. Budget staff and the operating personnel work under different bosses, and their performance is often evaluated by different people and different standards. They all desire to succeed, but one party's success often becomes the cause of the other party's failure. For instance, if a budget supervisor finds an error or shortfall in a particular production department, he/she is unlikely to go to the production supervisor directly for at least

---

[14]Chris Argyris, "Human Problems with Budgets," *op. cit.*, p. 98.

two reasons. For one, such direct communication may not be permitted by the company personnel policy. The two groups of people often communicate through a circuitous route. In addition, and more importantly, the budget supervisor gets no credit for sharing his/her finding with the factory supervisor directly. The budget supervisor's success lies in bringing the error to the notice of his/her boss, who then takes it up with his/her superiors, and so on up the company hierarchy. Once the information has traveled through the budget staff and to the top management, it travels down through the production personnel. Finding errors may win some points for the budget staff but causes much serious damage to the operating supervisor's morale and efficiency. The process illustrates how production and budget people start operating at cross-purposes.

Two additional factors can cause conflicts between the budget staff and operating personnel. First, in its pursuit of discovering errors, budget staff often develops an obsession of it. Secondly, it often becomes very defensive about its work. Rather than explaining the problem, it reacts negatively to any inquiries. It starts hiding under the maze of technical details. It blames the operating personnel for not understanding the budgeting process and criticizes them for the latter's ignorance.

A major ill consequence of the budgetary pressure is the creation of a *myopic* view among different operating people affected by the budgets. Since the operating supervisors are evaluated on the basis of success in meeting their separate budgets, they often operate unconcerned about the effects of their actions on the other departments and the company as a whole. The pursuit of narrow goals by each operating supervisor does not necessarily optimize performance of the whole company.

The top management has a major role to play if the conflicts between the budget staff and the operating people are to be resolved. Senior managers should understand the problems budgeting creates. Since the interdepartmental and staff-line conflicts are almost inevitable, the best management can do is to control the conflicts. It has to create an environment for all to operate harmoniously. Budgets can be an extension of management's leadership. Effort should be made by both the staff and line personnel to understand the budgets and each other's point of view. Their outlook toward budgets should change. It cannot happen on its own. It is an *educational process* of learning and letting others learn. All levels of management, budget staff, and the operating supervisors should learn about the budgeting process and how it affects human behavior before budgeting is introduced in an organization. Additionally, supervisors should undergo *training* in human relations. Such a training should be focused on the understanding of the underlying problems and not just on the superficial difficulties. The budget staff should also learn about the implications of budgets, on the workers (associates), the effect of pressure on people impacted by the budgets, and the effect of success and failure on employees (associates) and their families.

29.5 BUDGETS AND PARTICIPATION. Participation by all levels of management in preparing budgets has been generally recommended as a way of resolving many of the problems created by budgets. Support for participation can be found in all of the motivation theories. Budgeting offers an excellent opportunity to the top management to involve the subordinates (associates) in the affairs of a firm. In the following pages an attempt will be made to discuss several important aspects of participation, the careful consideration of which could contribute much to the success of budgets and budgeting.

(a) The Nature of Participation. Participation means the involvement of all levels of management and key employees in developing budgets. It is a process of joint decision-making where top management and the subordinates (associates), especially the middle-level and lower-level managers, freely discuss budget goals and expectations and reach a consensus (the Japanese style). In a participative system, both groups, the top management and the subordinates, understand that the proposals from the top management only form a basis of discussion and do not constitute the final decision. These are not dictates to be followed. Also, participation does not mean that the two groups will always be in complete agreement or that suggestions will always be accepted. It simply means that decisions will not be made unilaterally by the top management as is often done in the traditional environment. There will be full consultation with the subordinates before the higher-ups make a final decision. All genuine, reasonable, and experience-based input of the subordinates, no matter how different it is from the top echelon's expectations, will be seriously considered. Consideration does not mean just lip service or pretense. It means the subordinates' input will be incorporated in the budget to foster trust and openness among the employees. On the other hand, consideration does not also mean abdication of authority by the top management. The top management does retain the veto power when the subordinates' participation is frivolous and unreasonable. In a true participatory system, the subordinates become *associates,* and many successful corporations now address their employees that way. It has fused a sense of pride in the employees and fostered a team spirit.

Participation of subordinates can be successful only if it is true and sincere. True participation takes place when the subordinates do not feel inhibited and there is a give-and-take between the concerned parties. It also implies involvement of subordinates in substantial matters and not the creation of a facade. *Pseudoparticipation* is never a success and is soon recognized for what it is by the participants.[15] Pseudoparticipation leads to half-hearted acceptance and creates trouble later when the budget targets are not met.

In a true participatory system, preparation of budgets starts from the bottom of the hierarchy and moves upward. As the budget preparation moves up and down, it may go through a number of changes. When changes are suggested, they have to be justified, and that minimizes unnecessary changes.

(b) The Significance of Participation. Participation works because it requires joint decision-making where all levels of management provide input in the decision. When people participate in decision-making, they *internalize the goals.* They see those goals as their own goals. They perceive the goals as reasonable because the participants were themselves involved in setting them. The process provides intrinsic motivation to the participants. Participation is also an effective way of building trust among the employees.

The process of goal internalization ultimately results in a higher level of motivation among employees. As the following exhibit shows, an individual develops his/her goals through a complex process. To begin with, he/she brings to an organization his/her own personal, moral, social, and cultural values, which are part of an individual's upbringing and social life. These values are influenced by the socioeconomic

---

[15]See *ibid.,* p. 108, for some interesting observations.

and the legal and political environments. An individual also has his/her personal needs and ambitions in life. When an individual joins an organization, he/she brings those needs and ambitions with him/her and tries to match them with the corporate goals and other influences. The solid lines in Exhibit 29.1 establish that relationship.

Exhibit 29.1 also shows that an individual's goals are affected by the organization culture and the style of management leadership. Other influences—for example, the

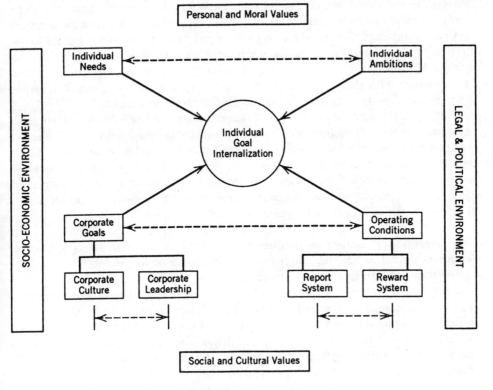

Exhibit 29.1   Individual goal internalization.

report and reward systems—also have an effect on the goal internalization. The interaction between these variables is denoted by the broken lines. In brief, an individual's goals in an organization are shaped by an interaction of four factors: individual needs, individual ambitions, corporate goals, and operating conditions. The intensity of these factors helps form an individual's goals at work and the extent of his/her internalizing them. When individuals participate in the budget preparation, they go through the entire process.

Participation in budgeting raises employee morale and commitment at the place of work. Employees develop a stake in the success of budgets and tend to work more efficiently. It creates a "we" feeling in the organization and checks the schism of "them" versus "us". Participation also encourages *cooperation* among the employees and makes them partners in the undertaking. Being a participant on an equal basis makes them feel important and gives the feeling that what they do matters. The participating employees also experience *job enlargement and empowerment,* which gives them self-esteem and satisfaction and creates a positive attitude toward the firm.

(c)   The Group Dynamics.   Participation by itself cannot affect performance. It influences productivity through a complex process called *group dynamics*. Group dynamics is the study of interacting forces within a small human group, i.e, how an individual's behavior is affected by the group.

People belong to different groups, including family, church, social, work, and so forth and these groups shape an individual's conduct within that group. At the place of work, an individual interacts with his/her superiors, subordinates, and colleagues. His/her performance very much depends on the values and attitudes of these groups and how committed that individual is to these groups. Human beings have a strong urge to "belong" and "connect," and this urge attracts an individual to different groups. His/her membership, which in most cases is informal, depends on his/her conformance with the group norms, his/her acceptance of the group values, the strength and cohesiveness of the group, and his/her own personality.

Participation in preparing budgets leads managers and subordinates to interact with each other, which increases group cohesiveness and morale. In a cohesive group where members value their membership, they are likely to accept the group norms. If participation increases group cohesiveness and if cohesiveness is rewarded for good performance, participation may lead to higher performance. In a way, participation self-perpetuates the wholesome environment that makes it work. It creates a virtuous circle, where success begets success.[16]

(d)   Organization Culture and Leadership.   Organization culture refers to the collection of shared values and beliefs that gives a feeling of community to the organization members. To be effective, participation has to fit in the organization culture and leadership style of the management. In an open and progressive organization where there is mutual trust and communication, participation will flourish. On the other hand, in an organization characterized by heavy-handedness of the top management and undemocratic ways of doing things, the seeds of participation can be planted but will have difficulty germinating and growing. Likewise, if the lower management is not used to working independently, participation would fail because the subordinates (associates) are conditioned to accepting the dictates of the top management.

Leadership is the process of developing a voluntary following for a common goal. Different managers have different leadership styles. There are aggressive managers, and there are weak managers. Both extremes could create problems in an organization. If the managers are not well trained in human relations, their behavior could discourage subordinates (associates) from coming forward with suggestions and taking initiative. Such managers, obviously, need training in winning trust and confidence of their subordinates. The overly aggressive managers can sometimes create the environment of *rejection* among the subordinates. Many of the subordinates may not be able to handle it and may feel discouraged from participating in the future. Effective participation requires a conducive environment where the subordinates do not come out of a budget session with a feeling of rejection. They should have the satisfaction of contributing something important in the preparation of the final budget.

---

[16]Selwyn W. Becker and David Green, Jr., "Budgeting and Employee Behavior," *The Journal of Business,* October 1962, p. 401; and see Gordon Shillinglaw, *Managerial Cost Accounting,* 4th ed., Homewood, IL: Richard D. Irwin, 1977, pp. 639–656.

While the overly aggressive managers have difficulty getting the subordinates to participate, the weak managers could also be equally unproductive. In the latter case, nothing could ever become final, and the participative system could degenerate into producing "rubber budgets." Employees soon learn that as long as a suggestion could be justified, it will be accepted and incorporated in the budget.

(e) Standards and Aspirations. Participation affects participants' aspiration levels differently in different situations. *Aspiration level* is the level of performance a person sets for himself for a familiar task. Common sense tells that "reasonably unattainable" standards are helpful because they raise the aspiration level of the employees.[17] Reasonable standards are easily internalized by the employees and lead to recognition and reward. The virtuous cycle is broken when the standards are unreasonably tight or too loose. In the case of standards that are difficult to attain with reasonable effort, the employees even get discouraged from making a normal effort. Because they cannot attain the standards with reasonable effort, the employees lose interest in working for them. Where the reward structure is strictly tied to the budgetary performance, it often leads to budgeting gamesmanship and cushioning to provide covers. Similarly, mediocre standards can also adversely affect employees' aspirations. There is no challenge in such standards. The level of aspirations and performance declines when the standards set for a person are below his/her personal goal. The lesson here is that the standards should be reasonable and challenging enough to get the best out of the employees. Senior managers must recognize the fine line between reasonable and unreasonable levels of performance.

The aspiration levels set by the management generally differ, from and in many cases exceed, those set by the employees (associates) themselves. Stedry ran experiments to see how actual achievements of the employees are related to budget and aspiration levels. He found that where the successful budget performance was rewarded and the failure penalized, performance was significantly influenced by the type of budget, the conditions of administration, and the way aspiration levels were set.[18] In another study, Bart found superior performance resulting when the attitudes of senior managers were consistent with the product managers' reward system.[19]

(f) Participation and Slack. Budgetary *slack* (other commonly used terms are padding, cushion, slush fund, hedge, flexibility, cookie jar, kitty, secret reserve, war chest, contingency fund/reserve[20]) could be another side effect of the participative process in budgeting. *Slack* is the amount of resources budgeted versus what is really needed to do the task in a proper manner. Even in a participative system, the managers are likely to resort to padding as it offers a cushion for covering errors and

[17]See Andrew C. Stedry, *Budget Control and Cost Behavior,* Englewood Cliffs, NJ: Prentice-Hall, 1960, for some of the ideas discussed in this section.

[18]See Andrew C. Stedry, *op. cit.;* and Nicholas Dopuch, Jacob G. Birnberg, and Joel Demski, *Cost Accounting: Accounting Data for Management's Decisions,* 2d ed., New York: Harcourt Brace Jovanovich, 1974, pp. 307–310.

[19]See Christopher K. Bart, "Budgeting Gamesmanship," *Academy of Management Executive,* 1988, pp. 285–294.

[20]*Ibid.*

shortfalls later. Slack gives flexibility to the managers. For instance, revenues may be underestimated and costs may be overestimated intentionally. Some slack is almost unavoidable—when rewards are too closely linked with performance—and may even be helpful in attaining the budgetary goals. When managers' performance is evaluated on the basis of their budget performance, they are able to attain their personal goals—for example, higher salaries, bonuses, and promotion—more readily if a reasonable amount of slack is present. The positive effect of meeting the budgets and personal goals generally outweighs the cost of inefficiency caused by slack.

A limited amount of slack is almost intentional and useful as it can help managers mitigate the budget pressure. But an unreasonable amount could be very costly to the firm and should be checked. A pragmatic approach lies in reviewing the budgets by the top management at some critical points. This way the top management could control unreasonable padding and still expect the subordinates to pursue reasonable goals of the organization.[21] Another approach is to reduce the inducement for padding. By de-emphasizing rewards based on budgetary performance, senior managers can reduce the temptation to pad.

(g)   Performance Reports and Rewards.   The importance of timely reporting and feedback in the success of budgets cannot be overemphasized. A firm should have an open, accurate, and understandable system of communicating performance of the managers by their responsibility. Such a system is known as *responsibility accounting*. Performance reports prepared under the system of responsibility accounting provide feedback to both the top management and the subordinates. They enable the management to adapt to the changing situation and take corrective actions on a timely basis. The subordinates also benefit from them because timely communication minimizes surprises. Performance reporting does not mean reporting only the unfavorable results. Reports on the favorable results are just as important for planning the future.

Responsibility accounting is an indispensable part of the budgeting system in a firm. A firm is generally divided into several responsibility units/centers under the control of separate managers. Each responsibility unit manager will usually have budgeted goals and resources to accomplish them. The budgeted goals are then broken down into operational targets by the period. Thus the budget for each unit indicates what is expected of each unit in any given period. At the end of each period, reports are prepared comparing actual results with the budget targets (computation of variances). Because these reports are prepared by the area of responsibility and not by activity or product, they help in identifying people responsible for the variances.

The conflict between sales and production people presents an interesting situation here. The former often push rush orders as long as the production people are willing to produce without charging extra for filling such orders. The latter do not like such emergencies all the time, and the situation creates conflicts and irritation between the two. Such conflicts can be easily avoided by charging rush orders the extra cost of producing the goods and also pointing out the reasons for cost variances. Both steps, the extra charge and the assigning of variances, will have the effect of making the future

---

[21]See Michael Schiff and Arie Y. Lewin, "The Impact of People on Budgets," *The Accounting Review*, April 1970, pp. 259–268; and Mohamed Onsi, *op. cit.*, pp. 535–548.

rush orders more acceptable to the production people and reducing the avoidable rush orders. Responsibility accounting can thus play a very positive role in budgeting.[22]

The performance reports under the responsibility accounting system should emphasize the principle of *controllability* of the items therein. When the budgeted and actual results are reported, they report only what the concerned manager at that level could control. Costs beyond the control of the manager will hardly serve any purpose if included in the report. Removal of uncontrollable items removes unnecessary clutter from the reports and helps management focus attention on relevant items. Reports by themselves cannot control costs. They help control costs by influencing the behavior of the people who are responsible for incurring those costs. The performance reports should be designed to serve the needs of management in this area.

There is, however, one danger in overemphasizing controllability of activities in performance reports. It may lead to compartmentalizing of responsibility on the part of subordinates (associates). The lower-level managers may start acting in a dysfunctional manner and ignore the overall or global interests of the firm. The performance reports thus contain powerful messages both to the top management and to the subordinates and can influence the latter's behavior. Therefore, such reports should be prepared with human sensitivity in mind.

One method of using performance reports effectively is to apply the principle of *management by exception*. This principle implies that management can be effective only if it is selective and attention is devoted to significant matters. By drawing management attention to every variance, the performance reports will lose their effectiveness. Thus, only significant and large variances are brought to management attention. This not only protects the effectiveness of the top management but also provides some flexibility to the subordinates. The subordinates also learn to look at the big picture and devote their time and energy where it matters.

The performance reports should not only clearly *communicate* but also *explain* what they purport to convey. Since most businesses have computerized their performance reporting, a word of caution could be added here. The computer printouts could be very cold, unintelligible, and frightening. Just because the budget/accounting staff understands the computer language and the accounting jargon does not mean everyone else also understands them. It is in everyone's best interest that only the relevant part of the computer printout be presented to the person concerned and that it be accompanied by proper explanation. The lesson is, where possible, make the reports *user friendly*. The purpose of the reports should be to help plan the future and not to blame and penalize people.

Effective participation presupposes *recognition and rewarding* of good performance. When the budgetees meet their budgets, they should receive prompt and fair recognition. The rewards should be equitably distributed and yet recognize differences in performance. If everyone receives the same reward for working at different levels of effort, there will be no incentive to work hard. Modern behavioral theories suggest that the concepts of *positive reinforcement and gain sharing* be followed in evaluating employees' performance. Efforts leading to positive reinforcement tend to repeat. Punishment of budgetary shortfalls cannot change things, but the recognition

---

[22]See Raymond Villers, "Control and Freedom in a Decentralized Company," *Harvard Business Review,* March–April 1954, p. 95.

of successful efforts may lead to their repetition. In fact, too much focus on failures makes the subordinates too cautious and thwarts their initiative.

(h)   The Role of Budget Staff.   The budget and the accounting staff members play a very crucial role in the participative budgeting system, especially now when the data accumulation and processing are computerized and Internet and Intranet have become part of business vocabulary. The budget staff's role is that of collecting information and coordinating budgets. Budget people simply report budget performance to the top management. However, they are often perceived by the operating personnel as if they are paid for finding faults with them and are thus considered adversaries. The budget people do not enforce budgets and still receive much criticism for budget failures from the line people. It is not unnatural for people to find scapegoats for their failures, and the budget staff is as good a scapegoat as the operating personnel can find.

The members of the budget staff need not be defensive about their role. Hiding behind the numbers or using accounting jargons does not help. Likewise, saying they are simply following top management's wishes does not help either. They should approach their role in a more careful manner and project their image as facilitators rather than number crunchers. They should take steps to change their image. The strategy of explaining their work and the reports they prepare can help. Good communication with the line managers can also increase the budget staff's effectiveness. They should emphasize that their role is to facilitate the task of operating people and not to find faults.

The members of the budget staff should exhibit the utmost amount of *patience* in their work. After all, they have to act as the first line of salesmen for budgets. They are the ones who coordinate the budgets. Finally, the budget people should try to simplify the worksheets and computer printouts they use and make them more intelligible to the operating people. Much can be said about standardizing the forms and data-inputting procedures the budget people use for collecting information. The budget office should collect only the information for which it has some perceivable need and not simply to look busy or keep others busy. Likewise, it should produce only the reports that facilitate the work of operating managers, not merely to justify its own existence.

29.6   CONCLUSION.   Today's economy is characterized by rapid technological changes, globalization of markets, shorter product cycles, deregulation, and intense competition. Recent developments like the total quality management and continuous improvement, activity-based management, balanced-score card, and just-in-time and computer-integrated manufacturing systems are revolutionizing the way management has to approach problems today. Business success and, in fact, its very survival depend on excellence. Budgeting has acquired even a more important role in today's economic environment. Budgets are universally used as instruments to convey management goals and expectations. They impact people and are impacted by people. Their role in motivating employees has also been generally recognized.

This chapter discussed both the traditional and modern behavioral assumptions as they affect budgeting. Budgets are known to create stress and are resented for that reason. Research shows that the system of participative budgets and removal of the underlying causes of stress can help resolve many of the problems budgets create in an organization. Participation works because the managers and their subordinates (associates) are able to internalize the budget goals better because the goals are jointly set. Goal internalization leads to higher morale and efficiency. De-emphasizing the linking of rewards with budgetary performance and educating about the role of budgets can go a long way in the lowering of budgeting stress. The important lesson of the chapter is that the people aspect of budgets (and budgeting) cannot be ignored if the management wants budgets to succeed in a modern complex organization.

29.7   THE BEHAVIORAL LESSONS OF BUDGETING

1. Budgets serve a variety of purposes in business, including planning of future, coordinating disparate goals, and motivating the employees (associates).
2. Maximization of profit at the subunit level does not always lead to profit maximization for the organization as a whole in the absence of goal congruency.
3. Budgets involve people at every level, and the people side of budgeting should not be ignored.
4. The traditional behavioral views—for example, the principal objective of the firm is profit maximization, goals are additive, people are motivated primarily by economic forces, and so on—are not very relevant in the modern setting.
5. The modern views of behavioral organization are that people have a variety of needs and motivations; they join an organization to meet their needs; the organization does not have goals, only the dominant group in the coalition has goals; and so forth. A single goal like profit maximization is difficult to establish and accomplish. Multiple goals such as satisfactory return on investment, market share, leadership in research and development, and customer service, and so forth, are more realistic goals in the present world.
6. Under the modern behavioral view, authority cannot be imposed. It is accepted from below.
7. People join an organization to meet their needs. Management's responsibility is to create an environment in which work should meet the needs of both the employees (associates) and the organization.
8. Imposed budgets create pressure on employees, and they resent it. The pressure leads to strife between departments and between staff and line personnel. Ultimately, morale and productivity suffer.
9. Modern management theories recommend that budgeting should involve people—those who will be directly impacted by the budgets.
10. Participation at all levels of management in budgeting helps resolve problems created by the budgets. Participation works because it helps participants better internalize the budget goals.
11. The success of participation depends on a variety of factors, including the nature of participation (real versus pseudo), organization culture and management leadership, group dynamics, performance report, and reward system.
12. De-emphasizing the link between rewards and budgetary performance can reduce the temptation for padding (cushioning) and budgetary stress.

13. Members of the budget staff play an important role in the success of budgets. They should attempt to win the trust and confidence of operating people by explaining and communicating their work in a clear and effective manner.

14. Educating about the role of budgets can help smooth relations and reduce irritation between budget staff and other members of an organization. Budget staff should be sensitive to human needs and aspirations.

SOURCES AND SUGGESTED REFERENCES

Atkinson, Anthony A., Banker, Rajiv D., Kaplan, Robert S., and Young, Mark S., *Management Accounting,* Upper Saddle River, NJ: Prentice-Hall, 2nd ed., 1997.

Berret, M. E., and Fraser, L.B., III, "Conflicting Roles in Budgeting for Operations," *Harvard Business Review,* July–August 1977, pp. 137–146.

Brownell, Peter, and McInnes, Morris, "Budgetary Participation, Motivation, and Managerial Performance," *The Accounting Review,* October 1986, pp. 587–600.

Burton, Alan, "Shareholder Value Budgeting," *Management Accounting* (London), June 1996, pp. 26–27.

Chalos, Peter, and Haka, Susan, "Participative Budgeting and Managerial Performance," *Decision Sciences,* Spring 1989, pp. 334–337.

Chandra, Gyan, and Singhvi, Surendra S., *Budgeting for Profit,* Oxford, OH: Planning Executives Institute, 1973.

Collins, Frank, "The Budgeting Games People Play," *The Accounting Review,* January 1987, pp. 29–49.

Cyert, Richard M., and March, James G., *A Behavioral Theory of the Firm,* Englewood Cliffs, NJ: Prentice-Hall, 1963.

Drtina, Ralph, Hoeger, Steve, and Schaub, John, "Continuous Budgeting at the HON Company," *Management Accounting,* January 1996, pp. 20–24.

Duston, Richard, "Off-the-Shelf Software Creates Custom Reports," *Management Accounting,* February 1996, pp. 48–54.

Ferguson, Dennis H., and Berger, Florence, "The Human Side of Budgeting," *Cornell Hotel & Restaurant Administration Quarterly,* August 1986, pp. 86–90.

Freeman, Eva, "Turn Your Budgeting Operation into a Profit Center," *Datamation,* January 1997, pp. 90–93.

Hirst, M. K., "The Effects of Setting Budget Goals and Task Uncertainty on Performance: A Theoretical Analysis," *The Accounting Review,* October 1987, pp. 774–784.

Horngren, Charles T., Foster, George, and Datar, Srikant M., *Cost Accounting: A Managerial Emphasis,* Upper Saddle River, NJ: Prentice Hall, 9th ed, 1997.

Johnson, H. Thomas, and Kaplan, Robert S., *Relevance Lost: The Rise and Fall of Management Accounting,* Boston, MA: Harvard Business School Press, 1987.

Kaplan, Robert S., "Knowing the Score," *Financial Executive,* November–December, 1996, pp. 30–33.

Madden, Donald L., *People Side of Planning,* Oxford, OH: Planning Executives Institute, 1980.

McGregor, Douglas, *Leadership and Motivation,* Cambridge, MA.: Massachusetts Institute of Technology Press, 1966.

Merchant, Kenneth A., and Manzoni, Jean-Francois, "The Achievability of Budget Targets in Profit Centers: A Field Study," *The Accounting Review,* July 1989, pp. 539–558.

Moseley, Owen B., "Sources of Human Relations Problems in Budgeting," Managerial Planning, July–August, 1979, pp. 36–38.

Munter, Paul, Collins, Frank, and Finn, Don, Game Play in Budgeting, Oxford, OH: Planning Executives Institute, 1983.

Rusth, Douglas B., "The Budgeting Process in a Multinational Firm," Multinational Business Review, Fall 1994, pp. 59–63.

Schiff, Michael, and Lewin, Arie Y., "Where Traditional Budgeting Fails," Financial Executive, May 1968, pp. 51–58.

Schmidt, Jeffrey A., "Is It Time to Replace Traditional Budgeting?," Journal of Accountancy, October 1992, pp. 103–107.

Shank, John K., and Govindarajan, Vijay, "Strategic Cost Management and the Value Chain," Journal of Cost Management, Winter 1992, pp. 5–21.

Sollenberger, Harold M., "The Five Phases of Budgeting; the Basic Budget Process Has Evolved into a Sophisticated Planning Tool," Credit Union Executive, Winter 1989, pp. 30–35.

Stewart, T. A., "Why Budgets Are Bad for Business," Fortune, June 4, 1990, pp. 179–190.

Welsch, G. A., Hilton, R. W., and Gordon, P. N., Budgeting: Profit Planning and Control, Englewood Cliffs, NJ: Prentice-Hall, 5th ed., 1988.

CHAPTER 33

BUDGETING IN THE HEALTH CARE INDUSTRY

Christopher S. Spence

Ernst & Young L.L.P.

CONTENTS

33.4 **BASICS OF HEALTH CARE BUDGETING**   1

(j) Position Review (New)   1

33.4 BASICS OF HEALTH CARE BUDGETING

Page 33•10, add at end of section:

(j) Position Review (New).   Typically, the largest component of a health care provider's expenses are employee expenses for salary and benefits. It is critical to control the growth and changes in staffing levels. In today's dynamic health care environment, patient volumes can change rapidly. Any changes in staffing levels related to new positions, open positions, or changes in scheduled hours should be reviewed for appropriateness by a position review committee. The position review committee typically includes members of senior management, budgeting, and human resources.

CHAPTER 34

BUDGETING IN THE BIOTECH INDUSTRY (New)

R. Malcolm Schwartz
Glenn A. White
Robert F. McElroy
Charles A. Clerecuzio

Coopers & Lybrand L.L.P.

CONTENTS

34.1 OVERVIEW OF INDUSTRY
SITUATION   1

34.2 KEY BUDGETING ISSUES   2

(a) Research and the "Capital Burn Rate" 3
(b) Sales and Marketing Support Levels   3
(c) Production Sourcing   3

34.3 CHALLENGES AT STAGES OF
THE COMPANY'S LIFECYCLE   4

(a) Financing and Start-up   4
(b) Research and Discovery   6
(c) Product Development   6
(d) Clinical Trials   8
(e) Product Approval   8
(f) Product Launch   8
(g) Manufacturing and Distribution   9

34.4 BUDGET FOCUS BY
FUNCTION AND AREA   9

(a) Research   10
(b) Operations   11
(c) Selling, General, and Administrative 11
(d) Facilities and Equipment   12
(e) Cash Budget   12
(f) Sales/Revenue Considerations   12

34.5 OTHER CONSIDERATIONS
AND TOOLS   12

(a) Lifecycle Accounting   12
(b) Technology Accounting   13
(c) Risk Analysis for Projects   14

34.6 SUMMARY   15

SOURCES AND
SUGGESTED REFERENCES   15

34.1 OVERVIEW OF INDUSTRY SITUATION. The biotech industry has grown to considerably more than 1,000 public or private companies over the last 20 years. The crowded industry competes for increasingly limited funding; most depend heavily on venture capital, having inadequate cash flows to generate significant interest among typical equity investors. In later stages of successful companies' evolution, equity

(IPOs) and debt may be options. Private investments in public entities (PIPEs) are now becoming common for later-stage funding. Nonetheless, $4.7 billion in public and private capital was raised in the 12 months ended June 1994. However, because investors are getting leery and the money flow is decreasing, good management practices—budgeting and planning among them—are very important, for both managing funds and attracting investors.

The industry has been hampered by uneven management, driven by greed to lure new investment and form companies that have little prospect of succeeding, and wracked by product failures. Even those relatively few companies with a more promising new product pipeline are faced with the difficulty of predicting the timing of Food and Drug Administration (FDA) approvals, which exacerbates the challenge of forecasting revenue and income streams. Following FDA approval, they still must face the challenges of physician acceptance and receptivity of the new products. Thus, following approval and introduction, the job of projecting sales volumes is still much more of an art than a science—which is very much counter to the mindset of the average research scientist, who likely has become the company leader.

Once the biotech company has dealt with the problem of projecting sales revenue, the next hurdle is projecting resource requirements and expenses for production operations and support functions. Other industries are somewhat more frequently blessed with some prior history of production capabilities, based on similar products, and thus have some basis for projecting manufacturing operating rates, yields, and costs. In biotech, each new product is likely to have substantially different production characteristics, making projection of operating rates and costs extremely challenging, to say the least.

Faced with these myriad unknowns and issues, these same biotech companies are faced with the need to develop credible forecasts for their operating plans. These plans are key to being able to prove and justify a need for investment from outside providers of capital.

This chapter discusses some of the key issues that should be addressed and included in the development of a budget for a biotech company. Specific consideration also is given to the different nuances that impact the biotechs based on where their products are in the lifecycle. Given the focus on the front, or development, end of the process, a brief discussion on the application of lifecycle accounting also is included.

34.2 KEY BUDGETING ISSUES. Given the backdrop of rather extreme uncertainty, biotech manufacturers are nonetheless faced with the same basic need to develop financial plans and budgets as are most of their counterparts in other industries. Forecasts of the expected revenue and expense streams not only support the important task of acquiring financing, but also provide a tool for measuring and managing the operational performance of the enterprise.

Key requirements in the development of the budget include the relatively obvious need to forecast sales (volumes, prices, and the resulting revenue streams); and the subsequent planning for the supporting resource and financial requirements to enable these sales, including capacity, labor, materials, and supplies. However, before reviewing the key elements of budgeting, it is useful to answer some important strategic and tactical questions addressing key operational considerations.

(a) Research and the "Capital Burn Rate". First and foremost, biotech companies depend on the development pipeline. Because the pipeline is key to their survival, they must plan for, manage, and maintain adequate resources to support their development efforts. Especially in the early stages of the lifecycle (discussed in further detail in section 34.3), it is critical that the plan be fully developed to support acquisition of adequate capital, and that this capital not be expended too quickly or ineffectively. That is, the early funding must frequently carry the biotech to a defined milestone before further funding can be obtained. This phenomenon is also frequently referred to as *controlling the capital burn rate.* Failure to manage the use and consumption of funds may result in the enterprise running out of financing and, worse yet, financing opportunities, before reaching the point of having a marketable product and the ability to generate its own funding through product sales.

(b) Sales and Marketing Support Levels. As the biotech enterprise initiates commercial operation, the development of a sales force will have to be addressed. To get the right message to the right market takes a more expansive effort than presentations at seminars and conferences by the president and other senior company officers and scientists. However, with a limited product line, an adequate level of both productivity and effectiveness cannot be expected (even) from a dedicated sales force. Therefore, consideration might be given to having products co-marketed by another manufacturer with an established sales force, already calling on the same market and therapeutic area (that is, disease segments such as hypertension, depression, or heart disease) as those for the new biotech's products.

Preceding formal introduction of the product, limited (within limitations imposed by the FDA) marketing and promotional efforts may be initiated, and consideration should be given to this area. Post-introduction, formal marketing and promotion will begin, and messages, literature, and other materials should be planned, created, and available at the point of product launch. Thus, early planning for the funding of these initiatives must be done to ensure that adequate resources are available to execute the plans.

To facilitate the promotional efforts surrounding products, market research should be performed to assess market potential for products, as well as possibly to test different concepts for messages and to develop a better understanding of what will be required to promote the product physically. Again, during budgeting it is important to consider and plan for all potential requirements, so as to allow for resource planning to meet downstream operational requirements.

(c) Production Sourcing. Long before the initiation of commercial production, the biotech company must decide how it plans to produce in order to meet the anticipated market demand. The first question is whether sales volumes are expected to warrant scale-up in any production facility, or if these needs can be met through production in the laboratory. Occasionally, demand for specialized products can be met through the laboratory or pilot facilities; if this route is used, it obviously can simplify the production question, as the operators already know how to produce the product. If larger production capabilities are projected, the next question to be addressed is whether production will be internal, or if contract manufacturers should be considered. The latter alternative, depending on the defined technology, may be quite viable, as there is a significant amount of underutilized capacity at a number of major pharmaceutical manufacturers today. Not only does this provide a relatively ready source of capacity, but these facilities are most likely FDA-approved for production, although specific approval for the new products still must be received.

Once the company decides it is going to manufacture its product internally, it must define and develop new capabilities to meet FDA compliance requirements, as well as the ability to meet cGMPs (current good manufacturing procedures). During the budgeting process, funding must be provided for the planned scale-up and production. If internal resources are not equipped to generate the definition of requirements and costs for this process, consideration should be given to hiring either an external consultant or a new employee to fill this role. In either case, a budget for the expenses associated with this role must be provided.

34.3   CHALLENGES AT STAGES OF THE COMPANY'S LIFECYCLE.   The budget focus of a typical biotech company evolves as the company transitions through its lifecycle. The journey from start-up to a fully integrated pharmaceutical company, expressed as a "lifecycle," is pictured in Exhibit 34.1.

Different functional areas, as described in section 34.4, will become the focus of budget considerations as the company evolves and grows. Managers must carefully direct funding to support the strategic needs of the organization for the current stage, and plan for the needs of future stages.

Each stage of the lifecycle carries intrinsic sources of uncertainty that give rise to risks that must be managed. There are costs associated with managing these sources of uncertainty, which must be considered when preparing annual budgets. The management of uncertainty involves deciding on an acceptable level of risk, managing the risks to reduce them to this acceptable level, determining the cost of managing the risks, and budgeting for the risk management in addition to any other contingencies.

(a)   Financing and Start-up.   The initial stages in the lifecycle of a biotechnology company are financing and start-up. Because financing involves raising initial funds that will be deployed through annual budgets beginning during the start-up stage, these stages can be examined together. For a company to move into the start-up stage, the quest for initial financing must have been successful. Today, this means securing a recurring stream of funding, or positioning the company strategically to generate early streams of revenue.

The focus of the company, and the budget, at this stage is to build the organizational foundation of the company and to attract research talent. Laying an organizational foundation does not mean building a large, cumbersome infrastructure or a bureaucratic overhead structure. To the contrary, the company needs to design its business processes so that they can function effectively with a minimal time commitment from the technical staff while limiting the support staff required. This often means early investments in technology, such as information technology, that can allow the company to leverage its human assets. These early foundational investments are more difficult to justify than science and research expenditures, from a budgetary point of view, but if made wisely they can significantly decrease a company's ongoing overhead costs.

Because base salaries at start-up biotechnology companies are often lower than at larger, more established pharmaceutical companies, compensation packages usually

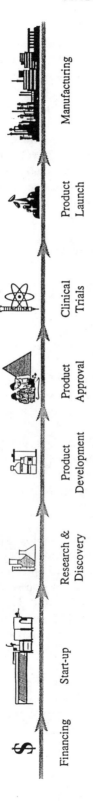

Exhibit 34.1 Biotech company lifecycle.

include equity or profit-sharing options. This style of compensation carries inherent risk and can be a hurdle in attracting top-notch talent; but can also be used to identify people with strong entrepreneurial spirits, which is a desirable quality for anyone involved in a start-up company.

(b)   Research and Discovery.   The focus of the research and discovery phase in the company lifecycle is to maintain a level, uninterrupted funding to allow the company to drive toward discovery of its first potential compound. The source of this funding, and the level of uncertainty it carries, can have a strong effect on annual budget preparation. Funding generated through predictable revenue from operations, such as contract research, carries a greater degree of uncertainty than cash in the bank. The greatest uncertainty during this stage comes simply from the serendipity inherent in the discovery process. This prevents accurate prediction of milestones and breakthroughs. The best way to manage this uncertainty is to design a targeted, focused research initiative. Often, research efforts veer off the main path and follow promising tangents. This causes an unnecessarily high capital burn rate and consumes precious resources. Companies should focus on a specific disease or family of therapies and direct resources in a very targeted manner. Companies developing an enabling technology should target a specific compound or class of compounds for initial prototyping of the technology. Once the technology has been proven, expansion to include other potential product classes can be considered.

The annual budget at this stage should be organized by research project (see Exhibit 34.2). All costs related to a specific project should then be tracked against the budget on a project-by-project basis. This enables both superior focus and budget control, and can provide warnings of projects that are beginning to drift from their targeted focus.

The discovery process can be accelerated through the use of advanced tools, such as combinatorial chemistry, computer-aided drug design, and new techniques and technology. This strategy requires accelerating some capital expenditures and/or technology license payments in order to reduce time-to-market and overall development costs.

(c)   Product Development.   The product development phase focuses on scale-up of the most promising compound(s), and development of a repeatable process for producing these candidate compounds. Standard operating procedures (SOPs) and other process and scale-up documentation are developed to facilitate technology transfer, as well as to provide an auditable trail of the development process. In the past, responsibility for cost of goods sold (COGS) fell upon the manufacturing group. Health care reform pressures, including requirements for early pharmacoeconomic justifications, have driven attention to COGS further back in the development process. Companies currently focus process development efforts on not only the technical efficiency of the process, but also the cost-effectiveness. The sources of uncertainty for this stage in the company's lifecycle are the challenges in developing an economical, reproducible process that can supply the market demand, and forecasting a good estimate of that market demand.

	Budget	*Actual*	*Variance*
Project Xi.			
Labor:			
Principal Investigator	(1) $100,000	(1) $100,000	0
Senior Scientist(s)	(2) 120,000	(2) 210,000	0
Scientist(s)	(3) 105,000	(2) 70,000	($35,000)
Laboratory Technician(s)	(3) 60,000	(4) 80,000	20,000
Assigned General Lab Labor	35,000	35,000	0
Subtotal Labor	**$420,000**	**$405,000**	**($15,000)**
Materials and Equipment:			
Special Materials	$150,000	$112,000	($38,000)
Special Equipment	250,000	325,000	75,000
Assigned General Materials	100,000	100,000	0
Assigned General Lab Supplies	50,000	65,000	15,000
Assigned General Lab Equipment	85,000	85,000	0
Subtotal Materials and Equipment	**$635,000**	**$687,000**	**$52,000**
Total Project Xi	**$1,055,000**	**$1,092,000**	**$37,000**
Total Projects:			
Labor:			
Principal Investigator	$320,000	$320,000	0
Senior Scientist(s)	384,000	400,000	$16,000
Scientist(s)	340,000	336,000	(4,000)
Laboratory Technician(s)	200,000	192,000	(8,000)
Assigned General Lab Labor	110,000	112,000	2,000
Subtotal Labor	**$1,354,000**	**$1,360,000**	**$6,000**
Materials and Equipment:			
Special Materials	$480,000	$510,000	$30,000
Special Equipment	800,000	790,000	(10,000)
Assigned General Materials	320,000	310,000	(10,000)
Assigned General Lab Supplies	160,000	155,000	(5,000)
Assigned General Lab Equipment	270,000	260,000	(10,000)
Subtotal Materials and Equipment	**$2,030,000**	**$2,025,000**	**($5,000)**
General R&D:			
Unassigned General Lab Labor	$40,000	$38,000	($2,000)
Unassigned General Materials	130,000	140,000	(10,000)
Unassigned General Lab Supplies	100,000	105,000	5,000
Unassigned General Lab Equipment	250,000	280,000	(30,000)
Unassigned R&D General & Admin	325,000	305,000	(20,000)
Subtotal General R&D:	**$845,000**	**$868,000**	**$23,000**
Total R&D	**$4,229,000**	**$4,253,000**	**$24,000**

Exhibit 34.2.   R&D project budget tracking.

Today, in addition to the scale-up hurdles in process development (which are typically more difficult to overcome in biotechnology processes than traditional pharmaceutical processes), the cost-effectiveness of the process and pharmacoeconomics of the product must also be considered. These risks can be managed by early investment in market research, and definition of the size and structure of the target market. This will provide the company with the upside potential of developing the lead candidate compound, as well as a basis for developing a cost-effective process and performing pharmacoeconomic studies. These activities also should receive early funding to avoid expensive scale-up development on processes that may later prove not to be economical.

(d) Clinical Trials. The focus of the clinical trials stage of the biotechnology company's lifecycle is to conduct the experimentation necessary to collect clinical data on the toxicology, potency, and efficacy of the product, to be used as a basis for FDA approval of the product.

The principal source of uncertainty during this stage is the success or failure of the clinical trials. As a product moves through the various clinical phases (I, II, and III), the cost commitment increases geometrically. The further into the clinical trial process a product fails, the greater the loss. The best way to manage this risk is to make a greater investment in earlier clinical phases, which will allow more thorough investigation and screening of compounds, and will increase the probability that only high-potential products proceed to the next phase of clinical development. This strategy will assist companies in minimizing phase III surprises. If pharmacoeconomic studies were not conducted during the process development stage, the budget for this stage should be constructed to allow for performance of these studies.

(e) Product Approval. The focus of the product approval stage of the lifecycle is preparation and filing of documents for FDA product approval, and for validation of the associated process, facility, and equipment. The assembly of documentation for filing and to support validation activities requires extensive labor resources. This can be mitigated to some degree, for the approval of drugs, through the use of information technology to perform a computer-aided new drug application (CANDA) filing. The labor resources saved, however, must be redeployed to some extent to support the planning and set-up of the various systems to support the CANDA.

The source of uncertainty for this stage of the lifecycle is FDA approval of the product filing and equipment, facility, and process validations. The best way to address this risk is to budget sufficient funds for well-planned and well-executed FDA filings and validations. The appropriate support resources should be contracted if they are not available in-house. This solution may be preferable to hiring the resources, especially for the first product filing. Although contracting will have a higher cost per hour than hiring, contract resources are easily released at the completion of the project; they can also be placed on hold if a delay is encountered, thus not generating any expense during such a holding period.

(f) Product Launch. The primary budgetary focus of the product launch stage of the lifecycle is to develop sales and marketing capability and to build sufficient inventory to support the product launch. For companies that choose not to build a sales and marketing function, these activities can be outsourced. In many cases, agreements may already be in place for products that are licensed out.

The chief sources of uncertainty for this lifecycle stage are the accuracy of market demand estimates and the ability to deliver product to satisfy that demand. The COGS of biotechnology products, as a percentage of sales, is much greater than for traditional pharmaceutical products. Comparing published fiscal year 1993 results for a group of leading manufacturers, cost of sales within pharmaceuticals is approximately 26%, compared to more than 38% for biotech. Coupled with the highly perishable nature of most biotechnology products, this makes building excessive prelaunch inventory an unwise strategy. A delicate balance must be reached. This concern, further exacerbated by conservative demand estimates, has resulted in early shortages for some new products. The best strategy is still to use relatively conservative estimates and to build a slight excess of prelaunch inventory to hedge the risk of demand being greater than expected. Market demand uncertainty may be somewhat mitigated by clearly defining and researching the target market. Allowances should be made in the budget at this stage for confirmation of the target market.

(g) Manufacturing and Distribution.   The final stage in the lifecycle is the manufacturing and distribution stage. The focus of the budget during this phase is on capital and labor expenditures to support the development and enhancement of ongoing manufacturing and distribution capabilities. This includes methodologies for forecasting demand (or, preferably, analyzing actual demand), planning capacity expansions, and managing the supply chain.

The major sources of uncertainty for this stage of the lifecycle are the accuracy of forecasts; competitive products entering or leaving the market, causing unplanned spikes in the demand pattern; and unexpected process problems that cause sudden shortages in supply. Managing these sources of uncertainty involves improving the accuracy of forecasts or gaining visibility of actual demand; continually collecting market intelligence regarding competitive products, to anticipate spikes in market share and demand; and utilizing advanced analytical techniques and data trending to predict and minimize process problems. Funds for these risk mitigation activities should be provided in the budget, at least as a contingency, to avoid having to "steal" money from other budgetary areas.

Exhibit 34.3 summarizes the focus of each stage of the biotech company lifecycle, the principal sources of uncertainty, risk management techniques, and budgetary considerations.

34.4 BUDGET FOCUS BY FUNCTION AND AREA.   Currently, most companies in the biotech industry have a functional organization structure, and have not transitioned to a more efficient process-based organization. As a result, budgets are still prepared along functional lines. Even if the company moves to a process orientation, it is still useful to consider requirements from the functional perspective. This presents key budget line items in each functional area for a vertically integrated biotech company. This is a "snapshot" budget of ongoing operations, as discussed in section 34.3. The budget for start-up companies can be very different. For companies with a lesser degree of vertical integration, such as contract research organizations, technology licensers, contract manufacturers, and co-marketers, line items and even entire functional areas may not appear.

Presented below is a summary, by the stage of the company's lifecycle of the primary budget focus, key sources of uncertainty; and how to approach and manage these risks.

Lifecycle Phase	Budget Focus	Sources of Uncertainty	Approach
Financing/ Start-up	Building organization & research capabilities	Aquisition of funding & of R&D talent	Solid business plan, attack empty niche market & obtain significant recurring funding
Research/ Discovery	Driving discovery & first potential compound	Serendipity of discovery	Target efforts (specific treatments/disease family) & use advanced tools (combinatorial chemistry)
Product Development	Defining process & scaling–up of key compound(s)	Scale–up hurdles, economic process development & market demand	Early funds for scale–up, good market research budget & early process economics
Clinical Trials	Conducting trials to show potency, toxicology, efficacy and bioavailabilty	Toxicology & therapeutic action results & pharmacoeconomics (emerging)	Allocate greater funds for more comprehensive Phase I & II trials to avoid Phase III surprises
Product Approval	Filing with FDA for product and facility approval	Regulatory agencies (FDA)	Significant funding to allow complete & well planned/executed NDA filing and facility validation
Product Launch	Building inventory and sales and marketing capabilities	Market size, market share, product demand & delivery lead time	Understand market demand and build sufficient inventory to fully launch product
Manufacturing & Distribution	Using capital & labor to build production and distribution capabilities and cGMP compliance	Competitive products forecasts and demand	Invest early to reduce COGS to strengthen position & concentrate on adding value added customer service

Exhibit 34.3.   Summary of the budgeting process by lifecycle phase.

(a)   Research.   Three major cost categories in the research function must be addressed in the budget: labor, materials and supplies, and fixed costs associated with equipment and facilities.

The first and most important cost category is labor. This includes not only scientists and technical personnel, but also R&D support staff, such as glassware washers and reagent preparation staff. This often represents the most significant cost category at biotech companies. When budgets are being planned, consideration must be given to anticipated new hires who might be added throughout the year. These new hires may be included in plans to increase staffing due to requirements at different phases of the development cycle. Associated expenses for benefits and employer costs, such as workers' compensation and health insurance, also must be included, as these vary either as a fixed rate per employee or as a percentage of the employees' salaries or wages.

The materials and supplies cost category includes items that will be consumed during or in support of performance of research and development activities. This includes chemical reagents, disposable items (latex gloves, pipettes, and the like), and consumable parts (such as filter cartridges and fractional chromatography tubing).

The third category addresses costs related to expenditures for equipment. Each year new equipment must be purchased to replace used, obsolete, and retired equipment, as well as for expansion of R&D operations. Although anticipated capital expenditures must be included in the capital budget, the operating budget must address the costs related to the operation and depreciation or amortization of these pieces of equipment. Annual maintenance contracts, emergency maintenance, and spare parts are also included in this cost category.

These cost categories, and especially the labor and materials/supplies groups, can be further partitioned by project. Some companies like to capture these costs by project to facilitate their recovery when the company begins to generate revenue, utilizing the lifecycle accounting techniques discussed in section 34.5(a).

(b) Operations.   Operational costs are incurred for the production of salable, or trade, materials. Some of the items will be the same as those in the research area, but their accounting treatment will be different. Budget line items for the operations area are typically divided into two broad cost categories: direct costs and indirect costs. Direct costs include all materials consumed in the manufacture of products, including materials and labor. A production unit of finished goods is exploded by means of a bill of materials (BOM), which links from finished goods to work in progress (WIP) and further back to raw materials (in units or quantities) and labor (manhours per unit related to the quantity produced); standard costs are then applied.

Indirect costs include all costs that support the manufacturing operations but are not directly consumed in the production process. These costs must be allocated to, absorbed into, or in some other way linked to finished goods produced, to be represented in the COGS or treated as fixed manufacturing overhead and expensed in that way. These indirect costs include such support activities as maintenance, purchasing services, supervision, and materials management. The operations functional area of the budget is unique, in that it is common to see this section of the budget, as well as product projections, calculated in terms of units, quantities, and manhours, which are then converted to dollars.

(c) Selling, General, and Administrative.   The sales, general, and administrative section of the budget represents an "all other expenses" category for biotechnology companies. This is different from many other industries because many biotechnology companies often do not develop sales and marketing capabilities. Thus, this category tends to be predominantly administrative overhead expenses. The items that typically are included in the general and administrative segment are executive management compensation, accounting and allied business functions, general clerical help, and general support functions such as information technology.

The sales component of this category includes direct and indirect expenses incurred in performing sales and marketing activities. Budget line items included in this cost category are compensation for sales and marketing staff, expense account allocations, product/service promotions, and market research. Compensation for sales and marketing personnel might include complex incentive and bonus packages in addition to base salaries, which introduces a degree of uncertainty into an otherwise straightforward cost category. Even expense account costs are more straightforward because they can be budgeted, on a headcount basis, as the responsibility of the individual salesperson. For most biotechnology products, promotion expenses can be predicted with a relatively high degree of certainty; in today's changing health care environment, promotion budgets must address service, as well as product, promotions. Market research is also part of the sales and marketing cost category; this includes outsourced services in addition to internal staff compensation and research expenses. Clerical and support staff expenses linked to sales and marketing activities are often broken out as a line item in the sales and marketing cost category, in lieu of being included in the general and administrative cost category.

(d)   Facilities and Equipment.   Facilities and equipment can be built, leased, or purchased; equipment can likewise be leased or purchased. Each of these options will result in different scenarios for budgetary requirements, specifically related to the magnitude and timing of investment and expense cash flows.

(e)   Cash Budget.   More so than at larger, more established pharmaceutical companies, biotechnology companies must maintain a delicate balancing act. The company must invest available capital to provide as high a return as possible, to continually extend the life of its capital burn rate, while at the same time keeping enough cash available to satisfy payables in a timely manner (to maintain a good credit rating). This usually involves timed deposits into cash accounts and careful timing of investments. Because these functions are performed by the financial group, that group is in the best position to budget the outward cash flows for the year.

(f)   Sales/Revenue Considerations.   As the biotech company plans for commercial introduction of its products, the demands of the new health care market and the managed care environment in general cause product sales frequently to be tied to the formulary of managed-care providers. Therefore, contracts between manufacturers and these managed-care providers frequently must be initiated to provide the access for sales. These contracts also specify the provision of discount rebates tied to the sales of products. This represents another key item to be planned; simple input of projected sales volumes and prices would overstate actual revenues, as it would fail to recognize these discounts and rebates. A truer assessment of net sales must be achieved by including these items.

34.5   OTHER CONSIDERATIONS AND TOOLS.

(a)   Lifecycle Accounting.   Lifecycle accounting is the accumulation of costs for activities that occur over the entire lifecycle of a product, from inception to abandonment by the manufacturer and consumer. Given that a number of products introduced in the biotech industry may be experimental or have a long developmental stage, companies adopting the lifecycle accounting approach will benefit, because this treatment considers the full costs from cradle to grave. In addition, because most of the cost of a new product is incurred after the design stage, lifecycle costing accounts for 100% of these costs, including the production, maintenance, and any associated regulatory or environmental expenses. Lifecycle costing also may indicate that a competitive product with high initial costs is a better alternative than one with low acquisition costs but higher operating, maintenance, or regulatory costs. However, it should be noted that all costs throughout a product's lifecycle must be considered in order to make a valid comparison of competing products or processes.

Another benefit of lifecycle costing is that it promotes a better matching of revenues and expenses. This is achieved by expensing certain activities based on the total planned number of units to be sold. A distinction, however, is that for management accounting purposes, all costs identified as benefiting the future and directly associated with management's plan are capitalized as incurred. This treatment of capitalizing-as-incurred requires that the expenditures be tied to a future product or program. The accountant or finance person should consider these types of costs (namely, preproduction costs such as R&D, planning, and start-up expenses) when preparing the company's annual budget or strategic plans for a biotech concern. The concepts of lifecycle costing are illustrated in Exhibit 34.4. The traditional GAAP model, shown as the "$ Spent" curve, dictates that project costs be expensed as incurred. The lifecycle model, however, represented by the "$ Committed" curve, capitalizes items as incurred, for those costs benefiting the future, which can be identified as part of a capital program linked to a future product or management objective.

A product cost study showed that over 90% was committed prior to Operations.

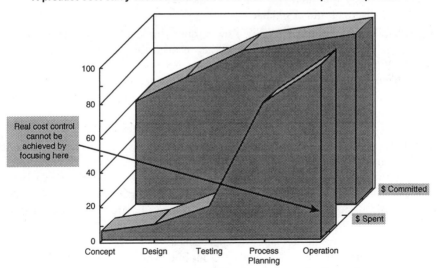

Life-cycle costing uses all costs from concept through discontinuance

Exhibit 34.4.   The concepts of lifecycle costing.

(b)   Technology Accounting.   Technology accounting embodies the management accounting concept that technology costs, which include plant, equipment, and information systems, should be treated as direct costs, similar to direct labor and material.

Many companies capitalize technology costs and amortize or depreciate them over the estimated useful life of the proposed technology; this method, which links cost to a fixed time period, tends to distort indirect overhead costs (which include amortization of the technology investment), because the fixed period often differs from the product lifecycle. An example of this is idle machinery that continues to amortize even though there is little or no production associated with that machinery.

The alternative approach is to amortize the technology costs over planned production runs, thereby matching costs more directly with products manufactured. This is accomplished by calculating a per-unit amortization amount, with the aggregate units identified as those involved in planned production or projected product demand. Those selecting this option should also consider the obsolescence of the asset's technology for the manufacturing process. This methodology also may lead to a different approach to GAAP, as direct production-based amortization replaces a time-based indirect allocation of costs. The financial executive or controller of a biotech firm should consider this alternative approach, because it more accurately spreads technology costs over the product lifecycles that the technology supports.

(c) Risk Analysis for Projects. The term *risk* as it relates to a biotech company's capital budgeting decision refers to the uncertainty involved in the potential outcomes of investment decisions and is also known as *strategic risk.* The possibility exists that these outcomes may result in real financial losses, requiring firms to analyze the risk using a variety of methods. These methods can be classified into two major categories, namely:

- Simple risk-adjustment (SRA) methods that rely on achieving a company's desired discount rate or payback period
- Probabilistic risk analysis (PRA) techniques that evaluate the uncertainties of critical variables and their probabilities, prior to any decisions made on risk-return/trade-off. Examples of these include sensitivity analysis, basic probability analysis, Monte Carlo simulation, decision-tree analysis, and capital asset pricing routines. These techniques are used by more sophisticated pharmaceutical companies.

PRA techniques require more rigorous analysis; however, they provide more quantitative information about the risk implied in the prospective project. It is the view of some practitioners that this additional quantitative data allows for greater insight into the nature of the risk and, ultimately, increases shareholder value (see chapter 11A for further discussions on the subject). Recent surveys conducted on capital budgeting issues indicate that companies have generally transitioned from theoretical discussion to practical use of risk analysis approaches.

The recent proliferation of financial modeling software has made it easier for companies to use more sophisticated risk analysis techniques in their evaluation of strategic investments. This is a positive trend, but this increased complexity has, in some cases, unfortunately led to less acceptance of capital projects, thereby reducing the number of investment opportunities presented, which ultimately impacts capital expenditure levels.

Biotech concerns must begin to develop a portfolio of risk analysis tools, and to use the simple with the sophisticated, in order to enable a more informed decision-making process on capital and strategic investments.

34.6   SUMMARY.   With all the complexities and challenges facing biotech companies, operational and financial budgeting may seem a trivial task. Yet, the ability to control one's destiny may lie in effective projection, measurement, and management of internal operations and expenses. As biotechs evolve and mature both in size and commercial focus, increased levels of financial sophistication will be required, both in internal resources and in tools applied. This chapter has presented points of concern and consideration for biotechs (and indeed for other start-up enterprises) so that they may begin with the right questions, and so as to include adequate funding plans for the breadth of resources required to effectively operate their companies.

SOURCES AND SUGGESTED REFERENCES

"Biotech Industry Alive, Proving Naysayers Wrong," *Chemical Marketing Reporter,* Sept. 26, 1994, at 19.

Berliner, Callie, and James A. Brimson, *Cost Management for Today's Advanced Manufacturing.* Boston, Mass.: Harvard Business School Press, 1988.

Brimson, James A., "Technology Accounting, " *Management Accounting,* Mar. 1989, at 47.

Goldberg, Robert M., "Health Care Reform and the Future of Biomedical Progress," *Journal of American Society of CLU & ChFC,* Sept. 1994, at 48–54.

Hamilton, Joan O.C., "Biotech: An Industry Crowded With Players Faces an Ugly Reckoning," *Business Week,* Sept. 26, 1994, at 84–92.

Hamilton, Joan O.C., "Warning: Don't Invest If You Have Heart Problems," *Business Week,* Sept. 26, 1994, at 88.

Ojala, Marydee, "Business Searching for Biotechnology," *Database,* Aug. 1994, at 74–76.

Pike, Richard H., "Do Sophisticated Capital Budgeting Approaches Improve Investment Decision Making Effectiveness?," *Engineering Economist,* Winter 1989.

Rotman, David, "Biotech Sales Flourish, But Cash Remains Scarce," *Chemical Week,* Sept. 28, 1994, at 13.

Simon, S.M. Ho, and Richard Pike, "Risk Analysis in Capital Budgeting Context: Simple or Sophisticated," *Accounting and Business Research,* Summer 1991, at 227–37.

Thayer, Ann, "Biotech Industry Readies for Reform and Renewal," *Chemical & Engineering News,* Oct. 3, 1994, at 17.

CUMULATIVE INDEX

Note: A page number with an "s" designation refers to a supplement page.

ABB. See Activity-based budgeting
ABC Budgeting (higher education budgets), 32.8
Absorption costing, 9.17–9.20, 9.21–9.22
Accounting. See also Cost accounting systems (manufacturing budget)
 nonprofit organizations, 31.11–31.13
  cash vs. accrual basis, 31.12
  depreciation, omission of, 31.13
  expenses vs. expenditures, 31.12–31.13
  fund accounting, 31.11
  responsibility structures, 31.22–31.23
  program budgeting and system of, 27.34
  responsibility accounting, 29.16, 29.18s
Accounting rate of return (ARR), 20.10–20.12
Accounting (FASB) risk, 23A.7s
Accounting services, 18A.10s
Account reconcilement services, 21.24
Accounts payable, responsibility for management of, 22.5
Accounts receivable
 balance sheet budget, 22.13–22.16
 responsibility for, 22.4
Accrual basis of accounting (nonprofit organizations), 31.12
Accrued liabilities, 22.35
Acid test. See Quick ratio
Acquisitions, 18A.22s
Activity-based budgeting (ABB), 18.8s, 27A.1s–27A.22s
 activity definitions, 27A.7s
 activity implementation, 27A.13s
 activity targets, 27A.13s–27A.14s
 bill of activities, 27A.13s–27A.15s
 budget options, 27A.20s
 budget report, 27A.21s–27A.22s
 calendar, 27A.15s
 customer requirements, 27A.4s
 definition, 27A.5s
 finalizing budget, 27A.19s–27A.20s
 implementation, 27A.20s
 interdepartmental projects, 27A.16s–27A.19s, 27A.20s
 links to strategy, 27A.8s–27A.13s
 performance reporting, 27A.20s–27A.22s
 planning guidelines, 27A.16s
 principles, 27A.6s
 process improvement by, 27A.4s–27A.7s
 process of, 27A.8s
 process reporting, 27A.22s
 ranking budget requests, 27A.19s
 sample, 27A.16s–27A.19s
 techniques and tools for, 27A.9s–27A.13s, 27A.14s, 27A.17s–27A.19s
Activity-based costing, 15.6s, 15.14s, 18.14s, 18B.6s, 18B.12s, 29.20s
 for payroll function, 18A.5s, 18A.27s–18A.28s, 18A.30s, 18A.31s

Activity-based investment analysis, 27A.8s
Activity-based management. See Activity-based costing
Activity (project planning), 14.5
Actual costing (manufacturing budget), 9.29–9.34
 deficiencies of, 9.34
 issues of material to production, 9.31–9.32
 labor operations performed, 9.32
 overhead, application of manufacturing, 9.32
 production completion and transfer to finished goods, 9.32
 purchase of materials, 9.29–9.31
 shipment of finished goods, 9.32
Actual cost of work performed (ACWP), 17.33
Actual costs, 9.29
Actual labor, 9.32
Actuarial services (for property and liability risk management program), 24.5
ACWP. See Actual cost of work performed
Adams, Gerard, 3.18
A delta t mapping, 18A.37s, 18A.39s
Administration, 15.2s
Administration of budget. See Organization and administration of budget
Administrative expense budget, 18.1, 18.9–18.10, 18.2s–18.14s, See also Distribution cost budget
 allocating expenses, 18.2s–18.3s
 strategic business units, 18.2s
 effectiveness-oriented costs, 18.12s
 efficiency-oriented costs, 18.12s
 factors impacting budget
  industry characteristics, 18.11s
  maturity of industry, 18.11s
  maturity of organization, 18.11s
  operating philosophy, 18.11s
  organizational structure, 18.11s
 levels of costs, 18.6s
 managing the budget, 18.13s–18.14s
  activity-based costing, 18.14s
  administrative charge-back to operating units, 18.13s
  benchmarking, 18.14s
  budget variance analysis, 18.13s
  hybrid transfer costing, 18.13s
  outsourcing alternatives, 18.14s
  performance measure, 18.14s
 preparation of budget, methods, 18.7s–18.10s
  activity-based budgeting, 18.8s
  comparison among methods, 18.9s
  expense/revenue basis, 18.8s
  factor costs, projecting, 18.10s
  gaining agreement, 18.10s
  historical-basis budgeting, 18.8s
  level of activity, projecting, 18.8s–18.9s
  relating resources to activities, 18.9s
  top-down versus bottom-up approaches, 18.8s, 18.10s

Administrative expense budget *(Continued)*
  zero base budgeting, 18.8s
  role of, 18.2s–18.7s
  scope of, 18.2s–18.7s
  types of expenses, 18.6s–18.7s
    capital asset costs, 18.6s
    depreciation, 18.6s
    expense, 18.6s
    leasehold amortization, 18.6s
    typical budget, 18.7s
    unique issues, 18.11s–18.13s
    value, identification of, 18.3s
      efficiency, 18.3s–18.6s, 18.12s
      effectiveness, 18.3s–18.6s, 18.12s
      functions included, identifying, 18.4s–18.6s
Admitted carriers, 24.16–24.17
Advertising
  distribution cost budget, 18.7–18.8
  expense, 15.9s
  sales and marketing budget, 15.3s
Aerospace industry, 3.26–3.27
Affidavits, 18A.33s
Agency insurance carriers, 24.3
AICPA. *See* American Institute of Certified Public
  Accountants
Airline industry, pressures and constraints for growth of,
  3.27
Allocated costs, 4.9
Alternate approaches (strategic planning cycle), 2.6,
  2.20–2.22
**American Institute of Certified Public Accountants
  (AICPA),** 6.1, 6.4
Annual profit plans, 4.1–4.11
  bracket budgeting 26.3, 26.21–26.22
  budgeting and, 4.8–4.11
    allocated costs, 4.9
    capital budgets, 4.9–4.11
    formats 4.9, 4.10
  cash budget and, 21.9
  development of, 4.2–4.7
    environmental outlook, 4.4–4.5
    forecasting vs. planning, 4.3
    goals and objectives, 4.5–4.6
    operating plan, 4.7
Annual profit plans *(Continued)*
  overview, 4.2–4.3
  situation analysis, 4.3–4.4
  strategic plan and, 4.2
  strategies and programs, 4.6–4.7
  forecasting and, 3.23
  international operations, 23.11–23.12, 23.13, 23.14
Annual program budgeting cycle, 27.19
Annuity, 20.5
Approval of budget by senior management, 12.7–12.8
Argyris, Chris, 29.10, 29.11s
ARR. *See* Accounting rate of return
Artificial intelligence, 28.4–28.5
Aspiration levels, 29.15, 29.17s
Assessment (program budgeting), 27.34–27.35
Assessments worksheet (strategic direction paper),
  23.5–23.6, 23.7
Asset based financing, 21.16
Asset ratio, 22.44

Assets
  financial, responsibility for, 22.4
  fixed assets
    balance sheet budget, 22.22, 22.24–22.27
    responsibility for, 22.5
  return on, 20.10, 22.7
Association for Manufacturing Excellence, 16.2, 16.8
Assumptions, budgeting, 7.9–7.10
Audit
  TQM implementation and, 26A.11s–26A.12s
Audit control (cash flow budget), 21.21–21.22. *See also*
  Internal control
Authoritative budgets, 29.3s
Authority, traditional flow of, 29.5, 29.6s
Automobile industry, 16.10, 27.7
Average collection period, 22.13–22.14, 22.16

Backwards phase (critical path method), 14.9–14.10
Bad debt
  hospital budgets, 33.23
  physician budgets, 33.38
Balance sheet budget, 22.1–22.52
  cash budget vs., 22.7
  cash shortfalls, 22.40
  changes in balance sheet, analysis of, 22.47–22.52
  definition, 22.2
  financial ratios, use of, 22.40–22.47
    leverage, 22.43–22.44
    liquidity, 22.42–22.43
    profitability, 22.44–22.47
  preparation of, 22.11–22.38
    accounts receivable balances, 22.13–22.16
    accrued liabilities, 22.35
    balancing cash figure (example), 22.38, 22.40
    cash and short-term investments, 22.11–22.12
    equity accounts, 22.35, 22.37–22.38
    fixed assets, 22.22, 22.24–22.27
    income tax payable, 22.33, 22.35–22.36
    inventories, 22.16–22.22
    notes payable, 22.27–22.28, 22.30
    other than current and fixed assets, 22.27
    prepaid expenses, 22.22
    trade payables, 22.30–22.31, 22.33
  profit budget vs., 22.7
  purpose of, 22.2
  responsibility for, 22.2, 22.3, 22.4–22.7
    accounts payable, 22.5
    accounts receivable, 22.4
    capital structure management, 22.6–22.7
    corporate taxes, 22.5–22.6
    financial assets, 22.4
    fixed assets, 22.5
    inventory levels, 22.4–22.5
    liabilities, 22.5
    notes payable, 22.5
Banking, sales and marketing budget, 15.15s–15.16s
Banks, leases and, 20A.8s
Bank wire transfer system, 21.21
Bayesian decision theory, 27.28
Behavioral aspects of budgeting, 29.1–29.19,
  29.5s–29.21s
  imposed budgets, 29.3, 29.3s
  modern view of human behavior and, 29.6–29.7,
    29.7s–29.8s

Behavioral aspects of budgeting *(Continued)*
motivation, 29.7–29.11, 29.8s–29.13s
expectancy theory, 29.8–29.9, 29.9s–29.10s
needs hierarchy, 29.7–29.8, 29.8s–29.9s
pressure devices, budgets as, 29.10, 29.11s–29.12s
role conflict and, 29.11, 29.12s–29.13s
X, Y, and Z theories, 29.9, 29.10s–29.11s
negotiated budgets, 29.4, 29.4s–29.5s
objectives of budgeting and, 29.2–29.3, 29.2s–29.3s
participative budgets, 29.3–29.4, 29.12–29.18, 29.4s, 29.13s–29.20s
aspiration levels, 29.15, 29.17s
budget staff, 29.17–29.18, 29.19s–29.20s
group dynamics, 29.14, 29.15s–29.16s
leadership, 29.14–29.15, 29.16s–29.17s
nature of participation, 29.12, 29.13s–29.15s
organization culture, 29.14, 29.16s–29.17s
performance reports and rewards, 29.16–29.17, 29.18s–29.19s
significance of participation, 29.12–29.14, 29.13s–29.15s
slack, 29.15–29.16, 29.17s–29.18s
standards, 29.15, 29.17s
stages in budgeting, 29.3, 29.3s
traditional view of human behavior and, 29.4–29.6, 29.5s–29.6s
Behavioral lessons, 29.21s
Belief graphs, 28A.3s
Bell Laboratories, 27.7
Benchmarking, 18A.35s, 18A.37s, 18A.38s, 18.14s, 18B.6s, 18B.12s
customer expectations, 26A.10s–26A.11s
payroll costs, 18A.3s, 18A.31s
and TQM, 26A.6s, 26A.14s–26A.15s
Benchmarks
activity-based budgeting and, 27A.11s
sales and marketing budget, 15.4s, 15.9s
Benefit/cost ratio. *See* Profitability index
Benefits administration
interaction with payroll, 18A.10s
Best practices, 18B.6s
Best-case budget, 13.14
Bidding on contracts, 23A.5s
Biotechnology industry, 34.1s–34.15s
budgeting by functional area, 34.9s–34.12s
budget issues, 34.2s–34.4s, 34.14s
facilities and equipment, 34.11s
financing and start-up, 34.5s
general overhead, 34.11s
investment in, 34.1s–34.2s
lifecycle, 34.4s, 34.9s
manufacturing and distribution, 34.8s
organization of company, 34.9s
product development, 34.7s
product launch, 34.8s
production sourcing, 34.3s
sales and marketing, 34.3s, 34.8s, 34.11s
sales revenue, 34.11s
Bonuses, 13.10–13.11. *See also* Compensation (executive)
B-O-P approach, 5.12
Boston Consulting Group matrix, 2.10, 2.11
Bottom-up approach (budget reviews), 7.4–7.5

Boulding, Kenneth, 3.25
Bracket budgeting, 26.1–26.23
in annual planning 26.21–26.22
applicability of, 26.2–26.3
benefits of, 26.22–26.23
budgetary control and, 26.3–26.4
consolidation of income statements with, 26.22
profit plan and, 26.3
sales and marketing budget, 15.12s
tactical budgeting model, 26.4–26.21
assessment of critical elements, 26.10–26.13
computer, application of, 26.13–26.16
flexibility in planning 26.16–26.18
identification of critical elements, 26.5–26.10
tracking and feedback, 26.18–26.21
Brainstorming, 27A.17s
Breakeven analysis, 8.4, 10.1–10.5
breakeven chart, 10.3–10.5
fixed costs, 10.2–10.3
manufacturing budget, 9.12–9.20
sales and marketing budget, 15.11s
variable costs, 10.3
Brimson, James A., 16.8
Brokerage insurance carriers, 24.3
Brokers, leases and, 20A.8s
Budget analyst, 5.2, 5.3–5.4
Budgetary control. *See* Internal control
Budget calendar, 7.9, 14.1s, 14.3s–14.4s
Budget centers, 26.2–26.5, 26.22. *See also* Expense centers; Profit centers
Budgeted cost of work scheduled, 17.33
Budget, factors impacting, 18.11s
industry characteristics, 18.11s
maturity of industry, 18.11s
maturity of organization, 18.11s
operating philosophy, 18.11s
organizational structure, 18.11s
"Budget game," 1.8
Budgeting
biotechnology industries, 34.2s–34.14s
calendar, 18A.49s–18A.50s
research projects, 34.5s–34.6s
tasks, 18A.49s–18A.50s
for TQM, 26A.1s, 26A.2s, 26A.19s–26A.21s
Budgeting approaches
payroll functions, 18A.27s–18A.31s, 18A.32s–18A.33s
Budget manager, responsibilities of, 12.1–12.8
Budget manual, 7.1–7.10
CEO's policy statement and, 7.2–7.3
changing budgets, procedures for, 7.6, 7.9
collection and consolidation of budget Information, 7.9–7.10
sample forms, 7.6, 7.7–7.8
corporate goals, defining of, 7.3
distribution of budget information, 7.10
responsibility for budget preparation, 7.3–7.4
review procedures, 7.4–7.5
use of budgeting information, 7.5–7.6
Budget objectives, 29.2s–29.3s
Budget plan template, 14.6s
Budget, preparation of 18.7s-18.10s
activity-based budgeting, 18.8s
comparison among methods, 18.9s

Budget plan template, *(Continued)*
  expense/revenue basis, 18.8s
  factor costs, projecting, 18.10s
  gaining agreement, 18.10s
  historical-basis budgeting, 18.8s
  level of activity, projecting, 18.8s-18.9s
  relating resources to activities, 18.9s
  top-down versus bottom-up approaches, 18.8s, 18.10s
  zero base budgeting, 18.8s
Budget report, 14.6s
Budget review panels, 27A.20s
Budget reviews. *See* Reviews, budget
Budgets, purpose of, 27A.2s, 27A.3s
Budget tracking, 17.2s, 17.35-17.36, 17.37
Budget variance analysis, 18.13s
Burden rate (research and development budget),
  17.29-17.32
Business cases, 11A.15s
Business direction/concept (strategic planning cycle), 2.6
Business gridding, 2.9, 2.11, 2.18-2.20, 2.21
Business organization, sales and marketing budget, 15.5s
Business plans, 11A.15s
  sales and marketing budget, 15.2s
Business segments (situation analysis), 2.7, 2.9
Business strategy. *See* Strategic management
By-product costs, 8.12

Cache programs, 28.6
Calendar, budget, 7.9
Capacity, 16.22-16.26. *See also* Productivity
  capital tools and, 16.33
  in continuous processes, 16.33-16.34
  cost changes and increase in, 16.31-16.33
  level of, 9.47
Capital, 11A.5s, 11A.13s
  company-wide profit goals and, 11.6-11.7
  cost of, 11.1-11.13
  divisional profit goals and, 11.7-11.13
  equity, 11.4-11.6
  EVA, 11A.9s
  executive compensation based on, 13.4, 13.8-13.9
  invested, 11A.9s
  investment, 15.2s
  market and, 11.3
  profitability and, 11.2-11.3
  programs, 11A.15s
  return on invested, 11A.7s, 11A.8s
  turnover, 11A.11s
  weighted average cost of capital and, 11.6-11.7
Capital asset costs, 18.6s
Capital asset pricing model (CAPM), 11.13
Capital burn rate, 34.3s
Capital intensive companies, 30.8, 30.10
Capital investment budgeting, 19.1-19.21
  in annual profit plan, 4.9-4.11
  comprehensive strategy and, 19.12
  computer, application of, 28.13, 28.14
  evaluation of projects. *See* Capital projects, evaluation of
  expenditures control, 19.18-19.21
  international operations, 23.4, 23.13-23.14
  nonprofit organizations, 31.31-31.32
  normal capital investments, 19.3
  operating budgets vs., 3.7-3.8
  postcompletion audit, 19.13-19.16

  empirical data, 19.14-19.16
  guidelines, 19.13-19.14
  reasons for capital investments, 19.2
  request preparation, 19.16-19.18
    capital request budgets, 5.11
    guidelines, 19.17-19.18
  search for new projects, 19.4
  special capital investments, 19.3-19.4
Capital investment committee, 22.5
Capital investment (definition), 19.2
Capital projects, evaluation of, 20.1-20.23
  accounting rate of return and, 20.10-20.12
  discounted cash flow rate of return and, 20.5-20.8
  input data for, 19.4-19.11
    cash flows with and without proposed project, 19.11
    cash inflows, 19.7-19.8
    cash outflows, 19.4-19.7
    economic life projection, 19.10-19.11
    inflation, 19.11
    sunk cost, 19.11
    tax implications of cash flows, 19.10
    transferred assets, 19.11
  lease-versus-buy analysis techniques, 20.20-20.22
    discounted cash flow, 20.21-20.22
    net present value, 20.22
  MAPI technique, 20.13
  net present value and, 20.8-20.10
  payback period, 20.12-20.13
  risk analysis technique, 20.14-20.16, 20.17, 20.18
  sensitivity analysis technique, 20.16, 20.18-20.19
  time value of money, 20.2-20.5
    compounding, 20.2-20.4
    discounting, 20.4
    present value, 20.4-20.5
  use of techniques in practice, 20.13
Capital request budgets, 5.11
Capital structure management, 22.6-22.7
Capital tools, productivity and, 16.33
CAPM. *See* Capital asset pricing model
Captive leasing, 20A.8s
Carter administration, zero base budgeting during,
  27.1s-27.2s
Cash, 15.3s
Cash basis of accounting (nonprofit organizations),
  31.12
Cash budgeting, 21.1-21.24, 34.11s. *See also* Cash flow
  annual budget and, 21.9
  balance sheet budget and, 22.7, 22.11-22.12
  environmental factors, 21.2-21.4
    industry trends, 21.3
    inflation rates, 21.3
    interest expense, 21.4
    operating expenses and, 21.4
    operating margins and, 21.3
  financial manager, role of, 21.5-21.9
    generation of investment income, 21.5
    measurement of results, 21.6-21.9
    planning and control, 21.6
  financing, types of, 21.15-21.17
    long term, 21.17
    short term, 21.15-21.17
  importance of, 21.4
  nonprofit organizations, 31.31
  objectives, 21.4

Cash budgeting, *(Continued)*
techniques for cash management, 21.18–21.24
audit control, 21.21–21.22
collection services, 21.18–21.19
concentration systems design, 21.19–21.21
disbursement techniques, 21.21
management information services, 21.22–21.24
time frame for, 21.9
Cash flow, 11A.2s, 11A.12s, 22.24
approaches to measurement, 11A.2s–11A.3s
budgeting, 11A.7s, 11A.14s
capital investments, 19.4–19.11
inflation, effect of, 19.11
inflows, 19.7–19.8
outflows, 19.4–19.7
tax implications, 19.10
with and without proposed project, cash flows, 19.11
discounted, in lease-versus-buy analysis, 20.21–20.22
discounted cash flow rate of return, 20.9, 20.12–20.14,
20.16, 20.18–20.19
discounting, 11A.4s–11A.5s
free, 11A.4s
leasing, 20A.12s
statements of, 21.9–21.15, 22.48
advantages, 21.10
disadvantages, 21.10
FASB 95 format for, 21.10–21.14
objectives, 21.9–21.10
Cash management information services, 21.22–21.24
Cash ratio, 22.42–22.43
Cash shortfalls, 22.40
Casualty insurance coverages, 24.10–24.11,
24.15–24.17
CD-ROM, 18A.46s
Center for Advanced Purchasing Studies, 18B.12s
CEO. *See* Chief executive officer
Certified Payroll Professional (CPP) program, 18A.32s
CFO. *See* Chief financial officer
Chandler, Alfred, 30.3
Chandra, Harish, 11A.16s
Change analysis (program budgeting), 27.18–27.19
Changing budgets, 7.6, 7.9
Check printing, 18A.48s
Chief executive officer (CEO), 2.2, 12.2, 17.5, 25.13,
25.16
budget policy statement of, 7.2–7.3
compensation of, 13.11–13.12
review of budget by, 7.5, 12.7
role of, in budgeting process, 1.3, 1.5
Chief financial officer (CFO), 12.7, 22.4–22.7
Child support payments, 18A.33s
Client/server environment, 18A.45s–18A.46s
Clinical trials, 34.7s
CMS. *See* Cost management systems
COGS. *See* Cost of goods sold
COLA. *See* Cost of living adjustments
Cold War, 16.5
Collection float, 21.7–21.8
Collection period, average, 22.13–22.14, 22.16
Collection services, 21.18–21.19
Collective bargaining agreements, 18A.19s
Committed costs, 8.8–8.9, 9.6
Company strengths, rating, 2.12

Company structure
as payroll cost factor, 18A.17s–18A.18s, 18A.27s
Compensation (executive), 13.1–13.21
budget incentives, pitfalls of, 13.11–13.13
corporate-level, 13.11–13.12
operating unit level, 13.12–13.13
long-term incentive plans, 13.19–13.21
optimal approach to, 13.13–13.17, 13.18–13.19
performance measures for, 13.2–13.10
capital charge, 13.9–13.10
cost of capital, accounting for, 13.4
earnings per share, 13.4
incentive plan costs, exclusion of, 13.3
net income after taxes and after extraordinary items,
13.2
operating unit performance measures, 13.8
overhead, exclusion of corporate, 13.8–13.9
return on capital employed, 13.5–13.8
return on shareholders' equity, 13.4–13.5
taxes, exclusion of, 13.2–13.3
structuring of reward opportunities, 13.10–13.11
Compensation programs, 18A.9s
Competition, 16.11
Compounding, 20.2–20.4
Computer Aided Manufacturing-International, Inc.,
16.8
Computer-integrated systems, 29.20s
Computers and computer applications, 28.1–28.16,
28.1s–28.3s
balance sheet budget preparation, 22.11
bracket budgeting 26.2, 26.13–26.16
capital budgeting model, 28.13, 28.14
choice of computer system, 28.2–28.3
portability, 28.2
training and support, 28.2–28.3
critical path method, 14.11
discounted rate of return, calculation of, 20.7
expert system artificial intelligence, 28.4–28.5
financial modeling, 28.3–28.4
fixed and variable cost model, 28.11–28.13
flexible budgets, 28.8–28.11
implementation of budgeting system, 28.15
master budget, 28.7–28.8
microcomputer factors, 28.5–28.7, 28.1s–28.2s
memory, 28.6, 28.1s–28.2s
peripherals, 28.6–28.7, 28.2s
software, 28.6, 28.1s
speed, 28.6, 28.2s
micro-mainframe link, 28.13, 28.15, 28.3s
profit calculations, 10.9, 10.11
risk analysis using 20.16, 20.19–20.20
software
acquisition and development, 18A.25s–18A.26s
budget plan template, 14.6s
budget report, 14.6s
choice of, 28.3–28.5, 28.6, 28.1s–28.2s
client/server envirinment, 18A.45s–18A.46s
costs, 18A.13s–18A.14s
CPM chart for budget schedule, 14.5s
decision support systems, 18A.46s
desktop integration, 18A.45s
financial modeling, 34.14s
in-house developed software, 28.5

Computers and computer applications, *(Continued)*
management's information system needs, 27.2s
microcomputers and, 28.6, 28.1s–28.2s
spreadsheets, 12.8, 28.3, 28.8, 28.10–28.11, 28.1s, 28.2s
top level tasks, 14.6s
Windows, 18A.45s, 28.2s
Computer service bureau (example of capital-intensive service company), 30.13–30.21
Concentration systems design, 21.19–21.21
Confidence factor, 26.11
Consolidation of budget information, 7.9–7.10
Construction
firm annual budgeting process, 3.14
TQM industry example, 26A.25s–26A.26s
Consultants, insurance/risk, 24.4
Consumable tools (manufacturing budget), 16.41–16.42
Consumer confidence, cash budgeting and, 21.3
Consumer packaged goods firms, sales and marketing budget for, 15.14s–15.15s
Consumer Price Index (CPI), 3.27–3.28
Contingencies, zero-base budgeting and adaptability to, 25.19
Contingency planning, 2.29–2.30, 5.12. *See also* Bracket budgeting
Continuing value, 11A.6s
Continuous improvement, 18A.41s, 18A.45s, 27A.9s
budgeting for, 18A.32s
TQM and, 26A.15s
Contribution analysis, 10.6–10.9, 10.10–10.11
higher education budgets, 32.7
Control, internal. *See* Internal control
Control, quality. *See* Quality control
Control charts
process, 26A.8s
Control Environment, 6.2–6.4
macrocontrols, 6.3
corporate culture, 6.3
external controls, 6.3
organization, 6.3
planning and reporting, 6.3
microcontrols, 6.4
Controllable costs, 8.9, 30.9
Cooperative advertising, 15.8
Copeland, Tom, 11A.6s
Core competency analysis, activity-based budgeting and, 27A.10s–27A.11s
Core processes, 26A.6s–26A.7s, 26A.13s–26A.14s
Corporate culture, 6.3
Corporate goals, 7.3. *See also* Strategic planning
Cost accounting, budgeting vs., 30.2
Cost accounting systems (manufacturing budget), 9.2–9.53
accumulation procedures, 9.22, 9.24–9.25, 9.27–9.29
impact on budgeting 9.24
selection, 9.25, 9.27–9.29
actual costing, 9.29–9.34
deficiencies of, 9.34
issues of material to production, 9.31–9.32
labor operations performed, 9.32
overhead, application of manufacturing, 9.32
production completion and transfer to finished goods, 9.32
purchase of materials, 9.29–9.31

shipment of finished goods, 9.32
decision factors in selection of, 9.3–9.4
failures of traditional, 16.8–16.9
full costing 9.22
options, 9.4, 9.5
overhead, 9.41–9.53
accounting procedures, 9.50, 9.53
actual costing, application to, 9.32
actual manufacturing overhead, 9.50, 9.51–9.52
converting budgets to overhead rates, 9.44–9.50
variances, 9.40–9.42
product associated costs, 9.4
standard costing 9.33, 9.34–9.37
budgets and, 9.34
criteria for judging success of system, 9.36
definition of standard costs, 9.34
purpose of, 9.35–9.36
setting standard costs, 9.36–9.37
valuation, 9.29, 9.30
variable costs, 9.4–9.22
break-even analysis data, 9.12–9.20
direct absorption costing data, 9.21–9.22
disadvantages of variable costing, 9.20–9.21
fixed manufacturing costs, identification of, 9.12
management tool variable costing as, 9.6–9.7
other uses for variable costing 9.10–9.12
overhead manufacturing, 9.6
product profitability analysis, 9.7–9.10
variance reporting 9.37, 9.39–9.43
labor variances, 9.40
manufacturing overhead variances, 9.40–9.42
material variances, 9.37
wage rate variances, 9.40
Cost-based pricing, 15.12s, 15.14s
Cost behavior, 8.1–8.17
breakeven analysis of, 8.4–8.8
fixed costs, changes in, 8.5–8.6
long-run budgeting, 8.7–8.8
relevant range, 8.6
short-run budgeting, 8.6–8.7
variable costs and contribution margin, 8.4–8.5
committed vs. discretionary costs, 8.8–8.9
controllable vs. noncontrollable costs, 8.9, 8.10
differential analysis of, 8.10–8.12
incremental costs, 8.11–8.12
joint product and by-product costs, 8.12
relevant costs, 8.10–8.11
direct vs. indirect costs, 8.9, 8.10
estimation of costs, 8.14–8.16
high-low method, 8.16
least squares method, 8.14–8.16
scatter diagram, 8.14, 8.15
fixed costs, 8.2
maximization of resources, 8.12–8.14
semivariable costs, 8.2
variable costs, 8.2
Cost-benefit analysis
nonprofit organizations, 31.18
program budgeting, 27.26–27.30
Cost center model (higher education budgets), 32.6
Cost differentiators, 18A.16s, 18A.17s, 18A.18s
Cost-effectiveness analysis. *See* Cost-benefit analysis
Cost elements, 27A.6s
Costing methods, sales and marketing budget, 15.6s

Cost management systems (CMS), 16.5–16.6, 16.8–16.12
  coordination of direct production and conversion, 16.9
  need for overview, 16.12
  profitability and, 16.9–16.12
Cost of capital. See Capital, cost of
Cost of goods sold (COGS), 34.6s
Cost of living adjustments (COLA), 3.27–3.28, 33.16
Cost/volume/price, 10.9, 10.11
CPI. See Consumer Price Index
CPM. See Critical path method
Creative thinking approaches, 27A.17s–27A.19s
Crime coverage, 24.12
Critical issues
  international business, 23.6, 23.8
  strategic plan, 2.16, 2.18
Critical path method (CPM), 14.4–14.11
  budget schedule, 14.5s
  computation in, 14.7–14.10
    backwards phase, 14.9–14.10
    forwards phase, 14.7–14.9
  computer software for utilizing 14.11
  controlling budget schedule with, 14.10–14.11
Crosby, Philip, 26A.3s, 26A.4s
Cross allocation method (cost redistribution), 9.45
Cross-border tax transfer, 20A.5s
Cross-functional teams, 18B.1s
Cross-rates, 23A.2s
Cross-walk reconciliation (program budgeting), 27.17–27.18
Currency option, 23A.4s
Current ratio, 22.42
Customer service
  activity-based budgeting and, 27A.4s, 27A.8s
  expense, 15.10s
  sales and marketing budget, 15.3s
Customer support services, 18A.10s
Customer surveys, 27A.9s–27A.10s
Customers
  expectations, 26A.10s
  identification, 26A.10s

Data capture, 27A.20s–27A.21s
  services, 18A.8s–18A.9s
Data center costs, 18A.12s–18A.13s
Data Resources, Inc., 3.16
Days' sales in inventory ratio (DSI), 22.16–22.17
DCFRR. See Discounted cash flow rate of return
Debt, cost of, 11A.6s
Debt ratio, 11A.3s, 11A.6s
Decision issues (strategic plan), 2.16
Decision package (zero-base budgeting), 25.5–25.12
  alternatives, formulation of, 25.5–25.6
  incremental expenditures and benefits, 25.6
  materials handling example, 25.8–25.12
  minimum level of effort, identifying 25.7
Decision support system, 18A.46s
Defect reduction, 18A.40s
Delphi technique, 27.31
Delta flow statement, 22.49–22.51
Demands(s)
  capacity vs., 16.23
  changes in, in manufacturing budget, 16.37
Deming, Dr. W. Edwards, 16.4, 26A.3s, 26A.4s

Deo, Prakash, 11A.10s
Departmental budgets. See also Divisional budgets
  bracket budgeting and consolidation of, 26.22
  health care, 33.5–33.6, 33.9, 33.33
  hospitals, 33.30–33.31
  nonprofit organizations, 31.22–31.23
  research and development, 17.28–17.32
    burden rate, 17.29–17.32
    coordination, 17.36, 17.38–17.39
    gross expenses, 17.29
Depreciation, 18.6s
  balance sheet budget, 22.24
  cash inflow and expense of, 19.7–19.9
  leasing, 20A.17s–20A.18s
  omission of, by nonprofit organizations, 31.13
Derivatives operations, 23A.4s
Desktop integration software, 18A.45s
Detailed plan (operational plan), 2.6
Deterministic models, 27.31
Differential costs, 8.10–8.12
  incremental costs, 8.11–8.12
  joint product and by-product costs, 8.12
Direct allocation method (cost redistribution), 9.45
Direct cost method, 15.16s
  absorption costing vs., 9.17–9.20
Direct costs, 8.9, 30.9
Direct deposit, 18A.19s–18A.20s, 18A.34s
Direct labor
  changed concepts of, 16.5
  definition, 9.3
Direct labor costs, 9.32, 16.42–16.45
  calculation of, 9.40
  measurement of, 16.44
  realism, importance of, 16.43–16.44
  wage incentives, 16.44–16.45
Direct material (definition), 9.3
Directors and officers liability coverage (D&O), 24.12
Direct writers, 24.3
Disbursement float, 21.7–21.8
Disbursement systems, 18A.9s
Disbursement techniques, 21.21
Discounted cash flow (lease-versus-buy analysis), 20.21–20.22
Discounted cash flow rate of return (DCFRR), 20.5–20.6
  advantages and disadvantages of, 20.7, 20.8
  computer calculation of, 20.7, 20.16
  net present value vs., 20.8–20.9
  payback period technique and, 20.12–20.13
  in practice, 20.13
  in risk analysis technique, 20.16
Discounting, 20.4
Discount rate, 11A.5s
Discretionary expenses
  fixed costs, 8.8–8.9, 9.4
  hospital budgets, 33.29–33.30
Distribution cost budget, 18.1–18.8
  advertising and sales promotion, 18.7–18.8
  analyses of, 18.3–18.4
  procedure, 18.6–18.7
  standards for, 18.4–18.6
Distribution methods, inventory levels and, 22.18–22.19
Distribution of budget information, 7.10

Dividends
equity vs., 11.5, 22.37–22.38
return on equity and, 13.16
Divisional budgets. See also Departmental budgets
final revision of, 12.7
initial budget department review, 12.3–12.6
data verification, 12.3
divisional budget assumptions and goals, analysis of, 12.5–12.6
previous forecast reliability, analysis of, 12.5
monthly submissions, 12.8
preparation of, 13.14
profit goals, 11.7–11.13
capital asset pricing model, 11.13
hurdle rates, 11.10–11.11
overhead, 11.9
portfolio effects, 11.9–11.10
revised consolidation of, 12.7
second budget staff review of, 12.7
senior management review of, 12.7–12.8
(D&O). See Directors and officers liability coverage
Document image processing, 18A.46s
Double-dip lease, 20A.13s, 20A.15s
Downloading of data, 28.13, 28.15
Drucker, Peter F., 16.2–16.3, 27.39, 31.2
DSI. See Days' sales in inventory ratio
Dummy activity (project planning), 14.5–14.7
DuPont Company, 27.7
DuPont formula chart, 30.3–30.5
Durability of finished goods, inventory levels and, 22.18
Dysfunctional behavior, 29.5, 29.6s

Earned value reporting, 17.33–17.35
Earnings diminution analysis, 24.7
Earnings per share, executive compensation based on, 13.4
Econometrics, 3.11–3.13, 3.16–3 17, 3.22
Economic life, 20A.11s
capital investment budget and projection of, 19.10–19.11
Economic order quantity (EOQ), 8.14
Economic risk, 23A.5s
Economic Value Added, 11A.7s–11A.12s
complementary measures and, 11A.12s–11A.14s
decomposition of, 11A.12s, 11A.16s
defined, 11A.3s–11A.4s
elements of, 11A.7s–11A.9s
formula, 11A.8s, 11A.9s
use for investment decisions, 11A.14s–11A.18s
Effectiveness-oriented costs, 18.12s
Efficiency variances (productivity variances), 9.40
80/20 rule (Pareto's Law), 16.41, 17.11, 17 13, 26.4–26.5, 26.15, 27.6
Electric utility, planning calendar for, 3.12–3.13
Electronic funds transfer (EFT), 18A.8s
Employee productivity, 16.32
Employee records
change inputs, 18A.7s, 18A.47s
Employees
TQM teams, 26A.13s
Employer Identification Number, 18A.19s
Encumbrance reporting (nonprofit organizations), 31.14, 31.30
Endowment earnings (nonprofit organizations), 31.7

Energy, economic effects of, 3.6, 3.20
Environmental analysis. See Situation analysis
Environmental Protection Agency (EPA), 3.26
EOQ. See Economic order quantity
EPA. See Environmental Protection Agency
Equitable Life, 3.22
Equity, cost of, 11A.6s
Equity, return on. See Return on equity
Equity accounts (balance sheet budget), 22.35, 22.37–22.38
Equity capital, determining cost of, 11.4–11.6
Euromarket, 23A.3s
Europe, program budgeting in, 27.11
Evaluation of employees, 29.17, 29.18s–29.19s
Event (project planning), 14.4
Excellence, activity-based budgeting and, 27A.6s, 27A.8s
Exception reporting (hospital budgets), 33.28
Exchange rate, 23A.1s–23A.2s
forecasts, 23.9
Executive compensation. See Compensation (executive)
Executory costs, leasing, 20A.14s
Exercise price, 23A.4s
Expectancy theory, 29.8–29.9, 29.9s–29.10s
Expected capacity, 9.47
Expense budget. See also Administrative expense budget
collecting data for, 7.6, 7.7
nonprofit organizations, 31.8
Expense centers, 6.5
higher education budgets, 32.6
Expense investments, 19.2
Expenses, allocation of, 18.2s–18.3s
strategic business units, 18.2s
Expenses, expenditures vs. (in nonprofit organizations), 31.12–31.13
Expenses, types of, 18.6s–18.7s
Expert system, 28.5
Expiry date, 23A.4s
External control, 6.3
Externally oriented nonprofit organizations, 31.3
Extra expense insurance coverage, 24.14
Extrinsic valence, 29.8, 29.10s

Factoring, 21.16–21.17
Falsification of information, 29.5–29.6, 29.6s–29.7s
Family Support Act, 18A.9s, 18A.33s
FASB. See Financial Accounting Standards Board
FASB 13. See Financial Accounting Standards Board Statement No. 13
FASB 95. See Financial Accounting Standards Board Statement No. 95
Fayol, Henry, 29.5, 29.5s
Federal government, program budgeting in, 27.8–27.11, 27.1s–27.2s, 27.3s
balancing resources, 29.1s
Carter administration, 27.1s–27.2s
format of, 27.19–27.22
annual cycle, 27.22
documents, 27.20–27.21
final submission, 27.22
Johnson Administration, 27.9
Kennedy Administration, 27.9
line-item budgeting, 27.2s, 27.3s
Nixon Administration, 27.9
phase-out of, 27.10–27.11

Federal government, *(Continued)*
  Rand Corporation, 27.8
  World War II, 27.8
Federal Reserve wire transfer system, 21.21
Feedback
  corporate planning cycle and, 2.4
  sales and marketing budget, 15.14s
  in strategic plan, 2.28–2.29
  strategic planning cycle and, 2.6
  tactical budgeting model, 26.18–26.21
Feigenbaum, 26A.3s
FIFO. *See* First-in-first-out system
Final operational plan (strategic plan), 2.22
Finance companies, leases and, 20A.8s
Finance departments
  efficiency increases, 18A.3s, 18A.5s
Financial Accounting Standards Board (FASB), 22.48
Financial Accounting Standards Board Statement No.
  13, leasing, 20A.5s, 20A.9s–20A.16s,
  20A.19s–20A.21s
Financial Accounting Standards Board Statement No. 95
  (FASB 95), cash flow statements using format of,
  21.10–21.14
  direct method, 21.12–21.14
  financing activities, 21.11–21.12
  indirect method, 21.12–21.13
  investing activities, 21.11
  operating activities, 21.10–21.11
Financial assets, responsibility for, 22.4
Financial institution costs, 18A.15s
Financial manager, cash budgeting and, 21.5–21.9
  generation of investment income, 21.5
  measurement of results, 21.6–21.9
  planning and control, 21.6
Financial modeling software, 28.3–28.4, 34.14s
Financial ratios, 22.40–22.47
  leverage, 22.43–22.44
  liquidity, 22.42–22.43
  price/earnings ratios, 11.2
  profitability, 22.44–22.47
Financial reports, budget formats and, 4.9
Financial risk, 23A.5s–23A.6s
Financial statements, leasing, 20A.2s
Financing, types of, 21.15–21.17
  long term, 21.17
  short term, 21.15–21.17
    asset based financing, 21.16
    factoring, 21.16–21.17
    trade financing, 21.16
Finished goods, inventory level of, 16.21–16.22, 22.18
First-half review, 5.9
First-in-first-out system (FIFO), 9.31–9.32, 24.14
First-quarter review, 5.8
Fixed assets
  balance sheet budget, 22.22, 22.24–22.27
  responsibility for, 22.5
Fixed costs, 8.2, 9.4, 27A.3s
  breakeven analysis applied to, 8.5–8.6, 10.2–10.3
  committed vs. discretionary, 8.8–8.9
  contribution analysis and, 10.9
  discretionary, 8.8–8.9, 9.4
  distribution cost budget, 18.6–18.7
  hospital budgets, 33.29
  manufacturing budget, 9.12, 16.45–16.46

  physician budgets, 33.36
  service company budgets, 30.8–30.9
Fixed efficiency variance, 9.42
Fixed/variable cost model, application of computer to,
  28.11–28.13, 28.2s–28.3s
Flexibility, 5.12
  in operational plan, 2.26
  in strategic planning 2.4
Flexible budgets
  computer, application of, 28.8–28.11
  hospitals, 33.28–33.30
Float, 21.7–21.8
Food and Drug Administration (FDA), 34.2s, 34.3s
  facility approval, 34.4s
  product approval, 34.8s
Ford Motor Company, 16.5
Forecasts and forecasting. *See also* Cost behavior
  annual profit plan, avoidance in, 4.3
  bracket budgeting, 26.19–26.20
  budget information and, 7.6
  economic, 3.11–3.13, 3.16–3.26
    impact of uncertainty, 3.20
    response to uncertainty, 3.21–3.26
    sources of economic data, 3.18–3.20
  of sales, in manufacturing budget, 16.19–16.20
  sales and marketing budget techniques, 15.12s
  strategic planning vs., 2.2
  timetables and, 5.7
  use of, in situation analysis, 2.6–2.7
FORECYT model, 3.2–3.3, 3.4–3.5
Foreign exchange rates, 23A.1s
  changes, 23A.6s–23A.7s, 23A.8s–23A.10s
  cross-rates, 23A.2s
  direct and indirect quotation, 23A.2s
  forecasting and risk, 23.9, 23A.5s
Foreign source income, 23.8–23.9
Forms costs, 18A.15s–18A.16s
Forms processing, 18A.48s–18A.49s
Forward exchange contracts, 23A.2s, 23A.4s–23A.5s
Forward operations, 23A.2s–23A.3s
Forward price, 23A.3s
Forwards phase (critical path method), 14.7–14.9
Fringe benefits (hospital budgeting), 33.20–33.21
Full costing
  manufacturing budget, 9.22
Full year estimate (international operations monthly
  report), 23.15
Functional expense reporting (nonprofit organizations),
  31.14
Functional organizations, 17.38
Functional plan (annual profit plan), 4.7
Functions of budgeting, 1.1–1.2
Fund accounting (nonprofit organizations), 31.11
Fund-raising (nonprofit organizations), 31.7–31.8
Funds mobilization, 21.20–21.21
Future costs, 8.10–8.11
Futures contracts, 23A.2s
Fuzzy logic, 28A.1s
  basic elements, 28A.3s
  fuzzy sets, 28A.1s

GAAP. *See* Generally accepted accounting principles
Gamesmanship, 29.6s
Gaming (program budgeting), 27.31

Gantt charts, 14.2–14.3, 14.1s–14.2s, 17.24, 17.26–17.27
 budget calendar, 14.3s–14.4s
 calendar schedule, 14.1s
 sample chart, 14.2s
GE/McKinsey strategic planning technique, 27.22
General Electric, 27.7–27.8
Generally accepted accounting principles (GAAP), 9.36
General Motors, 27.7
GNP. *See* Gross national product
Goal incongruence, 29.5, 29.6s–29.7s
Goals. *See also* Strategic planning
 corporate, 7.3
 within organization, 29.6, 29.7s
 participation and internalization of, 29.12–29.14, 29.14s–29.15s
 profit goals
  cost of capital and, 11.6–11.13
  long-run budgeting and, 8.7–8.8
 resource matching, 27A.14s
 setting 6.4–6.5
Going rate, 13.10
Government. *See also* Federal government, program budgeting in
 mandates, 17.13
 regulation by, 1.12, 3.6–3.7
Grants (to nonprofit organizations), 31.7
Graphic data (in international operations monthly report), 23.17–23.18
Graphics capability, 28.1s
Gridding. *See* Business gridding
Gross expenses (departmental research and development budget), 17.29–17.32
Gross national product (GNP), 3.3
Gross patient revenues
 hospital budgets, 33.21–33.22
 physician budgets, 33.37–33.38
Gross-to-net, 18A.7s–18A.8s, 18A.24s
Group dynamics, 29.14, 29.15s–29.16s
Group technology, 16.32

Hardware costs, 18A.12s–18A.13s, 18A.14s
Health care industry, budgeting in, 33.1–33.38, 33.1s
 See also Hospital budgeting; Physician budgeting
 cost control, 33.3–33.5
  educated consumer and, 33.5
  inflation and, 33.3–33.4
  managed care, 33.4
 current year projections, 33.6
 departmental requests, analysis of, 33.6, 33.9
 department managers, education of, 33.5–33.6
 management incentives and, 33.10
 position review, 33.1s
 review of departmental requests, 33.9
 strategic plan and, 33.5
 time table, development of, 33.5
 TQM example, 26A.26s–26A.27s
 turnaround reports, 33.6, 33.7–33.8
 variance reporting, 33.9
Health maintenance organizations, 33.4
Hedging, 23A.4s–23A.5s, 23A.6s
Hierarchy of needs, 29.7–29.8, 29.8s–29.9s
Hiese, Dennis, 16.15
Higher education, budgeting in, 32.1–32.16

ABC budgeting 32.8
annual budgets, 32.9–32.16
 assumptions, development of budget, 32.10, 32.12
 course identification and scheduling, 32.12–32.14
 organization, 32.9
 preparation of budget, 32.14–32.15
 review, modification, and approval, 32.15–32.16
 characteristics of effective budgeting, 32.5
 common maladies affecting, 32.3–32.5
 intramural funding, 32.5–32.7
 monthly budgets, 32.8–32.9
High-low method (cost estimation), 8.16
Hospital budgeting, 33.10–33.30
 advanced cost analysis in, 33.32
 allocation of deductions and allowances in, 33.32
 current year projections, 33.10–33.13
  analysis of, 33.13
  combination of year-to-date actual plus budget, 33.11
  combination of year-to-date actual plus inflated prior year of actual, 33.11, 33.13
  current year budget, 33.10–33.11
  simple averaging method, 33.11
 exception reporting, 33.28
 flexible budgeting, 33.28–33.30
 fringe benefits, 33.20–33.21
 full costed departments, 33.30–33.31
 historic data, gathering of, 33.10
 inflation and, 33.24
 monitoring performance, 33.25–33.28
  management review, 33.25, 33.28
  variance measurement and reporting, 33.25, 33.26–33.27
 nonsalary expenses, 33.21
 peer hospitals, comparisons to, 33.32–33.33
 physician budgeting. *See* Physician budgeting
 revenues and allowances, 33.21–33.24
  allowances (in general), 33.22–33.23
  contractual allowances, 33.22–33.23
  deductions, 33.22, 33.23
  gross patient revenues, 33.21–33.22
  net patient revenue, 33.23–33.24
  nonoperating revenue, 33.24
  other operating revenue, 33.24
  rate changes, 33.24
  spread methods, 33.24
 staffing and payroll, 33.14–33.20
  accrued vs. paid, 33.20
  base staffing and payroll, 33.15
  contract codes, 33.16
  hours other than base budget and overtime, 33.15
  overtime, 33.15
  pay increases, 33.16, 33.19–33.20
  productive vs. nonproductive time, 33.20
  variable staffing, 33.30
 units of service, 33.13–33.14
  ancillary units of service, 33.14
  inpatient routine units of service, 33.14
Human resources departments
 interaction with payroll, 18A.10s, 18A.12s, 18A.26s
Hurdle rates, 11.10–11.11, 11A.7s, 11A.8s, 17.16–17.17
Hybrid transfer costing, 18.13s
Hygiene factors, 29.9s

Iacocca, Lee, 26A.3s
ICLM. See Induced Course Load Matrix
Idle capacity variance, 9.42
Imposed budgets, 29.3, 29.3s
Improvement
   activity-based budgeting and, 27A.4s–27A.7s, 27A.19s
   continuous. See Continuous improvement
   process management approach to, 27A.6s–27A.7s
   process of, 27A.19s
Incentive payments (physician budgets), 33.36–33.37
Incentive performance, 16.42–16.43
Income profile, 26.13–26.14
Income taxes (in balance sheet budget), 22.33
   22.35–22.36
Incremental budgeting, 25.2–25.3
   higher education budgets, 32.3
   sales and marketing budget, 15.6s–15.7s
Independent leasing companies, 20A.7s
Index volume, 16.24
Indirect costs, 8.9
   administrative expense budget, 18.9
   manufacturing budget, 16.41–16.42
Induced Course Load Matrix (ICLM), 32.13
Industrial products firms, sales and marketing budget
   for, 15.15s
Industry trends, cash budgeting and, 21.3
Ineffective time, reduction of, 16.26–16.28
Inflation
   acceptance of, 16.11
   cash budgeting and, 21.3
   as environmental factor, 3.3, 3.20
   health care budgeting and, 33.3–33.4, 33.24
   projected cash flows and, 19.11
   replacement costs of fixed assets and, 22.25, 22.27
Information system, program budgeting and choice of,
   27.33
Initial cash outflows, 19.4–19.5
Inpatient revenues (hospital budgeting)
   ancillary, 33.22
   routine, 33.22
Insurance companies, leases and, 20A.8s
Insurance requirements, budgeting for, 24.1–24.18
   agents/brokers, use of, 24.4–24.5
   assessment of insurance needs, 24.6–24.8
      earnings diminution analysis, 24.7
      qualitative evaluations, 24.7
      risk reward index, 24.6
   casualty coverages, 24.10–24.11, 24.15–24.17
   consultants, use of 24.4
   crime coverage, 24.12
   directors' and officers' liability, 24.12
   property coverages, 24.9–24.10
   risk management and, 24.2–24.3
   risks, identification of, 24.13–24.15
   third-party administrators and, 24.5
      actuaries, 24.5
      claims administration and reserving, 24.5
      information reporting systems, 24.5
      legal representatives, 24.6
      loss control, 24.5–24.6
      program administration, 24.6
   types of insurance mechanisms and, 24.3
      agency/brokerage carriers, 24.3
      direct writers, 24.3

self-funded plans, 24.3–24.4
Insurance Services Office (ISO), 24.11
Integrated planning document (IPD), 23.4–23.5,
   23.9–23.14
   controlled units, restriction to, 23.9
   elements of document, 23.11–23.14
   exchange rate forecasts, 23.9
   purposes, 23.10–23.11
   review, 23.10
Interactive voice response. See Voice response systems
Interest expense (cash budgeting), 21.4
Internal control, 6.1–6.9. See also Reviews, budget
   bracket budgeting and, 26.3–26.4
   Control Environment and, 6.2–6.4
      macrocontrols, 6.3
      microcontrols, 6.4
   control loop, 6.7–6.8
   external control vs., 6.3
   planning systems for, 6.4–6.6
      assignment of responsibility, 6.5–6.6
      goals and objectives, 6.4–6.5
   reporting systems for, 6.6–6.9
      input control over, 6.7
      review and response, 6.7–6.9
Internal rate of return (IRR), 17.16–17.17. See also
   Discounted cash flow rate of return
International Accounting Standard (IAS) 17, 20A.4s,
   20A.9s, 20A.10s
International operations, budgeting for, 23.1–23.19
   alternative business structures and, 23.18–23.19
   capital expenditure budgets, 23.4
   headquarters operations, 23.18
   integrated planning document and, 23.4–23.5,
      23.9–23.14
      controlled units, restriction to, 23.9
      elements of document, 23.11–23.14
      exchange rate forecasts, 23.9
      purposes, 23.10–23.11
      review, 23.10
   monthly reporting procedures, 23.14–23.18
      abridged revision for general management, 23.15,
         23.17
      full year estimate, 23.15
      graphic data, 23.17–23.18
      manager's letter, 23.14
      twin currency income statement, 23.14–23.15
      variance analysis worksheet, 23.15
   operating budgets, 23.2–23.4
   reviews
      preliminary, 23.4
      procedure for, 23.10
   strategic direction paper and, 23.2, 23.5–23.9
      assessments worksheet, 23.5–23.7
      critical issues, enumeration of, 23.6, 23.8
      distribution of, 23.6, 23.8–23.9
      investment strategy matrix, 23.6
      statement of objectives, 23.5
Internet, 28.3s
Intramural funding, 32.5–32.7
Intranets, 28.3s
Intrinsic valence, 29.8, 29.10s
Inventory, 15.10s, 16.34–16.39
   determining ideal levels of, 16.21–16.22, 22.16–22.22
comprehensive inventory budget (example),

Inventory, *(Continued)*
  22.19–22.22, 22.23
    distribution methods, 22.18–22.19
    durability of finished goods, 22.18
    length of production process, 22.17
    raw materials, availability of, 22.18
    sales level, 22.16–22.22
  improvement of, as plannable core, 16.18
  responsibility for levels of, 22.4–22.5
Investment budgets. *See* Capital investment budgeting
Investment opportunity rate of return, 20.5
Investment programs, 11A.15s
Investment strategy matrix (international business), 23.6
IPD. *See* Integrated planning document
IRR. *See* Internal rate of return
ISO. *See* Insurance Services Office
Issues analysis (program budgeting), 27.15

Japan, 16.4, 29.9, 29.11s
JIT. *See* Just-in-time inventory management
JIT II purchasing, 18B.2s
Job order costing, 9.25, 9.27–9.29
John Hancock Insurance, 27.8
Johnson Administration, program budgeting during, 27.9
Joint-produced costs, 8.12
Juran, Dr. Joseph, 26A.2s, 26A.3s, 26A.4s
Just-in-time inventory management (JIT), 16.8, 22.18, 29.20s

Kaisen, 16.4
Kennedy Administration, program budgeting during, 27.9
Key success factors, 2.7
Klein, Lawrence, 3.18
Knowledge engineers, 28.5
Koller, Tim, 11A.6s

Labor
  actual, 9.32
  direct. *See* Direct labor
  variances, 9.40
Labor-intensive companies, 30.10–30.11
Labor-related costs, 18A.14s, 18A.15s
Lapsed time utilization (exhibit), 16.27
Laser printers, 18A.48s
Last-in-first-out system (LIFO), 9.32, 24.14
Law firm (example of labor-intensive professional services firm), 30.11–30.13
Leadership, 18A.50s
Leadership styles, 29.14–29.15, 29.16s–29.17s
Lease analysis, 20A.22s–20A.27s
Lease form, 20A.27s–20A.35s
Leasehold amortization, 18.6s
Lease pools, 20A.8s
Leases
  capital, 20A.9s, 20A.10s
  classification of, 20A.3s–20A.6s, 20A.21s
  operating, 20A.10s
  returns on, 20A.22s
  sources of, 20A.7s
Leasing, 20A.1s–20A.35
  advantages of, 20A.6s
  analysis, 20A.22s–20A.27s
  depreciation, 20A.17s–20A.18s
  disadvantages of, 20A.6s–20A.7s

  fair market value, 20A.15s–20A.17s
  FASB 13 and, 20A.5s, 20A.9s–20A.16s
    case example, 20A.19s–20A.21s
  financial statements and, 20A.2s, 20A.3s
  form, sample, 20A.28s–20A.35s
  international considerations, 20A.3s–20A.6s
  lessor selection, 20A.22s
  minimum payments, 20A.14s
  negotiation, 20A.21s–20A.22s
  process, 20A.3s–20A.6s
  purchase and, 20A.16s
  reporting, 20A.9s–20A.16s
  rules for, 20A.9s
  software for, 20A.9s
  terminology, 20A.9s, 20A.10s
Lease-versus-buy analysis, 20.20–20.22, 20A.16
  discounted cash flow, 20.21–20.22
  net present value, 20.22
Least squares method (cost estimation), 8.14–8.16
Legal representation (for property and liability risk management program), 24.6
Lessors, 20A.7s–20A.8s
Leverage, 11A.3s, 22.28, 22.30, 22.43–22.44
Leverage points, identification of, 2.18, 2.20
Liabilities
  accrued, 22.35
  responsibility for management of, 22.5
Licensing, software, 18A.14s
Lifecycle accounting, 34.12s
Life, economic
  capital investment budget and projection of, 19.10–19.11
  product life cycles, 17.3
LIFO. *See* Last-in-first-out system
Likely budget, 13.14
Line item budgeting, 18A.28s–18A.30s, 27.2s, 27.3s
Liquidity, financial ratios for measurement of, 22.42–22.43
Liquidity ratio. *See* Cash ratio
Local area networks, 28.3s
Lockbox services, 21.18–21.19
Long-range planning. *See* Strategic planning
Long-run budgeting, 8.7–8.8
Long-run performance, 29.7s
Long-term financing, 21.17
Long-term incentive plans, 13.19–13.21
Loss control services, 24.5–24.6
Lotus 1-2-3, 22.11, 28.8, 28.9

Macrocontrols, 6.3
Maintenance (manufacturing budget), 16.53–16.54
Managed health care, 33.4
Management, 1.1–1.14. *See also* Budget manager; Financial manager, cash budgeting and
  approval of budget by senior, 12.7–12.8
  and behavioral aspects of budgeting, 29.2–29.3, 29.5s–29.8s
  budgetary pressure and, 29.10, 29.11s–29.12s
  budget document and, 1.5–1.7
  budget staff and, 5.4
  compensation of. *See* Compensation (executive)
  contribution analysis and, 10.6–10.7
  control tool of, budget as, 1.8, 1.9–1.10
  corporate culture and, 6.3

Management, *(Continued)*
effectiveness of, 1.7–1.8
environmental analysis and, 1.10–1.12
evaluation standards for, 11.7
frequency of budget reviews by, 1.10
functions of budgeting process and, 1.1–1.2
health care budgeting, 33.10, 33.25, 33.28
impediments caused by, 1.7
insurance budgeting, 24.7
Japanese style of corporate, 29.9, 29.11s
and leadership styles, 29.14–29.15, 29.16s–29.17s
manufacturing budget
    misunderstanding of, by management, 16.11
    overhead costs, 16.47–16.50
organizational scanning and, 1.12–1.13
overview of budgeting process and, 1.2–1.5
performance standards and, 1.8–1.9
program budgeting, 27.6, 27.33
responsibility for budget preparation, 7.3–7.4
review, budgeting, 5.9–5.10
role conflict and, 29.11, 29.12s–29.13s
sales and marketing budget, 15.5
scientific, 29.5, 29.6s
standard costs and, 1.8
strategic planning and, 1.12–1.13
traditional vs. modern view of, 29.7, 29.8s
TQM program, 26A.12s, 26A.19s
universal principles of, 29.5, 29.5s–29.6s
variable costing as tool for, 9.6–9.7
variance analysis and, 1.8–1.9
zero-base budgeting, 25.13, 25.16, 25.17–25.21
Management approaches, 18A.50s
Management by exception, 29.17, 29.19s
Management by objectives (MBO), 17.6
Management of budget, 18.13s–18.14s
activity-based costing, 18.14s
administrative charge-back to operating units, 18.13s
benchmarking, 18.14s
budget variance analysis, 18.13s
hybrid transfer costing, 18.13s
outsourcing alternatives, 18.14s
performance measure, 18.14s
Management reports, 5.9–5.10
Management style
activity-based budgeting and, 27A.7s
sales and marketing budget, 15.5s–15.6s
value, 27A.18s–27A.19s
Manager's letter (international operations monthly report), 23.14
Mandl, Alex, 11A.12s
Manipulation of information, 29.5–29.6s, 29.6s–29.7s
Manpower budgets, preparation of, 5.5
Manual, budget. *See* Budget manual
Manufacturing
TQM industry example, 26A.24s–26A.25s
Manufacturing budget, 16.1–16.57. *See also* Cost
accounting systems (manufacturing budget)
cost management system, changing to, 16.8–16.12
coordination of direct production and conversion,
    16.9
overview, need for, 16.12
profitability and, 16.9–16.12
direct labor costs, determination of, 16.42–16.45
measurement, 16.44

realism, importance of, 16.43–16.44
wage incentives, 16.44–16.45
entrepreneurial approach, need for, 16.13–16.15
fear of change in preparation of, 16.12
floor and work-in-process control (review questions),
    16.54–16.55
indirect material costs, determination of, 16.41–16.42
inventory
    determination of required levels of, 16.21–16.22
    replenishment and, 16.34–16.39
maintenance (review questions), 16.53–16.54
as most significant part of total business plan, 16.7
overhead, 16.45–16.52. *See also* under
    Cost accounting systems (manufacturing budget)
    definitions, 16.45–16.46
    levels of, 16.46–16.50
    review questions, 16.50–16.52
plannable core, development of, 16.18
planned action budget, 16.16–16.17
pricing and inventory, changing concepts of,
product appearance, scheduling of new and revised,
    16.20–16.21
production requirements, determination of,
    16.17–16.18
program budgeting and, 27.7–27.8
publication of master schedule, 16.34
quality control (review questions), 16.52–16.53
raw materials requirements, determination of,
    16.39–16.41
    forecast accuracy, 16.39–16.40
    special commodity characteristics, 16.40–16.41
real shop capacity, establishment of, 16.22–16.28
    demonstrated capacity, 16.23–16.25
    ideal and controlled standard performance,
        16.26–16.27
    reduction of ineffective time, 16.26–16.28
sales history and forecast, 16.19–16.20
service companies, budgeting vs., 30.6–30.7
total quality control program, 16.28–16.34
    capacity increase, 16.31–16.33
    capital tools, 16.33
    continuous processes, capacity of, 16.33–16.34,
        16.35
zero-base budgeting and, 16.15, 25.4
Manufacturing Cycle Efficiency, 16.6
**Manufacturing operations as source of capital
    expenditure programs,** 5.11–5.12
Manufacturing processes, TQM and, 26A.9s
MAPI technique, 20.13
Marginal analysis (sales and marketing budget), 15.11s
Margin of safety, 10.3
Margins, cash budgeting and maintaining of operating,
    21.3
Market as gauge of financial performance, 11.3–11.4
Marketing, 30.2
Marketing budget. *See* Sales and marketing budget
Marketing expenses, 15.2s
Maslow, Abraham, 29.7–29.8, 29.7s–29.9s
Master budget, application of computer to, 28.7–28.8
Master schedule (manufacturing budget), 16.34
Material price variance, 9.37
Material purchases (manufacturing budget), 9.29–9.31.
    See also Raw materials
Material unit cost, standard, 9.36

Material usage variance, 9.37
Matrices. *See* Business gridding
Matrix organizations, 17.38–17.39
Maturity date, 23A.4s
MBO. *See* Management by objectives
McCarren Ferguson Act, 24.16
McGregor, Douglas, 29.9, 29.10s
McKinsey, 27.8
McKinsey/General Electric matrix, 2.10, 2.11, 2.18, 2.19
McNamara, Robert, 27.9
Mechanized GANTT, 17.24, 17.26–17.27
Medicaid, 33.3
Medicare, 33.3, 33.33
Member-oriented nonprofit organizations, 31.4
Memory (computer), 28.6, 28.1s–28.2s
Mergers, 18A.22s
Merit pay increases, 33.16
Microcomputer, 28.5–28.7, 28.1s–28.3s
   link with mainframe, 28.13, 28.15, 28.3s
   memory, 28.6, 28.1s–28.2s
   peripherals, 28.6–28.7, 28.2s
   program budgeting and, 27.2s
   software, 28.6, 28.1s
   speed, 28.6, 28.2s
Microcontrols, 6.4
Micromotions, 16.5
Microprocessors, 28.6, 28.2s
Middle-market firms, 24.1s
Mini-computers
   program budgeting and, 27.2s
Minimum lease payments, 20A.14s
Minimum level of effort (zero-base budgeting), 25.7
Mission/vision statement, 26A.13s *See also* Statement of objectives
Modeling
   program budgeting, 27.31–27.32
   software, 28.3–28.4, 28.1s
Modified accrual basis of accounting (nonprofit organizations), 31.12
Monitor (computer), 28.6, 28.2s
Monitoring profits of budgets, 5.8–5.10
Monte Carlo analysis, 17.21, 17.24
Monthly budgets (higher education), 32.8–32.9
Monthly management review meetings, 5.10
Motivation, 29.7–29.11, 29.8s–29.13s
   expectancy theory, 29.8–29.9, 29.9s–29.10s
   needs hierarchy and, 29.7–29.8, 29.8s–29.9s
   pressure devices, budgets as, 29.10, 29.11s–29.12s
   role conflict and, 29.11, 29.12s–29.13s
   X, Y, and Z theories, 29.9, 29.10s–29.11s
Multimedia, 18A.46s
Multinational companies, 23A.1s, 23A.10s
Multiple step-down (overhead costs), 33.31
Multiyear program and financial plan (PFP), 27.16–27.17, 27.21 27.22
Murrin, Jack, 11A.3s

Needs hierarchy theory, 29.7–29.8, 29.8s–29.9s
Negotiated budgets, 29.4, 29.4s–29.5s
Net income, capital investments and, 19.7
Net operating profit after tax (NOPAT), 11A.8s, 19.9
Net patient revenue, 33.23–33.24

Net present value (NPV), 11A.16s
   calculation of, for research and development budget, 17.16, 17.17, 17.19–17.21
   capital investment projects, in evaluation of, 20.8–20.10
   in lease-versus-buy analysis, 20.22
New York Stock Exchange, 11.4
Nine-month review, 5.9
Nixon Administration, program budgeting during, 27.9
Nonadmitted carriers, 24.17
Noncontrollable costs, 8.9
Nonmanufacturing processes, TQM and, 26A.9s–26A.10s
Nonprofit organizations, 31.1–31.35. *See also* Higher education, budgeting in
   accounting practices and budgeting for, 31.11–31.13
      cash vs. accrual basis, 31.12
      depreciation, omission of, 31.13
      expenses vs. expenditures, 31.12–31.13
      fund accounting, 31.11
   adaptability of budget, 31.9
   capital budgeting and, 31.31–31.32
   cash budgeting and, 31.31
   classification of, 31.3–31.4
      externally oriented organizations, 31.3
      member-oriented organizations, 31.4
   control of budget, 31.30–31.31
      reports, 31.30
      revision, 31.30–31.31
      variance analysis, 31.30
   development of budget, 31.25–31.29
      consolidated budget, 31.28
      final approval, 31.28
      responsibility units, 31.26–31.28
      revenue estimation, 31.25–31.26
      reviews and revision, 31.28
   effectiveness and control, measurement of, 31.8–31.9
      labor-intensive services, 31.8
      multiple service measures, 31.9
      service measurement, 31.8
      service timing, 31.8
   expense budgeting, 31.8
   long-range planning, 31.5–31.6, 31.15–31.17
      initiation of program planning, 31.17
      major objectives, definition of, 31.15, 31.17
      strategies for achieving objectives, identification of, 31.17
   organizational structure, 31.10
   participation in preparation of budget, 31.9–31.10
   planning of budget, 31.20–31.25
      adaption of program plans, 31.20–31.22
      assignment of duties, 31.24–31.25
      guidelines, preparation of, 31.24
      measurement tools, development of, 31.23–31.24
      responsibility accounting structures, establishment of, 31.22–31.23
   program budgeting for, 31.34–31.35
   program planning in, 31.17–31.20
      alternatives, analysis of, 31.17–31.18
      implementation plan, 31.19
      ongoing vs. new programs, 31.19
      selection of programs, 31.18
      in smaller organizations, 31.19–31.20

Nonprofit organizations, *(Continued)*
  reporting requirements, budgetary, 31.13–31.14
  encumbrance reporting, 31.14
  functional accounting, 31.14
  reimbursement procedures, 31.13–31.14
  responsibility center accounting for, 31.32–31.33
  revenue budgeting, 31.7–31.8
    endowment earnings, 31.7–31.8
    fund raising, 31.7–31.8
    grants and contracts, 31.7
  size of, 31.4–31.5
  standards for cost and performance in, 31.33–31.34
  time reporting, 31.34
  variable costing and flexible budgeting for, 31.33
  work measurement, 31.34
  zero-base budgeting for, 31.35
NOPAT. *See* Net operating profit after tax
Normal burden rate, 16.45
Normal capacity, 9.47
Norm bonus, 13.10
Notes payable
  balance sheet budget, 22.27–22.28, 22.30
  responsibility for management of, 22.5–22.6
NPV. *See* Net present value

Office of Management and Budget (OMB), 27.9
Ohno, Taiichi, 16.4, 16.8, 16.32
Oil companies
  annual budgeting process for, 3.15
  economic inputs for, 3.26
OMB. *See* Office of Management and Budget
Operating budgets, 5.11, 11A.16s
  capital budgets vs., 3.7–3.8
  international operations, 23.2–23.4
Operating expense reports, 5.11
Operating expenses, cash budgeting and maintaining of, 21.4
Operating exposure, 23A.8s–23A.10s
Operating investments, 19.2
Operating leverage, 22.24
Operating margin, 11A.11s
Operating/operational plan (strategic planning), 2.4, 2.6
  annual profit plan, 4.7
  role of budget within, 5.13
Operating unit(s)
  budgets by. *See* Divisional budgets
  performance measures, 13.8, 13.12–13.13
  performance targets for, 13.17–13.19
Operational costs, budgeting, 34.11s
Operations, 15.2s
  centralized versus decentralized, 18A.18s
  as fundamental area of business, 30.2
Operations research, 27.30, 27.32
Opportunities, defining, 2.12, 2.16
Organizational scanning, 1.12–1.13
Organization and administration of budget, 5.1–5.13
  capital budgets, 5.11–5.12
  flexibility, 5.12
  monitoring of progress, 5.8–5.10
  operating budgets, 5.11
  policy and procedures, 5.4–5.6
  production budgets, 5.11

  staff, 5.2–5.4
  timetables, 5.6–5.8
Organization culture, 29.14, 29.16s
Ouchi, William, 29.9, 29.11s
Outsourcing alternatives, 18.14s
Outsourcing, payroll functions, 18A.24s–18A.25s
Overabsorbed burden, 16.45
Overall float days factor, 21.7
Overhead
  allocation of, in hospital budgets, 33.31
  divisional profit goals and, 11.9
  executive compensation and corporate, 13.8–13.9
  manufacturing budget, 9.32, 9.41–9.53, 16.45–16.52
    accounting procedures, 9.50, 9.53
    actual manufacturing overhead, 9.50, 9.51–9.52
    converting budgets to overhead rates, 9.44–9.50
    definitions, 16.45–16.46
    levels of, 16.46–16.50
    review questions, 16.50–16.52
    variable costs, 9.6
    variances, 9.40–9.42
    wage rates, 9.37

Pallante, Thomas, 16.14
Pareto, Vilfredo, 17.11, 26.4
Pareto's Law. *See* 80/20 rule
Participative budgets, 29.3–29.4, 29.12–29.18, 29.3s–29.4s, 29.13s–29.20s
  aspiration levels and, 29.15, 29.17s
  budget staff and, 29.17–29.18, 29.19s–29.20s
  group dynamics and, 29.14, 29.15s–29.16s
  leadership and, 29.14–29.15, 29.16s–29.17s
  nature of participation, 29.12, 29.13s–29.15s
  organization culture and, 29.14, 29.16s–29.17s
  performance reports and rewards, 29.16–29.17, 29.18s–29.19s
  significance of participation in, 29.12–29.14, 29.15s
  slack and, 29.15–29.16, 29.17s–29.18s
  standards and, 29.15, 29.17s
Past costs. *See* Sunk costs
Past due accounts, collection of, 22.4
Pay
  biotechnology companies, 34.5s
  calculation of, 18A.8s
  earnings categories, 18A.21s
  frequency of, 18A.19s
  media, 18A.19s–18A.20s
  multiple programs, 18A.19s
Payables *See* Accounts payable; Notes payable; Trade payables
Payback period, 17.16, 20.12–20.13
Pay grade and step method (salary increases), 33.16, 33.19
Payment processing services, 18A.9s
Payor mix (hospital budgeting), 33.22–33.23
Payroll
  budgeting. *See* Budgeting
  company-unique practices, 18A.22s
  definition and functions, 18A.6s, 18A.8s–18A.10s
  department organization, 18A.27s, 18A.28s
  expense patterns, 18A.34s–18A.35s
  Human resources interactions, 18A.10s, 18A.12s, 18A.26s

Payroll *(Continued)*
  inputs, 18A.6s–18A.7s
  interactions with other company systems, 18A.22s
  legacy systems, 18A.25s
  model of process, 18A.11s
  outputs, 18A.8s
  planning, 18A.32s–18A.33s
  rework, 18A.33s–18A.34s
  services, 18A.21s, 18A.34s
  software, products for, 18A.12s
  as system, 18A.6s–18A.8s
  technology for, 18A.45s–18A.49s
  who fulfills function, 18A.23s
Payroll costs, 18A.3s–18A.5
  components of, 18A.12s–18A.16s
  cyclical patterns, 18A.34s–18A.35s
  factors affecting, 18A.16s–18A.22s
  recovery of, 18A.33s–18A.34s
  reduction, 18A.3s, 18A.5s, 18A.10s, 18A.17s
Payroll deductions, 18A.8s, 18A.10s, 18A.24s
  options, 18A.21s, 18A.33s
Payroll delivery services, 18A.9s
Pension funds, leases and, 20A.8s
Performance compensation. *See* Compensation
Performance measurement, 26A.15s
Performance reporting, 26A.15s–26A.16s
  activity-based budgeting and, 27A.20s–27A.22s
Performance standards, 1.8–1.9
Period, 11A.3s
Period costs, 16.45
Peripherals, computer, 28.6–28.7, 28.2s
Personal property, 24.13
PERT. *See* Program evaluation review techniques
Peters, Robert, 16.11, 16.13
Peters, Tom, 26A.3s
PFP. *See* Multiyear program and financial plan
Physical distribution
  expense, 15.10s
  sales and marketing budget, 15.4s
Physician budgeting, 33.33–33.38
  cash accounting 33.34
  comparative measures, 33.34
  compensation, 33.33, 33.36–33.37
  by department, 33.33
  fixed vs. variable expenses, 33.36
  involvement of physicians, 33.34
  nonsalary expenses, 33.35–33.36
  revenues, 33.37–33.38
  salary and fringe benefit expenses, 33.34–33.35
  by specialty, 33.33
Plannable core, 16.18–16.19
Planned action budgets, 16.16–16.17, 16.57
Planning. *See* Strategic planning
Planning charts, 14.3
Planning systems, 6.4–6.6
  assignment of responsibility, 6.5–6.6
  goals and objectives, 6.4–6.5
Planning tools, 20A.1s
PM. *See* Program memoranda
Pohlman, Jerry, 3.21
Policy statement, budget, 7.2–7.3
Population, as payroll cost factor, 18A.18s
Portfolio effects, 11.9
Portfolio management, 19.12

Position issues (strategic plan), 2.16
Positive reinforcement, 29.17, 29.19s
Practical capacity, 9.47
Practical income limits, 26.14
Preferred provider organizations, 33.4
Preliminary plan (operational plan), 2.6
Preliminary plan (strategic plan), 2.22
Prepaid expenses (balance sheet budget), 22.22
Preparation of budgets, 22.8–22.11. *See also under specific budgets*
  checklist, 22.8–22.10
  guidelines, 5.1, 5.4–5.6
Present value, 11A.5s, 17.17, 17.19–17.20, 20.4–20.5.
  See also Net Present value
  purchase versus lease, 20A.18s–20A.19s
Present value index. *See* Profitability index
Pressure devices, budgets as, 29.10, 29.11s–29.12s
  disadvantages of, 29.13s
Price/earnings ratios, 11.2
Price variance, material, 9.37
Price/volume chart, 10.5–10.6
Pricing
  adjustments, 15.8s
  cost-based, 15.12s
  exchange rate changes and, 23A.6s, 23A.8s–23A.10s
  penetration, 15.13s
  strategic, 15.12s–15.14s
  tactical, 15.12s–15.14s
Probabilistic models, 27.31
Probabilistic risk analysis (PRA), 34.14s
Procedure, budget. *See* Preparation of budgets
Process control charts, 26A.8s
Process costing, 9.25, 9.27–9.29
Process, definition of, 18B.3s
Process management, activity-based budgeting and, 27A.6s–27A.7s
Procurement process. *See* Purchasing process
Product approval, 34.8s
Product design and revision (manufacturing budget), 16.20–16.21
Product development. *See* Research and development
Production budgets, 5.11
Production process, inventory levels and length of, 22.17
Production requirements (manufacturing budget), 16.17–16.18
Productivity, 11A.10s–11A.11s, 16.5. *See also* Capacity
  capital tools and, 16.33
  of employees, 16.32
  variances, 9.40
Product life cycles, 17.3
  sales and marketing budget, 15.11s
Product profitability analysis, 9.7–9.10
Professional service companies, 30.7–30.8
Profitability index, 17.17, 20.9–20.10
Profit budgets, 22.7
Profit centers, 6.6
  bracket budgeting, 26.2
Profit plans, annual. *See* Annual profit plans
Profits/profitability
  capital costs and, 11.2–11.3
  cost of capital and
    company-wide goals, 11.6–11.7
    divisional goals, 11.7–11.13

Profits/profitability *(Continued)*
declining significance of, in budget, 16.9–16.12
long-run budgeting and profit goals, 8.7–8.8
maximization of, as principal goal, 29.4, 29.5s
net operating profit after tax, 19.9
price/volume chart and, 10.5
product profitability analysis, 9.7–9.10
ratios for measurement of, 22.44–22.47
Program budgeting, 27.1–27.39, 27.1s–27.3s
accounting system, 27.34
analyses, 27.26–27.33
comparison of approaches, 27.30
cost-benefit analysis, 27.26–27.29
operations research, 27.30
overview, 27.32–27.33
systems analysis, 27.26–27.27
use of modeling in, 27.31–27.32
assessment and organization, 27.34–27.35
failures in application of, 27.11
federal program format, 27.19–27.22
annual cycle, 27.22
documents, 27.20–27.21
final submission, 27.22
history of, 27.7–27.11, 27.1s–27.2s
federal government, 27.8–27.11, 27.1s–27.2s
industry, 27.7–27.8
information system, 27.33, 27.2s
nonprofit organizations, 31.10, 31.34–31.35
process phases, 27.12–27.19
annual calendar, 27.19
budgeting phase, 27.14
change analysis, 27.18–27.19
cross-walk reconciliation, 27.17–27.18
cycle of, 27.4
information systems, 27.19
issues analysis, 27.15
key elements, 27.14–27.15
multiyear program and financial plan, 27.16–27.17
planning phase, 27.12–27.13
programming phase, 27.13–27.14
program structure, 27.15
strategic and long-range plans, 27.15–27.16
systematic analyses, 27.19
program structuring 27.22–27.26
classification schemes, 27.24–27.25
development of programs, 27.24
hierarchy of programs, 27.23–27.24
lack of set formula, 27.23
problems, 27.25–27.26
in traditional budgeting, 27.23
residual benefits of, 27.38–27.39
staffing 27.35–27.37
tailoring of, 27.35
traditional budgeting vs., 27.4–27.5, 27.23
Program categories (program budgeting), 27.23
Program elements (program budgeting), 27.5, 27.24
Program evaluation review techniques (PERT), 14.4, 14.6–14.7, 17.24
Programmed costs, 16.45
Program memoranda (PM), 27.20–27.22
Program planning (nonprofit organizations), 31.17–31.20
alternatives, analysis of, 31.17–31.18
implementation plan, 31.19
ongoing vs. new programs, 31.19
selection of programs, 31.18
in smaller organizations, 31.19–31.20
Project screening. *See* Screening project
Property insurance coverages, 24.9–24.10, 24.13
Pseudo consultation/participation, 29.4s
Pseudoparticipation, 29.14s
Purchase, leasing versus, 20A.16s–20A.19s
Purchasing process, budgeting and, 18B.1s–18B.13s
creation of budget, 18B.11s–18B.13s
steps in process, 18B.11s–18B.12s
process approach, 18B.1s–18B.6s
implications of process approach, 18B.6s
process, components of, 18B.5s–18B.6s
process, illustration of, 18B.4s
process measures, 18B.6s–18B.11s
cost reduction capabilities, 18B.9s–18B.11s
product development capabilities, 18B.8s
production capabilities, 18B.8s
role of, 18B.6s–18B.7s
purchasing department, 18B.2s–18B.3s
suppliers, selection and control of, 18B.3s, 18B.7s, 18B.10s–18B.11s
classes of suppliers, 18B.7s
number needed, 18B.7s
value metrics, 18B.4s–18B.5s
Put options, 23A.4s

Quality circles, 29.11s
Quality control, 16.28–16.34
capacity increase, 16.31–16.33
capacity of continuous processes, 16.33–16.34, 16.35
capital tools, 16.33
review questions, 16.52–16.53
Quality function deployment (QFD)
activity-based budgeting and, 27A.11s–27A.12s
Quarterly review, 5.8
Quick ratio, 22.42

RAM. *See* Random access memory
Rand Corporation, 27.8
Random access memory (RAM), 28.6, 28.2s
Ranking process (zero-base budgeting), 25.12–25.13, 25.15–25.16
Rappaport, 11A.2s
Rate of return, 11.2. *See also* Discounted cash flow rate of return
accounting rate of return, 20.10–20.12
internal rate of return, 17.16–17.17
investment opportunity rate of return, 20.5
risk-free rate of return, 11.11
Ratios. *See* Financial ratios
Raw materials, 16.39–16.41
forecast accuracy, 16.39–16.40
inventory, 16.21, 22.18
special commodity characteristics, 16.40–16.41
RBRVS. *See* Resource based relative value system
Real estate brokerage, 30.7–30.8
Real property, 24.13
Recession, 3.20
Reconciliation services, 18A.10s
Reengineering, 18A.37s, 18A.39s, 18B.1s, 18B.12s
Reference tables, 18A.7s
Regional budget reviews (international operations), 23.4

Regression line, 8.14
Regulation, 1.12, 3.6–3.7
Reinvestment, 11A.4s
Relevant costs, 8.10–8.11
Relevant range (cost analysis), 8.6, 10.2
Replenishment (manufacturing budget), 16.34–16.39
Reports and reporting, 6.7–6.8
  administrative expense budget, 18.10
  behavioral aspects of, 29.16–29.17, 29.18s–29.19s
  capital investment budgeting, 19.19, 19.20–19.21
  health care industry
    exception reporting (hospital budgets), 33.28
    turnaround reports, 33.6, 33.7–33.8
    variance reporting, 33.9
  for internal control, 6.6–6.9
    input, control over, 6.7
    review and response, 6.7–6.9
  international operations, 23.14–23.18
    abridged revision for general management, 23.15,
      23.17
    full year estimate, 23.15
    graphic data, 23.17–23.18
    manager's letter, 23.14
    twin currency income statement, 23.14–23.25
    variance analysis worksheet, 23.15
  management reports, 5.9–5.10
  nonprofit organizations, 31.13–31.14
    encumbrance reporting, 31.14
    functional accounting, 31.14
    reimbursement procedures, 31.13–31.14
    time reporting, 31.34
  participative budgets, 29.16–29.17, 29.18s–29.19s
  research and development budget, 17.32–17.36,
    budget tracking 17.35–17.36, 17.37
    earned value reporting, 17.33–17.35
    organizational effects on data reports, 17.38–17.39
  third-party administrators, 24.5
  variance reporting 9.37, 9.39–9.43
    health care budgets, 33.9
    labor variances, 9.40
    manufacturing overhead variances, 9.40–9.42
    material variances, 9.37
    wage rate variances, 9.40
Requests for proposals, 18A.15s, 18A.26s
Research
  budgeting, 34.10s
  funding, 34.3s, 34.6s
Research and development budget, 15.2s, 17.1–17.39
  budget tracking, 17.35–17.36, 17.37
  coordination of project budgets, 17.36, 17.38–17.39
  corporate goals and, 17.3–17.5
  departmental budget, 17.28–17.32
    burden rate, 17.29–17.32
    gross expenses, 17.29
  earned value reporting, 17.33–17.35
  expense, 15.9s–15.10s
  industry life cycles and, 17.3
  monthly reports and, 17.32–17.33
  objectives, establishment of, 17.5–17.10
    basic requirements, 17.6
    corporate objectives, 17.7
    technological budget segmentation ratio, 17.9–17.10
    technological objectives, 17.7–17.9
  risk and, 17.5

sales and marketing budget, 15.3s
technological budget, 17.10–17.28
  project priorities, 17.13, 17.16–17.20
  project screening, 17.11–17.13, 17.14–17.15
  risk analysis and final project selection, 17.21–17.24
  scheduling, 17.24–17.28
  segmentation ratios, 17.9–17.10
  technology level and, 17.3
  zero-base budgeting applied to, 25.4
Residual value, 19.10
Resource based relative value system (RBRVS), 33.33
Resources
  allocation of, 11A.16s, 27A.14s
  maximization of, 8.12–8.14
  requirements and availability of, 1.7
Responsibility, assignment of, 6.5–6.6
Responsibility accounting, 29.16, 29.18s
Responsibility centers, 6.5–6.6
  higher education budgets 32.6–32.7
  nonprofit organizations, 31.26–31.28, 31.32–31.33
Responsibility for budget
  nonprofit organizations, 31.24
  preparation, budget, 7.3–7.4
Retailing, sales and marketing budget, 15.15s
Retro insurance plans, 24.3s, 24.11
Return on assets (ROA), 22.7
Return on capital employed, executive compensation
  based on, 13.5–13.8
Return on equity (ROE), 13.7–13.8, 22.45–22.46
  compensation of CEO and, 13.10–13.11
  corporate performance targets, 13.14–13.17
  operating unit targets, adjustment of, 13.17–13.19
Return on invested capital (ROIC), 11A.7s, 11A.8s,
  11A.11s
  tree, 11A.9s
Return on investment, TQM program, 26A.21s–26A.23s
Return on net assets (RONA), 20.10
Return on shareholders' equity, executive compensation
  based on, 13.4–13.5
Revenue budget
  collecting data for, 7.6, 7.8
  nonprofit organizations, 31.7–31.8
    endowment earnings, 31.7–31.8
    fund raising, 31.7–31.8
    grants and contracts, 31.7
Revenue center, 6.5
Reverse engineering, activity-based budgeting and,
  27A.12s–27A.13s
Reviews, budget
  consolidation of, 12.6–12.7
  divisional budget packages, initial review of, 12.3–12.6
    data verification, 12.3
    divisional budget assumptions and goals, analysis of,
      12.5–12.6
    previous forecast reliability, analysis of, 12.5
  divisional meetings, 12.6
  international operations
    preliminary review, 23.4
    review procedure, 23.10
  management, by, 1.10, 5.9–5.10
  procedures for, 7.4–7.5
    bottom-up approach, 7.4–7.5
    combination approach, 7.5
    top-down approach, 7.4

Reviews, budget *(Continued)*
review meetings, 12.6
senior management review
final, 12.7–12.8
preliminary, 12.7
Right-sizing, 18B.1s
Risk analysis, 20.14–20.16, 20.17, 20.18, 28A.2s, 34.14s
Risk assessment (program budgeting), 27.28
Risk consultants, 24.4
Risk-free rate of return, 11.11
Risk/reward index, 24.6
Risk(s)
insurance budgeting and management of, 24.2–24.3,
24.13–24.15
projects, selection of, 17.21–17.24
technological ventures, 17.5
ROA. *See* Return on assets
Rockwell International, 22.48–22.52
ROE. *See* Return on equity
RONA. *See* Return on net assets

Safety stock base, 16.39–16.40
Sales
inventory levels and level of, 22.16–22.17
limiting growth of, 22.37
production budgets and projections of, 5.11
Sales and marketing budget, 15.1s–15.16s
discretionary expenses in, 15.3s–15.4s
elements of, 15.3s–15.4s
links with other budgets, 15.2s–15.3s
operating factors in, 15.4s–15.5s
pricing adjustments, 15.8s
problems in, 15.7s
process, 15.2s–15.7s
purpose, 15.2s, 15.5s
selling expense, 15.8s
techniques for, 15.10s–15.14s
Sales force, 15.8s
Sales promotions
distribution cost budget, 18.7–18.8
expense, 15.8s–15.9s
sales and marketing budget, 15.3s
Salvage value. *See* Residual value
Samuelson, Paul, 3.18
Satisfier factors, 29.9s
SBUs. *See* Strategic business units
Scatter diagram (estimation of semivariable costs), 8.14
Scenarios, 3.21–3.23, 3.25–3.26, 27.31
Scheduling budget, 14.1–14.12
critical path method, 14.4–14.11
computational phase, 14.7–14.10
computer software for utilizing 14.11
controlling of budget schedule with, 14.10–14.11
Gantt charts, 14.2–14.3
manufacturing budget, 16.20–16.21, 16.34
planning charts, 14.3
technical budgets, 17.24–17.28
timetables, budgetary, 5.6–5.8
Scientific management, 29.5, 29.6s
Screening project, 17.11–17.13, 17.14–17.15
SDP. *See* Strategic direction paper
Security issues
corporate data, 28.3s

Segments. *See* Business segments
Self-actualization, 29.7–29.8, 29.8s–29.9s
Self-funded insurance plans, 24.3–24.4
Self-insurance alternatives, 24.2s
Self-insurance, 24.1s, 24.2s
Selling expense, 15.8s
sales and marketing budget, 15.3s
Semivariable costs, 8.2, 10.3, 30.9
distribution cost budget, 18.7
high-low method for estimation of, 8.16
scatter diagram for estimation of, 8.14
Sensitivity analysis, 11A.10s
capital expenditures, 20.16, 20.18–20.19
program budgeting 27.32
sales and marketing budget, 15.12s, 15.13s
Sequential allocation methods (cost redistribution), 9.45
Service companies, budgeting in, 30.1–30.21
clerical support staff, 30.9–30.10
computer service bureau (example), 30.13–30.21
cost characteristics, 30.8–30.11
definition of service company, 30.7–30.8
capital-intensive service company, 30.8
professional service company, 30.7–30.8
DuPont chart and, 30.3–30.5
financial planning and control, 30.1–30.6
law firm (example), 30.11–30.13
manufacturing company budgeting vs., 30.6–30.7
Service expense, 15.10s
Services, measurement of nonprofit, 31.8–31.9
Shared service centers, 18A.13s
Shareholder value, 11A.1s–11A.2s, 13.5–13.6
budgeting, 11A.15s–11A.18s
defined, 11A.2s, 11A.6s, 11A.12s
purpose of measuring, 11A.2s, 11A.4s
use as measurement of value, 11A.3s, 11A.4s, 11A.7s
Shingo, Shigeo, 16.8
Shop capacity (manufacturing budget), 16.22–16.28
demonstrated capacity, 16.23–16.25
ideal and controlled standard performance,
16.26–16.27
reduction of ineffective time, 16.26–16.28
review questions, 16.54–16.55
Short-run budgeting, 8.6–8.7, 29.7s
Short-run performance, 29.6, 29.7s
Short-term financing, 21.15–21.17
Simple risk-adjustment (SRA), 34.14s
Single-dip lease, 20A.13s, 20A.15s
Single-inventor lease, 20A.3s
Situation analysis (environmental analysis), 1.10–1.12,
2.6–2.18, 3.1–3.29
annual profit plan, 4.3–4.5
capital vs. operating budgets, 3.7–3.8
critical issues, identification of, 2.16, 2.18
definition, 2.5–2.6
description of environment, 2.6–2.9
business segments, selection of, 2.7, 2.9
key success factors, identification of, 2.7
direct environmental inputs to budgets, 3.11,
3.14–3.15
economic variables (survey results), 3.3, 3.5–3.7
economic vs. noneconomic factors, 3.2
forecasting and, 2.6–2.7, 3.11–3.13, 3.16–3.26
impact of uncertainty, 3.20

Situation analysis (environmental analysis) *(Continued)*
response to uncertainty, 3.21–3.26
sources of economic data, 3.18–3.20
FORECYT model, 3.2–3.3, 3.4–3.5
opportunities and threats, defining 2.12, 2.16, 2.18
and positioning of business, 2.9–2.12
business gridding, 2.9–2.10, 2.11
company strengths, rating, 2.12, 2.17
industry attractiveness, rating, 2.10–2.12, 2.13–2.15
specialized economic inputs, 3.26–3.28
Six Sigma program, 18A.37s, 18A.40s–18A.44s
Skinny-dip lease, 20A.5s, 20A.13s, 20A.15s
Slack, budgetary, 29.15–29.16, 29.17s–29.18s
Smed program, 16.32
Smith, Adam, 3.6–3.7
Software. *See* Computers and computer applications
Sorter, George, 16.13
Special studies (SS), 27.21–27.22
Speed, computer, 28.6, 28.2s
Spending variance, 9.41–9.42
Spot foreign exchange deal, 23A.1s
Spot rate, 23A.1s
Spreadsheet software, 12.8, 28.3, 28.8, 28.10–28.11, 28.2s
Spreadsheets, 28.1s–28.2s, 28A.2s, 28A.3s, 28A.8s
SS. *See* Special studies
Staff, budget, 5.2–5.4
in participative budgeting system, 29.17–29.18, 29.19s–29.20s
role conflict and, 29.11, 29.12s–29.13s
Staffing. *See also under* Hospital budgeting
clerical support staff in service companies, 30.9–30.10
program budgeting, 27.35–27.37
Standard costing (manufacturing budget), 9.33, 9.34–9.3 7
budgets and, 9.34
definition of standard costs, 9.34
purpose of, 9.35–9.36
setting standard costs, 9.36–9.37
standard cost system, 9.36
success criteria, 9.36
Standard costs, 1.8, 9.29, 9.34
Standards, performance, 1.8–1.9
Statement of cash flows, 21.9–21.15, 22.48
advantages, 21.10
disadvantages, 21.10
FASB 95 format for, 21.10–21.14
objectives, 21.9–21.10
Statement of objectives (international business), 23.5
Stedry, Andrew C., 29.15, 29.17s
Steel companies
economic inputs for, 3.11, 3.26
planning calendar for, 3.9–3.10
Steiner, G.A., 2.30
Step-down allocation (overhead costs), 33.31
Stern, Joel, 11A.3s, 11A.8s
Stewart, Bennett, 11A.3s, 11A.8s
Stock, sale of, 22.37
Stock prices, 11.5, 11.11, 11.13, 11A.3s
Storyboarding, 27A.18s
Strategic business units (SBUs), 27.8
Strategic direction paper (SDP), 23.2, 23.5–23.9
assessments worksheet, 23.5–23.7
critical issues, enumeration of, 23.6, 23.8

distribution of, 23.6, 23.8–23.9
investment strategy matrix, 23.6
statement of objectives, 23.5
Strategic management
activity-based budgeting and, 27A.8s–27A.14s
principles of, 27A.8s–27A.9s
tools for, 27A.9s–27A.13s, 27A.14s
Strategic planning, 1.8, 2.2–2.31, 5.12–5.13
alternate approaches, consideration of, 2.20–2.22
annual profit plan and, 4.2, 4.6–4.7
budgeting vs., 3.7–3.11, 3 .12–3.13
business direction and concept, 2.18–2.20
differentiated objectives, 2.18, 2.19
matrix position as guide, 2.20, 2.21
capital investment budgeting and, 19.12
contingency planning, 2.29–2.30
definition of, 2.2
description of environment, 2.6–2.9
as dynamic cycle, 2.5–2.6
feedback, 2.28–2.29
financial manager and, 21.6
forecasting vs., 2.2
health care industry and, 33.5
implementation problems, 2.30–2.31
in integrated planning document, 23.4–23.5
measurement of results, 2.28
nonprofit organizations, 31.5–31.6, 31.15–31.17
defining major objectives, 31.15, 31.17
identification of strategies for achieving objectives, 31.17
initiation of program planning, 31.17
operational plan, 2.22–2.28
consistency with strategic approach, 2.26
contents, 2.22–2.24, 2.26
successive commitments, 2.26–2.28
organizational scanning as part of, 1.12–1.13
in overall corporate planning cycle, 2.2–2.5
payroll budgeting and improvement, 18A.32s–18A.33s
program budgeting and, 27.12–27.14, 27.15–27.16
research and development, 17.3–17.9
basic requirements, 17.6
corporate objectives, 17.7
technological objectives, 17.7–17.9
situation analysis, 2.6–2.18
opportunities, threats and critical issues, 2.12, 2.16, 2.18
positioning of business, 2.9–2.12, 2.13–2.15, 2.17
zero-base budgeting and, 25.19–25.20
Strategic pricing, sales and marketing budget, 15.12s–15.15s
Strategic risk, 34.13s
Strategic statement (international operations), 23.11
Stretch budgets, 29.4s
Strike price, 23A.4s
Subsidiaries, debt of, 13.9
Success factors, identification of key, 2.7
Successive commitments, planning for, 2.26–2.28
Summaries, budget, 12.7
Sunk costs, 8.10–8.11, 19.11
Supplier costs, 18A.14s–18A.16s
Suppliers, selection and control of, 18B.3s, 18B.7s, 18B.10s–18B.11s
classes of suppliers, 18B.7s
number needed, 18B.7s

Swap operations, 23A.3s–23A.4s
Systematic analysis (program budgeting), 27.19, 27.32
Systems analysis (program budgeting), 27.26–27.27, 27.30
System shell, 28.5

Tactical budgeting model (bracket budgeting), 26.4–26.21
  assessment of critical elements, 26.10–26.13
  computer, application of, 26.13–26.16
  flexibility in planning, 26.16–26.18
  identification of critical elements, 26.5–26.10
  tracking and feedback, 26.2s, 26.18–26.21
Tactical issues (strategic plan), 2.16
Tactical pricing, sales and marketing budget, 15.12s–15.15s
Task level analysis, 27A.19s
Taxation, 11A.8s
Taxes and taxation
  and cash flow projections, 19.10
  corporate taxes, responsibility for management of, 22.5–22.6
  executive compensation and exclusion of taxes, 13.2–13.3
  income taxes (balance sheet budget), 22.33, 22.35–22.36
Tax payment services, 18A.9s, 18A.15s, 18A.19s
Tax reporting, 18A.9s, 18A.15s, 18A.18a–18A.19s
  W-2 forms, 18A.33s, 18A.35s
Tax withholdings, 18A.8s, 18A.19s
Taylor, Frederick W., 29.5, 26A.3s–26A.4s, 29.6s
Technology. See also Research and development budget
  budget for, 17.10–17.28
    project priorities, 17.13, 17.16–17.20
    project screening, 17.11–17.13, 17.14–17.15
    risk analysis and final project selection 17.21–17.24
    scheduling, 17.24–17.28
    segmentation ratios, 17.9–17.10
  level of, for industry, 17.3
  long- and short-range objectives, 17.7–17.9
    development, 17.8–17.9
    research and exploration, 17.8
    sustaining of funds, 17.9
  for payroll functions, 18A.45s–18A.49s
Technology accounting, 34.13s
Telephone companies, economic inputs for, 3.26
10k reports, 17.3
Theoretical capacity, 9.47
Theory X, 29.10s
Theory Y, 29.11s
Theory Z, 29.11s
Third-party administrators (TPAs), 24.5, 24.2s
  actuaries, 24.5
  claims administrators, 24.5
Third-party administrators (Continued)
  information reporting systems, 24.5
  legal representatives, 24.6
  loss control, 24.5–24.6
Threats, defining, 2.16
Timetables, budgetary, 5.6–5.8
Time reporting, 18A.8s–18A.9s, 18A.21s–18A.22s
Time value of money, 11A.4s–11A.5s, 20.2–20.5
  compounding, 20.2–20.4
  discounting, 20.4
  present value, 20.4–20.5

Tire industry, economic inputs for, 3.26
Tolerance control, 16.29–16.31
Top-down approach (budget reviews), 7.4
Total cash compensation, 13.10
Total Quality Control, 26A.8s
Total Quality Management (TQM), 18A.5s, 18A.36s, 26A.2s–26A.3s, 26A.28s
  application to processes, 26A.7s–26A.10s
  benchmarking. See Benchmarking
  budgeting for, 26A.2s, 26A.3s, 26A.19s–26A.21s
  customer focus, 26A.10s–26A.11s
  definitions, 26A.5s
  elements of, 26A.4s, 26A.5s–26A.6s
  examples, 26A.24s–26A.27s
  history, 26A.2s–26A.3s
  implementation costs, 26A.20s
  implementation phases, 26A.17s–26A.19s
  maintenance costs, 26A.20s–26A.21s
  model, 26A.11s–26A.16s
  paradigms, 26A.7s
  program management, 26A.12s
  return on investment, 26A.21s–26A.23s
  risks of, 26A.23s
  use in payroll function, 18A.35s–18A.45s
Toyota production system, 16.8
TPAs. See Third-party administrators
Trade financing, 21.16
Trade payables (balance sheet budget), 22.30–22.31 22.33
Traditional budgeting, problems with, 27A.2s–27A.4s, 27A.8s
Transaction costs, 18A.3s–18A.5s
Transaction exchange exposure (risk), 23A.6s–23A.7s
Trust, 29.15s
Turnaround reports (health care budgeting), 33.6
Twenty-four-hour coverage, 24.2s
Twin currency income statement, 23.14–23.15
Two-factor theory, 29.9s

Unabsorbed burden, 16.45
Uncertainty, quantification of, 20.15–20.16
Underabsorbed burden, 16.45–16.46
Unique advantages, identification of, 2.20
Units of service (hospital budgeting), 33.13–33.14
Universal principles of management, 29.5, 29.5s
Universities, 3.26, 31.23. See also Higher education, budgeting in
U.S. Department of Defense, 27.2, 27.7, 27.9
Usage variance, material, 9.37

Valence, 29.8, 29.10s
Valuation
  of business, 11A.2s–11A.3s, 11A.17s–11A.18s
    budgeting and, 11A.6s–11A.7s
    long-term, 11A.3s
    measurements for, 11A.1s–11A.18s
    short-term, 11A.3s, 11A.4s, 11A.10s
  cost accounting systems, 9.29
  for insurance coverage, 24.13–24.14
Value, 11A.4s
  book, 11A.9s
  continuing. See Continuing value
  creation of, 11A.10s–11A.11s, 11A.14s
  drivers of, 11A.9s–11A.10s, 11A.12s, 11A.16s
  measurement of, 11A.6s, 11A.8s, 11A.12s

Value *(Continued)*
  money. *See* Time value of money
  net present. *See* Net present value
  present. *See* Present value
Value analysis, 16.26
Value engineering, 16.26–16.28
Value management, 27A.18s–27A.19s
Value metrics, 18B.4s–18B.5s
Variable costs, 8.2, 9.4
  breakeven analysis and, 10.3
  contribution analysis and, 10.7, 10.9
  contribution margin and, 8.4–8.5
  distribution cost budget, 18.6–18.7
  hospital budgets, 33.29
  manufacturing budget, 9.4–9.22, 16.45
    break-even analysis data, 9.12–9.20
    direct absorption costing data, 9.21–9.22
    disadvantages of variable costing, 9.20–9.21
    fixed manufacturing costs, identification of 9.12
    full costing, as alternative, 9.22
    management tool, variable costing as, 9.6–9.7
    other uses for variable costing, 9.10–9.12
    overhead manufacturing, 9.6
    product profitability analysis, 9.7–9.10
  nonprofit organizations, 31.33
  physician budgets, 33.36
  service company budgets, 30.9
Variable efficiency variance, 9.42
Variance analysis, 1.8–1.9, 31.30
Variance reporting
  health care budget, 33.9
  hospital budgets, 33.25, 33.26–33.27
  manufacturing budget, 9.37, 9.39–9.43
    labor variances, 9.40
    material variances, 9.37
    overhead variances, 9.40–9.42
    wage rate variances, 9.40
Variance worksheet (international operations monthly report), 23.15
Virtuous cycle, 29.17s
Voice response system, 18A.21s, 18A.46s–18A.47s
Vroom, Victor, 29.8, 29.10s

WACC. *See* Weighted average cost of capital
Wage attachments, 18A.8s, 18A.9s
Wage incentives, 16.42, 16.44–16.45

Wage rate(s)
  standard, 9.37
  variances, 9.40
Warranties, 15.10s
Weighted average cost of capital (WACC), 11.6, 11A.5s
Weighted average pay rates, 33.19–33.20
Windows (computer program), 28.6, 18A.45s
Wire transfer services, 21.20–21.21
Wolf, Harold, 16.13
Worker's compensation, 24.11, 24.3s
Working capital (capital investment budget), 19.6
Working day, 23A.2s
Work-in-process inventory, 16.21
Workload, activity-based budgeting and, 27A.6s, 27A.8s, 27A.16s
  determining, 27A.14s
  non-service-related activities, 27A.15s
  special projects, 27A.15s
Workload drivers, 18A.17s, 18A.18s
Work packages, 17.33
World War II, program budgeting during, 27.8
Worst-case budget, 13.14
Worthington, Mac, 11A.14s
W-2 forms, 18A.33s, 18A.35s

X, Y, and Z theories, 29.9, 29.10s–29.11s

Yankelovich, 16.43

Zero balance accounts, 21.21, 21.22
Zero-base budgeting, 16.15, 18.8s, 25.1–25.21, 27.1s
  applicability of, 25.3–25.4
  contingencies, adaptability to, 25.19
  decision package, 25.5–25.12
    alternatives, formulation of, 25.5–25.6
    incremental expenditures and benefits, 25.6
    materials handling example, 25.8–25.12
    minimum level of effort, identifying, 25.7
  decision units, defining, 25.5
  detailed budgets, preparation of, 25.16–25.17
  nonprofit organizations, 31.35
  program budgeting and, 27.20, 27.29, 27.1s–27.2s
  ranking process, 25.12–25.13, 25.15–25.16
  strategic planning and, 25.19–25.20
  top-management decision making, 25.13, 25.16, 25.17
  traditional approaches vs., 25.2–25.3, 25.17–25.19